THE LEGACY OF VIETNAM

The War, American Society and
the Future of American Foreign Policy

CONTRIBUTORS:
DAVID M. ABSHIRE
RICHARD BARNET
SAM BROWN
ALASTAIR BUCHAN
ALTON FRYE
LESLIE GELB
PHILIP GEYELIN
MORTON H. HALPERIN
RICHARD HOLBROOKE
HUBERT HUMPHREY
IRVING KRISTOL
ANTHONY LAKE
ERNEST R. MAY
PETER OSNOS
LUCIAN PYE
EARL C. RAVENAL
JOHN P. ROCHE
EDWARD SHILS
JACK SULLIVAN
MICHEL TATU
MAXWELL TAYLOR
JOHN G. TOWER
PAUL WARNKE
ADAM YARMOLINSKY

THE LEGACY
OF VIETNAM

*The War, American Society and
the Future of American Foreign Policy*

Edited by

Anthony Lake

A Council on Foreign Relations Book
New York and London
New York University Press

Copyright © 1976 by Council on Foreign Relations, Inc.
Library of Congress Catalog Card Number:
ISBN: 0-8147-4964-x

Library of Congress Cataloging in Publication Data

Main entry under title:

The Legacy of Vietnam.

Includes bibliographical references.
1. Vietnamese Conflict, 1961-1975—United States.
2. United States—Foreign relations—1945-
I. Lake, Anthony.
DS558. L43   959.704'3373   75-13571
ISBN 0-8147-4964-X

0-8147-4997-6 (paperback)

Manufactured in the United States of America

COUNCIL ON FOREIGN RELATIONS BOOKS

Founded in 1921, the Council on Foreign Relations, Inc. is a non-profit and non-partisan organization of individuals devoted to the promotion of a better and wider understanding of international affairs through the free interchange of ideas. The membership of the Council, which numbers about 1,600, is made up of men and women throughout the United States elected by the Board of Directors on the basis of an estimate of their special interest, experience and involvement in international affairs and their standing in their own communities. The Council does not take any position on questions of foreign policy, and no person is authorized to speak for the Council on such matters. The Council has no affiliation with and receives no funding from any part of the United States government.

The Council conducts a meetings program to provide its members an opportunity to talk with invited guests who have special experience, expertise or involvement in international affairs, and conducts a studies program of research directed to political, economic and strategic problems related to United States foreign policy. Since 1922 the Council has published the quarterly journal, *Foreign Affairs*. From time to time the Council also publishers books and mongraphs which in the judgement of the Committee on Studies of the Council's Board of Directors are responsible treatments of significant international topics worthy of presentation to the public. The individual authors of articles in *Foreign Affairs* and of Council books and mongraphs are solely responsible for all statements of fact and expressions of opinion contained in them.

The members of the Board of Directors of the Council as of September 1, 1975, are: Robert O. Anderson, W. Michael Blumenthal, Zbigniew Brzezinski, Douglas Dillon, Hedley Donovan, Elizabeth Drew, George S. Franklin, Edward K. Hamilton, Gabriel Hauge (Treasurer), Nicholas deB. Katzenbach, Bayless Manning (ex officio), Harry C. McPerson, Jr., Alred C. Neal, James A. Perkins, Peter G. Peterson, Lucian W. Pye, David Rockefeller (Chairman), Robert V. Roosa, Marshall D. Shulman, Cyrus R. Vance (Vice Chairman), Paul A. Volcker, Martha R. Wallace, Paul C. Warnke, Franklin Hall Williams and Carroll L. Wilson.

Preface

The series of essays which make up this volume had their origin in the Committee on Studies of the Council on Foreign Relations in late 1971. That body—a committee of the Council's Board of Directors—began discussing the possibility of the Council sponsoring a study of the implications of U.S. intervention in the Indochina war for the future of American foreign policy. Inevitably, the Committee concluded, given the relationship between foreign policy and domestic politics, such a study would consider the war's impact on American domestic society as well.

Over the next year the design of the project took shape. Rather than engage a single author, and thus present only one point of view, the Committee opted for a volume of essays by many hands, thus running the risk—necessarily—of some lack of coherence, but gaining the benefits of diversity. In such an enterprise, much depends on the person chosen as editor, for it would be his or her responsibility to choose topics for individual contributions, find the authors, and work with them to produce finished, focused essays.

The Council was fortunate in its selection. Anthony Lake

brought to the task of editing this volume knowledge and experience both of Vietnam and of American government and politics. His first tour as a Foreign Service Officer, from 1962 to 1964, was as a Vice Consul in Hue and Saigon; his last, preceding his resignation at the time of the American invasion of Cambodia in 1970, was as Special Assistant to the Assistant to the President for National Security Affairs. Between were other Washington assignments concerned with Indochina, and two years as a graduate student at Princeton's Woodrow Wilson School of Public and International Affairs, which later awarded him the degree of Ph.D. During 1971-72 he was foreign policy coordinator for the Presidential campaign of Senator Edmund Muskie. Currently he is Executive Director of International Voluntary Services, a private analog to the Peace Corps with (incidentally) its own long history of service in Indochina.

Mr. Lake set about commissioning the essays in this volume during 1973. There followed the usual vicissitudes of a multi-authored book. The result is a collection longer aborning than either editors or authors would have preferred, but one which, by virtue of time passed, gave all concerned an opportunity to comment upon the close of America's involvement in Indochina, not merely upon the end of a chapter. Thus it appears at a uniquely appropriate time. The Council on Foreign Relations—it goes without saying—bears no institutional responsibility for any of the individual views expressed here. But its Committee on Studies is very pleased to place them before a larger audience. If their work in any way contributes to the task of re-examining the past and future roles of the United States in Indochina, in Asia, and, indeed, in the entire international system, Mr. Lake and his fellow contributors can be justifiably pleased.

Richard H. Ullman
Director of Studies

June 30, 1975   Council on Foreign Relations

Contents

Introduction

ANTHONY LAKE

Most Americans seem to feel about Vietnam now as Hemingway's Frederick Henry felt in *A Farewell to Arms.* "I don't want to think about the war," he said. "I'm through with it." But we are *not* through with it. For even if we do not want to think about the war, it has changed us, and we are condemned to act out the unconscious, as well as conscious, "lessons" we have learned.

No nation could undergo what the United States did in Vietnam without being changed. The physical costs are terrible to recall: more than 55,000 Americans dead in Indochina, 300,000 more wounded, over $150 billion spent. Recollections of the injuries we inflicted as well as suffered, and of the millions of people in Indochina killed, wounded, and made homeless remain enormously painful. It is no wonder that there is more "Let us forget" than "Lest we forget" in our national mood.

Beyond the emotions surrounding these memories, there is an intellectual reaction against trying to draw lessons from the war. After all, many observers now argue, American involvement in Vietnam was one consequence of overlearning the

lessons of Munich. "No more Vietnams," it is suggested, will
be as poor a prescription in other areas and at other times as
"No more Munichs" was in Vietnam. Were not the circumstances of Vietnam so exceptional that the American experience there provides the wrong history from which to derive
guidelines for the future of American foreign policy? This
warning may have validity as an injunction against overlearning some of the more specific, even technical, lessons of Vietnam. But our experiences in Indochina and their implications
must be studied for three reasons.

First, even if the specific details of Vietnam offer little
guidance to other foreign policy problems, we should examine
the broader conceptual, political, and institutional imperatives that led us into the war in order to understand our
present and future foreign policies—and even how our government (and, indeed, our society) works. As Henry Kissinger
put it, before joining the government in 1969:

> I don't know whether there will be "another Viet-
> nam." But I feel that we have to make a really prayerful
> assessment of what we went in there for, not to pin the
> blame on any people or particular set of conditions but to
> assess the whole procedure and concepts that got us in-
> volved there. We have to do this if we are not going to
> have another disaster that may have a quite different
> look but will have the same essential flaws.[1]

There is more, too, to be examined than the conceptual,
political, and procedural impulses that led us into Vietnam.
The second reason for such an examination is that we also
need to understand how the war has changed us and others.
What has been its role in the vast changes that have taken
place during the past decades in our institutions, our attitudes
toward each other, and our approach to foreign policy? What
effect have the war and American policy toward Indochina
had on other nations? How has the world context of American
foreign policy been altered?

A third reason for taking another look at the past concerns
the drawing of lessons for the future. Thucydides' view that

"events which happened in the past . . . [human nature being what it is] will, at some time or other and in much the same ways, be repeated in the future" may be debatable. But whatever the merits of debate about the meaning of history and how much can be learned from it, the fact remains that lessons—perhaps in the form of popular myths and broad clichés—*will* be drawn from the Vietnam experience.

These lessons—a Vietnam analogy that will amend or replace the Munich analogy—may provide implicit rather than explicit guides to action; they may be complex and contentious rather than the focus of a consensus; they may work themselves into the unconscious assumptions of our foreign policy debates as much as into our conscious calculation; and they may dictate the political limits of our policies as much as they decide the character of the policies themselves. The lessons can also be wrong. But they are no less important for that.

As others have noted, it is natural that just as generals of all nations tend to prepare for the last war, so statesmen generally work to avoid the most recent international disasters. The reasons go beyond the simple logic of learning from past mistakes. The personal careers of successful statesmen include a series of unrepeated substantive mistakes and repeated successes. As intelligent people, they derive general lessons from these experiences. Acting on imperfect information about complex choices, they were actually making good—and lucky —guesses. But in retrospect, a good or lucky guess becomes a wise decision. And a bad or unlucky guess by someone else becomes the stupidity of simple miscalculation. The past seems clearly ordered; the role of chance, the interplay of factors so complex that they are beyond control and even comprehension, is blurred and fades in one's memory. So patterns and laws are derived from accidental events that may have been coincidental.

The effects of experience are particularly strong in a democracy in which the President or Prime Minister is broadly accountable to the public. The central foreign policy clichés of the time and the simple lessons derived from recent experience delineate the general political boundaries of international action by the government. They also can provide political imperatives, forcing leaders into foreign actions they might otherwise have preferred to avoid. For example, once the supposed lesson of Munich had settled into the American public mind, no President and few other elected officials dared dispute the then dominant view that the United States could never remain indifferent to the loss of territory to Communist influence or control anywhere in the world. Coupled with the inflated sense of American power that followed the successes of World War II and postwar policies in Europe, this view meant that the political fortunes of American leaders were hostage to foreign events. As Nicholas Katzenbach has written:

> . . . Presidents became the prisoners of the cold war view of politics, even though each also contributed to it. The general public and congressional perception of the cold war—and, incidentally, of an exaggerated American power to influence and control events—made it virtually impossible for any President to be candid about the costs and risks of our foreign policy. The "China Syndrome" —the aftermath of Joe McCarthy—meant politically that it was easier to accept the premise of "no loss of territory" in the hope that his Presidency would not be called to account than to attempt to gain public and congressional acceptance that the premise might involve unacceptable risks and costs.[2]

It would be wrong, however, to underestimate the degree to which our political leaders were responsible for the existence of these public imperatives. Succeeding Presidents were willing partners in the creation and strengthening of those imperatives. Through belief, and in the process of rallying public support behind the tactical decisions they had made, they and their spokesmen trapped themselves with strong statements of strategic necessity.

On May 24, 1951, President Truman warned that:

> In Asia, in a vast area stretching from Afghanistan to Korea, free countries are struggling to meet communist agression in all its many forms. Some of these countries

are battling the communist armies of Soviet satellites; some are engaged in bitter civil strife against communist-led guerrillas; all of them face the immediate danger of communist subversion.

Soviet intentions with regard to these countries are unmistakably clear. Using the weapons of subversion, false propaganda and civil war, the Kremlin has already reduced China to the status of a satellite. The Soviet rulers have turned their satellite armies loose on the Republic of Korea. Communist rebellion is raging in Indochina. In Burma, the Philippines, and other places, communist inspired groups are stirring up internal disorder. In all countries, they are trying to exploit deep-seated economic difficulties—poverty, illiteracy and disease.

This campaign threatens to absorb the manpower and the vital resources of the East into the Soviet design of world conquest. It threatens to deprive the free nations of some of their most vitally needed raw materials. It threatens to turn more of the peaceful millions of the East into armies to be used as pawns at the disposal of the Kremlin.

Aside from immediate considerations of security, the continued independence of these nations is vital to the future of the free world.

Secretary of State Dulles sounded the same alarm in 1953: "If Indo-China should be lost, there would be a chain reaction throughout the Far East and South Asia." Ten years later, President Kennedy stated his belief in the domino theory and tied victory in Vietnam to Communist containment: "We want the war to be won, the Communists to be contained, and our men to come home. We are not there to see a war lost." In 1965, President Johnson described the stakes in Vietnam:

We are also there to strengthen world order. Around the globe, from Berlin to Thailand, are people whose well-being rests, in part, on the belief that they can count on us if they are attacked. To leave Vietnam to its fate would shake the confidence of all these people . . . in the

value of America's word. The result would be increased
unrest and instability and even wider war. We are also
there because there are great stakes in the balance. Let no
one think for a moment that retreat from Vietnam
would bring an end to conflict. . . . The central lesson of
our time is that the appetite of aggression is never satisfied. . . . There are those who say that all our effort
there will be futile—that China's power is such that it is
bound to dominate all Southeast Asia. But there is no
end to that argument until all the nations of Asia are
swallowed up.

The stakes, as portrayed by the President, had not been
reduced by 1970. As American units crossed the Cambodian
border on April 30, President Nixon warned: "If when the
chips are down, the world's most powerful nation—the United
States of America—acts like a pitiful, helpless giant, the forces
of totalitarianism and anarchy will threaten free nations and
free institutions throughout the world."

Yet, as Leslie Gelb has shown,[3] our Presidents and their
advisers have usually been aware that success in Indochina was
far away, if attainable at all. Still, prisoners of their own rhetoric, beliefs and political careers, they persisted. For Kennedy
and Johnson, successive escalations were required to stave off
disaster. For President Nixon, withdrawal had to be covered
by claims of "peace with honor." The pace of withdrawal
could not be so quick as to call forth the specter of the "pitiful,
helpless, giant."

As each President drummed up public support for his specific actions—the escalatory acts of Kennedy and Johnson and
both the escalatory and de-escalatory acts of Nixon—he in-
dulged in the rhetoric of American global responsibility. Thus,
the hyperbole accompanying each action strengthened the
public fears of defeat that forced Kennedy and Johnson to
take each next step in Indochina, and Nixon to hold out as
long as he could.

Many of the cold war lessons of Munich may still have force,
but they are likely to be contradicted by some of the emerging
lessons of Vietnam. Munich suggested a relatively simple,

positive injunction: As in the case of Nazism, early and force-ful action is required against Communist threats or minor tests of American will. The penalty of weakness would be felt in later difficulties on a larger scale. Most persons who had observed the consequences of the failure to intervene against Hitler in the 1930s—and had then fought successfully to defeat him—accepted the lessons wholeheartedly.

Vietnam, on the other hand, seems to many Americans to provide vague, negative injunctions against American sacrifice and expenditures abroad. Having observed the consequences of intervention in Vietnam and the American failure to gain a clear victory in the fighting, they conclude that the United States should avoid foreign wars not by nipping them in the bud, but simply by staying out of them.

While Vietnam recedes from the headlines and television news, and thus from our daily consciousness, the currents of American foreign policy debate remain confused. Both the positive impulses of Munich and the more negative warnings of Vietnam are in contention for public allegiance. Many Americans want to hear that we are still "Number One" in the world; President Nixon's warnings against hasty, unilateral retreat from Vietnam did well with the public; majorities usually supported the escalated American military actions in Indochina of 1970-72; and there are still many adherents to the view that those actions forced the agreements of January 1973. Yet polls show important public support for cuts in defense spending and little taste for the involvement of American military forces in the event of Communist-supported military attacks against even our closest friends and allies. Thus, in this period of contradictory political impulses about our foreign policies, Presidents may be buffeted between continued public expectations of foreign "success" and widespread doubt about the actions necessary to achieve it. As a result, political leaders could find more enticing than ever the unfortunate twin temptations to disguise the scope of American foreign activities from the public eye and also to overstate the present and future successes of American diplomacy.

In many ways, these years recall the years immediately fol-lowing World War I more than the period of the late 1940s.

Congressional opposition to the Administration on war powers and Cambodian bombing in 1973 recalled 1919 and the Lodge Reservations more than 1948 and the Vandenberg Resolution. Disagreement now between internationalists who welcome interdependence and those who prefer autarky recalls the debate over the League of Nations more than the near consensus behind American participation in the United Nations.

There are very important differences between the post-Vietnam and post-World War I periods, to be sure. In the first two decades of this century, only Latin America had seemed an area in which the security interests of the United States were automatically threatened by competitive foreign activity. Fifty years later, the United States has been motivated by the "illusion of omnipotence" and—perhaps more important—a sense of global omniresponsibility.

In 1919, Wilson toured the country to drum up support for the League of Nations. Today, a President can gain immediate access to a huge national audience on television. The effect of television on our foreign policies is paradoxical: it increases the President's power in foreign policy debates at home, but limits his ability to commit American resources and men abroad. At television press conferences and in dramatic, prime-time announcements of new initiatives, he can drive home the importance of his actions and the central concepts (simply phrased) that lie behind them. After almost every such Presidential address on Vietnam in the last decade, the President's approval rating rose in the polls. His critics have a hard time matching either his access to such an audience or the drama of his announcements. But televised news reports from abroad also place limits on the President's options. Specific news reports may appear to contradict Administration claims, as happened repeatedly during the Vietnam war. And a small event can fill a television screen so dramatically that it takes on more universal proportions. Televised films of the attack on the American Embassy in Saigon in 1968 left many Americans with the impression that all Vietnam was already in flames, although the Tet offensive was only in its first hours. The three C-130 transport planes sent to the Congo in 1967 so filled a television screen that they almost assumed the visual proportions of the Berlin airlift. (Ironically, the converse is also true: it is hard for television reporters to portray the full scope of a truly major disaster. Again, the difference between large and small events is lost.)

Thus, dramatic televised reports of foreign alarms and excursions seem to imply that the world is filled more with gore than with glory, that it is a place where American activity seems only to promote violence or anti-American incidents. One wonders whether colonial empires could easily have survived television. Imagine what the effects on British politics would have been of televised reports of the disaster at Isandlwhana, when a British army was annihilated by Zulu warriors. Or consider the impact in Belgium had there been televised exposés of Belgian brutality in the Congo in the nineteenth century. European antiimperialists would have been in a much stronger position if popular perceptions of empire had been molded by televised images as much as by the articles and speeches of returned explorers or colonial entrepreneurs like Cecil Rhodes.

There are other important differences between the foreign policy debates of 1973 and those following World War I. But three broad similarities are disturbing. The first lies in the reaction in both periods against idealism and reform.[4] In both cases, important liberals and conservatives joined in opposition to earlier excesses of intervention, painful adventures that had apparently been produced by a combination of self-interest and relatively disinterested ideals. In 1904, Theodore Roosevelt had declared that if a nation demonstrates that it

> knows how to act with decency in industrial and political matters, if it keeps order and pays its obligations, then it need fear no interference from the United States. Brutal wrong-doing, or an impotence which results in general loosening of the ties of civilized society, may finally require intervention by some civilized nation, and in the Western Hemisphere the United States cannot ignore this duty.

Whatever their true causes, American interventions in Latin America, including Mexico and Haiti, were portrayed partially as moral responses to internal bloodshed. American entry into the fighting of World War I was also wrapped in the language of moral obligation.

Similarly, the rhetoric of American involvement in Vietnam was couched in terms of the obligations of ideals. The implicit acceptance of the "White Man's Burden" before World War I was matched by acceptance, after World War II, of the "Free Man's Burden"; the interventionist thrust was the same. And disillusioned reaction has followed Vietnam, as it did World War I. Theodore Roosevelt's statement of 1904 must have echoed as strangely to the anti-interventionists of 1919 and 1920 as President Kennedy's Inaugural Address in 1961 now sounds to many after the agony of Vietnam. The liberal and revisionist critiques of past error in 1919 were remarkably similar to the critiques of their intellectual counterparts today. In 1919, some liberal critics of Wilson began to attack the proposition that any ideals could again justify such interventions in force. Going a step farther, revisionist scholars began to question the idea that Wilson's policies had been motivated, even in part, by idealistic principles.[5] And just as anti-interventionists like J. W. Fulbright and Senator Frank Church now join conservatives in opposing current levels of American bilateral economic aid abroad, so many of those opposed to Wilson's terms for American participation in the League were liberals. (In both cases, the motives seem to include frustrated idealism. Then, many liberals opposed the League because it rested on a vindictive treaty, not because they opposed its concept. Today, some liberal Americans oppose American aid not because they are against progress in the developing world, but because of their frustration and fear of bilateral American efforts there.)

By the 1930s, foreign policy idealists committed to an American role in international peacekeeping institutions were a distinct minority. As in the age of Watergate, the country's disillusion with foreign crusades had been strengthened by domestic scandal and economic disaster. The depression was psychological as well as economic. In May 1932, Walter Lippmann wrote of the drastic effects of "science and machinery and the modern city," and noted:

That a period of profound spiritual bewilderment had to ensue was inevitable. But this bewilderment has been greatly aggravated in the United States by what I believe may truthfully be called the moral apathy of those in high places. At the beginning of the decade the national government was attacked by brutal and conspicuous corruption. No clear word about it was spoken by those in high places. On the contrary, they sat silent, hoping that the people would forget, calculating that the evil would be overlooked. Is it surprising that public spirit weakened when it was demonstrated from the highest places that the corruption of government was not something that the citizens ought to care deeply about? [6]

The question now is whether the disillusion that leads some of our more intense domestic critics to conclude that the United States is inherently incapable of progressive action abroad will be as dominant an impulse as was the illusion that the United States could afford to "bear any burden or pay any price." They share one proposition. Both the illusion and the disillusion seem to reflect a belief that the United States must be unique. If it is not the most generous and responsible nation in the world, then it is the worst, whose strength and congenital inability to distinguish between safe and reckless actions, between humanitarian and political/military interventions, make it the most dangerous nation of all. The de facto alliance between the proponents of this jaundiced view and those conservatives traditionally opposed to American "giveaways" and "meddling" abroad could force a mean-spirited foreign policy that contradicts the implicit ideals of the critics who are most disillusioned by our Vietnam experience.

A second general similarity between the two periods is that foreign policy debates, then as now, were often considered to be between isolationists and internationalists. And, in both cases, this skewed the terms of the debate. In 1919 and 1920, it was more precisely a debate between nationalists and internationalists, with the position of the former conveying isolationist overtones. As Jean-Baptiste Duroselle has pointed out: "People were *nationalists* if they opposed the entry of the

United States into the League; they were *internationalists* if they favored it." [7]

It made little more sense in 1920 to call for literal isolationism—the severance of American ties to an interdependent world—than it does now. The manner in which the economic woes of 1929 echoed back and forth across the Atlantic in an intensifying spiral of depression demonstrated the point in distressing terms. The debate was about the character of American ties to other nations—their scope and the national advantages which they should convey. Few people were literally isolationists.

Similarly, charges of isolationism, neo- or otherwise, in today's debates make little literal sense. The debate concerns the nature of our foreign relations, not whether we should have them. And as in the years after World War I, there are powerful nationalistic impulses on both the left and right. For some supporters of the former, it is the nationalism of an America that devotes as much of its "welfare" efforts as possible to the perfection of its own society. For the latter, it is the nationalism of an America that seeks to deny global interdependencies in energy, food, and a host of other fields and that indulges in the rhetoric of being "Number One."

Both kinds of nationalism contain an isolationist impulse, although neither can produce an America that is physically isolated. The immediate threat is of an America that is isolated from the good will of others; a further danger is of an America that takes as little part in seeking international solutions to global problems as the United States did with regard to European problems in the 1930s. While what has been called the neo-isolationism of the left now seems most directly relevant to such a possibility, we should recall also the implications of "America First" in 1975, as in 1920. As President Harding put it:

> Call it the selfishness of nationality if you will, I think it
> an inspiration to patriotic devotion—
> To safeguard America first . . .
> To think of America first,
> To exalt America first.

Sentiments like these provided an essential contribution to the self-centered quality of American foreign policies between the two world wars. They could again.

A third similarity between these years and the years just after World War I lies in the lack of a consensus on foreign policy. All questions can be asked; none is yet answered definitively. Many questions are being asked now, rather than ten years ago, because of the reaction to the costs of the Vietnam war and our national relief from some of the fears of an aggressive Communist bloc—fears which inhibited challenges to the fundamental assumptions of American foreign policies after World War II and the Korean War. And it is precisely the unsettled character of current foreign policy discussions that makes them so important. Different and contending groups in the United States derive different lessons from the Vietnam experience and will apply those lessons when they hold power. Consider, for example, the differences that persist over the effect and importance of the bombing campaigns over North Vietnam, and the implications of this argument with regard to the relationship between force and diplomacy. It will be years, if ever, before a synthesis of these antithetical views emerges.

Thus, there is the opportunity to examine the lessons of Vietnam before debate ends and they become doctrine. That is the purpose of this book. Not a series of essays suggesting a set of lessons that *should* be drawn, it attempts rather to portray the ideas that are actually being assimilated into various approaches to American foreign policy. More than an examination of the American experience in Indochina, it considers also how those events have actually changed us and others.

The book presents original essays by authors of diverse backgrounds and points of view. The essays differ in style, in substance, and in method of expression. All of the authors have in various ways been concerned with the war in Indochina, and all, of course, have their own views on the role played by the United States in that war, on the impact of the war upon American society, and on its significance for American foreign policy in coming years. Some of the authors were

participants in the events about which they write. Their essays
provide personal reflections and evaluations drawn directly
from their own experiences. Other authors come from the
academic and journalistic communities; their essays are, in
most cases, more at arms-length both in conception and in
tone. The resulting diversity in style and approach is intended,
and indeed inevitable, in a collection of essays that reflects the
crosscurrents of America's Vietnam experience.

At the same time, it is impossible to include all points of
view in one volume, or even to achieve a perfect balance
among those approaches that are presented. Indeed, the definition of such a "balance" would require highly debatable
subjective judgments. All that can be hoped for is diversity,
and the reader should find the diversity of these authors
reflected in their disagreements. [8]

The book is divided into four sections. The first takes a look
at changes in the international system in the last decade or so,
and the effect of American participation in the Indochina war
on those changes. What role did the war play in the profound
shifts that have taken place in relations among the great
powers—such as American détente with the Soviet Union and
the Chinese People's Republic, the new state of flux in East-
West relations in Europe and within NATO and our other
alliance systems, the achievement of Soviet military parity
with the United States, and the retrenchment in American
military reach implied by the Nixon Doctrine? To most
Americans, any event so excruciatingly important to our national experience as the war in Indochina must have been of
global importance. This is clearly so with regard to the effect it
has had and will have on America's global policies. But how
has it affected relations among other nations? And how has
it altered their view of the United States, of our military
strength, our diplomatic skill, and our society itself? Two
foreign observers, Alastair Buchan and Michel Tatu, address
these and related questions.

Part II presents a series of essays exploring and debating the
effect and implications of the war for the United States and
how it makes its foreign policies.[9] The first pair of essays, by
Edward Shils and Peter Osnos, reviews the impact of the war

on our society. Shils provides a general review of changes in the attitudes of Americans toward one another, our government, and our institutions, and how the war contributed to a decline in the due given to authority in modern America. Osnos relates his observations of the legacy of the war in a typical American community—Riverdale, Maryland.

Beyond the broad effects of the war discussed by Osnos and Shils, what does our involvement in Vietnam suggest about how we make our foreign policies? The next four essays in the book examine the relationship between foreign policy and the broad political processes of the nation, with a natural focus on the twin issues of consensus and dissent. To what degree was the consensus of the 1950s and the early 1960s behind U.S. foreign policy (e.g., general agreement on the Munich analogy) shattered by Vietnam? By what process did these ideas take root in our political system? How were they challenged? Is a new foreign policy consensus now developing? *Should* one be developing? Irving Kristol and Leslie Gelb consider such questions in the light of previous American and European experience, while Sam Brown and John Roche describe and debate[10] the meaning of the dissent against the war that so dominated headlines and emotions during the height of American involvement.

The final four essays in this section are more narrowly focused on how key institutions have performed—and should perform—in the making of our policies toward Indochina and the rest of the world. Richard Holbrooke writes of the executive branch and the war—what roles the various parts of the bureaucracy played in the formulation of our Indochina policies, and what the performance of a bureaucracy in a democracy should be. His essay suggests reasons for the persistence of some of the myths in Washington about the reality in Indochina as he describes the interaction among the President, his appointees, and career officials. The next essay, by Phillip Geyelin, addresses important questions about the role of the press. Why did it take so long for the press as a whole to discover what reporters in Vietnam like Neil Sheehan and David Halberstam had learned in the early 1960s about official claims of success? How can a democracy, with a free press, pursue a limited war in which it must seek to scare the enemy by demonstrating it will stay the course, while reassuring the public that the course will be short and the costs low? What are the proper claims of "national security" on the press as the government seeks to use it for its own purposes in negotiations with the enemy? What are the institutional traps which make the press so vulnerable to the "truth" as interpreted by anonymous government officials? Alton Frye and Jack Sullivan then trace the effect of the war on relations between the Congress and the executive, as well as the performance of the Congress on the war. They present a useful summary of efforts by the Congress to reassert its prerogatives in the management of our foreign affairs and suggest the limits on, as well as the benefits of, a more assertive congressional voice. The last essay in this section, by Adam Yarmolinsky, examines the impact of the war on the military establishment and argues that our civilian leadership must inspire and lead—as well as control—it.

Part III turns to the substance of American policies and actions in Indochina, and the implications for our policies elsewhere. Three sets of issues are addressed: security policies, negotiating strategies, and American involvement in foreign societies.

Senator John Tower, Earl Ravenal, and Ernest May consider, from very different points of view, American security policies and the war. While they are in broad agreement about the nature of the security concepts that led us into the war, they disagree sharply about what conclusions should be drawn from our Vietnam experience. What does the war tell us about the limits of our security interests? How much is enough to defend them? What would be the consequences—at home and abroad—of underestimating our defense needs and of overestimating them? What are the dangers of the lessons about American security policies that various groups seem to have learned? These are tremendously complicated and broad issues, and the three essays do not pretend to explore them in detail. The point, as with other essays in the book, is to present through contrasting arguments some of the streams of thought now current as the meaning or meanings of the war settle into our national patterns of thought and attitude.

In a so-called era of negotiations, it is particularly instructive to review the negotiating processes which finally led to the withdrawal of American combat forces from Indochina. Examination of the difficulties encountered in the negotiations—each side's terms, different expectations, the misperceptions each held about the ability of the other to hold out, views of each other's intentions (e.g., fear of the other's attempt to "bargain from strength")—can illustrate more general negotiating issues. What does our Indochina experience indicate about the relationship among negotiating strategies, more general foreign policies, and U.S. military policies? For example, what does it suggest about building "bargaining chips" into the defense budget in order to negotiate from strength? About "linkages" among various negotiating issues? About alliance relationships in an era of negotiations? Maxwell Taylor and Paul Warnke suggest some alternative answers to such questions.

To conclude Part III, Richard Barnet, Senator Hubert Humphrey, and Lucian Pye write about the perils and benefits of American involvement in foreign societies in the light of experience in Indochina. What are the general purposes of such involvement? Is American civilian aid abroad necessarily the thin edge of a more general interventionist wedge? Should conditions ever be placed on our aid to insure its proper use by the recipient? Or to serve political ends? Are covert operations abroad ever justified? What attitude and actions should the United States take with regard to foreign violations of human rights? With memories of the carnage in Indochina still fresh, the issue of American assistance and interventions in the life of foreign societies is inevitably a difficult one. None of these essays suggests we can avoid involvement. They differ, however, on what the nature of that involvement should be.

The last section of the book is composed of essays by David Abshire and Morton Halperin. Each author was asked to consider the emerging Vietnam analogy, or analogies, which may be replacing the Munich analogy as a general guide or constraint for American foreign policies. Each author was also asked to do more than support the lessons he would draw from the war; instead, we solicited their views of the mistakes which may be made or avoided during the next decade as a result of the lessons that are now fashionable among various groups within the United States. Since different sets of lessons of the war seem to be emerging, as suggested by the disagreements in the other sections of this volume, it is not surprising that Abshire and Halperin find different kinds of dangers in learning too much from the war.

All of the essays in this volume, as well as the introduction, deal primarily in abstractions, which are the necessary short-hand for reality. Yet they can blur reality as much as they represent it. Behind the ordered array of options in a national security memorandum or the elegant generalities of a scholarly essay lies the real substance of our foreign policies: *people*, American and foreign, whose lives provide the final measuring stick for the success or failure of a policy. Indochina cannot be discussed without recalling the people there in the midst of their war.

Similarly, some of the most important new international crises now facing the United States and the world are intensely human problems: growing food shortages, worldwide increases in prices of oil and fertilizer, population growth, environmental damage and the like—as well as the alarming consequences of these problems for political and social organization in all nations.[11] Perhaps the greatest challenge to American foreign policy makers in the next generation will be to find constructive ways in which to cooperate with other nations in "managing interdependence"[12]—not only interdependence on security issues, but interdependence on questions of economic and ecological survival. We should recall that the decades after the Congress of Vienna provided an age of brilliant diplomacy and diplomatists. But the statesmen of the era, concentrating on their diplomatic chessboards, failed to come to grips with the social and economic problems that exploded in 1848 and afterwards.

The Vietnam experience may have so damaged American

confidence that it intensifies what could be a nationalistic reaction to problems that can only be solved through international action. The dangerous irony is that the global crisis in food, energy, and population could itself push Americans in a nationalistic direction, as it comes more and more to intrude into our everyday lives. The United States is discovering, after decades of what seemed like relative immunity from the economic and social consequences of events abroad, that it is just another nation—tremendously powerful, but almost as vulnerable to others as they have been to us. A foreign cartel can both drive up gasoline prices and invest a part of its members' profits here. Japanese managers train American workers on what can be done with a soybean. It seems backwards: During the age of Pax Americana, the stereotypical thought was that it was *American* government planners who made decisions that affected the lives of foreign peoples, *Americans* who dominated international institutions, *American* businessmen who trained others in more efficient—and even enlightened—business practices, and *American* investors who could buy a piece of another nation's action. Now, while this is still preponderently the case, the image of America as producer rather than recipient of international advice and influence is beginning to blur. While the United States has previously been prepared to accept the economic dependence of other nations on us, the question now is whether we are prepared to accept the fact of economic interdependence.

A natural response to the discovery that exogenous problems and people are threatening one's freedom of action —especially if one has thought of oneself as *sui generis*, even omnipotent—is to build barriers against the foreign influences. It would not be surprising if this were the dominant American response to intrusive global problems. Already the overwhelming popularity of the notion of achieving energy independence—even at a high environmental price—presents evidence of such a reaction. And American negotiating tactics on economic issues have often seemed to be concentrated more on the size of our slice of the international economic pie than on the question of what must be done to increase the size and quality of the pie itself.

Within the last year or two, the importance of meeting the challenges of interdependence has become an article of faith for most foreign policy analysts and practioners in this country. The question is whether concern about these problems will be translated into political pressures on our leaders to concentrate on their solution, as popular concerns about security issues provided political imperatives in the 1950s and 1960s. And, if so, what form will these new political pressures take?

The essays in this book suggest many ways in which the American experience in Indochina has and should have changed us. Most of them assume a welcome shift toward recognition of the limits to American power and responsibility. Such a shift requires more than a change in thinking; our unconscious attitudes toward ourselves and others are also changing. If Vietnam gives us more humility than self-hatred, caution rather than unconcern, then we shall have profited something from its horror. If we react with the nationalism of either an aggressive beggar-our-neighbors selfishness or a defensive mood of introspection, we shall continue to suffer from the experience. Today, far more than in the years after World War I, the global stakes in American reactions to disillusion are immense.

Notes

1. Richard M. Pfeffer, ed., *No More Vietnams? The War and the Future of American Foreign Policy* (New York: Harper Colophon Books), p. 13.

2. Nicholas deB. Katzenbach, "Foreign Policy, Public Opinion and Secrecy," *Foreign Affairs*, October, 1973. As Harry McPherson notes in *A Political Education* (Boston: Little, Brown, 1972), one of the clearest expressions of such public pressures came in an editorial in the *New York Times* on November 3, 1963: ". . . the loss of South Vietnam to the Communists could raise doubts around the globe about the value of U.S. commitments to defend nations against Communist pressure. . . . The impact on revolutionary movements throughout the world would be profound. At best, neutralism in the East-West struggle might spread. In much of Asia there might

be a feeling that the Communists—under the leadership and inspiration of Peking—represented 'the wave of the future.' "

3. Leslie H. Gelb, "The System Worked," *Foreign Policy*, Summer, 1971.

4. Chapter XIII of Robert Osgood's *Ideals and Self-Interest in America's Foreign Relations* (Chicago: University of Chicago Press, 1953) contains a particularly good description of this reaction after World War I.

5. See Osgood, pp. 313-18.

6. Walter Lippmann, *Interpretations, 1931-32* (New York: Macmillan, 1932), p. 27.

7. *From Wilson to Roosevelt: Foreign Policy of the United States, 1913-1945* (Cambridge: Harvard University Press, 1963), p. 30, italics added.

8. I should record here my gratitude to the staff of the Council on Foreign Relations for their assistance and advice in putting this project together. And I am particularly grateful to Ronald Steel and Leslie Gelb for their work as consultants on the book.

9. This section was to have included consideration of how American involvement in the war affected the state of the American economy, and vice versa, and the conclusions one might draw from this about the general relationship between foreign policy and domestic economic decisions. Unfortunately, last-minute problems prevented inclusion of such an essay.

10. I do not mean "debate" in a formal sense. The authors in each section were not shown each other's essays as they wrote, although, in most sections, authors were selected in part on the basis of their contrasting points of view. To maintain general coherence, the essays in each section were written in response to the same set of questions.

11. An excellent description of these problems and some possible corrective measures can be found in the Overseas Development Council's publication, *The United States and the Developing Countries: Agenda for Action, 1974* (New York: Praeger, 1974).

12. To use a phrase developed in an interesting extended essay by Miriam Camps, *The Management of Interdependence: A Preliminary View*, published in 1974 by the Council on Foreign Relations.

PART I

The Indochina War
and Change in the World

In the first essay Alastair Buchan considers what the war meant for the international system and the American place in it. Surely, one might suppose, any event which so dominated our own national life for so long must have been a dominant event abroad? After all, many of the key arguments about American involvement in the war concerned its importance to our relations with other allies and adversaries and to power relationships throughout Asia and beyond.

Buchan considers "the changing pattern of world politics" and reaches a conclusion that challenges what is probably the view of most Americans. "The blow to American idealism . . . the damage which military and political failure in Vietnam may have done to American influence," he writes, "are only aspects of a larger process of change; and the new structure of power relations in the world would not . . . be radically different if the United States had never become seriously involved in Indochina. . . ."

Buchan's detached perspective on the war may be beyond the emotional capacity of Americans scarred in one way or another by the experience. His essay also recognizes the importance of those scars and, therefore, concludes with some fears about the future.

Michel Tatu takes a close look at the war and two intricate *pas de trois* that were especially important in the period before the agreements of January 1973: among Moscow, Peking, and Hanoi; and among Moscow, Peking, and Washington. As Tatu notes, "It was an extremely complex situation—almost a model imbroglio of divergent interest, ulterior motives, and triangular interactions." Study of these relations is as important as they are complicated, for it concerns questions fraught with importance for the future. How much influence did American policies have on the dealings among North Vietnamese, Chinese, and Soviet leaders? What does this suggest about the importance and character of our relations with the two Communist powers on other issues?

Tatu reviews the "temptations" and "reservations" of both Moscow and Peking with regard to the conflict, and shows how a serious miscalculation on the part of Hanoi tempered Soviet support of the North Vietnamese at a pivotal moment. So, while Tatu credits skillful American moves toward Moscow and Peking as responsible "in large measure" for the "end of the 'American War' in Vietnam," circumstances beyond American influence had to be right as well. While he believes that Washington's new ties with China and the Soviet Union should be strengthened by the end of the American role in Indochina, Tatu concludes with the cautionary note that diplomatic circumstances—and American foreign policy—are hardly immutable.

Michel Tatu was long the Moscow correspondent of *Le Monde,* and is now its foreign editor. He is the author of *Power in the Kremlin.*

Alastair Buchan was Director of the Institute for Strategic Studies from 1958 to 1969, and is now Montague Burton Professor of International Relations at Oxford University.

The Indochina War and the Changing Pattern of World Politics

ALASTAIR BUCHAN

Sir Lewis Namier, the great British historian of a generation ago, used to warn his students of the danger of trying "to argue with history": of abstracting, that is, one event or sequence of events in a historical epoch in an effort to determine how world politics would have differed if it had not occurred. The past is a seamless web, he used to argue, of interrelated developments whose individual strands cannot be unraveled and examined separately. One does not have to be a historical determinist to accept the soundness of this view, and a great deal of the "oh, if only" historiography that now surrounds the American involvement in Indochina seems to me to be based on fallacious abstractions of parts of the national decision-making process at isolated points in time over the past quarter-century. The blow to American idealism which the protracted brutalities of the involvement occasioned and the damage which military and political failure in Vietnam may have done to American influence are only aspects of a larger process of change; and the new structure of power relations in the world would not, in my view, be radically different if the United States had never become seriously involved in Indo-

3

china, or even if it had been able to impose a peace settlement upon North Vietnam between 1964 and 1973. Much of the American literature of *mea culpa* is an aspect of what Denis Brogan first called "the illusion of American omnipotence," the belief that prevailed for nearly a generation, not only that American policy was all-determinant in molding the map of the world, but that the United States had a greater degree of choice at any point in time than was in reality the case.

This emerges particularly, I think, if one examines the history of American policy toward Indochina in the fifteen years before President Kennedy took office. Indochina had been on the American horizon ever since the Japanese conquest of it in 1941, and Roosevelt's attempts, during World War II, to evolve a future for it that would avoid a return of French colonialism are well known. But between 1942 and 1954 France could exert a degree of leverage on American policy which was a result of the fact that the United States had become a global power. Washington needed the goodwill of first Vichy and later de Gaulle in defeating the Axis powers in the Mediterranean and then in Europe. In the postwar years the key position of France—geographically in creating a system of military and diplomatic containment against the Soviet Union in Europe, and politically in relation to the German question—put the United States in leading strings to French policy elsewhere in the world. Acheson has been blamed for succumbing to French pressure for armaments to resist the Vietminh in 1948 and thereafter, and his memoirs show the reluctance with which he succumbed to it. But given what seemed to be the frailty of the European balance of power, he had little choice. France did not lose its power to influence American policy until the failure of the European Defense Community in 1954 forced or enabled Dulles to develop an independent American relationship with Germany.

By that time the French position in Indochina had collapsed, and one may legitimately ask why the United States became and remained so preoccupied with resistance to Communist penetration in an area where it had few economic and no direct strategic interests. Clearly the answer is in part ideological: the determination that communism should not undermine "free Asia" or overstep what Walt Rostow, who reflected a potent strand of liberal ideology, always referred to as "the World War II truce lines." But it was also closely related to an earlier decision, namely that Japan could not be held in thralldom for a generation and must be permitted to resume its independence, at least as an economic power. Economic stability for Japan meant access to the markets and raw materials of Southeast Asia; denial of them raised specters of resumed Manchurian or other adventures. The connection between the future of Japan and that of Southeast Asia was a matter of common agreement in Washington in the mid-1950s and was explicitly recognized in the National Security Council paper on the consequences of the Geneva Conference, which stated that "the loss of Southeast Asia would imperil retention of Japan as a key element in the off-shore island chain." [1]

Moreover, to the extent that Western policy in Southeast Asia during the 1950s represented the attempt to apply a containment strategy to an area for which it was unsuited, it was not of American inspiration alone. Although the "domino theory" emerged under that name in Washington in 1954, it was first publicly formulated by Britain's High Commissioner for South East Asia, Malcolm Macdonald, a strong friend of Asian nationalism, at a meeting of the Foreign Ministers of the Commonwealth, in Colombo in January 1950, when he warned of the effect that infiltration from China into Indochina would have on the security of Thailand and Burma. The Australian and New Zealand governments were extremely concerned after the Korean War about the possibility of Communist infiltration in Southeast Asia and exerted pressure on the United States to do something about it; the concurrence of both Australia and New Zealand in American policy in the area did not change until the early 1970s. Eden and Dulles might dislike each other, and might disagree on the feasibility of military intervention in Vietman in 1954 or about trade with or recognition of China. But the British (who were particularly concerned about the future of Malaya) and the Australians (who were particularly concerned that Indonesia might come within a Communist sphere of influence) had the same basic concern with the containment of communism in Southeast Asia, which lasted in the British case until about 1964 and in the Australian case until considerably later.

I do not mean that the United States could not have resisted the pressures or entreaties of its allies if it had chosen and if there had been a settled official and political consensus in the fifteen years after V-J Day that under no circumstances should it dabble in the politics of Southeast Asia. In hindsight, the European balance does not now seem to have been so precarious in the late Stalin or post-Stalin era as it seemed then. But given the fact that the Western alliance in the Truman and Eisenhower years was a coalition in which the United States was as dependent on its major allies for bases and other facilities as they were on it for economic and strategic support, it would have taken a bold act of policy to ignore their views about Southeast Asia, especially as they coincided with its own. By deliberate acts of policy, alternative trading partners could have been developed for Japan—in Latin America, for instance. All I would suggest is that the original American preoccupation with Indochina was a normal outcome not merely of domestic pursuits but of earlier decisions about its relations with other countries.

II

But this does not provide an answer to the central question: To what extent was the American involvement in Indochina, during the period when decisions were made about it unilaterally in Washington, a prime factor of change in the nature of the international system? First, a point of definition. One can argue that American policy toward Indochina has been made more or less unilaterally ever since 1954, despite nominal consultation with SEATO or other allies during the earlier years; Britain, for instance, was hardly consulted about the decision to abandon the attempt at Vietnam-wide elections in 1955 and 1956 which the Geneva Conference called for, though it was the cochairman of the Conference. American relations with Diem were entirely bilateral throughout. But since the situation in Vietnam was relatively quiescent in the later 1950s and the situation in Laos, the focus of crisis in

1960-61, was stabilized by a multilateral agreement in 1962, I think we are justified in limiting ourselves principally to the period between Kennedy's encouragement of the overthrow of Diem in November 1963 and the uneasy armistice of 1973, the period of deepest U.S. involvement.

Certainly, if one compares the structure of power and influence in the world then and now, the contrast is a very striking one. In 1963 the United States was not only the most powerful state at every level on which state power is exerted but also the most magnetic society. It had a superiority over the Soviet Union in strategic weapons of the order of ten to one, and Kennedy had recently used that margin of strength with skill and prudence to settle the Cuban missile crisis. It produced nearly half the world's wealth; it was the major source of development aid; it was the forcing house of innovation in almost every aspect of science and technology. Its policy decisions were central not only to those of its forty-odd allies but of many formally nonaligned countries as well. Though it was clear that its racial problems had become more serious with the urbanization of the black minority, the United States was still the world's greatest experimental society; it had led the world in the expansion of higher education; and there seemed to be a flexibility in its approach to new social problems which older societies could not match.

The Soviet Union had just suffered a major reverse over Cuba and was heading into an internal political crisis. The Sino-Soviet dispute was reaching the height of its first phase, which arose from conflicting ideological views and national interests (as contrasted with the tensions arising from the border crisis and from security considerations in 1969). China exerted only a limited influence in parts of Southeast Asia and little elsewhere. De Gaulle had vetoed Britain's first application for entry into the European Economic Community, which had itself progressed little further than the removal of various internal trade barriers. To virtually all the West European countries the NATO relationship was more important than the Community. Japan was only just beginning to become an economic power in its own right.

Twelve years later only parts of this landscape are still recognizable. True, the United States is still the world's most powerful state at every level of material power. But the Soviet Union has achieved "parity" in the number of strategic weapons it deploys (which includes numerical superiority in land-based missiles), even though the total of nuclear warheads the United States controls is still larger than that of its "adversary partner." The Soviet Union is also a global power in the sense that it was not ten years ago, with an ocean-going navy and alliances with India, Egypt, Iraq, and Somalia. Equally important, China is now a full member of the international community, has resumed its seat in the U. N. Security Council, has a strategic force in the process of building, and has identified the Soviet Union as its prime adversary. As a consequence of American initiatives between 1969 and 1972, there is now a triangular political relationship between the United States, the Soviet Union, and China, in which developments in the relations of any two of the partners affect the relations of each with the third.

The United States remains the core power of the system of alliances which it constructed in the early period of the cold war, in Europe, in Asia, and with the Latin American states. Among other things it has a virtual monopoly of strategic power, for the size of the British and French nuclear forces remains small, their future in doubt. Moreover, the possibility that allies like Japan or Germany might assert their independence by becoming nuclear powers is still a fairly remote one. The United States still stands, therefore, in the same central relationship to its allies as it did a decade ago.

Yet, even in NATO, the relationship between the United States and its allies has become one of *primus inter pares* rather than one of dominance. American military power continues to be decisive because of the integrated military system upon which European security rests, and the close link between conventional and strategic deterrent power. But the level of the American military commitment is now a matter both of debate in Washington and negotiation with the Soviet Union. And in East Asia the change—now that Vietnam has completely fallen—seems likely to be marked. Almost certainly the American military presence will be removed from mainland Southeast Asia, and probably reduced in the Philippines, perhaps in Korea as well. Basic American alliance commitments in East Asia may remain (though that with Taiwan may soon be wound up), but the effect of the measured American withdrawal—foreshadowed by the Nixon Doctrine of 1970—will be to leave the United States simply a strong Pacific power, as it was in the earlier twentieth century, and not the dominant one that it has been since the Korean War.

And on other planes of power than the military, the structure of interallied relationships has changed profoundly. The principal allies now exercise considerably more initiative than a decade ago, whether it be the West German government's *Ostpolitik*, Japan's development of its own relationships with both China and the Soviet Union, or the European Community's relations with the African and other developing states. And the contrast is even more marked in economic and monetary relationships. The United States began to have an adverse balance of payments overall as early as 1958, but it was not until 1964 that other countries began significantly to accumulate surpluses of dollars. By 1970 the American balance of trade was in deficit, primarily with Canada and Japan, and three devaluations of the dollar between the end of 1971 and the middle of 1973 have made it certain that the Western monetary system will have to be reconstructed, if it is to be reconstructed at all, on a different footing from that which has obtained since 1946, in which the U.S. dollar has been its basic currency. Japan has been for several years the world's third strongest economic power; the enlarged European Community has a combined GNP of $750 billion. To cap these difficulties, a major increase in American overseas investment to take advantage of lower wage levels in Europe and elsewhere has not only increased balance-of-payments difficulties but disrupted domestic employment in some areas. Finally, the United States is becoming less and less self-sufficient in raw materials, most particularly in oil, for whose supply it has become increasingly dependent on the Persian Gulf states, even though Europe and Japan are more dependent still.

So marked has been the change in the structure of world

politics over this period, so changed is the position of the United States, that it is not surprising that the fact that this process coincided with frustrating and ultimately unsuccessful intervention in Southeast Asia should make many Americans feel that Vietnam—its cost, its slaughter, the domestic tensions it created, its ultimate failure—was the prime cause of their change of fortune.

III

What a great nation perceives to be a fact is itself an important determinant in international politics; I shall return at the end to this point and to its profound implications for the present and future. But if one sticks to the process of change on the world scene that has occurred over the past decade or so and assesses underlying causes as a historian might do, a strong case can be made that the effect of Vietnam upon the most basic elements of transformation has been either marginal or at most indirect. It is generally agreed that the greater pluralism of the international system in the mid-1970s by contrast with the mid-1960s has resulted from a convergence of two motive forces in particular: first, the Sino-Soviet conflict, which has made each of the mainland powers identify the other as its principal adversary, and thus move to make limited accommodations with the United States and other centers of power; second, the ending of American dominance within the non-Communist world, most particularly in its alliance systems—at every plane of power except the strategic—and a consequent redefinition of American interests.

I am not an expert on the Sino-Soviet dispute, but it seems to have a quality of inevitability which is more than simply the product of hindsight. Once the fears generated in the Chinese leadership by MacArthur's handling of the Korean War had subsided, once it became clear that the presence of the U.S. Seventh Fleet in the China Sea was not a prelude to an American invasion, the conflict of interest between two states that are hostile for reasons of geopolitics and race began to assume an ideological form. And the first signs of this occurred as early as 1958, or even 1956, while the American involvement in Indochina was still quite small. One can, of course, argue that the growing American presence there after 1962 or so, plus the tendency of both Kennedy and Johnson to treat China and the Soviet Union as equally hostile powers, at least in Indochina, created for about six years a synthetic unity of action between Moscow and Peking. Though the Chinese have no great respect for the North Vietnamese, whose leadership was more interested in relations with Moscow for military and other aid, they could not ignore the possibility that a large American military force near their southern border might be the prelude to an American onslaught on China itself, in which case they would need Soviet assistance. In other words, the Vietnamese involvement of the United States had the effect of delaying the time when Moscow and Peking would begin fully to develop containment strategies around the world vis-à-vis each other.

One can also argue that the Vietnam conflict, by reinforcing a hostile and threatening image of China in the eyes of large parts of the Administration, the Congress, and the public (though clearly some people in the Administration, notably the CIA, always doubted the real influence of Peking on Hanoi), delayed the moment when, in the interests of its security, China could put out feelers to the United States for an improvement of their relations and prevented the United States from exploiting the Sino-Soviet rift to improve its bargaining position with Moscow. But this argument can only be applied to the early and mid-1960s, because after 1966 the onset of the Cultural Revolution, whose inner springs were primarily domestic, really closed Peking to intercourse with the outside world until 1969.

Finally, one can argue that Vietnam delayed the opening of serious discussions between Washington and Moscow on détente, strategic arms control, European security or the Middle East; and by delaying them made it harder to achieve serious progress or to align superpower interests. This is a more substantial point. It was clear throughout the second half of the 1960s that the Soviet interest in trade and technological collaboration was rising, and that a political price could have been explored if the United States had been able to devote sufficient time and diplomatic effort to it. Many Europeans were also convinced that the muted American reaction to Soviet intervention in Czechoslovakia in 1968 was a consequence of Johnson's preoccupation with Vietnam. He often seemed like a hunter caught in his own trap, anxious to stabilize and improve superpower relations or to take other broad initiatives, yet obsessed with the next day's bombing targets in a remote corner of Asia.

Yet there are strict limitations even on this argument. The summit at Glassboro in 1967 made clear that the Soviet leaders were not prepared for serious arms-control negotiations until their strategic armory was larger, nor for discussions on the Middle East while it seemed that they had the whole radical Arab world in thrall. Their approach to European security questions changed markedly after the Prague summer. It was the re-entry of China into the international system, not American frustration in Vietnam, that changed the name of the game.

And by the time the great-power relationship had become a triangular one that included China, there was an agenda of Soviet-American business to be disposed of which had only an indirect relation to Vietnam. For one thing, the Soviet attainment of parity in strategic weapons was a consequence of decisions taken in Moscow after the Cuban missile crisis, though continuing tension in Southeast Asia may have created an incentive to keep the program going, even when its cost rose. From what has been published about the SALT negotiations between 1969 and 1970, it is clear that rising congressional resistance to defense expenditure as a whole, which was a direct consequence of Vietnam, did have a bearing on American negotiating positions about the mutual abrogation of ABM systems. But what really gave the SALT negotiations their impetus was technological developments, the ABM itself and the multiple warhead, which had been under development for over a decade. Certainly Vietnam and the rapid increase of American defense costs from 1965 onward made the United States anxious to stabilize the strategic confrontation with the Soviet Union. But this was a political as much as a fiscal calculation, which went back to Robert McNamara's early days in the Defense Department before serious expenditure on Vietnam had started.

This brings one to the other principal motive force of change, the redefinition of the American role in the world. The first point to make is that the present situation—in which Japan and the European Community are important economic, and increasingly important political, actors in an international system that is in general more plural in nature—is one that the United States was nominally anxious to bring about ten and even twenty years ago. There may be an unresolved ambiguity in American policy in that the United States wishes its allies to assume more initiative and a greater share of the general burdens of the West in such things as development aid or conventional military power but is most reluctant to devolve any strategic responsibilities on them, or recently even to treat them as serious coalition partners on issues such as the Middle East. Yet no American Administration has committed itself either to the goal of a bipolar world or to permanent dominance within its alliance systems in the way that the Soviet Union has and still does. But the way in which a more plural or polycentric system has come into being was not of American choice, and Vietnam did have an important, if indirect, bearing on the course of events.

It is true that Charles de Gaulle was a phenomenon quite independent of his time. It is also true that Gaullism, as an attitude of mind that gathered weight not only in France but in other countries in the 1960s—Romania, for instance, or India or Iran—was a reassertion of nationalism in an era of greater strategic stability than the cold-war years, so that middle powers felt greater freedom to assert their automony. But carnage in Vietnam, an area which the French felt they understood better than the Americans—though with little reason, for it had been the most neglected of all French colonies for two generations—helped give a national basis to de Gaulle's personal defiance of American leadership, and made it harder for governments like those of Britain, Germany or Italy to defend their continued acceptance of that leadership. Vietnam certainly widened de Gaulle's personal influence in the world beyond the borders of France.

Elsewhere in Europe as well as in Japan, Vietnam aroused popular opposition, though originally this was intense only with the student generation. It also made governments uneasy

that they might become embroiled in an Asian conflict in
which they had no interest. Ironically, it is clear from the
Pentagon Papers and other sources that one of the prime
reasons why Kennedy and then Johnson, together with Dean
Rusk and in particular Robert McNamara, argued that first
the Vietcong, and later North Vietnam as well, must be defeated at almost any cost, short of the use of nuclear weapons,
was the maintenance of the credibility of American guarantees
to the allies of the United States. Yet neither the European
NATO countries nor, as far as I can see, Japan felt that their
security was in a real sense enhanced by American persistence
in honoring a self-engendered promise to a small Asian ally.
Germans in particular tended to feel that Vietnam was dis-
tracting the attention of Washington from both the risks and
the opportunities developing in Europe as the Sino-Soviet
conflict made the Soviet Union more edgy about its position
in Eastern Europe and readier to contemplate accommodation with the West. If the British were concerned about the
risks of American failure in Vietnam, this was largely because
of their own interests, in Malaysia and Singapore, and not
from acceptance of arguments about the credibility of American strategic guarantees. The British role at the apogee of the
Vietnamese conflict is not a shining one: growing reservations
about American policy and fear of its consequences, coupled
with a reluctance to stand up to the United States on the issue,
because the position of sterling was at that time so dependent
on the support of the dollar. But though Vietnam may have
diminished European confidence in the American decision-
making process, it did not affect the conviction of European
governments that the Atlantic alliance was essential to their
security.

Very naturally, the impact of Vietnam has been much
greater in Southeast Asia and Australasia than in Europe or
Northeast Asia. Since 1973, and now more clearly after the
dramatic denouement in Cambodia and Vietnam, the Thai
can hardly rely on their American alliance through SEATO.
They, with Malaysia and the Philippines, are already moving
to establish ties with Peking, and in general the nations of
Southeast Asia are bound to search for a policy or norm that

accepts the area as one accessible to the influence of all the major powers—provided that none tries to claim a hegemonial position—in place of an American-led system of containment directed against the mainland powers. Australia and New Zealand will join in this concept, even though the ANZUS alliance will probably retain some contingent importance for them.

Economic historians may well argue for some time how significant a role the Vietnam war played in weakening the external economic and financial position of the United States. Clearly, from 1965 onward the fact that defense expenditure rose rapidly but that there was no significant increase in taxation contributed to inflation in the United States, and this tended to drive American investment overseas toward cheaper labor markets and weakened the competitive position of American exports and ultimately of the dollar. Japan also profited directly from American procurement there for Vietnam. But it seems to me that the weakening of the American economic position was primarily due to more rapid advances in Japanese and European, than in American, productivity during the 1960s and early 1970s, as well as to the refusal or inability of first the Johnson and then the Nixon Administration to place controls on overseas investment, and only secondarily to any economic distortions that may have been caused by the war in Vietnam.

Finally, there is a factor that is nonetheless real for being impossible to measure accurately, namely, diminishing respect for the United States as a society on the part of Europeans, Japanese, Latin Americans, Asians, even Russians. Certainly, the student unrest to which the war gave rise played a part in this, though such unrest had its counterpart in many other developed countries for quite different reasons—the over-crowding of the Japanese and French universities, and the antiquated structure of authority in the German universities, for instance. The eruption in the 1960s of many domestic issues in the United States—increased racial tension, concern with the decay of the cities, greater awareness of poverty and welfare problems—was a consequence, it seems to me, not of Vietnam but of some twenty years' preoccupation, on the part of élites and those controlling the purse strings in Congress, with foreign rather than domestic issues. Vietnam simply exacerbated problems that would have risen to the top of the agenda at that time in any case; and it was not Vietnam alone but a host of other external commitments which made it impossible for the Administration to switch its focus when the issues changed. Undoubtedly the costs of Vietnam cut sharply into funds available for Great Society programs. But even if these programs had been fully funded, there would have been a heavy proportion of failures—even the wealthiest society cannot wipe out deep-seated problems in the space of a few years.

IV

The most lasting international consequences of Vietnam —and not only for Americans—may well be on Americans' perceptions of themselves, of the world, and of the proper role of the United States in it. The fact that a conflict which lasted for nearly a decade, killed 55,000 Americans and over a million Vietnamese, and represented the first palpable failure of American arms in the history of the Republic, happened to coincide with the emergence of a number of endemic domestic problems and a loss of American strategic and economic predominance, has had the consequence of reinforcing the view of many Americans that the world is an ungrateful place. The fact that the American involvement was liquidated by a President whose interests were in international affairs, and that he was returned to office by a landslide in 1972, partly because the Vietnam war had itself created severe disarray within the Democratic party, may have simply delayed political expression of a fundamental change in public priorities, rather than averted it; the present Congress shows marked tendencies in the direction of downgrading all effort abroad, and the trend seems to go beyond the impact of the new "Class of 1974" or even of the recession.

One must be careful, however, to recall Namier's dictum. How much of the current decline of public confidence in Washington is really a consequence not of Vietnam but of Watergate, or of the sudden elevation to the Presidency of a mild man who has neither the gift nor the taste for exercising its authority and powers on a broad front? How much is it a consequence of the accidental conjunction of domestic recession and debacle in Indochina?

One can also argue that the completeness of the recent debacle wipes the slate clean, that the self-deception of the years of striving for "peace with honor" between 1969 and 1973—involving the invasion of Cambodia and the bombing of Haiphong—or of the phony armistice of the past two and a half years, were as damaging in terms of American political and moral self-confidence, if not of lives, as the earlier war years. Logically, the American polity should now be ready to address its enormous ingenuity, energy and humanity to the transformed agenda of world politics, to the negotiation of the new multilateral armistices or nonaggression pacts that will be needed to govern access to food, energy and raw materials, to order trade and monetary relations, to control North-South as well as East-West conflict.

But the concealed consequences of wars often linger in the public consciousness long after the dead are buried. And I am haunted by that famous quotation from Max Weber: "Interests (material and ideal), not ideas, dominate directly the actions of man. Yet the 'images of the world' created by these ideas have very often served as switches determining the tracks on which the dynamism of interests kept the action moving." The Vietnam war may have been such a switch point in the whole public conception of the nature of American society, and of its relationship to other societies. Unlike the Civil War, which left simply a void of grief and anger in a country whose external relations were still quite limited, the Vietnam war may lead—especially in a period when the United States is in a more competitive position, strategically with the Soviet Union, economically with Europe and Japan—to a harsher definition of American interests. It could also lead to a gradually pervading sense of national pessimism based on the belief that the United States is simply a big power, with as much capacity for harm as good, like other big powers in history, and not the distinct and buoyant civilization that it has been during most of the first two hundred years of the

Republic's history. I do not say this must be so, and as someone who regards America as his second home I hope I may
be wrong. But it will take a span of remarkable domestic
leadership in politics, in the universities, the states, and the
cities, to restore the self-confidence, the social generosity, and
the breadth of view that since Roosevelt's day have been
associated with the word "American."

Notes

1. *United States-Vietnam Relations, 1945-1967* [The Pentagon
   Papers] (Washington: GPO, 1971), Vol. 10, p. 732. This
   document is not included in the unofficial Gravel Edition of the
   Pentagon Papers.

Moscow, Peking, and the Conflict in Vietnam

MICHEL TATU

The conflict in Vietnam was less traumatic and wrenching an experience for the Communist world than for the United States and the West as a whole. But it was still a source of grave problems for the Communists. In view of the context of the war, this is hardly surprising. The conflict involved three Communist nations, two of which—the Soviet Union and China—were increasingly in a state of rivalry; indeed, the escalation of the conflict coincided with the open break in their relations. The third, North Vietnam, behaved in a manner almost totally independent from both of them. Finally, the conflict placed all three countries in opposition to the United States, the major capitalist power—and this at a time when the rivalry between the Russians and the Chinese was shaping the relations of each nation with Washington.

Thus, it was an extremely complex situation—almost a model imbroglio of divergent interests, ulterior motives, and triangular interactions. And if from 1969 to 1973 the considerable skill of the Nixon-Kissinger diplomacy wrested profit from this situation, it was not in the simplistic way that some had thought at the beginning. Convincing Russia and China to stop aiding North Vietnam and to push it toward peace was not enough. The proper blending of circumstances was also necessary; the triangular interplay had to produce a mix of compelling pressures which pointed toward a settlement at the very same time—and at the right time.

To be sure, this juncture held only for a while. The Watergate affair and President Nixon's resignation, the consequent weakening in the conduct of American policy and in executive-congressional relations, the crumbling of the Thieu regime's power in Saigon and its intrinsic military weakness resulted in draining the 1973 agreement of its substance, leading in the end to the fall of South Vietnam. The Paris Agreement nevertheless marked a stage in the history of this war, and we will concentrate on the period which led to its conclusion.

Our emphasis, then, will be on the shifts that occurred in Soviet and Chinese support of North Vietnam, for it is basically these changes that led to the agreements of January 1973. But bear one point in mind: The shifts should not mask or diminish the reality of the support. Whatever their disagreements and reservations, the Soviet Union and China did aid Hanoi throughout the war. There could be no question that they would do otherwise.

Since Western dollar estimates of the aid are, a priori, debatable, we shall cite no figures. We shall merely note that the North Vietnamese and the combatants in the South apparently never lacked food, munitions, fuel, or such heavy matériel as tanks, rockets, and artillery. At least until North Vietnamese ports were mined in 1972, the Russians and Chinese furnished Hanoi with large quantities of all it needed to survive and fight. The Soviets concentrated on heavy and sophisticated equipment, such as antiaircraft missiles, and hence their aid had a higher monetary value. Chinese aid emphasized complementary goods: foodstuffs and light arms.

Verbal support, too, was constant. Not a word of criticism of the North Vietnamese appeared in the Russian or Chinese press at any time during the war. There were charges only in the intensity of the verbal support, in the degree of warmth of the diplomatic backing, and in the quality of the war matériel that was furnished.

In this regard, a major limitation on the military support must be noted. The Soviet Union, which alone among the Communist powers could provide ultramodern war matériel, contributed tanks, anti-aircraft missiles in varying quantities, and rockets of varying ranges. But never did the Russians supply piloted aircraft or weapons that could threaten the American aircraft carriers in the Gulf of Tonkin. The will to avoid any escalation of the conflict that might lead to a Soviet-American confrontation remained constant throughout the war. Such restraint is inevitable in the thermonuclear age. It should, therefore, be seen as a permanent limitation. We are more interested here in specific nuances, actual shifts in the degree of support. There are more of these with regard to the Russians than to the Chinese.

II

Ambiguities in the Soviet position stemmed from the fact that the Vietnam war could be viewed in two different ways —not only as a local affair giving rise to certain reservations, but also as a tempting opportunity.

1. The *reservations* arose from the fact that Moscow did not have sufficient control over the war to be fully committed to it. In addition to their wish to avoid a confrontation with the United States, the Soviet leaders could not approve of all of Hanoi's war aims. The Soviet Union did, of course, proclaim its support for "wars of liberation." Khrushchev had reaffirmed that support in a January 1961 article in *Kommunist,* which John Kennedy took as a grave challenge. But the same article, while encouraging "wars of liberation," contended that "local" wars had to be avoided. And that is precisely what the Vietnamese conflict became, in Soviet terms, once the United States was massively engaged. Did Hanoi's goal of reunifying Vietnam under the direction of the workers' party justify a war of that type? Yes, if a victory over the United States could be achieved in a reasonable time and without a risk of escalation. No, if the entire international situation, and particularly Soviet diplomacy, had to be subordinated to that objective for a lengthy period. This was never stated officially, but it is precisely the key to how Moscow reacted each time the conflict took a critical turn.

Furthermore, the North Vietnamese objective violated the fundamental rules of peaceful coexistence. Not merely proclaimed, these were rules that governed practice elsewhere: The countries of the "socialist community" had to be defended, by force if necessary, but the extension of communism to new territory, though desirable, was not worth a war. Hanoi had to be protected, but helping it to raise the red flag in Saigon was a more doubtful venture (unless, once again, this end could be achieved without too much difficulty, as was the case in 1975).

The Soviet leaders, rather distrustful of any nationalism other than their own, had betrayed their basic thinking as early as 1956, when they took the misconceived step, seriously irritating Hanoi, of proposing the admission of both Vietnams to the United Nations. That effort was short-lived. But Moscow has been following a policy of consolidation rather than conquest vis-à-vis the other divided countries as well—Korea since 1953 and Germany since the very start.

It is ironic to note that the German situation, unlike the Korean, is exactly the reverse of the Vietnamese situation. The man insisting, like President Thieu in Saigon, that his country remain divided and that a separate state be established has been Honecker, and before him Ulbricht, the allies of the Soviet Union. And those who have refused, like the North Vietnamese leaders, to recognize the other part of the country, calling it an artificial creation and seeking (only in words, it is true) to do away with it, have been the West German "revenge seekers," unceasingly opposed by Moscow. The context, of course, is different in the two cases; and, in any case, the Kremlin is not in the habit of being embarrassed by contradictions. But the fact remains that the Soviet Union could not lend unconditional support to Hanoi's cause.

2. At the same time, the conflict held out *temptations,* opportunities to be seized. The Soviet Union was tempted, whenever the situation appeared to favor the North Vietnamese, to chalk up a point against the United States by giving the extra help needed to produce a victory for which the Soviets could claim credit. That was the case after the fall of Diem in 1963, during the Tet offensive in 1968, and undoubt-

edly in 1971 as well as in 1974. More generally, there were considerable periods during which Moscow felt that the war was serving its interests, seriously weakening its American rival without demanding excessive sacrifices of the Soviet Union. Those were the periods when the conflict seemed circumscribed, with little chance of escalating.

But there was another, more far-reaching temptation. It had to do with China. The growing rivalry with Peking induced Moscow not only to flaunt its solidarity with Hanoi, but to push the fortunes of its own particular pawns in the fray as well. In the event of a victory by the Communists and their allies in South Vietnam, or even more in Laos and Cambodia, the most desirable outcome could be a "Greater Indochina" linked preferentially with the U.S.S.R. and able to limit Chinese influence in Southeast Asia. A good way to pursue this end was to give Hanoi better aid than the Chinese did in hopes of convincing the North Vietnamese leaders, as well as Leftist forces throughout the world, that Soviet aid was the aid that counted in Vietnam. This temptation was particularly strong in 1971, as we shall see below.

III

Understandably, the ambiguities of the Chinese position were the reverse of the Soviet ambiguities. One might summarize by saying that Peking's natural inclination was to commit itself to the North Vietnamese, but that "second thoughts" soon developed, growing stronger as the "temptations" grew stronger in Moscow.

1. The *inclination to support* the North Vietnamese was natural. It was an Asian conflict, in an area very close to China, where the Americans appeared as intruders. Moreover, Mao Tse-tung saw in the conflict (or thought he could see, for the context was quite different) the prototype of the people's war, with the surrounding of the cities by the countryside and the waging of all-out guerrilla warfare. This was the type of war he himself had successfully fought to achieve power, and he had become its theoretician on the international stage. Aware of the reservations in the Soviets' support of North Vietnam and of the embarrassment that these reservations were causing

them in world opinion, Mao was all the more eager to support not only Hanoi, but the indefinite protraction of the conflict. His reasoning was that the Soviet Union, which could have done so much, did not wish to go too far, whereas China, with much more limited possibilities, was doing all it could. That explains the more strident tone of China's verbal support. China claimed to be allied with Vietnam "like the lips with the teeth" and to be ready to support the Vietnamese with "the greatest national sacrifices."

In point of fact, the sacrifices were limited. Mao, rather than Ho Chi Minh, was responsible for the thesis that in a people's war "one relies on one's own strength." Dean Rusk was therefore correct in saying at the time that the Chinese were prepared to fight "to the last Vietnamese." Peking's commitment remained indirect throughout; the only exception occurred during the bombings of the Johnson period, when the Chinese sent 40,000 men to help repair North Vietnam's railways.

Geographic proximity also made China more willing than the Soviet Union to take risks in defense of North Vietnam. Several times during the conflict, Peking made it known discreetly that Chinese troops would cross the border in the event of an invasion of the North that endangered Hanoi and its regime. The situation recalled that of Korea when Mao decided (reluctantly, as we now know) to dispatch his troops to prevent the defeat of North Korea and the installation of American troops on the Yalu.

2. Hence, Chinese *reservations* did not stem from fear of the United States, as was the case with the Soviets, but rather from the very temptations to which Moscow was prey. China had little to gain from the unification of Vietnam under the aegis of Hanoi, and still less from the establishment of a "Greater Indochina" dominated by North Vietnam. Like all great powers, and like the Communist powers in particular, China has always preferred dealing with divided neighbors to having overly vigorous nations on its doorstep, even if they were officially its allies. Stalin had similar thoughts; after the war, he had nipped in the bud the idea of a Balkan Federation put forward by Dmitrov and Tito, who at the time were perfectly orthodox Communists. There was no reason for Mao Tse-tung

and Chou En-lai to react differently to North Vietnam's "mini-imperialism," particularly when Hanoi's feelings toward Peking were anything but satisfactory to the Chinese leaders.

The Vietnamese have historically mistrusted their big northern neighbor. They do not forget that they were forced in the past to repel Chinese invasions. In the great schism dividing the Communist world today, the Vietnamese have sought to maintain their impartiality; but there are reasons for suspecting that their hearts are with Moscow rather than with Peking. In the 1920s and 1930s, Hanoi's leaders were formed by the French Communist party, a branch of the Comintern, and closely aligned with the Soviet Communist party. Though Asians, they have ways of thinking, methods of work, and concepts of politics that are closer to those of the Soviets than to those of the Chinese. Thus, they carefully refrained from imitating, or even approving, the Chinese Cultural Revolution; and they approved the Soviet intervention in Czechoslovakia, which China loudly condemned. Moreover, do not geography and circumstances make it advisable for North Vietnam to counteract the pressure of China's proximity by adopting a more friendly attitude toward the U.S.S.R., just as Romania, to buttress its independence from Moscow, has sought a rapprochement with China?

For all these reasons China's leaders, whatever they might say, could not align themselves unreservedly with Hanoi. Indeed, their reticence could only grow as they saw the Soviet Union take advantage of its position as the main supplier of heavy equipment to strengthen its stance in North Vietnam. Even the ideological sympathy felt in Peking for a "people's war" was dampened by the nature of the Soviet aid, which transformed the character of the war. No longer a thoroughly independent struggle, waged by local political and military means, it became a more classic type of war, waged with heavy weapons and tending to strengthen the influence of the great powers, particularly the Soviet Union.

Reacting in similar vein to the Middle East conflict, the Chinese have criticized Arab governments for downplaying the "people's war" and relying too heavily on Soviet deliveries of sophisticated weapons. A great power like the Soviet Union may give the impression, they have contended, that its support can swing the balance; but the long-run results of its aid is to create a dependence which enables Moscow to neutralize the conflict and frustrate the hopes of the "rebellious peoples."

A crucial effect of the Sino-American rapprochement, which began in 1971, was to restrain further the natural tendency of the Chinese to support the North Vietnamese and to strengthen China's reservations. These changes occurred to the extent that Nixon succeeded in convincing China's leaders that the achievement of their great national objective—the evacuation of American troops from Taiwan—required a reduction in regional tensions, i.e., an end to the Indochina war. On a more general plane, the rapprochement gave a further twist to the triangular interplay among the three hostile great powers. As the Soviet Union became a little more hostile and the United States a little less hostile in Peking's view, a divided Vietnam, with American influence persisting in the South, seemed preferable to a unified Vietnam in which Soviet influence predominated. That is the key to the distinct cooling in Chinese support for North Vietnam in late 1971

IV

These contradictory sentiments—"resolute" support and masked hesitation—alternated in both Moscow and Peking throughout the war, but the shifts were most marked at the war's most critical points. Two of those points were also significant for Sino-Soviet relations. They were the 1965-68 bombings of the North under President Johnson and the 1971-72 turning-point in the war.

The former period raised a major question, debated in the American press and by American commentators, concerning the Communist world: Would not the U.S. escalation of the war, the bombing in the North and the dispatch of a massive expeditionary force to the South, be deemed so grave a provocation by the Soviet Union, and still more by China, that they would forge their unity anew in order to meet it? In other words, did the escalation not imply a formidable threat to the United States, not only in Indochina, but throughout the world?

Unfortunately, it is not certain that this question, with all its implications, was posed in President Johnson's immediate entourage. If, as the White House seemed to think at the time, the Chinese were pulling the strings in the Vietnam war and the war served only their interests, Mao would have reacted to the escalation by drawing closer to the Russians, who were urging him to do just that. If the Chinese were as anti-American and as desirous of a total victory for Hanoi as the Administration believed, they would have welcomed all means of helping the North Vietnamese resist the United States. They would, for example, have encouraged a greater Russian commitment by making the necessary minimum of concessions to Moscow. But just the opposite happened, and the schism deepened.

The fault did not apparently lie with the Russians. In the spring of 1965, after the start of the bombings, Moscow exerted pressure on Peking by launching a major campaign for unity of action in support of North Vietnam. The language used was skillfully moderated. Instead of calling upon the "dogmatists" and other "revisionists" to rally to its banner, the Soviet Union proposed a temporary silencing of differences as a basis for "concrete measures" in support of North Vietnam and in reply to "imperialist aggression." The campaign was welcomed by the Japanese Communist party and other Communist parties which had generally been rather cool to the Soviets.

It is now known with virtual certainty that some Chinese leaders were likewise inclined to respond favorably to the Soviet appeal. During a visit to Peking in the spring of 1966, a Japanese Communist party delegation held lengthy discussions with its mayor, Peng Cheng, apparently one of the strong men in the Chinese party, a close ally of President Liu Shaochi, and a serious candidate in an incipient struggle for power. It was later learned that the joint communiqué drafted following the discussions, in referring to aid for Vietnam, echoed the Soviet "unity of action" slogan. On Mao's orders, the communiqué was never issued, and Peng Cheng soon fell from power.

The Cultural Revolution, which was then beginning, had

largely domestic motivations, chief among them the struggle for power. Its international significance was to answer a key question: Which should China consider the main enemy—the United States or the Soviet Union? Mao thought it should be the Soviet Union, and his point of view was victorious. This choice flowed from global strategic considerations—a profound mistrust of Great Russian imperialism; an aversion to the paternalistic, domineering methods used by the Russians in the international Communist movement; and perhaps the hope of an eventual settlement of old accounts with Russian expansionism in Asia. Compared to such considerations, the Vietnam war, as important as it was, did not amount to much. At most, it delayed a Sino-American rapprochement for a few years. But such a rapprochement had been in the cards since 1960, when the great schism burst into public view.

It took a large dose of cynicism on Mao's part to impose his viewpoint. He had to reject a unity of action that would have significantly facilitated things for the North Vietnamese and that was strongly supported by many Western Communist parties, which necessarily were more idealistic. But the Soviet leaders, despite the "nobility" of their appeal for unity of action, were not motivated by sentiment either. The escalation in Vietnam offered them an opportunity to refurbish the façade of the Communist movement on conditions favorable to them, to place China on the defensive, and to move toward the world conference of Communist parties that had been their primary objective since 1963. (The conference was finally held in 1969, but preparatory meetings took place from 1965 on.)

Still, Moscow extracted several concessions from Peking. One of them was Chinese acceptance in 1967, at Hanoi's urgent entreaty, of an agreement with the U.S.S.R. permitting the use of Chinese railroads for the transit of Soviet war matériel to North Vietnam. For technical as well as political reasons, transshipment failed to acquire major significance. A considerably larger volume of supplies was sent by sea to Haiphong and, at least until the end of 1969, to Sihanoukville in Cambodia.

The beginning of the second significant phase in the war was marked by the Sino-American ping-pong match in the spring of 1971, and then by Kissinger's first trip to Peking. From then on, Sino-Soviet rivalry played a crucial role in the development and outcome of the conflict.

Although the Sino-American rapprochement created a sensation in the world and reinforced Nixon's prestige, its early effects were not all beneficial to the United States. The Soviet Union, understandably concerned by what it perceived as an effort at encirclement and collusion by its two main adversaries, intensified its international activities to a disturbing degree. In Asia particularly, it sought to close a ring around China and to score points against the United States. Such was the case in the Indian subcontinent, where the Indo-Soviet treaty, signed in the summer of 1971, was followed a few months later by the Indian victory over Pakistan, humiliating China and embarrassing the United States. Pursuing the effort to encircle China, Gromyko visited Japan belatedly in January 1972, this time achieving little.

The Soviet effort in Hanoi was still more serious. In early 1971, several factors were pushing the Soviet leaders closer to North Vietnam:

1. Their influence among the Communist forces in Indochina had somewhat declined, together with the level of fighting in the aftermath of the Tet offensive, and even more as a result of Prince Sihanouk's entry into the Chinese camp following his overthrow in 1970. Chou En-lai took advantage of this fact to sponsor a "conference of Indochinese peoples" in 1970. Held in China, the conference was intended to coordinate the efforts of the peninsula's four anti-American movements or governments—the Democratic Republic of Vietnam, the Provisional Revolutionary Government, the Pathet Lao, and Sihanouk's supporters. Through the latter group in particular, China hoped to play a more active diplomatic role in the region, to the detriment of Moscow, which had failed to develop a relationship with Sihanouk.[1] The time had now come for the U.S.S.R. to move forward again.

2. The Sino-American rapprochement offered just the opportunity Moscow needed, for it irritated and worried Hanoi. In the summer of 1971, the North Vietnamese press for the

first time indirectly criticized the Chinese, decrying "selfish great power interests" and "American plots to divide the anti-imperialist front." Such criticism had hitherto been reserved for Soviet restraint in supporting North Vietnam. Here was a chance for the Soviet Union to reverse roles, placing the Chinese on the defensive by arguing that the Soviets were better supporters of the Indochinese struggle. Here was a chance to nourish again the long-range vision of an anti-Chinese, pro-Soviet North Vietnam dominating the Indochinese peninsula. But even if this maximum result should be out of reach, the Soviet leaders could not pass up the opportunity they saw in the Chinese eclipse in Hanoi to consolidate their own positions.

3. Finally, the rapprochement with North Vietnam served as a warning to the United States. "Move closer to our Chinese enemies and ignore us if you wish," the Soviet message appeared to say, "but we are in a position to aggravate your difficulties in Vietnam and to remind you that the solution you are seeking to the conflict is to be found just as much in Moscow as in Peking."

The third point was, of course, not the main one, for Brezhnev was interested not in a confrontation with the United States, but in the development of his own dialogue with the United States. He took the initiative in the fall of 1971 to call for a summit meeting with Nixon. He probably would have been more cautious in lending aid to North Vietnam if he could have foreseen the grave escalation with which his future guest would respond to the North Vietnamese offensive the following May. The Soviet leader may have miscalculated. But it must be recognized that he had valid reasons for drawing closer to the North Vietnamese; and the only way he could do so was to deliver the weapons Hanoi wanted. In other words, he had to lift Moscow's embargo on certain types and quantities of arms.

Another possible explanation, compatible with the above, is that the North Vietnamese cited the South Vietnamese operation in February 1971 via Route 9 in Laos, attacking the Ho Chi Minh Trail, as evidence that the Soviet Union had better help them prepare for an invasion of North Vietnam.

Since the South Vietnamese operation was not successful, the argument lacked persuasiveness, but it fell on receptive ears in Moscow.

In any event, in the spring of 1971 Soviet military supplies began arriving at North Vietnamese ports in quantities never before seen there. One year later, eyewitnesses reported that North Vietnam, and particularly the areas around Hanoi and Haiphong, had become a full-fledged arsenal, stocked with massive quantities of ammunition, fuel, and artillery pieces. The tanks could be explained as necessary for reinforcing the North Vietnamese army; but the many SAM missiles were rather surprising, since no one prior to late March 1972 expected the Americans to renew the bombing. As the suppliers of all this matériel, the Soviets must have suspected that it would be put to use, i.e., that there would be an offensive in the South. But they undoubtedly hoped that the offensive would take place in January or February 1972, coinciding with Nixon's trip to Peking and embarrassing the Chinese leaders. They may also have thought that the extent of their aid to Hanoi had given them some degree of control over North Vietnamese policy. The resolutely pro-Soviet and somewhat anti-Chinese tone of the Hanoi press in early 1972 lent credence to the view that a solid friendship now bound the two countries and would be reflected in the behavior of the North Vietnamese Politburo.

Given this background, Hanoi's decision to unleash the great offensive in the South on March 30, 1972, just a few weeks before Nixon's visit to Moscow, had consequences of the utmost gravity. If the offensive proved not to be a military success, it was an even greater error on the diplomatic front. Having already annoyed the Chinese by transparently, if indirectly, criticizing their rapprochement with the United States, North Vietnam had now deeply irritated its principal protector, the Soviet Union, as well.

The author has overwhelming evidence to confirm the claim that the Soviet leaders were not informed, let alone consulted, prior to North Vietnam's massive offensive. It is affirmed in Moscow that General Batitsky, chief of the Soviet Union's anti-aircraft forces, was given not the slightest hint of the

coming offensive during his talks with North Vietnamese civilian and military leaders in North Vietnam shortly before
March 30. The North Vietnamese Politburo undoubtedly had
good reasons for its discretion. Brezhnev, had he know of the
plans in advance, would most likely have urged that the
offensive be postponed at least until Nixon's departure from
Moscow. But, for reasons still undisclosed, Hanoi did not wish
to wait. Perhaps it wanted to strike a decisive blow well before
the American elections; perhaps it was concerned with the
consolidation of the South Vietnamese Army; perhaps it
hoped to extract from Washington, before the withdrawal of
more American troops, the concessions that General Thieu
was not prepared to offer.

   For the Soviets, this was the moment of truth—and maybe
of disillusion—on Vietnam. Seen from Moscow, it was intolerable that a small country, even if an ally, should obstruct
one of the greatest undertakings of postwar Soviet diplomacy
—the first visit of an American President to the Soviet
Union. It was particularly intolerable in this case, for North
Vietnam had acted without consulting its protector, who had
just done so much to help. This showed, or confirmed, that the
ally was not reliable, that it acted too independently, and that
the dream of a large opening for Soviet influence in an Indochina unified under Hanoi's leadership was unrealistic.

   The Soviet reaction might have been different if the offensive had quickly achieved decisive successes, leading to the
collapse of the South Vietnamese Army and to Washington's
resigned acceptance of a fait accompli. Moscow could then
have forgotten its bitterness toward Hanoi, or at least ex-
ploited Hanoi's success by taking credit for it. But with President Nixon's violent reaction to Hanoi's initial successes, and
particularly with the mining of the ports on the Gulf of Tonkin, events took a different turn. Coming just three weeks
before his visit to Moscow, the President's actions, interpreted
throughout the world as a challenge to the Russians, posed a
serious problem. Some Soviet leaders, including Ukrainian
party chief Shelest, apparently urged a postponement of
Nixon's visit. But Brezhnev managed to keep his arrangements

intact, and Shelest was removed from his Ukrainian party post shortly before Nixon's arrival. Brezhnev's attitude stemmed from the great importance he attached to the Soviet-American summit and to the development of trade with the United States. Furthermore, he did not wish to leave the Chinese alone in their contacts with the United States, and he considered a dialogue with Washington indispensable to his European policy—which also reflected his fear of China in the East. Finally, it was Hanoi that had administered the initial humiliation to the Soviet Union, and Brezhnev could not permit a small country in the socialist camp to dictate Soviet policy. Hence, at least for the foreseeable future, the Soviet Union abandoned the temptations described above. Convinced that the war had lasted too long and should be brought to an end, it returned to its earlier posture of reluctant ally.

In the wake of its strategic error, North Vietnam confronted an entirely new situation. Until then, it had found at least one advantage in Sino-Soviet rivalry: When either of the great Communist powers reduced its support for Hanoi, the other took up the slack, causing the first to fear it would fall behind. But, beginning in 1972, both Moscow and Peking, for different reasons, wanted a settlement to the conflict. This did not lead to a reconciliation between China and the Soviet Union, however. As between 1965 and 1968, the Chinese only reluctantly agreed to the transshipment of Soviet aid and, after a few months' delay, to the opening of southern Chinese ports to Soviet ships. Thus, with the March 30 offensive bogged down despite terrible losses, with its allies pressing it to compromise, and with prospects of an unlimited blockade and bombing, North Vietnam decided to negotiate. The breakthrough, represented by Le Duc Tho's proposals to Kissinger on October 8, 1972, resulted from this combination of circumstances.

Admittedly, Hanoi's strict independence of both of its protectors is also a major element in the international framework. If North Vietnam should now decide to move fully into one of the two camps—which would more likely be the Soviet camp—the Soviets would again be tempted to seek an anti-

Chinese platform in southern Asia. But has North Vietnam
been fighting so bitterly for thirty years just to become an
instrument of a great power?

Notes

1. The dilemmas arising from the Sihanouk case show the extent
   to which Sino-Soviet rivalry affected the two nations' responses
   to Indochina. Sihanouk's alignment with Peking caused Moscow to refuse recognition of his government-in-exile until very
   late, though the Soviets were placed in an untenable position by
   Marshal Lon Nol's repeated failures. Similarly, China supported non-Communist Sihanouk so vigorously because he was
   hostile to Moscow and because Peking needed him as a counter
   to future domination of the peninsula by the North Vietnamese, whose relations with Sihanouk were strained.

PART II

The Indochina War and Change in the United States

The War and American Society

As Alastair Buchan suggests, "the most lasting international consequences of Vietnam . . . may well be on Americans' perceptions of themselves, of the world, and of the proper role of the United States in it." These perceptions are not simply the product of the published wisdom of foreign policy sages; they are inseparably bound to the changes in attitude and behavior that have taken place within American society as a whole since the early 1960s. No one can measure with precision the influence of the war on these changes. It is clear, however, that the experience helped produce new approaches among Americans to each other, to their leaders, and to their institutions. This will inevitably alter the political processes behind, and therefore the substance of, our foreign policies.

In the first two essays of this section, Edward Shils and Peter Osnos consider some of the most important changes of the past decade; the former with regard to American society as a whole, the latter as they took place in a "typical" community near Washington, D.C.

Shils finds that the war helped stimulate and strengthen a number of trends within America which have common, complementary effects: the erosion of the legitimacy of authority, and the polarization of opinion between traditionalists and progressives. The federal government—and, to varying degrees, other authorities in our society—have been trapped between their tendency to take on more responsibility and their inability to meet the goals they set, all the while scrutinized by a suspicious public, press, and, most importantly, television newscasters. Television has also, in Shils's view, politicized the American public and therefore polarized it between the adherents of the "progressive outlook" and those of the "traditional outlook." While the war and Watergate have combined with other factors to place the traditional outlook on the defensive, Shils concludes that it will remain strong. The progressives, however, may lose the unity engendered by opposition to the war.

Shils believes that restoration of civility in American society is necessary to ameliorate the impact of continuing divisions, and that civility depends on the restoration of the legitimacy of authority. Since he doubts that this can come soon, he fears that American society may be "in perpetual disorder," an "enduring inheritance from the war in Indochina."

Peter Osnos studied the impact of the war on Riverdale, Maryland, a town whose population is preponderantly of the "traditional" outlook. Even here, one finds the politicization and doubts about authority that alarm Shils but which, viewed in a different light, may indicate something more hopeful—greater participation by Americans in the workings of their democracy. Osnos could discover little impact of the war on people's lives; indeed, Vietnam seemed in the process of becoming a dim memory, which may explain why so few people of those he interviewed seemed interested in finding scapegoats for the war. But he found that it had changed their attitudes in ways even they barely recognized. Beyond a disillusion with government and the modesty with which they viewed the American role in the world, there was a more active personal view, learned, perhaps, from observation of the impact of antiwar activism. The leader of Riverdale's antibusing movement told Osnos that "the war forced a lot of people to start speaking out. We never thought there was anything we could or should do about that, but we saw there might be something we could do closer to home. Busing seemed like something we could handle."

Both Shils and Osnos found that the impact of the war on America was more general than particular. Vietnam seems to have touched our citizens less directly than we believed (largely because of television); it had, however, affected our society as a whole. This view parallels the findings of surveys by Potomac Associates in 1971 and 1973.[1] According to these polls, most Americans take more comfort in the state of their own affairs than in the state of society as a whole. It may be that this collective psychological depression is one of the most important consequences of our years in Vietnam.

Peter Osnos is the Moscow correspondent of the *Washington Post*. He joined the *Post* in 1966, and has served in London, Washington, and, for two years, Indochina.

Edward Shils is Professor of Social Thought and Sociology at the University of Chicago and Fellow of Peterhouse, Cambridge University. He is also Honorary Professor of Anthropology at University College, London. He is the author of various works, including *The Torment of Secrecy* and *The Intellectuals and the Powers*.

Notes
1. Albert Cantril and Charles W. Roll, Jr., *Hopes and Fears of the American People* (New York: Universe Books, 1971), pp. 51, 52; William Watts and Lloyd D. Free, eds. *State of the Nation* (New York: Harper, 1974), pp. 258-63.

American Society and the War in Indochina

EDWARD SHILS

In modern societies, wars impinge on the entire population much more gravely than did wars before the French Revolution. Since the rise of citizen armies, large numbers of young men are removed from civilian society in wartime, their attachments are disrupted and opportunities closed, and they are subjected to dangers which they and their families feel acutely. The large expenditures required to maintain the armed forces and the diversion of resources place great strains on the society as well as the economy. And war greatly intensifies the relationship of the citizenry to the ruling authority.

The diffuse and widely dispersed patriotism which is characteristic of modern societies is rendered more salient in time of war.

The center of society—governmental authorities and the symbols of national life—is more visible in modern societies than it was in the past. It has become more significant to the citizenry—a category which scarcely existed in oligarchical and autocratic societies before the modern age—and draws to itself sentiments which aristocratic and mostly illiterate societies with less prominent centers could not arouse or attract. At the same time, despite the endemic and inexpungible presence of patriotism the center of society has come into disrepute among many highly educated persons. Patriotism, since early in the twentieth century, has been thought by many intellectuals to be atavistic or archaic, associated with a tribal outlook which lacks moral sensitivity. In twentieth-century Western societies, this disparagement of patriotism has been temporarily. softened in wartime when, especially in the beginning, the solidarity of each of the contending national societies has typically increased. For a time other problems tend to be put aside. But if the war goes badly or if it drags on without decisive issue, national solidarity and the patriotism of intellectuals particularly diminish. Where there is freedom of expression and association, political discussion and contention become especially clamorous.

In modern liberal-democratic and more or less civil societies, the conduct of war leads government to arrogate to itself more powers over more spheres of life. As a result, it becomes both more visible and more available for criticism. Wars, in fact and in imagination, give the government the ultimate power over life and death. The good name of governments, their reputations for efficacy, probity, and solicitude, are placed at risk. The legitimacy of governments, on which the effective exercise of authority in civil society rests, is always at risk; faltering or unsuccessful conduct of a war threatens legitimacy further. When the prospects of military victory are slight, or when armies are being defeated, the legitimacy declines. Resistance to authority increases, class conflict becomes exacerbated, strikes occur in great number. Where there is still freedom for the expression of such views, there is talk of revolution. Disobedience to the law increases. Soldiers desert. Patriotism acquires harsher tones, and hostility towards patriotic symbols becomes more widespread.

Lost wars release all sorts of accumulated animosities. Anger over the uncompensated suffering caused by war—even in countries which do not suffer invasion or prolonged enemy occupation—and resentment against authorities, who purported to be strong and turned out to be weak, come surging forward. It is not just the rulers at the peak of the society who are rejected; all authorities—police and civil service, parents, teachers, and clergy—are in varying degrees repudiated because they were involved in the abdication of authority from the powers which it claimed for itself.

Even in societies of which the armed forces have been successful, the situation shows tendencies in the same direction. Where the reigning authorities have blundered and the war was fought in long and sanguinary battles in which, although they eventually culminated victoriously, great losses were suffered by the victors as well as by the vanquished, the reputation of authority is tarnished. The openly critical attitude towards authority, characteristic of liberal-democratic societies, has an expansive potentiality. The more governments undertake to do, the more numerous their publicly perceived errors will be. Because wars heighten the probability of mistakes and failures, they heighten the dangers to which governments are subject.

American forces were not defeated in the military action in Indochina, but neither were they victorious. The restrictive aims as well as the strategy and the conditions under which the war was conducted precluded decisive victories in the field or a conclusively successful outcome to the war as a whole. It was a war of uncertain legitimacy, for it was never officially "declared," and it went on for nearly a decade, involving more and more American soldiers. Television made the war even more present to civilians as it brought distant military operations into millions of homes with an immediacy never seen before. The discrediting of the earlier optimistic announcements of "body counts" of the slain enemy and the succession of unsuccessful programs of "pacification" contributed to a general conviction of the hopelessness of the undertaking and to disbelief in the truthfulness and efficacy of the authorities in government and the armed forces. As the war continued so issuelessly, it gave rise to more and more dismay. The fate of sons, husbands, and kinsmen serving in Indochina was a cause of perpetual worry. The inability to gain victory was humiliating. And the increasingly theatrical opposition to the war was exasperating and embittering to those whose patriotism was already severely affronted by the powerlessness of American power in the field.

II

The popular response to American participation in the war in Indochina occurred in a setting of certain major changes in American society. These changes began before the war, but they soon fused with responses to the war, giving them a special quality.

The youth culture was one such change. It was a powerfully asserted demand by adolescents and by young men and women that they be free to find and form their life-styles as impulse and taste prescribed, without regard for traditional restraints and the discipline of ambition and convention. It was given much prominence by the visibility of pop culture on the television and its audibility on radio and sound recording. The concurrent increase in the number and proportion of young persons attending universities and colleges conferred a high standing on the culture of a generation which was denying the validity of the culture and social outlook of the older generation and the institutions it controlled.

A second notable change was the urgency with which it came to be believed that the amount of poverty in the country was very great and that it had to be speedily and definitively eliminated. The poor were seen as possessing rights which had not been previously acknowledged.

Still another of these changes was increased insistence of the black section of American society that its full civil rights should be acknowledged; that it should possess greater economic opportunity and should be more integrated into American society. It demanded greater equality in all important respects with the white section of the society, and the claim was supported by influential sectors of the white population.

There occurred at the same time a very considerable change in attitudes toward sexuality in American society. This was a further stage in the fading of American puritanism which resulted from the Great Depression. Obstacles to the publication and distribution of works of pornography were almost eliminated. Public discourse was modified to accommodate this new mode of preoccupation with sexuality in all forms, normal and perverse. Distinctions and boundaries related to sexual differences were bitterly attacked. Manliness ceased to be a virtue outside the "archaic" sectors of American society.

The foregoing changes all have in common an enhanced appreciation of the value of the individual. They are variants of a new type of individualism. A second set of changes runs in a somewhat contrary direction. They are connected with the expansion of the powers of the center of American society and the saturation of its peripheries.

The growth of the new individualism gained force at a time when the federal government was continuing the long-term trend of adding to its powers. The older regulatory powers, the social security system, and the more active intervention in economic policy introduced before World War II continued. This was followed by the enlarged role of the federal government after that war as a result of accepting responsibility for full employment. In the 1960s the federal government accepted responsibility for the comprehensive improvement of the situation of the black members of society and for the closely allied elimination of poverty, for the provision of housing, for the support of scientific research, and thus for the support of a major sector of the activities of universities, as well as for the support of various higher educational activities alleged to be connected with national defense. Armaments and the maintenance of the armed forces, together with all these other activities, took large parts of the national income.

These increased activities far outran those of state and municipal governments and indeed made them into dependents of the federal government. The increased dependence of state and municipal governments reduces the power of the state and local political machines. Naturally, all this made the federal government far more visible to the citizenry.

An accompaniment of the growth of the regulatory functions and of the provision of services by the federal government in spheres previously left in the hands of state and local governments or in private hands, or in no hands at all, was the growth of the prominence and power of the executive branch of the federal government at the expense of the legislative branch. The power of the President and of his entourage in the executive office of the President has expanded with few reversals since the 1930s. The federal civil service had never been highly esteemed in the United States. It grew greatly as government increased the scale of its activities, but its prestige did not increase. Preoccupations with security, domestic and foreign, generated unprecedented provisions for intelligence and counterintelligence. Genuine necessities were encrusted by many demands which were fictitious. From the remnants of the Office of Strategic Services and G-2, the intelligence services grew into the largest intelligence-gathering operation ever established in a liberal-democratic country. Intelligence-gathering activities received a mighty stimulus from the technological potentialities of electronics realized in highly sensitive devices of perception, recording, and data processing. The security-consciousness inherited from World War II and sustained by the long tension with the Soviet Union and the inherent secretiveness of a large bureaucracy collided with the resentment of the legislative against the executive and brought to a high pitch conflicts about secrecy and publicity. With the government as prominent in public consciousness as it was, its secretiveness was not easily bearable. It was least bearable by the organs of mass communications which had helped to dramatize the prominence of the federal government. The local was partially displaced by the national in the public's conception of American society.

The belief that practically nothing is beyond the power of government, that it is omnipotent, is not only accepted by most of the people but even by many radical critics of government. And yet, at the same time, the traditional attitude of distrust toward government, and particularly toward most politicians, has persisted in various forms. The course of the war in Indochina and of the accompanying domestic events confirmed this distrust, but did not diminish the demands for governmental intervention and provision. The exacerbated demands of the various parts of American society only increases the likelihood of exposure of failed undertakings. And failed undertakings are what the organs of public opinion are determined to expose.

All this places federal governmental authority in a difficult position. Before World War II, American security services—secrecy-keeping and intelligence-gathering—were obscure and generally unnoticed by the public. Governmental secrecy was disapproved of, but there was little interest in it. World War II, the development of nuclear weapons, and the persistent distrust of the Soviet Union after the war increased the stock of secrets. For about a decade following 1945, the federal government built up a large apparatus for the creation and protection of secrets, primarily about national security. Several major congressional committees made their fame from the belief in the sacredness of secrets and the danger of their unauthorized disclosure. Even when the apprehension of subversion was dissipated, it was still generally accepted that certain activities of government should be maintained in secrecy; this applied particularly to the armed forces and the intelligence service. But this was contrary to the tradition of distrust of governmental authority and to the tradition of the openness of everything in American society to the curiosity of the press. The two traditions persisted, but in moderation.

The crisis of confidence in government attendant upon the war in Indochina, the desire to end the cold war and to blame the United States for its existence, the rancor of radical students and teachers against the Central Intelligence Agency (CIA) and the armed forces have helped to restore and intensify the avidity with which the press seeks to penetrate the veil of secrecy. As government came more and more under suspicion of falsehood and secretiveness during the second half of the 1960s, the demand for freedom of information began to grow greater. The disclosure of the CIA's subsidy of various spurious foundations, which then made grants to the National Student Association, the Congress for Cultural Freedom, and other intellectual bodies, helped to discredit governmental secrecy further. The purloining of the Pentagon Papers was another blow against secrecy and the credibility of government. It was taken for granted that the government was hiding heinous crimes under the protection of secrecy. The widespread support for Daniel Ellsberg for breaking his oath of secrecy testified to the discredit into which government had fallen. Its ineptitude, even in protecting its secrets, and its inability to prosecute successfully one who had so massively betrayed the obligation he had earlier accepted, were evidence of power unworthy of and unable to command respect.

The paradox remains. Disrespect for government moves hand in hand with greater demands. A disrespected government renders itself even more subject to censure as new tasks are put upon it which it cannot refuse. The great affair of President Nixon's tapes has appeared to many to vindicate their distrust of government.

III

Like most of the great changes in American society, recent trends have been vociferously discussed. America is a clamorous country. Laudation is exaggerated; complaints are exaggerated. American politicians speak hyperbolically; their critics speak hyperbolically. Quite apart from crudity of perception, characteristic of both the proponents and the antagonists of the inherited order, the tradition of raucous rhetoric makes for simplification and exaggeration.

Even in relatively eventless times, public discourse within the United States tends toward hyperbole. But the United States has not known relatively eventless times for nearly half a century. In the period of great changes brought in by the Great Depression of the 1930s, every important step away from the previously accepted pattern has been accompanied by acrid contention. This was accentuated in the 1960s. The never-gratifying participation of the United States in the war in Southeast Asia—coming as it did in a time of many domestic conflicts about primordial things such as sex, age, and race, and with the federal government more prominent in the public mind than it had ever been—aroused very strong passions. Television reporting always stressed what was most passionate. Riots in black districts, demonstrations, virulent denunciations, altercations with police in universities, and meaningless and menacing military operations all possessed features most amenable to the traditions of hyperbolic representation.

Authority appeared very unfavorably in these accounts: brutal, cowardly, propitiatory, half-hearted by turns, its weakness
and ineffectiveness were as visible as the ostensibly justified
destructive and righteous indignation of demonstrators and
rioters. In scenes of battle abroad, soldiers were shown in
bewildering and unconquerable circumstances, where no
operation was visibly and definitively successful. Ruins,
maimed bodies, and perplexed and worried young American
soldiers were the staples of the television reports. At home,
smouldering buildings in black districts, glowering young
black faces, policemen wearing protective equipment making
them look like monsters, students running from pursuing
policemen or chanting taunts in a carnival atmosphere were
steady features of television for some time. The news commentators, like the televised reports themselves, showed as
much sympathy with the rioters and demonstrators as animosity against the forces of order.

It is an old tradition of American newspaper reporting,
which television has inherited, to be critical of office-holders.
This tradition has been accentuated by the "liberationist"
intellectual culture of the television profession, which abhors
commercial values while being immersed in the commercially
dominated world of television production. Criticizing American society through photographic reporting of its failures
offered compensation for the degradation of working for a
base and commercially motivated institution. Members of the
profession lent themselves with special gusto to photograph-
ing, reporting, and annotating the discomfiture, ineptitude,
and ineffectual brutality of the establishment.

Although the members of the television profession were not
radicals who sought to infiltrate the mass media, they had
inherited the tradition of muckraking from the printed press.
Golden opportunities were available to them—there was so
much that was violently dramatic to display, and the audience
was so large and so fixed on the medium of television, as the
audiences of the printed word had never been, that it would
have been a wanton disregard of opportunities for satisfying
and distinctive professional performance to be better balanced and less melodramatic. Whatever their motives, their

interpretation of important events made a profound mark on American society in the 1960s: it was a sense that American society was degenerating into an uncontrolled disorder which authority could not halt.

Television gave the American people vivid images of certain aspects of the war in Vietnam—certainly not the only significant aspects—which they could never have got from reading newspapers and periodicals. It made them see the war as a meaningless destruction of lives and landscape, carried out by young men like their own sons living in mortal danger. Television helped to politicize the American people; it showed them terrible things which were linked to the poor judgment and devious character of the politicians, military men, and university presidents. As much as, if not more than, any other factor, television contributed to the changing of Americans' image of their own society. The media of mass communication, and particularly television, nearly obliterated the image of what was quiet and orderly and decent in American society and replaced it with an image of a society which was the scene of angry debate and vast and violent disorder. American society was made to appear adrift in a stormy sea full of shoals; those who had presumed to govern it seemed helpless in the storm. This was the message. Television did as much as any technological device could do to dissolve the belief of American society in the legitimacy of those to whom its major decisions had been entrusted.

The 1960s were years in which these authorities, who governed the central institutions of American society, faced problems with which they could not deal very effectively. American has always been a difficult country to govern, and it prospered because it was generally able to avoid the situations in which people had to be kept under strong and concentrated authority. Nonetheless, the American people and their guides and leaders had for some decades been demanding a more active federal government from which they desired more services but to which they were not so willing to give more obedience or respect. The strength of local governments declined through their own poor standards and traditions and the policies of the federal government, which never showed reluctance to add to its tasks. The universities underwent an expansion of their activities not unlike that of the federal government; their administrators were increasingly willing to go on adding to their tasks. The military authorities, their self-confidence bolstered by their accomplishments in World War II, assumed that no enemy could withstand the arms given them by American technology, but they were disabused in Indochina.

The displacement of professional politicians by amateurs in the Democratic and Republican party campaigns in 1972 was an indication of the rejection of the older exercisers of authority in party politics. The discrediting and general dislegitimation of the old gang was a part of the movement which was strengthened in the failures of the government and its armed forces in Indochina. Opposition to the war spurred the efforts of highly educated persons to influence and obtain nominations and gain elective office. In doing so, they overpowered many of the conventional machine politicians, disrupting the older type of party organizations. They threw the Democratic party, which since the 1930s had been the party of progress, into a state of disarray. In the Republican party, the extension of petty zealotry beyond the traditionally elastic limits of political competition seems also to have been the work of a similar body of politicized amateurs heartened by the generally faded reputation of the professionals.

In the 1960s, authorities of all kinds confronted difficult problems of the black population, of the overextended universities, and of the war in Indochina which were beyond their powers. Their inefficacy greatly damaged popular belief in their legitimacy. The agitation of intellectuals, in and outside the universities, scientists as well as social scientists and literary men, middle-aged and even the old as well as young joined in this derogation of political, academic, military, and economic authority, while making the adversaries of authority—the North Vietnamese and Vietcong Communists, university students, black rioters, even in a few extreme cases muggers on the streets and adolescent gangster-terrorists—into paragons of virtue and the bearers of hope for the future. Interestingly enough, this agitation had a profound influence on many of those against whom it was conducted. Politicians, army officers, police chiefs, and, above all, university administrators began to echo the beliefs of their adversaries, to confess to the defects of which they were accused, and to praise those who denounced them.

IV

Radical "politicization" led to the polarization of two outlooks: the progressive and the traditional. Ever since the Administration of Franklin Roosevelt, there had grown up in the country a sharper distinction between the traditional and the progressive outlooks. But the differences continued to be blurred by the overlapping of the two major political parties. And the two were not diametrically opposed to each other, since they had differed only in the intensity of their stress on various aspects of a commonly espoused individualism. Both the "party of progressive outlook" and the "party of traditional outlook" affirmed the value of the individual. One stressed the value of the expansive, sentient, affective individual; the other valued the expanding individual disciplined by purpose, institution, and necessity.

As the two streams separated in the 1950s and the 1960s, the progressive outlook moved toward a degree of egalitarianism which went beyond equality of opportunity to equality of result. It opposed not merely massively unequal rewards; it opposed unequal results as such. It had always been populistic and plebiscitary by inclination. It became secularist in its attitude toward religious issues and organizations. Earlier progressivism in nonsexual matters had had close ties with Roman Catholicism. The progressive outlook came more and more to believe in the omnipotence of the state, but it was hostile toward professional politicians and toward any concentration of authority. It asserted the normality of all sexual practices and minimized the differences between males and females. It believed in the coming of plentitude. It derided or was indifferent to the patriotic symbols of nationality. It was hostile toward those who espoused more traditional views on all the wide range of topics which engaged its interest.

The traditional outlook had for a long time held the ascendancy in the United States, but the Great Depression, the decline of the agricultural class, and the effects of World War II had shifted it into a more progressive position. The disorders of the 1960s and particularly the contention against the prosecution of the war in Indochina renewed its adherence to the traditional elements in its outlook. This is perhaps the deepest effect of the association between the party of progressive outlook and the opposition to the war.

The traditional outlook was characterized primarily by a resistant mood. It had long taken for granted that individuals must work for their livelihood and that they should be rewarded in accordance with their bargaining power and the scarcity of their skills and abilities, which the traditional outlook equated with merit. The traditional outlook accepted the pattern of the paternally centered family, the division of tasks between males and females, and the virtues of masculinity and femininity. It accepted inequalities of rewards and powers although it was less sympathetic with inequalities in the distribution of deference. It accepted the inevitability of scarcity. It accepted inhibition and restraint. It accepted the claims of traditional Christian doctrine and the appropriateness of religious observance. It accepted representative institutions, although it too was skeptical about professional politicians. It was, above all, patriotic.

Of course, both the party of the progressive outlook and that of the traditional outlook were very heterogeneous. Neither was officially constituted, and their beliefs have not been officially promulgated. The traditional outlook, having less support among articulate intellectuals educated in the noneconomic social sciences, in literature, and in philosophy and having less of a body of intellectually respectable literature to invoke, was not in a position to argue its case very effectively. Its difficultues were furthered by the fact that most of the institutions—the universities, the press and television, and the book publishing industry—through which its case, if it could be articulated, could be presented were dominated by the party of the progressive outlook. (Espousal of these outlooks corresponded very roughly to the division between levels of education, occupational strata, and variations in regional and metropolitan residence.)

There is, however, one major difference from the past. This is the greatly increased size and visibility of the party of the progressive outlook. Whereas before the Great Depression of the 1930s, the party of the progressive outlook was confined to the world of literary and artistic intellectuals, bohemians who overlapped with them, a very few academics, even fewer businessmen, some metropolitan lawyers and journalists, and perhaps some members of the still small advertising industry, the situation is now very different. (Another sector of the party of progressive outlook had been found among farmers and professional persons in the Northwest, but in certain respects this sector was also very traditional in its outlook.) The numbers of the groups who were and are the main bearers of the progressive outlook have greatly expanded. (The tertiary, particularly the professional, occupations—learned and minor—have grown from being a very small minority into a very substantial one, which Colin Clark long ago pointed out as a feature of advanced societies.) The increased numbers and influence of the adherents of the progressive outlook and the lack of intellectual articulateness and suppleness in argument of their traditional opponents encouraged the former group, as it became more extensive in its following, to become more intense in its espousal. The progressive outlook also became more comprehensive in its substance, almost to the point of becoming an ideology. The large number of educated persons associated with it and their wide professional spread enabled the party of progressive outlook to formulate views on nearly every aspect of life and to find spokesmen for almost every sector of society except in the working and clerical classes. It became a coalition, the objects of whose interests ranged from the economy to sexual gratification. Its large size and its public prominence increased the self-confidence of assertion by its proponents, whereas before the breach in the front of a rigoristic puritanism occurred, the party of the progressive outlook felt itself to be beleaguered in a hostile land, fearful and resentful of its overpoweringly oppressive opponents. Now it became contemptuous of its opponents and confident that it had them on the run.

Its proponents increased very greatly their influence in American society at large through television and journalism and through university teaching. In both areas, they had very large audiences, and in the latter, the audience formed a self-perpetuating community with a self-extending culture which carried long past the university student years. University graduates became university teachers and journalists and television broadcasters. The influential role they played in mass communications and in the academic world had a mutually reinforcing effect. This made them believe that the movement of history was all on their side and that they were opposed only by an unreasonable, antiquated remnant fighting a last-ditch battle.

V

The lines separating the two parties began to be more sharply delineated by the middle of the 1960s; but the party of traditional outlook was very slow in finding itself. Partisanship in attitudes toward American military action in Indochina for a considerable period lay generally along the same line as that dividing the traditional from the progressive outlooks, but there was very little articulated confrontation of the two outlooks.

Antagonism toward the government's policy in Indochina began in the universities among teachers and students. Outstanding journalists who had been swept along by the glitter of the Kennedy Administration and who began by supporting the American involvement lost their enthusiasm for it under President Johnson's less charismatic Administration, and they returned to their professional propensity to uncover falsifications, ineptitudes, and corruption in the conduct of politicians.

Antagonism to the war had its main strength among the more educated. It gained strength among congressmen, but that was slower. It made more rapid or at least more dramatic advances among clergymen of nearly all the major denominations. They had already been animated by the civil rights movement, and it was easy for them to move into the support of resistance to conscription. The black civil rights movement became more radical and in doing so ceased to confine itself to exclusively black concerns. Black moderates, sensing a danger of losing their following, assimilated some of the radical's attitudes and rhetoric. To their denunciations of white society, the black radical leaders added the denunciation of the war in Indochina. The presence there of black soldiers gave particular point to their interest and increased their vehemence.

Until the late 1960s, the progressive party had the arena of public talk pretty much to itself. Whatever their immediate influence on the actual conduct of the war, attitudes of disapproval of the war made steady progress within intellectual circles, gaining a larger following, becoming more vociferous, resorting to more drastic methods, and attracting the support of more elements of the heterogeneous party of progressive outlook.

In the face of this, the party of the traditional outlook could not respond very coherently. There were very few persons to speak for it. Its working-class adherents were discomfitted by the indecisiveness of the fighting, and they were troubled by the fact that their young men who were not registered university and college students were being steadily called up for military service and sent to Indochina. The rising figures of casualties and the disappearance of many into North Vietnamese prisoner-of-war camps generated anger. But at the same time, resentment against the progressive outlook was being consolidated. The agitation against the war among university students and teachers was resented. Attendance at universities and colleges had always been looked upon as a privilege which few in the working or lower middle classes received; it caused offense to them that the privileged should foul the national nest. It was shocking that self-evident truths should be denied by raucous university students and teachers with long hair and motley dress, by vehement and untidy young women, by blacks and by Roman Catholic priests and radical Protestant clergymen. There was distress that the United States and its symbolic embodiments in the national flag and the military uniform should be abused and desecrated.

On the campuses, many teachers did not take an extreme position in denouncing the government, but there were few who argued that the United States was doing the right thing.

There was a vigorous campaign against defoliants, chemical and biological warfare, and the use of napalm, generally coming out of the scientific departments. University teachers were signing newspaper advertisements, manifestos, and open letters against the war, and in large number. Practically no one was taking a contrary standpoint.

Among the students—at least among the audible voices—there was practical unanimity in opposition to the war. Whatever the opinion among the reticent, among the outspoken there was much energetic hostility. In the course of their opposition, the students turned the universities upside down for a time. As long as they aimed at the federal government, they had the support of a majority of their teachers and administrators. Their activities, mainly demonstrative, were regarded as extremely "photogenic" by television producers. Until the demonstrations at Kent State University, which ended in several deaths, the students went steadily forward without a serious reverse. The altercations with university and municipal police generally drew much blood for small wounds, and the publicity given those wounds was part of the victory.

The support which they had from their elders in opposition to the war made for a greater responsiveness to their other demands. For the most part, the universities and colleges fell over before them. They did not have to fall far, since they were already leaning in the same direction. On the way, the students gained a few incidental victories, forcing themselves into some of the various governing bodies of universities, bullying their compliant teachers and administrators into instituting intellectually preposterous innovations in curricula, and making appointments of their choosing.

All these events were being slowly imprinted in the minds of adherents of the traditional outlook. State legislators began to remonstrate. California's governor, with considerable support, began a vendetta against the University, and Dr. Clark Kerr was dismissed from the presidency. Gestures of a similar character were made in other states, and in Congress ineffectual efforts were made to take revenge on students and administrators. Generally, however, the party of traditional outlook could not muster its forces and retreated on many parts of the line.

The 1968 national convention of the Democratic party in Chicago represented a turning point in the movement of opinion. The party of progressive outlook gathered its hosts there to overcome the traditional leadership of the Democratic party. Beyond the "confrontation" on the floor of the convention, they undertook to confront the "reactionary mass" of the traditional outlook in Grant Park. Hippies, pacifists, socialists, propagandists for a North Vietnamese and Vietcong victory came together and challenged the Chicago police. The provocation was deliberate and successful. The police responded as they were desired to respond, and the television services showed the entire country what the establishment was like—heavy-handed, monstrous, brutal, and incompetent. It was a great success for progressivist propaganda. But it also precipitated a strong reaction, inarticulate but embittered, among the working and lower middle classes who were less well educated, many of whom were of Eastern, Central, and Southern European ancestry and in whose culture American patriotism had been one of the accomplishments of assimilation.

With the election of Nixon to the Presidency, the country became more profoundly divided. Vice-President Agnew's speeches attacked those of progressive outlook more directly and more prominently—albeit crudely—than anyone had done until that time. The counterattacks of the local police against the Black Panthers, the trial of the Chicago Seven, and the trials of Black Panthers in New York and New Haven were not very skillful efforts by authority to strike back at the progressives. The declaration of intention by the Nixon Administration to reform the welfare services was another such retaliatory action, impelled also by the traditional disapproval of dependence on governmental bounty. The passing of the crest of the wave of governmental enthusiasm and support for scientific research and especially for academic scientists was another aspect of the determination of the party of traditional outlook to hit back at the progressives, among whom were many famous scientists. The Health, Education and Welfare Department's demand that universities produce "positive action programs" to show that they were establishing quotas for blacks, Spanish-speaking Americans, etc., was part of the same pattern of response. It was especially attractive to the Nixon Administration, since, in this case, the progressives of the universities were being hoisted with their own egalitarian petard.

The war dragged on with the government reluctantly yielding to the pressure of criticism from the outside and from Congress. It now committed itself to bringing the war to a halt as soon as it could be done "with honor." On the one side, the radical wing of the progressive party demanded that the United States forces be withdrawn unilaterally and without any commitment from the North Vietnamese and Vietcong leadership. Figures of celebrity, notoriety, and distinction became patrons of the Vietcong; journeys to North Vietnam and testimony on its behalf became part of the technique of progressivists, while the traditional outlook, inhibited by legal restraint and the fear of arousing even more progressivist antagonism, stood by helplessly, but with deepening resentment.

On the other side, the President, with widespread support from politicians and believing that he had the mass of the working and lower middle classes with him, refused to take an action which would be an acknowledgment of defeat.

Nonetheless, depite widening cleavages as the bloc of traditional opinion became consolidated behind the President and the Vice-President, the country became more quiet. Large-scale demonstrations against the war decreased in size and frequency. Riots in the black quarters of the large cities diminished in size and practically halted. The Black Panthers subsided and then publicly renounced their revolutionary intentions. The uproar in the universities also calmed down; there was a brief campaign of bombings by the Weathermen, and then that too subsided.

It is difficult to say why this "pacification" of the country took place. It certainly was not the result of more conciliatory attitudes on either side. Neither of the parties spoke in an idiom of national reconciliation. Animosity remained deep;

vehement hatred did not diminish. Nonetheless, the country was quieter than it had been. Perhaps, one reason was that the Republican Administration was so alien to the party of progress that its adherents thought they could gain nothing from it. President Nixon spoke relatively little and avoided press conferences in which he would have had to respond to the insinuating questions of progressivist journalists. It is quite possible that the older sense of isolation and impotence which American intellectuals had so long experienced had been reactivated, and with it the belief that they lived in a society which was obdurately unsympathetic with what they desired. The decline in the number of young men called up for military service and the reduced threat of conscription associated with the prospect of an entirely volunteer army also reduced the agitation of university and college students. It is possible that diminished opportunities for employment of holders of advanced degrees also caused a greater sobriety among the students.

But whatever the causes of the greater quiet, it was certainly not because of more sympathy with the traditional outlook on the part of the proponents of the progressive outlook. The outburst in the spring of 1970 when American forces began to conduct operations in Cambodia showed the direction in which sentiments lay. But there was soon a relapse into quiet.

The Presidential election of 1972 demonstrated where opinion had been brought by the cleavage over the war in Vietnam. President Nixon stood for patriotism; he was against the "disrespectable" classes who lived on governmental "charity" without working; he was against public sexual expression and abortion; he was in favor of more forceful action against criminals; he was against busing; he was against amnesty for draft evaders and deserters; he was for a Supreme Court which would not go in the progressive direction of the Warren Court. He was for "law and order," he was for "peace with honor," for an undefeated—even if unsuccessful—American army. He was on the side of patriotism and religion. He seemed to embody the beliefs of American society of the period before the deluge of the Great Depression. He won the election by a large margin. Yet, at the same time, the working and lower middle classes in the big cities did not go completely over to their long-standing enemy, the Republican party. President Nixon's success was not matched by his congressional Republican running mates. The working and lower middle classes still favored the traditional populism of the Democratic party—even though they disapproved of the indulgence shown by its national leaders toward the blacks and kindred ethnic groups, homosexuals, and evaders of the draft. They were still attached to the Democratic party as it had been shaped and defined by Franklin Roosevelt, Harry Truman, and Lyndon Johnson, but they could not bear to support those elements which proclaimed the more extreme tenets of the progressivist outlook.

The war in Vietnam exacerbated and made more intense the cleavage in American beliefs between traditional American individualism and the newer progressivist appreciation of a form of individuality, which regards every impulse and desire as worthy of gratification, with the extreme egalitarianism and hostility to and dependence on authority which are associated with it. I think that this polarization of these two fundamental and antithetical views of life and society will not soon be replaced by the pattern of intermingling and fusion which prevailed from the late 1930s until the end of the 1950s.

VI

Many other effects—direct and indirect—of American participation in the Indochina war are worthy of mention. They are all ramifications of the cleavage between the traditional and progressive outlooks.

The problem of the balance of payments of the United States began well before the deeper involvement in Indochina and the inflation was also of earlier origin. Nonetheless, the war aggravated both conditions. These and the devaluation of the dollar (the position of which had appeared to be as irrefragable as American power), coming in the same period as civil disorders in black quarters and on university campuses, the unceasing prevalence of robbery and drug addiction, the continuing agitation against the war, and the prospectlessness of the war itself, gave rise to an apprehension that American society was coming down in ruins. In many conventionally patriotic persons, it produced feelings of anguish and a sense of being bereft. It was made even harder to bear by the apparent gratification with which this humiliating condition was viewed by some of the most visible antagonists of the party of the traditional outlook.

Another consequence of the war has been the partial expulsion of science from the pantheon of American civil deities. The ranks of the progressive party were split by this. The use of napalm and defoliants in Vietnam, passionately denounced by certain progressive scientists, entailed an attack on science and scientists. Traditionalists had long accepted science as a source of benefit to the health and prosperity of the American people. The progressive party agreed with this, but in its opposition to the war and its drawing to itself of the supporters of anticapitalism and aestheticism, it became ambivalent. The campaign against the pollution of air and water, the poisoning of animal and plant life, and the defacement of the landscape attracted the support of persons hostile to industrial capitalism and to the conduct of the war in Indochina. Scientific technology was made responsible for these affronts to the quality of life.

Another effect is to be seen in higher education. In many universities and colleges, especially among the younger staff members, there is a substantial body of radicals who have become hostile to the traditions of their subjects. The desire for a "critical science," for "people's science," for "critical sociology" and similar innovations expresses animosity against the intellectual substance of higher education. They have not found many adherents among their contemporaries. More important, however, is their dislike of the idea of the university as an institution for intellectual training and research because it postulates the legitimacy of intellectual authority and because it trains young persons for élitist careers. Elitism is, after all, one of the most hated features of a system of authority. The populism and aestheticism of the progressivist outlook has serious implications for the standards of university governance, appointment, curriculum, etc., and for the relations between universities and government. The influence of such attitudes (precipitated by the broadening of the progressivist front in the opposition to war) on academic opinion and on the public and governmental image of the universities is likely to be real and, probably for some time to come, injurious to the relations between universities and government.

The populism of American intellectuals has become more pronounced and more pervasive as a result of the opposition to the war. Antiélitism has taken large strides. It is part of the abdication of responsibility by those called to positions of authority in American society. It is part of the loss of nerve which authority experiences when its legitimacy loses some of the acknowledgement which it needs. The rancor of the period of the war has furthered the retreat of the "Wasps" not only from moral ascendancy but also from their former dominance over the imagination of the intellectuals. American society is developing a hole in its center.

In the religious life of the country, the acrimony over the war has left open wounds. Many Protestant and Roman Catholic clergymen have become more radically political and more estranged from the members of their congregations and parishes. The efforts of clergymen (inspired by profound movements in the churches but heightened by the conflict over the war) to address themselves to the young and the outcast by innovations in doctrine, worship, and ritual maintain the deepened cleavage between the two parties of the traditional and the progressive outlooks.

The contention about the free expression of sexual impulses—by no means a creation of the acrimonious disputes about the war—has been sharpened by increased dissension between the two currents of opinion. For one thing, the homosexual liberation and the women's liberation movements as well as the general advancement of pornography were fortified by association with the powerful movement against the traditional outlook and by the general dislegitimation of institutional authority, which the war helped to consolidate. All this removed the lid from American society. Anything could be "got away with." It became easy and safe to defy authority. In this situation, almost every refusal of the traditional ethos was fostered. Pornography has now become linked with civil liberty more intricately and intensively than before, and the connection will not be easily sundered.

The misdeeds grouped under the name of Watergate and the self-righteous counterattack which has followed from them are connected, in varying degrees of indirectness, with the war in Indochina. They are the excrescences of an old American tradition of a frail probity in public life, but they are also much affected by the cleavage of the two outlooks. Like much else in the public life of American society since the second half of the 1960s, they should be seen as the products of prior beliefs exaggerated by the angry conflicts over the war in Indochina.

The present disarray of the party of the traditional outlook—I do not mean just the Republican party as such —through the discredit of the President and Vice-President who embodied its ideals is very great. But that disarray is not a prelude to evaporation. There is too firm an anchorage of American society in the corpus of belief inherited from the past for the traditional outlook to be obliterated by its momentarily dispirited state. The Nixon Administration, whatever its achievements and failures in domestic policy, did arouse and set in train a marked reaction against the party of progressive outlook. The decisions of the Supreme Court regarding the powers of the police in dealing with persons suspected of criminal actions and the present state of busing shows that the traditional outlook and its agents have not lost the momentum given them by this reaction. The surge of the right-to-life movements and those which aim at the restoration of capital punishment might not lead to success on a grand scale, but they are not doomed to certan failure either. The slowly regrouping antipornography and antivice forces show that the traditional outlook is not going to fade away.

On the other side, the party of progressive outlook, even though its advance was slowed down by the end of American military activities in Indochina, has made many stable gains on many fronts. Women's rights are more definitely established than they were earlier. Much of the force behind the movement for women's rights came from the general loosening of attitudes and the diminished legitimacy of those who previously wielded authority in all spheres of life. Likewise, much progress has been made in improving the position of blacks in America.

The battle between the two outlooks will continue. The question is whether it will continue with the acerbity and hatred which has been stirred up in the center of American society, or whether the two antagonists will become more civil and appreciate the affinities which bind them together into a common society. The rehabilitation of civility depends on the restoration of the legitimacy of authority in American society.

Will the passing of the travail of the war rehabilitate the legitimacy of governmental and other authority? Many elements of the progressivist outlook are fundamentally derogatory of authority. The ideas of participatory democracy have been added to the older ideas of populism and grass roots democracy; they have been joined by bohemianism, animosity against businessmen and politicians, and muckraking. These ideas had been alive for a long time, but previously they were scattered; they were not consolidated until the polarization which occurred in the course of the contention about the war. As the war recedes as an issue, then some of the elements will lose their prominence and hence will be less powerful. The diverse elements of the progressivist outlook will lose their present unity and their mutual reinforcement will weaken.

But the legitimacy of authority is a subtle and ramified phenomenon. It is especially complicated in a liberal democracy where it must be subject to rational scrutiny and criticism. The legitimacy of authority can never be wholly destroyed, but it can be enfeebled. If the leaders of institutions are in doubt about the righfulness of the institutions they rule, their own incumbency, and their own actions, they reduce the readiness of the citizenry to acknowledge their legitimacy. If the citizenry believes that no authorities are legitimate, the self-confidence of existing authorities is cut down. The diffuse and pervasive antiélitism to which every more-or-less educated politician, administrator, civil servant, journalist, publicist, and academic now purports to be committed, is a perpetual solvent of legitimacy. The antiélist attitude, which has long been characteristic of American populism, has now become a much more widespread and open profession of faith. Even literate businessmen are antiélitist. Rationally and morally, the whole scene is farcical.

Yet it does express a state of mind which is genuinely averse to the ascendancy of some human beings over others. There are moral merits in this state of mind, but no society could function if it were ever brought to actual realization. It is in fact practically impossible that it could be brought into realization.

The exercise of authority is inevitable in society, and its more-or-less effective exercise is necessary. In American society great responsibilities have been placed on authority, but there is a deeply rooted tendency not to acknowledge its rightfulness. The tendency is especially pronounced in the educated classes. Politicians and others called upon to perform the tasks which can be exercised only by the use of authority are very sensitive to the criticism contained in this reluctance to acknowledge its rightfulness. This tendency, which brings to a high point an old American tradition, was intensified by the disputes about the war. It might continue even after the war and the Watergate complex of events, which is its aftermath, have passed. If it does continue, it will keep American society in perpetual disorder, and it will comprise our most memorable and enduring inheritance from the war in Indochina.

The War and Riverdale

PETER OSNOS

A few weeks after the last American GIs left Vietnam, when the pictures of returning POWs were still vivid in our minds and the impression that the fighting was really ending was still widespread, I went to a town called Riverdale, Maryland, to find out something about the legacy of the war in the United States. In those quiet, early spring days just before the Watergate case and related scandals broke open and two years before Indochina's climactic battles, the country appeared to be heading into a period of relative calm. And glad we were of it. Our war years, after all, had been tumultuous, marked by riots, massive demonstrations, bombings and shootings; many related to the war directly, others indirectly, few not at all.

And yet, for all the upheaval, looking back to the spring of 1973, we really knew very little about the impact of the Vietnam war on American society, the impact of those years of unrest and controversy. What we didn't know, and could not reasonably ask until our troops were finally withdrawn from the fighting, was how people had been changed by the confrontations at home and abroad that had figured so prominently for so long. Every reliable poll had shown that, as the war dragged on, it steadily lost support among all segments of the population until the conflict became probably the most unpopular war in American history. That much we did know. But what were the consequences of that unpopularity? How did the war reflect on the institutions and leadership we held responsible for it? What about our national self-image? Had the war actually intruded in our daily lives? And if so, how much? Those were my questions as I set out for Riverdale.

What I found in a month of interviews was that the war, despite its length and cost to the nation, had little direct impact on individual lives, at least that people could identify. On the other hand, the war apparently did have a substantial effect on people's attitudes. I found, for example, that Vietnam had caused considerable disillusionment with government and other "institutions"—particularly diminishing belief in the wisdom and truthfulness at the top levels of Washington officialdom. The years of frustration seemed also to have raised doubt among many over whether the United States should or could assert its will internationally. I found, too, people who had learned from the antiwar protests that they could make a difference by challenging policies they opposed, whether liberal or conservative. But for all that, I discovered in Riverdale that the war itself—the origin of people's feelings— was very quickly being forgotten, to the extent that people often no longer realized the influence the conflict had on their thinking.

I had chosen Riverdale for my project because it appeared to me to represent a reasonable crosssection of the American majority—middle-income, middle-aged, middle-brow, and predominantly white. Riverdale, as it happens, is only a few miles from downtown Washington, D.C., but the people who make their homes there are not the policy-makers, the big-time lobbyists, or the supergrade bureaucrats. They are the clerks and technicians, the artisans, salesmen, and schoolteachers whose residence on the edge of the nation's capital has little to do with their lives.

In 1970, according to the U.S. census, the people of Riverdale had a median income of $10,698 per family, their median education was 12.2 years, and they were about evenly divided between white-collar and blue-collar workers. Riverdale voters have traditionally been Democrats, but in the 1972 election Richard Nixon outpolled George McGovern by a margin of 2 to 1.

At Riverdale's center is an old incorporated town of about 5,000 people that has all the trappings of village Americana: a mayor, a town council, volunteer firemen, a police department with a dogcatcher, barbershop gossip, and flagpoles in more than the occasional front yard of gabled homes that still have porches. Around the town since World War II has grown another Riverdale, a federal postal zone and election district governed by a county administration. There are 15,000 people or more living here in subdivisions and swaths of garden apartments, linked by major arteries, lined with shopping centers, used-car lots, gas stations, quick-order eateries, big and bustling churches, and drive-in banks.

In all, the two Riverdales provide a setting instantly recognizable to the outsider—sufficient in both diversity and familiarity to satisfy my criteria for the national norm.

It is not, I realize on reflection, especially surprising that people in Riverdale did not generally connect the war directly with their own lives. Dating from 1961, more than 2.5 million Americans served in Vietnam, about 55,000 were killed, another 300,000 were wounded (half of them seriously enough to be hospitalized), and some 600 were captured. The war's direct consequence on these men and their families is obvious. But for the rest of the country, the war years meant no added danger to life or property, nor was there any widespread fear of enemy attack (as opposed to the Korean War years when civil defense was a national mainstay: as a schoolboy then, I was issued a dog-tag that I had to wear at all times and was required with all my classmates to huddle under our desks in frequent air raid drills).

In fact, in most cases, the Indochina war involved no disruption at all of our regular routine. There was no rationing, no shortages of consumer goods—the energy crisis and the recession, the paper and plastic shortages did not become a problem until after our troops were withdrawn—and income generally went up faster than the cost of living in spite of inflation as high as 6 per cent a year. By recent standards it was a time of economic ease. Probably the only major intrusion in the way we went about our daily lives was the draft, which caused considerable and understandable dismay among those eligible, but even the draft did not ultimately mean peril for most people. At the height of the Vietnam build-up, according to Pentagon figures, the draft reached only about 2 per cent of those eligible to serve. Only about 40 per cent of the GIs sent to the combat zone were draftees through 1970. (The figure dropped sharply after that.)

The point is that, on the whole, the Vietnam war required little of us, certainly when compared to the national commitment and sacrifices of World War II. As a country we could easily absorb the cost in both money and lives. On several occasions in Riverdale, I was told that the violence of the war was of no account in a society where as many people are killed in traffic accidents every year as died during the whole of our involvement in Vietnam.

Perhaps that is in part the reason why it was so easy for Riverdale to forget the men who died in Vietnam. The names of the nine young men from the town who were killed were not inscribed on any plaque or scroll. I finally culled them from a computer print-out at the Pentagon entitled: "List of Casualties Incurred by U.S. Military Personnel in Connection with the Conflict in Vietnam." The mayor of Riverdale had never heard of any of these men; neither had three town policemen. The pastor of the First Baptist Church of Riverdale could remember a funeral or two, but he couldn't recall any names. The parish priest of St. Bernard's Church knew of no one who had died in the war, so he called the priest who had preceded him, but he couldn't think of anyone either. Riverdale's county councilman thought of someone, but that name didn't show up on the Pentagon's list. The hazy recollection of a few neighbors, a few tradesmen, and a scoutmaster was that survivors of the dead GIs had moved away. The cost of involvement, I concluded, had been community. Another reason Riverdale could not mourn its dead is that it no longer knew who they were.

A telephone survey of Riverdale residents commissioned by

the *Washington Post* for a series of articles on local reactions to the war (of which my project was a part) gave further support to the idea that the consequences of the war were not something people tended to see as personal. In answer to the question on what had most affected their lives in the previous decade, 63 per cent of the sample (anyone over age eighteen who answered the phone) cited "cost of living/inflation" and only 20 per cent of them listed the war. The rest of the answers were divided in smaller percentages among a number of categories, including civil rights and crime. However, when it came to picking the things that had most importance for the country as a whole over the past decade, then Vietnam was considered equal to the cost of living, with civil rights and crime slightly behind.

To draw this distinction regarding Vietnam—between what people saw as being of national significance and what they related to themselves—is central to understanding what I encountered in Riverdale. To a considerable extent, people had been able to turn off on the war altogether by setting it aside as, in effect, the country's problem rather than their own—something for the politicians to worry about. When I told people that I was in Riverdale to talk about the war, the response, even among those who later proved to have the most outspoken views, was almost invariably "why bother?" As it was explained to me, Riverdale had for a time in the mid-1960s gone all out in support of the war because that is what they expected of themselves as Americans. But then, as they saw that their government and its allies had neither the will nor the means to win, people became confused about why we were in Vietnam and indifferent to the cause.

"So many patriotic Americans felt that if the war needed to be fought, why hadn't we done it, gotten it over with, and gotten out," said the Reverend R. Herbert Fitzpatrick, pastor of the First Baptist Church, Riverdale's largest. "After a time," he went on, "I had the feeling that most people weren't even truly aware that we were engaged in a war. It did not reach into their lives and hearts like previous wars. I've heard those with husbands and brothers over there say that if they got killed, it would be in vain. There wouldn't be any glory in it. It didn't seem worthwhile somehow for a war without any real purpose."

The fact is that even by the spring of 1973, the Vietnam war had already been largely forgotten by many people, even though the recent cease-fire agreement and troop withdrawal had pushed the conflict again to the forefront of the news. Out of four members of the executive board of the Riverdale Parents and Teachers Association I interviewed one evening, only one could identify Nguyen Van Thieu as the President of South Vietnam. And only the same person, a middle-aged housewife, was able to identify Ho Chi Minh as the pre-eminent figure of Vietnamese communism. A series of follow-up questions met with similar ignorance. But I detected no embarrassment on the part of the PTA board. "I had seen the names in the paper," said the chairman of the welfare committee, a mother of three, wife of a heavy-equipment operator, and sister of a Vietnam veteran, "but I lost interest. I saw no point in it. It was strictly a politicians' war."

As I mentioned earlier, there were those I spoke to who no longer even recognized how profound an impression the war had made on their thinking. They were unaware, at least until it was pointed out to them, how greatly the war might have influenced the way they responded to the issues that did touch them personally—busing, for instance, and the cost of living. If, as so often happened, a person said his chief concern was rising prices, then a connection between inflation and the war might eventually emerge, but it did not suggest itself automatically.

Take, for example, the case of Dan Maurer, leader of Riverdale's active antibusing movement, who told me at the start of the interview that the war had virtually nothing to do with his life. "Unless you had a husband or a brother in the Vietnam thing," he said, "it was easy to forget about it. But when they started talking about your son and daughter and what they're going to do with them, well that takes precedence over something that is far away and doesn't touch you personally." And yet, as we talked, he began to see a relationship between the war and his role in the busing dispute. "The war," he said, "forced a lot of people to start speaking out. We never thought there was anything we could or should do about that, but we saw there might be something we could do closer to home. Busing seemed like something we could handle."

In acknowledging, then, that attitudes prompted by the war were frequently submerged and that people did not regard Vietnam as a pressing concern to themselves, the fact remains that attitudes and beliefs were altered. There was in Riverdale an unmistakable sense of disillusionment, a tarnished view of America and a new—or at least redoubled—wariness of the instruments and personalities responsible for the nation's destiny. I did not encounter anyone calling for vengeance or singling out any particular group or person for special blame. Once they got around to talking about the war, people spoke in generalities. But they were troubled.

Cary Bloom, a forty-nine-year-old salesman who is a past commander of the Riverdale area post of the Veterans of Foreign Wars, described the country's situation this way: "The war weakened the cement that has always bound us together, the mortar has been kind of jarred loose by this war. The general faith in the institutions of our country has been shaken. I feel strongly about it. It would worry me if we went into another war because the fabric we had in World War II just doesn't seem to be there and I just wonder how we would support another war."

Again, the telephone survey conducted for the *Post* (by Peter D. Hart Research Associates of Washington) basically supports my own conclusions. Sixty per cent of the sample said that the war had contributed greatly to the growing lack of confidence in national leaders; of the remainder many said the war had at least some effect on the erosion of confidence. "The people of Riverdale are proud of being Americans," I was told by Father Charles Wilk of St. Bernard's Church, "very proud of being Americans." Yet a sizable minority (36 per cent) said that, because of the Vietnam involvement, they were less proud of the country than they had been. Fifty-five percent of the sample said they now felt the decisions to enter the war had been wrong, and 40 per cent said the war had persuaded them that the United States could not police the world.[1] In my conversations I found that the longer I talked to people, the more reflective they were and the more critical they were likely to become.

Some of the comments I collected make the point about their questioning attitudes clearly:

Charles Harp, a thirty-year-old businessman, said: "There's a mistrust of institutions. It's not just the government, it's other things. I don't think our parents would ever have assumed that General Motors and ITT could do something wrong. Now we all know that institutions have faults."

Harp spoke also about the recognition that the United States was not able to impose its will despite its great strength. "There is an image we all grew up with, that the American soldier with his gun and his flag draped over his back and God protecting him could not be defeated—that he was always in the right. It was our opinion that once we got into something it couldn't last very long."

Royal Hart, a commercial photographer who has represented Riverdale in county-and state-level offices for about ten years, said: "You've got the 'dropout' mentality now, mostly among the young. They just don't have confidence in our institutions, in being able to make changes and rely on the word of politicians. Their perception of the country was formed in the war years. That's probably been Vietnam's biggest impact."

Kathy Ferguson, a senior at Parkdale High School said: "When I was a little kid we had idols, superpeople. They aren't anymore. I guess the war took care of that, and the assassinations. For years we were told the war was going to end real soon. We were promised, but the government just did it to keep us quiet."

And a government worker who preferred to remain anonymous offered this view: "We all realize now that elected leaders are capable of doing things that are not in the best interests of the United States. We know that if a man is elected to the Presidency of the United States, that is no guarantee that he will lead us to the right solution. As a result, I guess, we have all become more suspicious, more aware."

It may well be this increased suspicion of government and the greater questioning of official judgment that Dan Maurer, the antibusing leader, was referring to when he said the war "forced a lot of people to speak out"—not, as observed, about the war itself, but about matters of immediate concern. No issue in recent memory disturbed the residents of Riverdale more than the court-ordered busing of school children. Residents strongly opposed any shifts; the antibusing sentiment in the town, as elsewhere in the country, led to an overhaul of the school board in the 1973 election. "We talk about the silent majority," said the Reverend Fitzpatrick of the First Baptist Church (whose school almost doubled in size after the busing order took effect), "well, people aren't being so silent anymore. And that's an effect of the war. The reason so much was heard about liberalism is that liberals made themselves heard. If conservatives make more noise, then we might see a different trend in our lives." As a consequence of the war, people in Riverdale apparently no longer feel obliged to obey all the directions of local and national government as the price of patriotism.

The young people of Riverdale require some special attention. It is commonly believed that the war—the draft and the peace movement—played a greater role in the lives of the young than it did in their parents' lives. Nothing I heard in Riverdale contradicted this. "I suppose the whole hippie movement, the long hair and permissiveness, was a protest against the establishment," said Ott Wuenschel, a student counselor at Riverdale's high school, "a way of expressing their feelings. They thought the war was pointless, that they were being led to slaughter. It might have been different if they felt they were protecting their country." The high school students I spoke to for the most part said they were antiwar and liberal, compared to their parents, who tended to be prowar and conservative. "It's almost like two different towns," said one seventeen-year-old.

But granting some differences between the generations, I don't think differences in attitude should be exaggerated. For instance, the seniors at Riverdale High School said they were as opposed to busing as their parents were, and they protested plans with more feeling than they could ever muster about the war. "Busing has much more of an effect on us than the war," observed Scott Piechowicz, a long-haired seventeen-year-old who said he was strongly opposed to Vietnam. "It's more local." In the *Post*'s survey, 62 per cent of the under-thirties in the sample said the cost of living had affected them most in the previous decade; only 24 per cent cited the war, about the same results as for all age groups. The young, no doubt, emerged from the war years skeptical of "the establishment," but so, as we've seen, did many other people in Riverdale.

My interviews were completed before the full furor over the Watergate scandals. Although that subject was mentioned in some conversations, it did not predominate as it might have a few months later, further obscuring Vietnam as a topical issue. My suspicion is that the impact of Watergate was to accentuate the existing disenchantment with government and officialdom that I had traced to the war.

That Riverdale is representative of national attitudes on the matter of confidence in leadership is borne out by a major survey conducted in the early fall of 1973 on behalf of the Senate Subcommittee on Intergovernmental Relations. Prompted by Watergate, the survey (carried out by Louis Harris and Associates) recorded very substantial drops in public confidence in political leadership and institutions, such as the military and big business, as compared to a similar survey in 1966. In particular, the percentage of Americans who expressed a "great deal of confidence" in the executive branch of the government dropped from 41 per cent in 1966 to 19 per cent in September 1973. For the first time since Harris began taking such surveys a decade ago, a majority of the sample said they felt a sense of alienation and powerlessness. Years of discontent over a war few people understood and even fewer believed in have apparently left their mark, regardless of what other factors may have contributed to the gloomy mood of Americans.

What, then, is the legacy of Vietnam? To judge from my inquiries in Riverdale, it is likely to be foremost in Americans' feelings about government and institutions generally and about our national responsibilities and capacities. The people of Riverdale seem less prepared to accept on faith what others decide is best for them. They seem, too, to be less intent on seeing our standards imposed elsewhere, mostly because that has turned out to be so much trouble. These attitudes may linger even though the memory of Vietnam, the place, the stakes, and the toll, fades.

Perhaps historians will someday conclude that the Vietnam war was the unfortunate but logical culmination of United States policy in the 1950s and 1960s. The war burrowed its way into our consciousness, seeming a natural extension of a policy of intervention already in force. The people of Riverdale I think would not let that happen so easily again. Today, American troops are withdrawing from worldwide bases, and old dogmas are being abandoned. In part, that is so because of changes in the configurations of international relationships. In part, it is because American society has had enough of the strain.

Notes

1. The *Post* survey was taken in four communities near Washington. On most questions, the results elsewhere were essentially the same as those for Riverdale. However, Riverdale was the only one of the four where less than a majority said the war had affected their feelings about American inability to police the world.

Consensus and Dissent

The consensus that supported—and even forced—American foreign policies since World War II has been shattered. Now one hears debate about what the nature of a new consensus should be. The assumption seems to be that this is an interim period before a return to the normalcy of broad agreement on new basic principles of foreign policy. But is such consensus "normal," and do we need one?

Irving Kristol and Leslie Gelb suggest some untraditional answers. Kristol argues that consensus in America has been rare; rather, there has been a series of alternating and conflicting "ideological impulses" in American foreign policy, "with stretches of uneasy ideological equilibrium in between." Neither of the two traditional streams of thought, isolationism or interventionism, works now. The former is possible only for a "pure" republic, modest in size and ambition. And interventionism is rejected by the "cosmopolitan" élite which for a generation after World War II pressed it upon the rest of the nation.

The great question now, Kristol argues, is whether Henry Kissinger can bring us to a different, more European conception in which foreign policy is viewed with "realism" rather than with the moral fervor of ideologies. And what is needed, Kristol concludes, is public "confidence" in, rather than consensus behind, our foreign policies.

The views of Leslie Gelb are very different. He believes that consensuses have been a dominant feature of American foreign policy-making, and that the consequences has been a tendency toward conformity and rigidity of thought and policy. A consensus makes it the more likely that our policies will be guided by doctrines—often with a name attached. "Doctrines," Gelb argues, "become the symbols with which the power-holders can manipulate the public, but in the end, they trap and undo even their authors." He would prefer that the consensus of the last decades be replaced only by specific consensuses on specific issues, openly arrived at through open debate.

Kristol writes that, for the moment, we have practically all dissent and no consensus. But to Sam Brown, a former leader of the antiwar movement, foreign policy dissent, as he would define it, has been crushed. Tracing the history of the movement, he finds that it was torn between those who sought to influence the decision-makers through sustained and decorous pressure and the more militant activists who tried to use the war issue to "educate" the American people about the nature of our nation's general approach to the world. In describing this split, Brown defines a basic trap from which dissent in America finds it difficult to escape. Even when large numbers of Americans agree with the substance of the dissenters' point of view—as many finally did about the war—the *style* of the dissenters puts them off. So the choice for the protestors is to mute their voices or, in frustration, to become more shrill or even violent. And, as the latter course is taken, the more distant public support becomes. Together with the counter-moves of the government, this trap, in Brown's view, spelled the doom of the movement and the effort to force fundamental change in American foreign policy.

The essay by John Roche is written from the other side of the issue. A former aide to President Johnson, Roche agrees with Brown that the protestors had little effect on policy, without sharing Brown's dismay. What mattered, Roche says, is that the public came to see the war as "pointless"—but not "immoral" or "obscene." And when "realists," like Walter Lippmann, Hans J. Morgenthau, and George Kennan, were joined in their opposition to the war by influential members of Congress, neither President Johnson nor his successor could continue to pursue a war with no deadline.

It may be that the protest movement had more of an effect than Brown and Roche indicate; at least it kept forcing the war issue into the consciousness of the public in the mid-1960s. There can be no doubt that their essays disagree strongly about the importance of its failures.

Irving Kristol is Henry Luce Professor of Urban Values at New York University and coeditor of *The Public Interest.*

Leslie H. Gelb is a diplomatic correspondent for the *New York Times.* After serving on the staff of Senator Jacob Javits, he was director of Policy Planning and Arms Control at the Pentagon (1968-69) and a Senior Fellow at The Brookings Institution.

Sam Brown is Treasurer of the state of Colorado. He was the Coordinator of the Vietnam Moratorium Committee (1969-1970) and was active in the campaign of Senator Eugene McCarthy in 1968.

John P. Roche is Henry Luce Professor of Civilization and Foreign Affairs at the Fletcher School of Law and Diplomacy, and was Special Consultant to President Johnson during 1966-68. His latest work is *Sentenced to Life: Reflections on Politics, Education and Law.*

Consensus and Dissent in U.S. Foreign Policy

IRVING KRISTOL

It is commonly—and, on the whole, correctly—observed that American politics is nonideological when compared with the politics of Western European nations. These latter achieve stability by effecting an equilibrium among competing ideological parties; the United States achieves stability by searching for a consensus which each competing party then tries to represent. The distinction cannot be pressed too far: Ideology and consensus are never completely divorced from one another. The ideologies of European parties are influenced by a natural desire to win an electoral majority, and the American consensus is always taking new shape as a result of the ideological impulses within its parties. Still, the difference is real enough and justifies the casual ascription of a "pragmatic" temper to American politics and of an "ideological" character to European politics.

And yet, when it comes to foreign policies, it is no great exaggeration to say the situation is almost reversed. Foreign policy in Europe tends to grope for a national consensus, whereas in the United States it is shaped by alternating ideological impulses, with stretches of uneasy ideological equilibrium in between. Occasionally, one such impulse will be so powerful as to represent a popular consensus; but that consensual condition will not prevail for very long. In Europe, every government will insist that its foreign policy is "realistic," and the controversy will revolve around the question of whether it is actually so or not. In the United States, the issue of "realism" is one that concerns only a handful of scholars and analysts. The debate over American foreign policy is more usually in terms of whether it is "correct" or not; i.e., whether it truly expresses the ethos of the American Republic and its political traditions. Indeed, to say of an American Secretary of State that he practices realpolitik is to insinuate that he is perhaps being delinquent vis-à-vis some prescriptive set of American ideals.

The ideological character of American foreign policy is obscured by the fact that it has very little to do with the conventional twentieth-century contest between left and right. The two opposing ideological impulses in the United States have been, from the beginnings of the Republic, "isolationist" vs. "interventionist"—peculiarly American categories that have no exact counterparts elsewhere. It is true that in Europe the left has traditionally been more insular in its thinking because it is so intent on the reconstruction of the domestic order, whereas the right has traditionally had close ties with the spirit of nationalism and is much concerned with a national presence on the international scene. But though this vaguely resembles the isolationist-interventionist dualism of American politics, it is not really the same thing. In the United States, the issue is always who is being most loyal to the original "American promise," who is best fulfilling the covenant which Providence (or its secular equivalent, History) has struck with the American people, who is most adequately expressing the moral mission of the Republic. And, in arguing this issue, left and right can be either isolationist or interventionist, depending upon circumstances. For both, any suggestion of mere realism in foreign affairs is uncomfortably "un-American."

In its purest forms, the isolationist/interventionist debate revolves around the question of whether the American Republic can best contribute to the redemption of the human race by (a) perfecting itself so marvellously as to provide an irresistible model for other peoples, or (b) intervening, to one degree or another, in the affairs of other peoples so as to assist the world in its movement toward the American model. Of course, the reality of American foreign policy has never incarnated either of these pure forms—the world is just too recalcitrant for such incarnations. Still, these ideals have profoundly influenced American foreign policy, and it is never possible fully to comprehend this policy without some reference to them.

The trouble is that, with the advent of the nuclear age, and with the natural growth of the United States into the status of a world power, the ideological polarity behind American foreign policy has less and less connection with actuality. A world power—one may even say this is the definition of a world power—will influence events, will affect the destinies of other peoples, as much by what it does *not* do as by what it overtly does. The very existence of a world power creates conditions of dependency and interdependency—and also engenders the obligations (moral, political, and economic) which flow from such conditions. The American Republic today is an "imperial republic," a phrase which sounds like an oxymoron to American ears, but which is by no means an odd or monstrous political reality, as the histories of Rome and Venice clearly reveal. And this radically changes the terms of the debate.

The change has been noticed, of course, but has not always been correctly interpreted. After World War II, it simply seemed as if the interventionist impulse had finally and definitively predominated. But interventionism, like isolationism, is more a kind of political romanticism than a political theory, strictly speaking. The failure of American foreign aid programs and the disillusioning experience in Vietnam made the limitations of interventionism only too evident, and isolationism suddenly began to regain public favor. But the Middle East war of 1973 and the resulting energy crisis showed that isolationism was no live option either. So, for the moment, it is fair to say that American opinion on foreign policy is practically all dissent and no consensus. Nor is any consensus likely to emerge until Americans come to think about foreign policy in a way very different from their past habits of mind. The importance of Henry Kissinger is that he has tried, carefully and tentatively, to legitimize such a new way of thinking about foreign policy. Whether he has succeeded is not at all clear. Both interventionists and isolationists remain suspicious of his deviations from the two traditional norms, and it would take very little for these suspicions to be translated into destructive hostility.

II

In recent years the debate over the future of American foreign policy was charged with intense and urgent feelings attached to a single experience: the Vietnam war. For many, especially among our younger citizens, *all* of American foreign policy is now being perceived in the light of this event. That it was an illuminating and highly instructive event is beyond question. But one can reasonably doubt that it makes sense to understand American foreign policy in terms of Vietnam, rather than trying to understand Vietnam in terms of the more enduring imperatives which shape, and will continue to shape, American foreign policy. These imperatives place irksome limits on both the interventionist and isolationist impulses—which is probably why so many Americans dislike the very notion of enduring imperatives, and tend to regard them as some kind of unconstitutional restraint on their liberties.

The ironies implicit in any attempt to define the future of American foreign policy so as to solve yesterday's problem, i.e., Vietnam, is well illustrated by the "war powers" act which Congress passed, over President Nixon's veto, on November 7, 1973. This new law requires that the President report to Congress within forty-eight hours of committing American troops abroad. Within sixty days—or ninety days, if the President certifies to Congress that he needs the additional time—the President must bring the troops home, unless Congress has specifically authorized otherwise. Moreover, Congress can at any time end the troop commitment by a concurrent resolution, which does not require Presidential signature. That is the law, passed after much acrimonious debate. What are its likely effects?

One possible, and plausible, answer is that it would have no effect whatsoever. After all, though the law assumes that American Presidents decide to send troops overseas in an arbitrary and capricious way, whereas Congress is more prudent and deliberative, there is really no evidence for any such assumption. Presidents do take congressional and public opinion into account when making these decisions; moreover, there is little doubt that, had such a law been in existence in 1962, Congress would have given the necessary sanction to President Kennedy and, later, to President Johnson. It did in fact give such sanction on many different occasions. True, it now wishes it hadn't, and the proposed law embodies this retrospective wish. But as the memories of Vietnam begin to fade in the years ahead, and as new crises arise with no obvious parallel to Vietnam, there is far more likely to be concord than discord between Congress and the executive on any issues of military intervention. There are not many instances in American history—I cannot offhand think of one—when the President insisted on sending American troops abroad *against* the expressed wishes of a majority in Congress. Crises in foreign policy do tend to develop a consensus, albeit temporary, and the executive usually operates within the consensus.

Another possible answer is that the law would have exactly the opposite effect of that intended. A President who thought it important to intervene quickly in some part of the world, and who was uncertain of the support he might receive in Congress, might look at that sixty-day deadline and decide that he would have to intervene massively so as to ensure a quick success. In other words, such a law would mean that military intervention abroad, when it occurred, would be on a large scale rather than on a limited one. And what if the President misjudged the situation, and his massive intervention, after sixty days, had not reached a military conclusion? Would Congress really decide that, say, an army of 50,000 American soldiers should promptly surrender? Or should withdraw helter-skelter, suffering great losses and humiliations? Or that the American government should promptly sue for peace on the enemy's terms? None of these alternatives is likely. So the law would, in the end, make disengagement and withdrawal less easy to accomplish, not more.

In short, there was an "agonizing reappraisal" of American foreign policy, a bitter quarrel between President and Congress, and eventual legislation which seemed to signify an isolationist turn after an interventionist misadventure. And yet, one has good reason to think, the whole business was really beside the point. Just how emphatically beside the point may be inferred from the fact that the single most important element in the post-Vietnam situation was ignored: the replacement, by an earlier Act of Congress, of an army of conscripted citizens by an army of professional soldiers.

Indeed, it may well be the case that the most significant lasting consequence of the Vietnam war for American foreign policy will have been the creation of a large, professional, standing American army. Yet in debates over foreign policy, this matter is either ignored or regarded as peripheral. Only a few observers—most notably, Joseph Califano, Jr.—have warned that a volunteer army will have very significant implications for American foreign policy. These implications will all be in the direction of increasing the executive's discretion with regard to military intervention, whenever or wherever he thinks necessary.[1]

In a sense, the creation of a large, professional army may be regarded as symbolizing a new stage in the history of the American Republic. Political philosophers have traditionally insisted—and American political philosophy has traditionally agreed—that republics, if they are to maintain their republican purity, should be served only by a "citizen's army" which is motivated by a selfless devotion to the public good. But this belief was itself based on the assumption that such a citizen's army would fight (and would be most willing to fight) either in defense of the republic (the isolationist idea) or in defense of democratic ideals (the interventionist idea). Where, however, a republic takes upon itself a major responsibility for stabilizing the international order, such a vulgar policing function can only be performed by a professional army. A republic which has assumed that responsibility and that international role has ceased being a "pure" republic and has become an "imperial" republic. Practically all republics in the history of Western civilization have experienced this transformation, the only exceptions being those (e.g., Switzerland) which were too small and weak even to think of playing a serious international role. It is ironic that, in the United States in the 1970s, it is those who have been most bitterly disillusioned with our imperial experience in Vietnam, who are dismayed at the prospect of sending American boys to fight in dubious battle overseas, and who feel most urgently the desire to recover a condition of republican, neo-isolationist purity—it is these very people who have also created the major bulwark of an imperial republic, i.e., a professional army.

The imperial republic emerges out of the pure republic, not because the population as a whole, or any class of the population, or any particular leaders, are seized with a lust for grandeur. Rather, it is the consequence of all sorts of feelings and actions which, at the time, seemed perfectly natural, perfectly reasonable, and so far from being inharmonious with the vision of a pure republic as to appear to be its logical corollary. The traditional prescription for preserving republican purity is so harsh that it can never be sustained for long. Thus, political philosophers in the past who thought seriously about republics (e.g., Aristotle, Montesquieu, Rousseau, Jefferson) agreed that a pure republic ought *not* to be a large, wealthy, and powerful nation—for power naturally brings with it a sense of responsibility and a perception of responsibility by others, which leads to foreign entanglements. In the abstract, one could possess the power and resolutely abhor the responsibility—but this is to diminish one's humanity, in one's own eyes as in others'; it requires a kind of fanatical devotion to bare principle that does violation to our most human and humane sensibilities. This is but another way of saying that a pure republic may be the best of all possible societies, but it does not encompass all the virtues inherent in our humanity. In pursuit of these other virtues—compassion, world peace, world order, and the mitigation of barbarism—republicans find themselves moving inexorably away from the pure republic they still adore.

In addition, philosophers of republicanism have for the most part agreed that a pure republic should have as little trade and commerce as possible, even as little in the way of cultural relations as possible, with the rest of the world. Isolation is recommended not merely so as not to create vested interests in foreign policy (though this is one reason), but primarily in order to diminish *all* contact with the outside world. Such contacts are dangerous because they create sentiments of affection and detestation toward other nations which will lead to our feeling implicated in their destinies. A pure republic, to maintain its purity, must engender among its citizens sentimental attachments only to itself. Otherwise, a republican foreign policy will slowly find itself assuming large responsibilities toward other nations and peoples: protecting them, assisting them, reproving them, resisting them. Moreover, such foreign entanglements will frequently become a cause of contention and create divisiveness among the republic's population, which will not always have a unanimous judgment as to the merits or demerits of other nations.

The history of American foreign policy over the past century has witnessed the evolution from the isolationism of a pure republic to the active commitments of an imperial republic. This movement was led by the best-educated and most cosmopolitan section of the American people, who felt that it was positively shameful for a great power (which the United States had certainly become) not to use its resources to help create a better world. The mass of the people followed only reluctantly, skeptical as to the supposed virtues and vices of foreign regimes, and instinctively anxious about the effects of foreign entanglements upon the institutions and the way of life of the old American republic. This isolationism of so many Americans was sharply rebuked by the interventionists as lacking in idealism and compassion, and as having an antiquated and absurdly narrow view of America's destiny. Still, it is instructive to observe in retrospect how percipient the isolationist critique was. It warned that an imperial status would result in an aggrandizement of the powers of the Presidency, an enormous military budget supported by unprecedentedly high taxes, involvement in morally ambiguous enterprises overseas, incessant domestic controversy over particular foreign policy issues, etc. These warnings were dismissed with something like contempt; they were seen as mere symptoms of cultural lag on the part of provincial America, the product of crude nostalgia rather than enlightened foresight.

World War II saw the unambiguous victory of a new interventionalist consensus on American foreign policy, which lasted for two decades. At the heart of this consensus was the threat of a Communist world encircling the United States, a specter the American people found so horrifying as to overcome their traditional isolationist inclinations. Even so, there was little enthusiasm among the bulk of the American people for their new imperial role; the mood was rather one of stoical resignation. It was among the cosmopolitan élite that enthusiasm was to be found: in the universities, in the media, among the college-educated generally. With the Vietnam war, both the enthusiasm and the stoicism suffered a severe shock. One might call it a shock of recognition, a realization of how difficult it was to reconcile an imperial role with the traditional idealistic premises of American foreign policy.

III

It is important to realize that the reigning interventionist consensus after World War II did not really represent a candid recognition of the United States' imperial status, nor did it imply an acceptance by populace or politicians of the burdens that accompany such a status. True, among a rather small circle of foreign policy experts there developed an interest in sophisticated realpolitik—or at least an academic version of realpolitik, with complicated theories about the strategic and tactical games which were assumed to take place on the international checkerboard. But the average American knew little and cared less about such theories; had he taken notice of them, he would doubtless have found them sinister or downright immoral. For the American public, the interventionism to which they had reconciled themselves had nothing to do with realpolitik. On the contrary, it was seen as a continuation of the "idealistic" foreign policy of Woodrow Wilson and Franklin D. Roosevelt. The idea was that American power would help establish the permanent hegemony of the "peace-loving" nations, and this in turn would create a world order in which the liberties of nations and peoples would be protected. It was understood that this might occasionally require a military involvement overseas, but it was always taken for granted that any such involvement would see the "free world" defending itself against "aggression" from the enemies of freedom. It was also taken for granted that such military involvement, however costly, could not be long-lasting, since American power would be massively deployed to decide the issue on the side of right as against wrong.

The Korean War put the internationalist vision to a severe test, which it barely passed. One forgets—as the foreign policy establishment forgot in the years that followed—how unpopular the Korean War was. Its moral aspect was clear enough: The United Nations affirmed the "rightness" of U.S. intervention, and of our allies, by sending some troops, and ratified this moral affirmation. But the war simply dragged on too long. Americans felt that if they were in the right, they therefore had the right to use whatever force was necessary to win quickly and decisively. This sentiment was and always had been an integral part of the internationalist outlook, which *never* contemplated long, limited wars with ambiguous conclusions. In truth, the idea of a democracy fighting such wars with a conscript army has an inherent absurdity in it. Democracies fight wars with enthusiasm, not with strategic theories, and their conscript armies are supposed to be motivated by a cause, not by professional pride. By the time the Korean War ended, most observers agreed that the main lesson to be learned from it was that the American democracy could not again be expected to tolerate a long, bloody, limited war. It took only a little more than a decade for this lesson to be forgotten.

Though it is obvious that Vietnam has to be regarded as a failure of American foreign policy, it is important to have a frank comprehension of the causes behind this failure. To begin with, it was a longer and much costlier war than anyone anticipated. The North Vietnamese fought with a fanaticism and skill that made nonsense of Lyndon Johnson's hopes that a relatively modest effort could achieve, if not victory, then some sort of compromise settlement. Hanoi's premise—that a long and bloody war would create discontent and divisiveness within American society—turned out to be more true than the Pentagon's premise that a very high casualty rate (by American standards) would cause Hanoi "to come to its senses." The American democracy, it turned out, was not able to sustain a long, bloody, limited war overseas—what, in the days of the British Empire, was called a "frontier war"—especially when this war was fought with a conscript army. Such a war did not have a place in either the interventionist or isolationist vision of American foreign policy. According to the interventionist view, American power was such that it could not happen; according to the isolationist view, American interests were such that it should not happen.

The second important feature of the Vietnam war was that, in its ten years' duration, the entire context of international affairs changed. Even as the Soviet Union approached nuclear parity with the United States, and China developed its own nuclear capability, the threat of Communist world domination seemed to diminish. Both Russia and China turned inward to struggle with their enormous domestic problems, and each of these Communist powers came to regard the other as posing the most urgent threat to its own (a) military security, and (b) doctrinal orthodoxy, and hence political legitimacy. It was anticommunism, after World War II, which had persuaded isolationist Americans to go along with an interventionist foreign policy. To the degree that the Vietnam war ceased to be viewed as part of a larger war against world communism, to that same degree the war came to lose its meaning for many Americans.

Moreover, the diminution of the Communist threat gave rise to a new spirit among our European allies, one which, in turn, quite simply shattered the interventionist dream of a "free world" united to oppose communism and to establish an international order acceptable to American opinion. As the threat of Soviet aggression became or seemed to become more remote, and as China, too, appeared to lose its appetite for "people's wars of liberation," the nations of Western Europe turned inward, concentrated on economic growth, and lost interest in playing a major role in world affairs.[2] The United States had never conceived of its intervention in Vietnam as being a lonely venture; it assumed, rather, that this intervention was a natural extension of the alliance politics of the postwar period, and that it was acting as a representative of the "free world." European indifference to our Vietnam predicament, which soon turned into European hostility toward our Vietnam involvement, made American policy in Southeast Asia appear of doubtful legitimacy and pointless in intention. All Americans soon began to wonder: What on earth are we doing in Vietnam? In such an atmosphere, the pressure for a quick settlement and withdrawal became overwhelming.

IV

After Vietnam, American foreign policy is a shambles. The postwar consensus derived from liberal internationalism is now under powerful attack from the very class of people—the educated, idealistic "cosmopolitans" who constitute what Gabriel Almond calls the "attentive public"—which created and sustained it, while the bulk of "provincial" America has no more enthusiasm for it today than was the case yesterday. *Everyone* is now a dissenter on American foreign policy, and one cannot imagine any crisis in world affairs, short of an overt military attack upon American territory, to which the American government could respond with the assurance of enthusiastic congressional and popular support.

The Middle East crisis in the fall of 1973 is in only superficial contradiction with this judgment. Israel has always been a somewhat special case for American foreign policy; it is an outpost of liberal democracy and Western values in the Middle East, with a strong claim on the conscience of American Christians and the loyalty of American Jews. Moreover, President Nixon appears to have had strong and positive feelings about Israel, largely because the Israeli government, whatever its private opinion about our Vietnam intervention, never publicly criticized it. So it was possible, when the Yom Kippur war broke out, for the United States quickly to airlift large quantities of war matériel to Israel. But that action just about

reached the limits of possibility. Had the war continued for
any length of time—i.e., had the Israelis been less successful on
the battlefield—the fear of involvement would surely have
resulted in a diminution of support, military and political.
Moreover, had the Russians intervened more directly, it is
unimaginable that the United States would have responded
with a corresponding counterintervention. Fortunately, the
Soviet leaders could not quite believe that this was the case.
They could not believe that President Nixon's military alert
was less meaningful than it appeared. In a way, one can say
that, at that moment, President Nixon was reaping the benefits of his bombing of North Vietnam, undertaken and
sustained despite congressional opposition and with little
popular support. But that harvest was a one-time affair. In
retrospect, it is clear that the President would have found it
extremely difficult to initiate, and could never have sustained,
a military engagement with Soviet forces in the Middle East.
Congress and public opinion would not have accepted it,
especially as all our allies would have violently opposed it. The
subsequent reappraisal of American-Israeli relations, after the
failure of Secretary Kissinger to negotiate an Israeli-Egyptian
détente, more accurately reflects the basic impulses behind
American foreign policy today.

The aftermath of the Middle East crisis—the oil embargo,
the energy crisis, and the mad scramble by our European allies
for separate and preferential agreements with the oil-producing shiekdoms—revealed the degree to which the free world is
in utter disarray. NATO, the cornerstone of our interventionist foreign policy, is gradually disintegrating. Our European
allies are no longer convinced that the United States would
risk even a limited nuclear war in the face of Soviet aggression.
They are not at all sure, given Soviet nuclear strength, that
they want to become nuclear battlefields in any case, and no
longer believe (it is so convenient no longer to believe) that
the Soviet Union has aggressive intentions toward them. The
United States, for its part, still officially talks as if it had the
will to live up to its NATO and SEATO commitments, but
public opinion polls suggest that there may be a huge distance
between official rhetoric and political reality.

In such a state of confusion, callow ideas and wishful thinking will seize the day. Fantasizing is the post-Vietnam fashion. Thus, the United States Senate has actually passed, by a huge majority, something called a "National Commitments Resolution." This expresses "the sense of the Senate that a national commitment by the United States results only from affirmative action taken by the executive and legislative branches of the United States government by means of a treaty, statute or concurrent resolution of both Houses of Congress specifically providing for such a commitment."[3] A moment's reflection would reveal that such an effort to define legalistically the national interest or national security, by specifying each commitment which enters into the calculation of national interest, is inherently absurd and ineffectual. Commitments, especially those of a great power, emerge from events as these unfold in unpredictable ways. There is no way of knowing beforehand where or what kind of commitment the United States will feel it necessary to make, or where, or when, since this will largely depend on the actions of other nations. Indeed, this very uncertainty is what makes it necessary for the United States to have a foreign policy at all, and to negotiate with both friend and foe about the exact scope of any particular commitment, in any particular place, at any particular time, in any particular set of circumstances. A degree of ambiguity and uncertainty is as indispensable to the making of foreign policy as it is to the playing of a game of chess. It is not uncommon, in a chess game, for one little isolated pawn suddenly to become the pivot around which the entire game centers, a pawn which, under other circumstances, one would sacrifice without a qualm. There is just no way in which one could precisely define beforehand, or even precisely define at any moment, the extent of one's commitment to this pawn or any other piece.

But need one play the game of international politics at all? This is the question being raised by the neo-isolationist reaction to our Vietnam experience and to the interventionist premises which made that experience possible if not inevitable. Senator Fulbright insisted that the United States should shun any kind of unilateral action in foreign affairs and should use international institutions as the vehicle of its foreign policy. In view of the absence of such institutions, or the extreme fragility of those few that do exist, this approach represents a marriage of convenience between Wilsonian internationalist rhetoric and practical isolationism. Others are more candid and quite simply revert to the doctrine classically expressed by John Quincy Adams: The American people should be "the well wishers to the freedom and independence of all, the champion and vindicator only of its own," and the American nation will modestly "recommend the general cause of liberty by the countenance of her voice, and by the benignant sympathy of her example." [4]

Now it must be said about this isolationist possibility that it is not, in the abstract, *utterly* utopian. We can have such an isolationist foreign policy if we are willing to be the kind of nation, the kind of pure republic, to which such a policy would be appropriate. In such a nation, all citizens would be indoctrinated from an early age to a condition of indifference (or as close to indifference as possible) toward foreign peoples and foreign nations: American Jews would have no powerful sentiments of attachment toward the state of Israel or other Jewish populations overseas; American blacks would be discouraged from any sense of identification with the peoples of Africa; the American Irish would have no special feelings about the fate of Ireland; in short, the process of "Americanizing" our heterogeneous population would have to be more radical than was ever previously the case in our history. In addition, and as Jefferson explicitly recommended, university students would be discouraged from travelling abroad or from conceiving any overly strong attachment to, or curiosity about, foreign cultures and foreign societies. Businessmen would similarly be discouraged from travel abroad or investment abroad; America's commercial contacts with the outside world would be reduced to an absolute minimum. "America First" would be the rule in all our affairs, as we defiantly buttressed ourselves against the world, its temptations, and its corruptions.

All of these isolationist policies were in fact envisaged by Thomas Jefferson as the necessary and correct policies for the

United States to pursue. Otherwise, he feared, we would decline from a pure republic to an imperial republic, as Athens and Rome had done before us. An imperial republic is more prosperous and more cultured than a pure republic; it is more powerful; it is, or can be, a center of world civilization in a way that a pure republic, inherently provincial, can never be. But an imperial republic, he thought, will be deficient in republican virtue—in single-minded and selfless attachment to, and devotion to, one's own political community—and will therefore eventually breed the agents of its own destruction: selfishness, avarice, the love of luxuries, intellectual frivolity, artistic self-indulgence, a diminished reverence for the laws of God and man. An eighteenth-century London or an eighteenth-century Geneva? The choice is an exclusive one.

And that choice was definitively made long ago. It was made when the American people decided that they preferred to be a large, commercial, prosperous nation, rather than a small, agrarian, "spartan" community. Inevitably, that definitive choice gives rise to recurrent nostalgia for a world we have lost, a possibility never realized, and the isolationist temper has been a continual presence in American life, sometimes flaring up into bitter dismay at the destiny we have chosen for ourselves. Such dismay is very noticeable today. It is real; it is authentically American; it is, at this late date, pointless and purposeless. Strategic disengagement from the world, with all of its implications—a lowered standard of living, an inward-turning culture, a provincial civilization, and an austere lifestyle—is not a policy for the 1970s at all, but a dream born of frustration. It is, quite literally, reactionary and escapist.

The United States in the 1970s is and will wish to remain a world power, economically and militarily, and a cosmopolitan center of world civilization. As such, what it does not do will be as consequential, for itself and for the world, as what it does do; there is no way it can rigidly delimit and predefine its responsibilities, which flow ineluctably from its power. A wealthy man who watches a poor neighbor starve to death cannot disclaim responsibility for the event; a powerful man who watches a weak neighbor being beaten to death cannot avoid being accused (if only through self-accusation) of culpability. If you don't want such responsibilities, then don't become rich and powerful. If you wish to unburden yourself of such responsibilities, then cease being so rich and so powerful. No one has ever been able to figure another way out of this dilemma.

V

If one assumes, as I believe one must, that the United States will remain, and will wish to remain, a rich and powerful nation for as long as it can, then certain consequences follow. One such certain consequence is that power to make foreign policy will continue to flow to the executive.

It has already been pointed out that as a result of Vietnam a serious effort is under way to reestablish congressional control over foreign policy, and a great many people seem to think that this is a real possibility. Yet this goal could only be achieved if (a) Congress became radically different from what it now is, and (b) foreign policy became radically less significant than it now is. It is hard to envision either of these things happening, and it requires a truly immense leap of the imagination to envision both of them happening.

For Congress to play a positive role in foreign affairs, as distinct from acting as a negative check upon the executive, it would have to become what it once was long ago, a deliberative body. In such a body, the members are thoroughly informed of the matters under discussion, and they debate these matters at great length in an atmosphere congenial to calm and rational decision-making. This means, in turn, that the business of government has to be circumscribed (there are limits to how well-informed anyone can be about many issues), and the congressional agenda has to be brief (there are limits of time, as well as information). Once upon a time, these conditions prevailed. A historian of nineteenth-century America finds that congressional debates are an important source, an indispensable source, of information about governmental policy, foreign or domestic, and about varying opinions with regard to such policy. With each passing decade, however, the *Congressional Record* becomes less interesting. The important congressional debates take place either in private meetings of its committees or in the public forum provided by the mass media. (Future historians will surely consult the tapes of such a television program as "Meet the Press" with more diligence than they will apply to the *Congressional Record*.) But even the important debates in Congress are no longer so very important. The truly important ones take place *within* the executive branch: in the National Security Council, the State Department, the Treasury, and the other departments and agencies of the executive, all of which are now huge bureaucracies. They control most of the available information about any policy issue, and they have the time, energy, and personnel to concentrate on the intricacies of any particular policy issue. Indeed, today the real struggle for power over foreign policy is between the executive and these bureaucracies. There is little reason to think that the situation will be otherwise tomorrow.

So the question posed to the American nation is not whether the United States will remain a world power (it will), nor whether the President will remain the prime mover of our foreign policy (he will), but *how* the President will shape the foreign policy of this great power. And here we do indeed confront a serious problem, which is not really a problem of foreign policy at all, or of the Presidency at all, but of American national purpose and of the consensus that shapes and defines this purpose.

The old consensus—the liberal-internationalist-cold war consensus of 1945-65—has collapsed. In retrospect, the startling fact is that it existed at all and lasted as long as it did. That consensus represented a most extraordinary coalition of American opinion, without significant precedent in American history and almost certainly not to be repeated in our lifetime. American foreign policy has *always* engendered more controversy than during this period. What we witnessed, under Truman, Eisenhower, and Kennedy, was a convergence of two ideologies—of liberal internationalism and anticommunism—which represented quite different sectors of American society and contradictory currents of American opinion. People who disagreed sharply over domestic issues and who had incompatible visions of what a good American society would look like were nevertheless able to join hands in their foreign policy consensus. This odd consensus finally collapsed for two reasons. First, because those in its left and liberal wing found its domestic aspirations and ideals unpleasantly constrained and frustrated by its foreign policy commitments. These aspirations and ideals involved increasing government spending on domestic social programs, which, in turn, was incompatible with a large defense budget. And second, the coalition collapsed because the conservative wing found that liberal internationalism had a conception of the national interest that was so vague and idealistic it had lost contact with the reality of national feeling and sentiments. These sentiments approved of an anticommunist foreign policy but were not much interested in any such larger mission as the preservation of international order or the modernization of the underdeveloped nations. Perhaps, if our Vietnam intervention had been brief and militarily decisive, the coalition could have sustained itself for a while longer. But that long, expensive, and morally ambiguous war (South Vietnam being no obvious part of the "free world") was intolerable. Under this strain, the coalition broke and the prevailing consensus on American foreign policy was shattered.

It is against this background of dismay and incoherence that the significance of Henry Kissinger is to be estimated. He has been the first American Secretary of State to have to operate without *either* a consensus on foreign policy *or* a polarization over foreign policy, a polarization which, whatever its difficulties, at least provided basic points of reference and a field of maneuver for the statesman. He is in the process of constructing a foreign policy for the United States *ex nihilo*; or, to be more precise, he is in the process of constructing a foreign policy for an imperial republic which is reluctant to confront the fact that it *is* an imperial republic, and whose foreign policy traditions are not really appropriate to its new condition. Inevitably, he is regarded with some unease and even suspicion.

This suspicion is implied in the frequent comparisons between Kissinger and Talleyrand or Metternich. Neither of the latter figures is an American hero, since it is not at all clear that their policies flowed from a set of strong moral convictions. To put it another way: American foreign policy, whether isolationist or interventionist, has always been highly moralistic in its posture and rhetoric. Americans are quick to assume, therefore, that when a policy is not moralistic it is probably not moral. This is an erroneous, if unsurprising, confusion.

As a matter of fact, it can be argued that no nation can, for any length of time, carry out an immoral foreign policy: i.e., a policy which is not congruent with the values inherent in, and expressed by, its domestic arrangements, political or social or economic. The word, realpolitik, will apply to particular moments or events when this congruence is (or seems to be) disturbed—when, for reasons of dire necessity or extraordinary opportunity, a nation acts in a way that is inconsistent with its political traditions and values. But no nation ever has had a foreign policy based simply on realpolitik, just as no polity has ever proclaimed, as one of its basic values, cynicism or hypocrisy or opportunism. Both Talleyrand and Metternich had political ideals, and their policies were in the service of such ideals. Only, in American eyes, they were such modest ideals—modest in substance (i.e., lacking in ideological or quasi-religious pretensions) and modest in form (i.e., lacking in righteous enthusiasm)—that somehow they do not seem like ideals at all. Hence, the aura of amorality which Americans perceive and shy away from.

What Henry Kissinger symbolizes, as Secretary of State, is the Europeanization of American foreign policy—a process already visible in the writings of George F. Kennan, whose heir Kissinger can properly claim to be. He also symbolizes the end of the idea of "American exceptionalism." This idea was at the root of both isolationism and interventionism, each of which in its own way conceived of the United States as a "city upon a hill" and "a light unto the nations." But the emergence of the United States as a world power, its transition to an imperial republic, means a coming-of-age in which such utopian visions no longer fit the reality. American foreign policy will certainly continue to reflect the values of our liberal democracy. But it will now have to encompass other values, too (international stability, regional balances of power, etc.) which, in the eyes of the purists, will be seen as compromising American values. In a sense, this purist perception will be correct: it is impossible to define a nation's interests without taking its values into account, and there is no such thing as an accommodation to other nations' interests without a compromising of values. This is as true in the destiny of a nation as it is in the life of an individual. A doctrinaire refusal to compromise one's values is the sign of the perpetual adolescent. The sign of maturity, on the other hand, is a prudential management of one's values in a world which permits *no one*'s values to be fully achieved.

How the American people will react to this unprecedented situation is, of course, the interesting question. To talk of consensus (or dissent) in foreign policy is, in this connection, beside the point. Consensus is what sustains an ideological foreign policy, and no great power—not the United States, not Russia, not China—can have a foreign policy that fits neatly into an ideological *Weltanschauung*. For a foreign policy which consists mainly in the prudential management of one's values, it is confidence in one's political leadership, and in the political system as a whole, which is most needed. The American democracy has never been noted for having confidence in its political leaders; distrust of politicians, a heritage of the radical republicanism of the eighteenth century, goes very deep in the American grain. Nor have the opening years of the 1970s, the Watergate years, given us reason to think that such confidence will, to the average American, seem merited or plausible. Nevertheless, it is only with the overcoming of this crisis of confidence that American foreign policy can hope to become reasonably effective, both in terms of America's political values and of the necessities of a world which gives these values no providential privileges.

Notes

1. In *The New Republic* for April 21, 1973, Joseph Califano writes: "A defect in the proposal for the volunteer army is that it could make it too cheap and easy for national leaders to make the initial decision to wage a war. . . . By removing the middle class from even the threat of conscription, we remove perhaps the greatest inhibition on a President's decision to wage war."

2. See George Ball, "Europe's Isolationism," *The Listener,* May 24, 1973.
3. Quoted by Leslie Gelb, "Domestic Change and National Security Policy," *The Next Phase in Foreign Policy* (Washington; D.C.: The Brookings Institution, 1973).
4. See Walter Z. Laquer, *Neo-Isolationism and the World of the Seventies* (New York: 1972).

Dissenting on Consensus

LESLIE H. GELB

Finally, back in the summer of 1973, the Congress passed and the President signed legislation barring further American combat activities in Indochina. It was anticlimactic by then, evoking sighs of relief rather than hurrahs, but necessary nonetheless. The night before passage, President Nixon dispatched a letter to Capitol Hill, telling the legislators how irresponsible they were and warning them that if anything henceforth went wrong in any part of the world, it would be their fault.

At the same time, Henry Kissinger was saying something much more important. In one of his rare public appearances as the National Security Adviser to the President, Kissinger said: "The present ordeal of the whole nation is too obvious to require commentary." His solution was consensus: "The consensus that sustained our international participation is in danger of being exhausted. It must be restored."

Since becoming Secretary of State, Kissinger has frequently reiterated this plea for a new consensus. It seems a beautiful vision: All Americans pulling together to create "a new stable structure of peace," making this a better world and fending off dangers without war. But his plea raises questions of process no less than of substance. Despite or because of its traditional allure in our country, the notion of consensus itself merits examination.

To me, it is undeniable that American immersion in the Vietnam war was the product of an American consensus to do so, and the indifference of many in the face of this consensus. Whether you believe that the war was necessary or evil, whether you believe that the consensus was manipulated or relatively spontaneous, the point remains. The widespread belief that South Vietnam should not be lost to communism generated and sustained that war.

This consensus crippled dissent. Strikingly, this was so even after the summer of 1968, when a majority of Americans first came to the conclusion that the war was a mistake and that the United States should withdraw. For at the same time, most Americans continued to hold that a Communist takeover by force in Vietnam was still unacceptable. The consensus, thus, even surmounted the general conviction that the war made little sense!

Before proceeding further, the meaning of consensus requires some illumination. The Random House Dictionary defines it as "general agreement or concord"; a secondary definition is "majority of opinion." This essay strongly leans on the first definition and eschews the second. For American foreign policy in the past quarter-century, consensus has meant widespread agreement among executive branch officials, legislators, journalists, social scientists, labor leaders and the like on the general principle that the United States should take the necessary steps to prevent the advance of communism. This consensus was not invariable or always omnipotent. Cuba was an important exception.

Some people might prefer the term "bipartisan support of foreign policy." This, too, is acceptable as a definition, so long as it is not restricted to Congress—and so long as it is not confused with familiar notions of "going along with the President" and "politics stopping at the water's edge." Again, consensus is used here to define broad agreement on an overarching belief that actually motivated most American leaders and followers in their specific actions. It is not meant to connote the absence of conflict, but to underline the fact that differences were submerged, ignored, and managed. Put another way, this is an essay about consensus as it is embodied in doctrine and acquires the character of a political imperative.

So the question, then, leaps out: With the Vietnam experience to look back on, should we really want another consensus? Would the United States and the rest of the world actually suffer, as Kissinger suggested, without Americans firmly backing another American global vision? Or would we all be better off without one? To answer these questions, the post-World War II consensus itself has to be dissected. What were the origins of that consensus and how was it preserved and extended? What did the consensus consist of? Why was dissent so ineffective? How would the policy-making process look and work without a consensus on basic policy propositions?

On origins, the battle between the Wallacites and the Churchillians in 1946 is a fair place to start. Henry Wallace, gentle and dogmatic, supported by a vast array of liberals, was arguing that the United States had to learn to live with Russia and eschew power politics. Winston Churchill, fierce and articulate, evoking perhaps louder echoes than he desired in America, was calling forth images of an "iron curtain" and insisting that Moscow only understood force. The battle ended with victory for the Churchillians in March 1947, when President Truman invoked the doctrine of containment. Invoking the confrontation between freedom and totalitarianism and vowing to meet either direct or indirect aggression, President Truman set us on the course of containment of communism for the next twenty-five years.

The substance of the subsequent American consensus on preventing the spread of communism in Vietnam is well known: the fearsome combination of the belief in the indivisibility of peace, the notion of monolithic communism, the fear of another Munich, and the nightmare of a McCarthyite right-wing reaction. But why did American leaders seek a consensus in the first place? Why was anticommunism the choice?

Why did the defeat of the Wallacites at the hands of the Churchillians, despite the stir caused by these early doves, seem such a foregone conclusion?

First, there *had* to be a consensus on foreign policy. Americans, while they would struggle with each other to define it, could not do without it. There is something about America's past, something inherent in our form of democracy, particularly with respect to foreign policy, that makes it appear ultimately necessary and natural to have consensus. Americans, like the devoutly religious and like the twentieth-century Communists, must have a clear sense of right and wrong.

This has not been an absolute feature of our past. But it has been more characteristic of the United States than of other western democracies. It would not be much of an exaggeration to say that most French leaders, with the notable exception of Napoleon and De Gaulle, have not been preoccupied with gaining a consensus. The persistence of the multiparty system in France has indicated a keen interest in preserving differences—sometimes to the point of stalemate. The British have not expressed their acceptance of differences through a multiparty system, but the tolerance of dissent has been strong nonetheless. They have enshrined the principle of majority rule. But this meant nothing more nor less than having half plus one, entitling the government to have its way until the other party was able to form a majority. No special moral value was placed on the majority; it was a legal and political concept. And again, few British leaders made a determined effort to transform this majority into the broad-gauged agreement that characterizes consensus. Indeed, it often seemed that British leaders found very large majorities cumbersome when it came to carrying out consistent programs. There would be too many that would have to be pleased.

But for Americans, a majority has not been enough. Difference, even with losers of elections, had to be accommodated, the fewest possible toes had to be trodden on, and as many as possible had to be brought into the fold. In France and Britain, majorities meant legitimacy, but not in the United States. Legitimacy in the United States has never been con-

ferred simply by election—either by half plus one or the so-
called 60 to 40 landslide victory. Consensus, not election,
conferred legitimacy to act abroad.

President Franklin Delano Roosevelt won large mandates
in the 1932 and 1936 elections, but it was still an uphill fight to
guide the Congress and the American people toward world
involvement. President Truman would never have gained approval for the Marshall Plan or Point Four—or perhaps even
for NATO—without prior widespread approval for the containment doctrine. The nation did not follow Lyndon B.
Johnson into Vietnam simply or primarily because he smashed
Goldwater in the 1964 election. Election provided the opportunity, not the right, to act. Presidents have needed consensus
and have set out either to create it or to reinforce the existing
one.

Second, in addition to the requirement for consensus, it was
preferable that the consensus be negative. The goal of stopping communism was easier to understand and sell than more
complex slogans like "making the world safe for democracy"
and "building stable government through economic development." Our leaders, to be sure, dressed up the negative in
positive terms. But negative injunctions have almost invariably been more compelling in American politics. What was
the Monroe Doctrine but a warning to foreigners to "keep
out of the Americas"? What was isolationism but a stricture
to Washington "to keep out of the world"?

Americans like to believe, and with good reason, that they
have made sacrifices to better the world. But do-goodism, it
seems, rarely has been the key selling point. The best recent
example of this is the yearly battle over foreign economic aid.
Only when the aid bill was packaged as a substitute for American troops, or as a weapon in the battle against communism,
has the bill fared well in Congress. Thus, when the Wallacites
sought to portray the possibility of a world free from power
politics, a world of noble aims, their pitch turned out to be no
match for the vision of barriers painted by the Churchillians—
and the political onslaught mounted against them.

Third, besides being negative, the postwar American goal
was bound to be specifically anti-Communist. At bottom,

American foreign policy goals have been based on rejection of things alien—and nothing was more alien to the United States than communism. The United States has been seen as a land of hope and promise. But even beyond that, Americans have pictured their country as *sui generis,* fundamentally different from the rest of the world. On a surface level, it began with Americans simply not having a particular taste for pomp and ceremony or the status symbols of class and royalty. But basically, Americans in politics have tended to define things as alien by reference to their economic system. Many factors come together to forge a nation's foreign policy. But linking all of these factors in American history was one proposition: Anything from abroad that threatens the continuation and growth of what is regarded as the values associated with our political-economic system is anathema. The threat could be foreign or domestic, but was usually seen as both. British imperialism, for example, was often seen as a major threat because it closed off foreign markets to American traders. After World War II when Britain lay shattered, the Soviet Union was seen as the only likely threat to American security. American leaders expressed their fears of Moscow in terms of Communist ideology and large Communist parties in Western Europe, and bundled these together in a vague balance-of-power concept. But the nightmare was not one of a Soviet military attack against the United States or even Western Europe. It was the nightmare of being isolated through a Soviet political takeover of Europe, leading, in turn, to the economic strangulation of the United States. Such was the common perception among élite groups at the time when the new American foreign policy consensus was taking shape and gaining political support.

The core political struggles in American history, at least with regard to foreign affairs, have not been over whether there should be or would be a consensus, but over who would define it. Those who won the battle to shape consensus in these seminal postwar years had everything going for them. They had the "negative factor" and they had the Communist issue of a threat to the economic system. Their idea was simple and American.

Everyone knew when the consensus had taken hold—at least among the élite or opinion-making groups. The new beliefs were chanted throughout society. The news media, academics, legislators, would-be legislators, Kiwanis Club members, and schoolteachers outdid each other in proclaiming their loyalty to the new holy words. Anyone who disputed them was simply dismissed.

The general anti-Communist consensus was well established in the early 1950s. Throughout most of the decade, Vietnam and Indochina were backwater issues. Dien Bien Phu and various Laotian crises called Indochina to the public mind, but, for the most part, this area of the world was ignored even by élite Americans. Nevertheless, to the extent that Indochina did receive attention, the prevailing assumption was that communism had to be stopped there as well. A glance at the executive branch documents in the Pentagon Papers, or occasional congressional speeches, or editorials, will bear this out. For most of the 1950s, however, the situation in Indochina was not so desperate as to require a full testing of the depths of this consensus. This ends-means test would not have to be applied until the early 1960s and again in 1965.

It was at this stage, in the 1960s, that the consensus on Vietnam made its presence felt. The political struggle that ensued was not over the consensus itself, but over how best to achieve the given ends. Political opponents began to wrestle not over the sanctity of the holy words, but over who was a better interpreter of scripture. Each claimed the conch, as did the boys in *Lord of the Flies,* on the grounds that he was a better high priest. The rhetoric of every postwar Presidential election, until 1972, never came to grips with the assumptions of containment. Time after time, the debate was over who was tougher or who might be more sensible. At the point where questions became assumptions, the consensus had been set.

In the process, the framework for debate closed in. Those who disagreed or felt queasy found they had to make their case within the bounds of the consensus. Alternatives became increasingly unacceptable. What was being done became the only thing that could be done.

This is why I find the "turning-points" thesis about United

States policy and Vietnam so unpersuasive. Scholars have written about several periods in the Vietnam story when, they say, our leaders could have decided either to get out or go in more deeply. Among these periods were: 1950 when the Chinese Nationalists were driven off the mainland; 1954 at the time of Dien Bien Phu; 1955 when the French began to leave Vietnam; 1961 when President Kennedy took over with a clean slate; and again in 1965 in the wake of President Johnson's landslide victory over Senator Goldwater and before we began bombing North Vietnam and sending in combat units. With the exception of the Dien Bien Phu instance, which is filled with enormous complexities, none of these, in retrospect, have the properties of a turning-point.

A turning-point, to have any real meaning, must be a situation in which it is quite conceivable that the decision will go either way. But in none of these periods were the odds anywhere near even. The remarkable fact about each of these stages in the Vietnam story is how quickly American leaders made their choice to take the next step. Indeed, a look at the Pentagon Papers, the memoirs, and the congressional debates shows that the issue was never whether we should get out or do nothing. The issues were how much more we had to do to prevent a Communist takeover and when to do it.

There was little or no difficulty in maintaining the consensus. Nearly everyone was trapped or in the throes of trapping himself. For bureaucrats, it was the effectiveness trap. For politicians, it was the rhetorical trap. For Presidents, it was the necessity trap. On the effectiveness trap, President Johnson made it plain even to his closest lieutenants that to stay in the Sun Court they would have to operate within a very narrow terrain. Everyone got the message. George Ball described it well in a television interview: "What I was proposing was something which I thought had a fair chance of being persuasive . . . if I had said let's pull out overnight or do something of this kind, I obviously wouldn't have been persuasive at all. They'd have said 'the man's mad'." It remains remarkable how few were willing to plead insanity.

On the rhetorical trap, the *Congressional Record* is lined with protestations of fealty to the President in his fight to keep

Vietnam out of Communist hands. Many legislators would privately say in 1966 and 1967 that they had their doubts, but could not bring themselves publicly to back away from their record. The most that many of them managed to do was to attack the President's handling of the war and to urge "negotiations." But virtually all of them were quick to add that they did not mean concessions that would allow Communists into the Saigon government.

On the necessity trap, Presidents were adept at frequently using the technique of telling their questioners that they had no choice. They had to do what they were doing or face the options of humiliating defeat or risking World War III. President Johnson's memoirs are replete with the phrase "no alternative." President Kennedy before him used the same line. Theodore Sorensen records the President's thinking on Vietnam in November 1963 as Kennedy "was simply going to weather it out, a nasty, untidy mess to which there was no other acceptable solution."

And just as people were trapping themselves, they were using the consensus to trap and isolate others. The conservative isolationists of the 1950s like Senators Allen Ellender and Richard Russell could be ignored. Those like Senator J. W. Fulbright who, in the early 1960s, protested the war as immoral were scrambled together by the Administration and the news media with personalities like Stokely Carmichael and the flag burners, damaging their respectability—and thus their ability to maintain successful opposition to policy. Inside dissenters like George Ball could be made into "devil's advocates," and the only opponent less formidable than a self-proclaimed devil's advocate is an eighty-year-old woman boxer. Internal dissenters like Clark Clifford could also be frozen out of the action. And if worse came to worst, these opponents could be thrown a bone—like a bombing halt, a call for free elections, or a cease-fire. Whatever the opponents advocated could be incorporated into a Presidential speech, and, with a few wrinkles, also be made unacceptable to Hanoi. But Presidents could say enough so that it always looked as though they were trying to do what the something-short-of-surrender dissenters wanted. Dissenters who said we should not get in-

volved in the first place or, later, that our involvement had
been a mistake and we should withdraw were tragically few in
number until the Tet offensive of February 1968. Indeed,
most "dissenters" were in fact operating wholly within the
policy consensus.

Apart from the "fringe" people who actually challenged
basic assumptions, different groups were, from time to time,
thought of as dissenters. In the 1950s, it was the military. But
they were not questioning basic assumptions; they were simply
saying that Vietnam was a distraction, the wrong war, and that
we should instead go for the jugular in Moscow and Peking. In
the early 1960s, it was the Governor W. Averell Harriman-
Roger Hilsman school. But they were not saying the American
commitment to Vietnam was wrong; they were arguing that
too much emphasis was being given to the military side of the
war and not enough of the political struggle and to pacification. In the late 1960s, the pacification clique was joined by
others who wanted to limit American involvement and begin
turning over more of the responsibility for fighting the war to
the South Vietnamese. The few who privately went further
kept their public arguments within the framework of the giv-
ens—again, the effectiveness trap. These people were not
really dissenters at all. They were people who by and large
wanted to go down a different road to get to the same place, or
whose arguments lent them that appearance.

In many ways, this "alternative road" group was cynical in
its substantive thinking, yet naïve politically. Some among
them, like Assistant Secretary of Defense John McNaughton,
wrote memos about being a "good doctor." Like the good
doctor, we would show that we tried hard to save the patient,
so when the patient died, it would be clear that Washington
was not to blame. But in political terms, to do more and to get
"our noses bloodied," another McNaughton phrase, would
in the end make it more and not less difficult to extricate
ourselves.

If neither the true-dissenters nor the alternative-roaders
proved very effective in changing policy, how was it that we
finally did get out? Was it the street marchers and the draft-
card burners? I think not. Their methods never seemed to

strike a responsive political chord in the country. If anything, the reverse was true. Nor did the intellectual critiques of the war as either a mistaken application of valid American foreign policy or the inevitable consequences of mistaken policies carry much weight. Perhaps in the end most Americans came to feel as the true dissenters, but this is not apparent either. Richard Nixon and Henry Kissinger still were able to carry on the war for four more years after it seemed the American exit was imminent. Passionate opposition and intellectual arguments, in the end, counted for very little and changed few minds.

The argument that finally prevailed at the end of the Johnson Administration was the weight of dead Americans. The war had gone on too long, and too many Americans were being killed. As with all wars that endure beyond public expectations, voices of dismay came to have an impact in the end. President Nixon realized this soon after his inauguration. Whenever the pressure for withdrawal would reach flood proportions, he would announce another troop cut and reduce draft calls. For a time he would be praised for "getting us out," and then the tide of criticism would recede for many months. As the American troop levels and draft calls got lower and lower, many dissenters went back to sleep. The carpet-bombing of North Vietnam, it must be remembered, was not an unpopular act.

Finally, the combination of American bodies and public frustration with a war that wouldn't end did bring the Nixon Administration to withdraw from direct combat in Vietnam. Yet to the end, it seems to me, the public did not reject the consensus behind the war in any intellectual or conceptual sense. Through the voice of the congressional majority, their message was simply "we've had enough." To say that the dissenters won out in the end is to slight the overwhelming fact that the United States propped up a political minority in Saigon for over twenty years at an enormous cost in lives and dollars, and continued to offer it massive aid.

The dissenters really did not have a chance. Given the force of consensus in American history and the politics of foreign policy, they were bound to be losers. Thus, looking at our colonial past, the historian Daniel Boorstin writers: "In New England the critics, doubters, and dissenters were expelled from the community; in England, the Puritans had to find ways of living with them." Boorstin went on to say that the American Puritans "transcended theological preoccupation precisely because they had no doubts and allowed no dissent." The early Puritans believed they knew what was right. The only permissible questions were how to achieve the foreordained goals—in other words, questions about tactics.

At best, dissenters in America are thought to be eccentrics; at worst, they are equated with the devil. The new American Puritans, the holders of the containment conch, had little difficulty convincing most Americans that those who opposed Vietnam policy were the enemy.

This situation is intolerable. In my opinion, our historical passion for consensus is as fraught with dangers for our future as it has been in our past. We were not served well either by the isolationist doctrine of the 1920s and 1930s or the containment doctrine of the 1950s and 1960s. The former led to a consistent pattern of underreaction and the latter to a persistent pattern of overreaction.

An overall policy consensus generates political paranoia and intellectual rigidity. The witch hunts, the suspicion, and the intolerance are well known. But equally important is what the consensus does to analysis of foreign problems and descriptions of American alternatives.

Facts are forced to fit the theory, and all the facts begin to look alike. Threats to Greece and Turkey are said to be a replica of Munich. The "loss" of China is seen as a rerun of Roosevelt's "give-away" to Stalin of Eastern Europe. The Korean War becomes another Manchuria. Vietnam is analogized into an Asian Berlin. And regardless of the uniqueness of each, all are considered as interrelated threats emanating from the Kremlin's Pandora box. Discrimination, which is the essence of sound policy, is lost, and policy choices are reduced to a single unchanging response—stop communism.

But it is one thing to demonstrate the insidiousness of consensus as embodied in doctrine and quite another to think out how we would do without it. The absence of consensus would certainly allow for more fine-tuned analyses of world problems and a wider real list of policy options. It could mean avoiding another Vietnam, different in form but similar in doctrinal determinism. But would not the price for these probable advances, this new intellectual and political flexibility, be too high? Specifically, what would happen to any semblance of policy consistency? And would there not simply be policy paralysis?

I would argue, first, that too much stress has been placed on the need for policy consistency. What good reason is there for having a doctrine that allows no military involvement anywhere, or that presumes military involvement everywhere a military threat exists? It seems perfectly reasonable to me both to be prepared to use force to deter and defend in Europe, and to hold to the notion of no Asian land wars. Similarly, we could easily visualize a situation, say, in which Washington should be prepared to provide arms aid to the Indonesian government but not to the Thai government. And I can readily see the rationales for helping Israel without also having to prop up the Saigon regime. Any Administration should have foreign policy goals—goals that can be debated publicly—but it should eschew all-encompassing doctrines that determine actions toward their pursuit.

Doctrines demand too much consistency. If a President has invested much political capital in an overall doctrine, how could he then proceed to intervene in Vietnam without also intervening in the Dominican Republic? Just so did President Truman send the fleet to protect the defected Chinese Nationalist government on Taiwan when he needed the political support of the conservatives for his defense of South Korea. He should have been able to fight in Korea without having also to undertake so broad a commitment by the United States against the new government in Peking.

The absence of consensus embodied in doctrine would, indeed, lead to some loss of consistency, but what is lost in consistency is, in my opinion, more than compensated by what is gained in discrimination. The harder question is what to do about the probability of policy paralysis—for some kind of consensus is often required to act in a particular situation.

With no agreed doctrine that has political backing, how could any government even begin to function? How would bureaucrats charged with implementation know what was expected of them? How could allies and adversaries know what to expect of us?

Here, it is necessary to underline the point implicit in the foregoing analysis, namely, that the problems arise from having an overall policy consensus—a Truman Doctrine, an Eisenhower Doctrine, the doctrine of flexible and controlled response, or the Nixon Doctrine. Having these *kinds* of doctrines is what I am suggesting should be avoided. These are public relations exercises designed to limit rational and critical discussion of policy—and they achieve this purpose. These Presidential doctrines and what they lead to in the way of political paranoia are the nub of the problem. They are the traps to be shunned—for the good of the President and the country.

But consensus on specific issues or policy areas will and should occur. Through the inevitable confluence of ideas, bureaucratic politics, and domestic politics, particular policies will emerge for particular areas and issues. It will certainly take Presidents, their lieutenants, bureaucrats, and others longer to hammer out those specific compromises in the absence of a doctrine. But is time of the essence in most diplomatic situations? The news media rather than the demands of events usually compel rapid decision. And even if a particular matter is time-urgent, why should the American response be foreordained by a doctrine?

The Cuban missile crisis is a perfect example of doctrine becoming a political imperative. It is not at all clear why President Kennedy and his advisers assumed they had to act so quickly. To be sure, more missiles were arriving from Russia; but some, it seemed, were already there, and even if they were not, would that difference have been so insurmountable? With more time and without the political pressures of doctrinal paranoia, perhaps President Kennedy would not have taken us into a situation in which he felt the chances of nuclear war were one in three.

The consensus on a particular policy question that will

emerge may or may not be a good one, depending on many variables. But when it is not deduced from some larger, untouchable whole, it can be reexamined. The President and the nation are to the better if there are no good arguments for changing the policy, if the reasons for the particular policy are sound ones humanistically, pragmatically, and factually. But the point is that, under these circumstances, policy can be changed because altering it does not necessitate reordering the cosmos.

Yet, creating the kind of more relaxed and less structured circumstances I find desirable does require a significant change in attitudes and some minor institutional reforms. I have few illusions about the difficulties of bringing about change. Indeed, by disposition, I find slow but steady change more satisfactory than facing an unknown new world. But one factor that always stands in the way of any change is uncertainty about what would be expected of us and how the system would work in a new situation. The following is a sketch of what the foreign policy process would look like and how it could work without a doctrine and the attendant political pressures.

At the most mundane and yet profound level, there would have to be tolerance of all views. Our dogmatism is only exceeded by our self-righteousness. Why do our Presidents, for example, have to be right every single time and pretend everything they do is consistent with everything else they do? Someday, it might not even take great political courage for a President to behave with a sense of fallibility.

Presidents would have to resist the siren songs of their advisers to write that speech defining the new doctrine. Establishment academicians would have to risk being irrelevant once again, by challenging assumptions and refusing to operate within the consensus. Politicians would have to watch their rhetoric. George McGovern's plea in the 1972 Presidential campaign to "come home, America" is typical of how electoral rhetoric could have become governmental policy. The press and columnists would have to be less critical of delay in the government's reactions to foreign events and more critical of doctrinal pronouncements by Presidents and their lieutenants. Going to this direction would be, in my veiw, neither against human nature nor, after a while, bad politics.

Besides changing these attitudes, executive branch leaders would have to institutionalize dissent, not domesticate it. For example, departments should not set up separate groups of devil's advocates which can be easily isolated and ignored. It has to be made known that dissenters can have their day in court *without prejudice*. It would not be difficult to see if departmental leaders are serious about this. But dissenters would also have to be serious—if they believe something is fundamentally wrong and they cannot change it from within, they should quit.

Opening up executive agencies to serious consideration of policy alternatives would also go far toward alleviating the pernicious aspects of "the leak." Leaks occur because there is no mechanism for open and orderly expression of views within the bureaucracy. Leaks come from all sides; there is no way to stop them. Trying to block them only leads to bad feelings and more leaks. Executive branch leaders do themselves a disservice by letting alternative information and alternative policies reach the Congress and the public through the leak. Because everyone understands that the leak is something that leaders seek to suppress, it only serves to make what the government is trying to do appear more illicit and unjustified. It is in the Administration's interests to make information and policy alternatives known as an integral part of its own public presentations.

Congress, in this new situation, would have to be the ultimate noise-maker and policy-maker of last resort. The Congress does best as an institution, in my judgment, when it questions the goals of the Administration and forces the executive branch to bring out the facts, to think policies through in public, and to face a range of political realities. It is when liberals expect more than this of Congress that they become disillusioned with Capitol Hill.

The pressures on legislators to make foreign policy bipartisan are, of course, enormous. But most legislators seem to get talked into a form of bipartisanship that never quite existed and should not exist. This is the notion that politics stops at the water's edge, and that the Congress should get behind Administration policies, rather than ask questions or insist on answers and even compromises from the Administration as the price of agreeing to particular policies. Too often, the Congress buys consensus for the sake of consensus, and to avoid responsibility.

But bipartisanship as practiced by one of its orginators, Senator Arthur Vandenberg, does not fit the myth of politics stopping at the water's edge. Vandenberg did make it clear that he welcomed consultations by the executive branch with members of the Congress. Yet when Secretary of State Kissinger urges consensus and bipartisanship on the Congress, he and the Congress would do well to recall Vandenberg's ambivalence and look at the way Vandenberg actually practiced bipartisanship. "When and where it is possible," he said, "in clearly channeled and clearly defined projects, for the legislature, the executive and the two major parties to proceed from the beginning to the end of a specific adventure, so that all are consulted in respect to all phases of the undertaking, I think it is a tremendously useful thing." But, Vandenberg added, "to think that can be done as an everyday practice in regard to all of the multiple problems of international import which now descend upon the State Department every day, in my opinion is totally out of the question."

Vandenberg pressed his realism a step further into the realm of pure politics. "The Republican Party has this dilemma: if it does not cooperate in the world, it will be blamed for destroying the peace, as in 1920. If it cooperates too much with the Democratic administration, it will be charged with having no policy of its own." His solution was to support President Truman's European policy where "we could lose everything," and attack him on Asian policy where, he said, "there is no solution I can think of anyway."

Yes, this was crass politics. But politics cannot be separated from foreign policy—especially in a less structured situation without an agreed doctrine to hide behind. The doctrines of the past did not eliminate politics; they channeled and narrowed what was considered to be legitimate debate. Within this limited framework, the politics of foreign policy remained bitter. Without doctrine, the politics will continue to be bitter but the range of legitimate debate can broaden immeasurably.

Administration leaders obviously do not like this kind of situation. It makes everything harder for them. It runs counter to the essence of what power-holders seek—consensus and the legitimacy which consensus provides. This legitimacy, in turn, is the very stuff of power. Legitimacy helps to insure that those who oppose what the executive branch wants to do will either keep quiet or can be rendered ineffective.

Having a new consensus, whether it be a Nixon Doctrine, a Kissinger Doctrine, a Kennedy Doctrine, or a Jackson Doctrine, is not a consummation devoutly to be wished. Such doctrines do not mean the end of partisanship. And no new doctrine can adequately come to terms with the variety of world problems. Doctrines become symbols with which the power-holders can manipulate the public, but in the end, they trap and undo even their authors.

The Defeat of the Antiwar Movement

SAM BROWN

The headlines about demonstrations and trials implied that great events were taking place. And they were, as antiwar activists finally helped make the war an issue for all of America. But so little of America was changed. The movement was worthwhile for its impact at the height of American involvement in Vietnam—an involvement, we should remember, which still continues. Yet our protests against the war had a broader purpose, and we failed. For we seem to have had little lasting influence on the nature either of American society or its approach to the world.

Before considering the reasons for our failure, I should set aside the old and not truly relevent arguments about our motives. Some observers saw the rebirth of domestic communism and some a new fascism. David Broder worried about the attack on the Presidency, and Walt Rostow worried about the attack on the President. Each observer conjured some new motive for dissenters.

But in the main, dissenters had few ulterior motives. They were persuaded neither by the debates of foreign affairs scholars about the likely impact of U.S. withdrawal nor by the

claims of radicals. Rather, they were people who abhorred the
continuation of the destruction, who were appalled by U.S.
support for the revolving Saigon governments, and who were
sickened by what they saw on television every night.

This simple, humane motivation was not entirely applicable, however, to the active leadership. The most active of the
participants and leaders of the antiwar movement spent endless hours debating and refining obscure ideological points. In
addition, thousands of hours were spent attempting either to
attach or detach every other contemporary cause seeking to
gain the thrust and strength of the antiwar movement. View-
ing the leadership as monolithic and conspiratorial, the
government responded, as we now know from Watergate testimony, in an increasingly hostile and paranoid fashion.

Although the antiwar movement had strategic goals (sometimes simply the cessation of the bombing, sometimes the
ending of imperialism, but mostly something in between), it
accomplished very little of what it set out to do. The reasons
for its failure are rooted in the history of the movement itself;
they led directly to its isolation and ultimate failure.

The history of the antiwar movement can be divided
roughly into three parts, and the seeds of its internal and
external difficulties were there from the beginning. The first
period lasted from 1961 to 1967; a second period extended
from 1967 through 1972; the third, since the signing of the
agreement for reduced U.S. combat participation in January
1973.

The earliest phase of the antiwar movement laid the
groundwork for its later frustration. During this period
(1961-67), which began with ban-the-bomb activism and led to
the anti-Vietnam-war activity, only the most committed were
involved. In the Senate, only Morse, Gruening, and Clark were
dependable. There were no major Kennedy-era defections to
the antiwar movement, and local teach-ins leading to the
National Teach-in on the War in 1965 were the most active
expression of support and involvement of the academic community. Organizationally, the movement was a poorly funded,
loosely knit collection of activists with a floating leadership
which formed ad hoc, event-oriented coalitions. The general

conception of the antiwar effort, both in the media and the public, was of a student movement with no political base, talking about an issue which was only of academic interest.

This slow beginning was not so surprising, since the issue did not lend itself to the organization of popular pressure. There was no crisis or East-West confrontation to jar awareness of the U.S. population. There was virtually none of the economic pressure that might have grown out of a direct threat to the dollar or to the interests of a major industry. There was little ethnic pressure, since no bloc comparable to the Irish or Jews was involved, and the racial aspect of the war was never a widely understood issue. These were discouraging obstacles for those who sought to expand and strengthen the influence of the movement.

The result was a marked loss of faith among the antiwar leadership. The basic optimism and idealism of the Port Huron Statement of 1961 (about peace and participatory democracy) had disappeared by 1967; instead, there was a deep-seated cynicism.

About that time, a shift in public attitude began. Television brought death into American homes every night; the bodies in Vietnam increasingly became U.S. soldiers. Liberals began to defect from the policy: a rush of people from the Kennedy Administration, led by Richard Goodwin, were joined by economists and students of foreign relations. Concurrently, the draft became a serious problem for the sons of the upper-middle-class Americans. Then, in February 1968 the Tet offensive shattered the myth of U.S. military superiority; in March the voters in New Hampshire disproved the myth of the war's popularity.

Within the antiwar movement, two schools of thought had emerged. One was to broaden the base of the movement by using traditional political means such as elections and mass public demonstrations. The other was to shut down the machinery of war through draft resistance, sit-ins, fasts, disruptions of troop movements, and so on. For almost half a decade, each method gathered support and lived in uneasy alliance with the other.

By the end of 1972, the second period had passed. In place

of outrage and activism, there arose a widespread belief that organization against the war in Indochina was impossible. As American participation in the conflict became increasingly indirect, TV coverage of the continued fighting became sporadic and public interest declined. It was as if the war as an issue had fallen through a time-warp to the early 1960s; we were still in Vietnam, but once again it did not seem to matter, and the years of activity seemed to have left little residue.

There is little institutional impact from the antiwar movement. The defense budget is at, or above, war levels. SANE, AFSC (American Friends Service Committee), and similar permanent organizations are not significantly stronger. And although peace has become a much-used term in the official lexicon, government policy was not deeply affected.

Congress is now sensitized to the issue of Vietnam; few in the whole nation believe any longer that a "Vietnam" is the kind of situation in which we ought to be involved. Yet there is little reason to believe that mass dissent could be readily organized if we did enter a comparable situation. Although it seems that most people would prefer to avoid another Vietnam, this past adventurism was ultimately undermined as much by Nixon's lack of barstool credibility as by the antiwar movement. Ford has wide latitude to act in the name, if not necessarily the interest, of the U.S. people in further military activity. Inflation, foreign manipulation of oil prices, and our sagging international reputation present possible pressures for new adventures.

In order to understand why we came through the trauma of the 1960s so little changed, it is necessary to look not at the limited accomplishments of the antiwar movement, but at the reasons for its failures.

Internally, the splits in the movement were severe. The fundamental split was between those who saw the war as an inevitable product of our culture and economic system and those who saw it as an aberrational episode. Virtually all the antiwar leadership was of the "inevitable by-product" school, while most of the participants in marches and campaigns were of the "aberrational-occurrence" school.

Consequently, the language and intent of the leadership

often were not understood by potentially sympathetic audiences. I remember attending a march in 1965 at which both
Norman Thomas and Carl Oglesby spoke. Thomas spoke in
terms of moral outrage, about rescuing the national soul. As
the son of a religious, Midwestern family, I could identify
easily with his ministerial pleas. Oglesby talked about U.S.
imperialism with language that set my teeth on edge. Within a
year, I read Oglesby's speech in essay form and found myself
agreeing with it. Within two years, I found it hard to restrain
myself from using his language. I had come to believe it but
feared it would be offensive to potential supporters.

This fundamental split had numerous ramifications. One
was that every march, demonstration, or sit-in was preceded by
weeks of haggling about speakers, about the tone of the slogans, statements, handbills, and so on. The pressure within the
leadership toward a more-radical-than-thou stance was very
strong, but the desire of some leaders was for broadening
rather than narrowing the base of opposition to the war.
Therefore, a delicate compromise was sought between an approach sufficiently strong to satisfy militant elements of the
leadership and one not so strong as to drive away potential
participants. The tension was constant and consumed many
hours which could have been used more productively.

The second fundamental reason for the failure of the antiwar movement was overdependence on upper-middle-class,
draftable young men. This is a notion I resisted for a long time,
considering it conservative-liberal nonsense. Many of the
people I knew best were resisters, conscientious objectors, or
people who had been deferred for medical or educational
reasons. I reasoned that since they remained active in the
antiwar effort, others would still be active whether or not the
draft affected them.

The advent of the predominently poor and increasingly
black "volunteer" army shot down that idea. Tens of thousands of antiwar participants, parents as well as sons, disappeared along with the draft.

Third, agents provocateurs and the costs of legal defense
made organization against the war much more difficult. The
Chicago Seven, Harrisburg, and Ellsberg trials consumed more

than $2 million that might otherwise have gone into the creation of long-term citizen-organizations or political campaigns. It remains an open question, however, whether the funds could have been put to more productive use in that period if they had been available. As the movement waned, these trials and other forced diversions became the substance and the organizational focus of antiwar activity.

Fourth, there developed within the movement a strong sense that politics was a useless activity at best, and perhaps even harmful. By 1970, many of the people who had developed skills in the antiwar movement that might have been translated into campaign assets wanted no part of the electoral process. This antipolitical tendency was part of a generalized antileadership bias inherent in the diversity of the movement. When no individual led, more people felt equal and thus more involved. While this prevented personality cults from developing, the result was not the strong new sense of shared responsibility and communal leadership for which many hoped.

Finally, there was the lack of a common, broad analysis of the problem. The more political elements of the antiwar movement wanted people of all persuasions on other issues to join in opposition to the war. Thus, we tried to appeal to potential supporters on the basis of the lowest common ideological denominator; we did not try to force acceptance of a complex analysis. We avoided linking antiwar efforts to demands for abortion rights, the legalization of marijuana, or any other cause-of-the-week. That would have required a broad concept which could demonstrate their relatedness, and the general public had not accepted any such analysis.

We never gained acceptance of a political analysis which would have placed the behavior of the U.S. government—and the momentary successes and defeats of the antiwar movement—in perspective. Instead, opposition to the war depended largely on moral outrage. This reinforced a sense of superiority in times of apparent success and left us with no underpinnings in time of failure.

Only political organizations with great wealth or patronage, such as the major political parties, or ethnic, racial, and "shared experience" groups can survive this lack of theoretical grounding. Power and community can become substitutes for theory, but we had neither power nor community.

Without a larger analysis, the ethic in the movement in the late 1960s became one of "do-your-own-thing." Consequently, there was a nonjudgmental attitude by the majority toward the foolishness of a few. Some people decided to swim in the reflecting pool while 500,000 others marched decorously for peace. But the drama in the aberrent acts was given equal time on the evening news and allowed people to avoid dealing with the questions raised by the marchers. And it left people an easy excuse for not participating.

Even on the issue of violence, there was little willingness by antiwar leaders to take a strong stand. Some wanted simply to reaffirm a nonviolent commitment and say nothing about specific acts of (purportedly) antiwar groups which led to violence. This became the dominant mode. A few favored denouncing specific acts of violence in which antiwar people were involved. This second course of action never received serious consideration. There was a widespread fear of a new McCarthy era; it was argued successfully that ADA (Americans for Democratic Action) liberals had been helpful to Joseph McCarthy by distinguishing themselves from more radical elements and leaving them defenseless. No one wanted to be in the comparable position when it came down to the nitty-gritty this time. The argument for strong and specific denunciation of violence was most frequently voiced by Allard Lowenstein, whose influence was resisted by militant leaders through *ad hominem* attacks.

In essence, many of us thought that the acts which we were encouraged to denounce were either acts of agents provocateurs or were at least precipitated by law enforcement agencies. The media appeals for "responsible" behavior on the part of the antiwar movement had no impact. (They came, after all, from papers and people who, by and large, had no sympathy for the movement or its goals.) In fact, with the exception of the University of Wisconsin bombing and some Weatherpeople craziness, there was little sentiment for denunciation and, in hindsight, little to denounce.

These observations on the past are easier for me to accept

than are their implications for the future. Some of the points pressed by the antiwar movement have been integrated into the mainstream of American thinking. Vietnam may have opened doors to rapprochement with Russia and with China, and less American proclivity to behave like a colonial power. The direct influence of Vietnam dissent may be felt in the form of new limits on U.S. foreign policy options elsewhere in the world.

But I think there is not likely to be great dissent in the next few years, about Vietnam or any other foreign adventure. Our attention is turned inward to deal with economic instability in family budgets as well as in the nation, and the leisure time of the young has been constricted since the affluent days of the 1960s.

The one hope is that since dissent over Vietnam was less likely than over U.S. military action elsewhere, its existence was in fact an indication of a fundamental moral vitality of this nation.

We are a society which depends for its life on a general regard for law and the appearance of democracy. The idea that all was well with our system was fundamentally challenged by the antiwar movement, as we insisted that the rules were constantly being violated by the people charged with upholding them. And the revelations of the Pentagon Papers and Watergate did show that the strength and morality of our government was being undermined daily by the most prestigious of our citizens.

The most serious question is whether such a reaction against the corruption of our society is inevitable in our democracy. Were the antiwar movement and the response to Watergate rooted in a healthy and continuing public concern about the actions of our leaders, or were they temporary revulsions spurred by crisis headlines and TV images? Will the same concern for justice that ran through so many Watergate editorials now be applied to all the apparent inequities of American life—and in American actions abroad? Or will the outrage at Watergate melt away like the antiwar movement, leaving no structural change in its wake? The answer is not clear, and thus all the more important.

The Impact of Dissent on Foreign Policy: Past and Future

JOHN P. ROCHE

At the outset, certain key propositions have to be established. The first is that dissent is not a monolithic concept; different individuals and groups object to specific policies for widely disparate reasons. The classic example in the area of domestic policy was the last-ditch defense of prohibition by preachers and bootleggers. In this sense, as we shall see, dissent from our intervention in Southeast Asia was founded on many varied premises. What the protesters had in common was a target, an individual who, by the nature of his office, wore a bull's-eye on his back: the President of the United States.

Needless to say, neither Lyndon Johnson nor Richard Nixon enjoyed their experiences as point-man. Indeed, President Johnson considered it extremely unfair to find himself simultaneously attacked by the right for not "nuking" Hanoi and by the left for not dumping Saigon. In an ideal world, his point would have been valid, but anyone who believes we live in an ideal world is ipso factor no candidate for President. Suffice it to say that neither Johnson nor Nixon was dragged screaming into the White House.

The second aspect of dissent that should be noted for the

purposes of this essay is that I do not limit the category to the professionals, the articulate spokesmen for various anti-Vietnam movements. In fact, it is my contention that inarticulated objections to Vietnam, gradually building up in the mass of the population, were far more significant in policy terms than the rhetorical blasts of the antiwar militants. And they were on a completely different wavelength; the war was not "immoral" or "obscene," but pointless. American soldiers (generally from their socioeconomic levels) were getting killed and wounded —and for what?

Essentially, in historical terms, this was a reversion to the conditioned reflexes of pre-WorldWar II isolationism. These people were vigorous patriots, they despised the overt anti-Americanism of some of the antiwar militants, but they simply could not understand why half a million Americans were inconclusively fighting somewhere at the other end of the world. An extremely able representative warned me in 1967 that his constituents (mainly blue-collar and working class) were signing off. Their slogan, he said, was "let the gooks fight it out."

With these preliminary points in mind, let us turn to the protest movement and explore its various components. Immediately one discerns three distinct categories: the "ideologues," the "opportunists," and the "realists." Sorting out the varieties of radical experience is beyond the scope of this work, but the general characteristics of the Trotskyites, Maoites, etc., was that they were not "doves" (in the vocabulary of the era) but "Hanoi hawks." That is, they opposed our intervention because they believed that the Democratic Republic of Vietnam was a historically progressive regime engaged in "liberating" the South from "imperialism and colonialism."

Another group of ideologues refused to carry Vietcong flags. They were the authentic pacifists who wanted peace in Indochina, not a Hanoi or a Saigon victory. Unfortunately, perhaps because of the very character of their convictions, they were out-shouted and out-maneuvered in various organizations and eventually denounced by the Hanoi hawks for their major proposal: an in-place cease-fire.

If the leadership of the antiwar movements tended to be usurped by Hanoi hawks, the great bulk of the constituents

can best be described (in a nonperjorative sense) as opportunists. As a one-time activist in the movement to block American
intervention in World War II, I had some sense of the motives
of the college students who poured into Washington to
protest. Most human beings have a natural tendency to define
as unjust any war in which they may get shot. This tropism can
be overcome very quickly by a Pearl Harbor—it is not a matter
of cowardice—but the war in Vietnam had no Pearl Harbors.

In 1966 a British journalist was stunned by what he took to
be my cynicism when I observed that the antiwar movement
would wither away in two weeks if we ended the draft. This
was not cynicism: for a quarter of a century I have been
teaching young people, and I have noted that one area in
which they have the edge on their elders is the speed with
which they can convert self-interest into high moral theory.
Having been rather good at it myself, I don't see this as
heinous—but I do feed it into the computer. In any event, the
end of the draft and the withdrawal of American ground
troops obliterated the student antiwar mobilization. When
President Nixon mined Haiphong and resumed full-scale
bombing, there was barely a whisper on the nation's campuses.

If the students provided the action, the whooping, and the
jumping so beloved by the media, the most serious body of
opportunists were those professional politicians and former
officials who participated in what I have called "the defection
of the Jacobites." Here the focal figure was the late Senator
Robert Kennedy who, with powerful friends and allies
throughout the country, began undermining Lyndon Johnson
on Vietnam. There was nothing remotely unconstitutional
about Robert Kennedy's desire to replace Johnson in the
White House, but his de facto break with the President in
1966 triggered a remarkable barrage from eminent political
figures with the standard refrain: "Vietnam would not have
happened if only Jack were here."

President Johnson took this very hard, particularly since it
coincided with the outburst of Dallas demonology. A new
conspiracy theory on the assassination of John Kennedy
seemed to surface every week, culminating in the rancid

MacBird, a play which had Johnson masterminding the murder. One speech by Robert Kennedy, who had been Attorney General when his brother was shot, could have defused the whole ugly business; the Kennedys' could have consented to the release of the autopsy photographs, which confirmed the Warren Commission's findings. But there was no action; the "Jacobites" just stood by and sardonically watched the lunatic picadors jab President Johnson.

Let me repeat: The defection of Robert Kennedy (even though he played his hand very cautiously) was a decisive event in the antiwar saga. At last the antiwar forces had a senior, legitimate political figure who could not be written off as a Hanoi stooge or some species of eccentric. While in public, Kennedy, to the despair of his would-be troops, wobbled back and forth, the word was passed that "he is with us." In the event, it took Senator Eugene McCarthy's good showing in the New Hampshire Democratic primary to flush Kennedy out, but from that day until his tragic death he provided the political charisma that the antiwar organizations had so long needed. Moreover, Kennedy's appeal reached deep into the inarticulate sector of American opinion.

Finally, there was an antiwar ambience (it was hardly an organized group) that I have called the realists. Walter Lippmann, Hans J. Morgenthau, and George Kennan come to mind. Neither ideologues nor opportunists, their objection was that Vietnam simply wasn't worth the price. From their viewpoint, American national interest was harmed by the endless, inconclusive struggle, and the costs (both physical and psychological) were preposterously out of proportion to any conceivable benefits. It's worth noting that, like George Ball, who shared many of their attitudes, they were strongly Eurocentric. These individuals, who never marched or engaged in movements, had nonetheless a very significant impact on élite opinion. Indeed, as the years went by, an increasing number of establishment figures came around to this viewpoint. Initially supporters of the war, they decided—as the bills mounted —that we had made a mistake. Their criticism, however, was utilitarian, not moral, in character. In attacking the war as a blunder, any one of this persuasion could not (except in First Amendment terms) say it was immoral or obscene. These terms do not exist in the utilitarian dictionary.

So much, then, for those whom we might call the articulators of dissent. It was a noisy experience to live through—in 1968 the White House resembled the Alamo—but what remains to be analyzed is the extent to which dissenters in this category influenced policy. One can hardly bring empirical techniques to bear on such a subjective question, but firsthand experience in the Johnson White House leads me to certain conclusions. First, the public noise-makers, the student demonstrators, had no direct impact. Partly Johnson brushed them off because he had made a fundamental strategic error in handling public opinion. Politicians, like generals, fight the last war, and from 1965 on the President was convinced that the real attack on his policies would come, on the Korean model, from the right. Thus, when the assault came from the left he was totally unprepared. (So was I; I had made the same miscalculation.) However, his generally low opinion of liberal political competence—"Conservatives can't make speeches," he once told me, "and liberals can't count"—led him to downplay the mass meetings, Pentagon mobilizations, and similar conventicles.

On the other hand, though admittedly they made him grit his teeth, Lyndon Johnson had great respect for those I have called the realists, or at least for some of them. The problem was he knew they had a point, but he could not admit that for all intents and purposes the Joint Chiefs of Staff had him caged. When you make an announcement to the effect that everything our boys in Vietnam need, they're going to get, you are setting yourself up for a military sandbagging. By 1966, Secretary Robert McNamara had lost his predominance in the Pentagon and the Joint Chiefs were riding high. Ironically (as we shall see), their Chairman, Earle Wheeler, did more than any dissenting group to demoralize American opinion on the war.

But the body that Johnson took most seriously was, as one might suspect, Congress. By 1966, senators and representatives, who were used to ignoring exhortations from ideologues, were getting ominous reactions from the plain folks who never went to college, avoided public meetings like the plague, hated hippies, loved America—but wanted out. I was picking this up from my own connections and on March 27, 1967, sent President Johnson a memorandum arguing in part that

> [North Vietnamese] present "insane" military operations are designed not to "win" the war, or to cut I Corps off from the rest of Vietnam, but simply to kill more Americans at *whatever cost* in North Vietnamese. To a dedicated old Bolshevik a weekly headline in the *Times* "U.S. Deaths Reach New All Time High" is worth 5000 dead peasants from the PAVN . . . . In short, Ho is not counting on the peaceniks but on the isolationists in the United States and believes (correctly) that coffins are more significant propaganda than leaflets.

It was at this level that dissent really got to President Johnson. One old congressional friend after another would tell him: "Mr. President, I'll vote appropriations, but I can't publicly defend the war." (Even Senator George McGovern did not vote against Vietnam appropriations until 1969.) I am absolutely certain that by the summer of 1967, Lyndon Johnson knew that something had gone desperately wrong with the war. To put it oversimply, the military would not fight the kind of war he wanted and were furious because he would not let them fight to their own specifications. Regrettably there was no George Marshall as Secretary of Defense to cover the President's flank—one of Harry Truman's greatest blessings. Even MacArthur was known to salute Marshall.

To summarize, by the end of the summer of 1967, opposition to the Vietnam war had convinced the President that a new policy was in order. Nobody contemplated simply pulling out; indeed, polls indicated that if the Communists took over in South Vietnam, the President would be held to blame. First, though with agonizing delay between the announcement of McNamara's resignation (November 29, 1967) and his replacement (February 29, 1968), came a new Secretary of Defense, Clark Clifford, who combined immense talent with long experience as a bureaucratic in-fighter.

Second, Johnson, who had told me flatly shortly before Christmas that all the Joint Chiefs wanted was "more of the same" and that he wasn't going to give it to them, began an intricate political maneuver. Its objective was to convey to the American people that everything in Vietnam was just fine, but he could be trusted to clean up the mess. This maneuver had three components: (1) a major victory over the North Vietnamese in the upcoming winter-spring offensive; (2) an offer to negotiate, combined with some kind of bombing halt; and (3) a massive effort to de-Americanize, or Vietnamize, the war.

This is not the place to recount the weird outcome of this scenario, except to note that we won an incredible military victory at Tet which one of Wheeler's Machiavellian ploys destroyed. As the back-channel messages between Wheeler and Westmoreland amply document, the Chairman, seeing an opportunity to increase his budgetary leverage, blackjacked the General into making a preposterous bid for 206,000 more troops. After Westmoreland, who was a bit baffled, explained that he had won, that he didn't need reinforcements, Wheeler flew out to Clark Field to show him the light. Westmoreland was instructed to base his request on the following "worst case": (1) the collapse of South Vietnamese army; (2) the removal of Korean troops; and (3) the injection of four fresh North Vietnamese divisions.

When the 206,000 figure was leaked—against a background of Johnson proclaiming a notable victory—the balloon went up in domestic politics. A furious Johnson (who knew nothing of Wheeler's private dealings with Westmoreland—luckily for the former) now had literally no room to maneuver. On March 31, 1968, he made the negotiations offer and took the veil. Secretary Clifford began a vigorous effort to make the Army of the Republic of Viet Nam into an army: for example, contracts for automatic weapons (M-16s) for the South Vietnamese were finally signed in the spring of 1968. (The Nixon program was merely an intensification of Clifford's policy, though the Republicans have claimed credit for originating Vietnamization.)

The articulate dissenters have taken credit for "dumping" Johnson and altering the war policy. The difficulty with this is that Nixon's only real change in policy was the rapid withdrawal of American troops. On the other hand, the new President dropped more bombs on Indochina than Johnson did. The qualitative change in our policy was a reversion to the military wisdom of the 1950s: "No land wars in Asia." The American people, in sum, were quite prepared to bomb North Vietnam, but they did not want American draftees killed in substantial numbers for some abstraction called self-determination. By 1975, Indochina was simply blacked out on their mental maps.

In other words, to reiterate, the potent dissent against Vietnam was not moralistic or guilt-ridden: most Americans find nothing intrinsically immoral about fighting totalitarians. They just don't want to get involved unless the shooting is on their street. (Recall in this connection that in 1941 Nazi Germany declared war on the United States.)

Parenthetically, perhaps the most distinctive impression made by the articulate dissenters was on the advertising men who became Richard Nixon's palace guard. It took me some time to comprehend it, but Haldeman and others genuinely believed that a left-wing revolution was a distinct possibility; whereas those of us who have known the cast of characters (a few insane fanatics excluded) for a decade or more knew that, although they could make quite a racket, the militants were incapable of organizing a two-car funeral. When the FBI and the CIA independently confirmed the view that there was not substantial evidence to demonstrate their connections with Communist powers, this was taken as proof that the security agencies were out of touch with reality. Enter: the "plumbers," toppling the first domino on the road to Watergate.

To conclude, the protest movements as such (those groups I have styled as the articulate dissenters) had only marginal influence on American policy, though they were naturally accused of hindering negotiations, giving aid and comfort to the enemy, and similar sins. This is an old accusation: it was also leveled against Representative Abraham Lincoln during the Mexican War and by President Lincoln against the Peace Democrats during the Civil War. (President Franklin D. Roosevelt once went so far as to award an Iron Cross to a journalist he found particularly obnoxious.) This argument does not (and never had) impressed me: it assumes stupidity on the other side of the Hill.

I assumed that Ho Chi Minh, Pham Van Dong, and their Soviet friends made a pretty careful analysis of American political realities and realized that if the war was increasingly unpopular, so were the anti-American antics of the militants. The key dissenting group was the "continental patriots," whose position never achieved high moral ground but was vividly expressed to me by my friends at the firehouse: "End the ———ing war . . . and shoot the ———ing draft-dodgers." But the vital point to keep in mind for the future is that they were not just sick of intervention in Southeast Asia; they signed off virtually across the board.

Indeed, in the perspective of American history, the surprising thing was that we made any global commitment in the wake of World War II, and that the average American was prepared to stay the course for a quarter of a century. With Vietnam, the trumpet called retreat. This was vividly demonstrated in a *Time* Louis Harris Poll, "The Limits of Commitment" (May 2, 1969). Asked about their willingness to use force to repel a Communist *military* invasion, 57 per cent agreed with respect to Canada, 52 per cent for Mexico, but no other area came close to a majority. (the figure for Israel, for example, was 9 per cent, and even West Germany mustered only 38 per cent. Subsequent polls have reinforced Harris's findings.)

The implications for American policy-makers are obvious and were quickly picked up by President Nixon. The new Chief Executive realized that he had to walk a high wire because the American people wished neither to lose nor to fight the Vietnam war. "Peace with honor" was in essence a plea for time to extricate ourselves from Indochina. It was successful: After the student spasm triggered by our invasion of Cambodia and the simultaneous killings at Kent State University, vocal dissent became limited to certain senatorial rituals, e.g., the Hatfield-McGovern "amendment to end the war." But the President believed—correctly as it turned out—that the American people would support strong measures (such as mining Haiphong harbor and resuming the bombing) if they were presented as a way of "winning" peace. However, as he clearly realized, there had to be a pay-off for these draconian moves; he could not escalate indefinitely.

Meanwhile the President formulated the Nixon Doctrine, which is a most interesting rhetorical exercise, one which accurately reflected the mood of the American people. The Doctrine, in summary, announced: (1) We are as a nation committed abstractly to that slightly disconcerting abstraction, the "free world"; (2) we want to help our friends work out their own problems and will provide material support; but (3) when it comes to the crunch, they are on their own. Put differently, the public's definition of American self-interest has reverted to continental, or perhaps hemispheric, dimensions.

The polls on American attitudes towards the Yom Kippur war, for example, strikingly resemble those taken in 1940-41. In the same way that an overwhelming majority wanted Britain to win World War II, but only a minority wanted to get the United States mixed up in the hostilities, the public response to a Gallup Poll (December 23, 1973) indicated 54 per cent favoring Israel, but a 7 to 5 margin *against* sending arms to the Jewish state. A 1975 Gallup Poll indicated only 10 per cent support for rescuing Israel from overwhelming assault.

This withdrawal syndrome was probably in the works anyhow. A generation has arisen in the land that knew not Hitler or Stalin (over half the population has been born since 1946) and, while in real power terms the world today is more bipolar than it was in 1946, there is the appearance of fragmentation, the illusion that polycentrism has altered the balance of terror. Yet the war in Vietnam clearly supplied a catalyst, a traumatic revulsion. Not against immoral or obscene wars—as the anti-war intelligentsia would have it—but against any war that did not directly result from an attack upon our turf.

Superficially this isolationism has its attractions. The President, Congress, and the American people could devote themselves to establishing (to paraphrase the late Joseph Stalin) affluence in one country. A "Fortress America" strategy would presumably eliminate confrontations in such exoteric locations as Laos, the Congo, the Horn of Africa, or the Persian Gulf; the knowledge that the United States was no longer protecting the playground could stimulate West Europeans and the Japanese to assume some hitherto overlooked responsibilities.

However, without denying that American statesmen have to live with this armadillo complex, it also presents great risks. I opposed intervention in 1939-41, survived Pearl Harbor, and spent three years retaliating. Today, for most of us, resurrection would be a precondition for retaliation to a nuclear Pearl Harbor.

Bureaucracy and Democracy: The Executive, the Press, the Congress, and the Military

The next set of essays examines the performance of the government and the press on the war, and the effects of the war on those institutions. They also suggest some reasons for the persistence of American involvement in the longest war in our history.

Richard Holbrooke divides officials of the executive into three parts: the President, the bureaucrats, and "something-in-between" or the President's men. He shows how successive Presidents have maintained the same basic U.S. commitment and objective in Vietnam; how they and their appointed allies within the government, together with a few senior career officials, designed new strategies; how the tactics were defined by the parochial clashes of the bureaucrats, often including some of the President's men acting as bureaucrats; and how all combined in self-serving and self-deceiving internal assessments of the war that, finally, served no one well.

Self-deception was the Siamese twin of deceiving the public, a subject addressed by Philip Geyelin in his essay on Vietnam and the press. He considers how the press allowed itself to be used—not to inform the public, or even simply to make the government look good—but as one instrument of the government's Vietnam strategy. The problem was that it had to be used in impossibly contradictory ways: to scare Hanoi about our toughness and willingness to go the route without, however, scaring an American public fearful of how long that route might be.

Why did it take so long for the press to refuse to go along? According to Geyelin, the explanation has to do with the nature of the "news media" in America. For all the talk of their awesome power and irresponsibility, our news-gatherers are remarkably pliable. The initial impulse, at least, is to accept a responsibility to report for the record and more or less at face value not only what the government says it is doing, but what the government says are the results of what it is doing. His essay describes the powers of the government over the press and the traps in which the government finds itself.

In the end, however, the effort to use—or misuse—the press in contradictory ways had to fail. The losers were the press, the government, and therefore, all of us.

Alton Frye and Jack Sullivan suggest that lack of information was an important reason why the Congress provided little brake on Administration policies throughout the 1960s. (One might add, parenthetically, that information is power; power brings responsibility; and few sought responsibility for or even about the war.) Frye and Sullivan trace the history of the congressional role on the war, and how Vietnam helped create a new mood of assertiveness on Capitol Hill. After providing a useful summary of the measures taken by the Congress, they conclude that it has offered the President a more balanced alliance rather than a challenge. "On the President's acceptance or evasion of this proffered alliance," they write, "hang the future harmony and effectiveness of American foreign policy."

The effect of Vietnam on the American military, as Adam Yarmolinsky finds, was primarily to instill a sense of frustration. The armed forces were asked to fight a war and to design tactics in accordance with limited strategies adopted by civilian leaders. Now, Yarmolinsky writes, military prestige and self-confidence have suffered even while the cost and influence of the military estabishment have increased. This is part of a dilemma raised by Yarmolinsky's essay: How does civilian leadership assert its constitutional authority over the armed Forces without further eroding military self-confidence, especially when the military can argue that it suffered from the step-by-step indefiniteness of civilian policy-making on the war? A proper sense of pride within the military can only be restored after restoration of a sense of purpose. As Yarmolinsky argues, the burden is on our strategists and policy-makers, in and out of government, civilian and military, to think through and demonstrate what purposes the military should be serving in coming years—one of the issues addressed in the following section of this volume.

Richard Holbrooke served as a Foreign Service Officer in Vietnam at the U.S. Embassy and with AID in the Delta. He was then assigned to the White House, to the Paris peace talks, and to the Peace Corps as Country Director in Morocco. He is now Managing Editor of *Foreign Policy*.

Philip Geyelin is editor of the *Washington Post*'s editorial page and author of *Lyndon B. Johnson and the World*.

Formerly staff director for Senator Edward W. Brooke, Alton Frye is now a Senior Fellow of the Council on Foreign Relations and Director of the Institute for Congress Project of the Carnegie Endowment for International Peace. He is the author of *Nazi Germany and the American Hemisphere* and *A Responsible Congress: The Politics of National Security*.

Jack Sullivan is a senior staff consultant to the House Committee on Foreign Affairs. A congressional staff member for the past thirteen years, he lectures frequently on the role of Congress in foreign affairs.

Adam Yarmolinsky is Ralph Waldo Emerson University Professor at the University of Massachusetts. He served in the Pentagon and White House between 1961 and 1966. His most recent book is *The Military Establishment, Its Impacts on American Society*.

Presidents, Bureaucrats, and Something In-Between

RICHARD HOLBROOKE

Presidents and bureaucrats, bureaucrats and Presidents, work together in a strange mixture of close collaboration and mutual self-interest, mutual fear and distrust, and frequent deception. Presidents may view the career services with skepticism and even contempt, but they need the bureaucrats to govern; and so every President finds a few career men he can, and must, trust, from Robert Murphy under FDR to Alexander Haig under Richard Nixon, and assigns to them delicate and important tasks. Every President looks for a few bureaucratic allies and hopes the "permanent government" will make him look good.

Yet even when Presidents use personally selected and trusted career officials, and even when they publicly profess a great respect and reliance on the career services, their basic attitude toward the "permanent government" is inevitably one of distrust.

The careerists serve the President, whoever he is, loyally, discreetly, obediently—but usually keeping a polite, safe distance. Anyway, that's the way they explain it. "We are the professionals," say the soldiers and diplomats, "our advice is nonpolitical"; and it is important to recognize that most dedicated members of the career services believe above all else about themselves that they are in fact professional and nonpolitical.

Presidents understandably see things differently. The permanent government often comes to resemble a permanent threat to Presidential ambitions and objectives. They see, and often bitterly complain in private, about entrenched fiefdoms, foot-dragging, opposition to change, fights to preserve or enlarge bureaucratic power. Presidents suspect the State Department, the Pentagon, and the CIA of leaking information to upset carefully laid Presidential plans. Simultaneously, they see timidity, fear, indecisiveness, and rigidity within the ranks. Ambassadors are either too independent or too cautious. Generals may at any moment tell congressmen or journalists that the Administration is weakening our national security. Presidents complain about the ignorance of the careerists—then withhold vital information from them, setting up elaborate mechanisms to bypass established chains of command.

If Presidents see political bias in the career services, however, they are probably missing the important point. Kennedy, seeking new ideas, often complained that the Foreign Service was too conservative. Nixon seems to have distrusted it (and wiretapped some of its members when they worked for Kissinger) because it was too liberal. "They are both wrong," observed a former Foreign Service Officer, "the Foreign Service is just the Foreign Service." By this he meant that the essential quality of the foreign policy bureaucracies, both civilian and military, is not ideological, but self-perpetuating, self-preserving, self-protecting. The bureaucracy is just the bureaucracy.

Presidents come and go; they may visit China, have nuclear confrontations with Russia, or change visa regulations. But the smart bureaucrat knows that long-run survival in a career service does not necessarily come from short-run success. Close identification with a President is heady wine, but it is not always good for your career, unless, like Charles Bohlen and Llewellyn Thompson, personal standing with the President is part of a successful but regular *climb* through the career ranks. Besides, Bohlen did pay a price under the Republican Administration—Dulles exiled him to Manila.

Presidents can never really trust the bureaucrats they inherit, the bureaucrats who will outlast them. That is understandable. No President should rely on the career services; they have become far too big, with too many vested interests, to respond as Presidents would wish. They cannot be relied on for rapid response, for honest reporting, for thoughtful advice, for innovative thinking, or for unquestioning loyalty.

But who can? The President sets our goals, as we shall see. In Vietnam and elsewhere, great policy objectives come from the top, shaped as a result of the domestic political debate and consensus, or lack of consensus, not as a result of the "games bureaucrats play." Yet the bureaucracy is vitally important for at least two reasons: first, no President can create policy in a vacuum—he must get information on which to base his assessments and decisions, and these sources must at least include the bureaucracies. Second, once policy is formulated it must be carried out, and here bureaucracies—fighting jurisdictional wars, dragging their feet, or simply misunderstanding their instructions—can divert, deflect, or change policy in ways which no President finds acceptable, and many do not understand until it is too late.

Encouraged by ambitious aides, Presidents blame many of their own failures of leadership on poor "implementation" by the government. They grapple with the question of how to get the government to respond; some set up elaborate committee structures, others create secret bypass mechanisms. Kennedy, for instance, dreamed of a secret group of thirty people who would run things without telling the Pentagon and State; Nixon and Kissinger actually did it, although on the domestic side, at least, a few criminal acts were committed along the way in the name of national security.

It is important to bear in mind that:

> • The President is quite separable and distinct, as a personality and as a factor in events, from *everyone* else in the government, including his closest advisers.

• His interests, in the most personal and hence most important sense, are different from everyone else's.

• He is, by definition, the most successful man in American political life, having attained the most powerful job.

• He is the focal point of everyone else's hopes and fears and frustrations. He is only a man, but he is unique; and, in an unhealthy way, he has become a national lightning rod.

• Almost all other men normally live in some fear of him; and fear is not a healthy basis for good working relationships. Yet, it can produce results, so all Presidents exploit the fear factor to varying degrees.

• He is unavoidably isolated in the office of the Presidency.[1]

Harry Truman, who seems to have had a deep understanding of the ambiguous nature of his office, summed it up in two comments: first, the famous sign on his desk—"The Buck Stops Here"; and second, his wonderful lament for his successor: "Poor Ike. He'll sit here and say 'Do this. Do that' and nothing will happen. It just won't be like the Army at all."

Obviously this ambiguous relationship with the bureaucracy is unsatisfactory, and into it every modern President has brought a growing number of his own men, "President's men," to help run the country. This is the crucial middleman layer of the government—those who should hold it together and make it work. And in many of its recent failures, including Vietnam and Watergate, it is precisely this ill-defined but vital middle level that has performed the worst.

In a government which functions well, one in which the President is well-served and protected, one in which the information flow upward is honest and the implementation of policy downward and outward is coherent, this middle group of political appointees must play a vital role. They must be the links that join the President to his huge and unwieldy machine. If the President is the driver and the bureaucracy the engine of the giant government machine, then the President's men must be the steering wheel, the drive shaft, the brakes,

and the safety devices. In Vietnam, the President's men
—especially under Kennedy and Johnson—did a remarkably
poor job, and in so doing reduced the information flow upward
to the President, narrowed potential understanding of the
problem, and simply served their President badly. Yet, if men
in these critical positions failed themselves and their country,
it must also be said that each President had ample warning
signals that things might be off-course, and each chose to
ignore or minimize them. Presidents get the advice and advisers they want—and ultimately deserve. In Vietnam, the
system worked [2]—but within it men failed, made serious errors
of judgment, and contributed greatly to our long agony.

It is not easy to define this middle group. A career official is
a career official, and the President is the President, but what is
a "President's man"? Everyone else, would be one answer, but
further discussion is required. David Halberstam described
one generation of them, the Kennedy-Johnson group, as "the
best and the brightest." It is an aptly ironic phrase, for every
President, looking for men he can trust to advise him and carry
out his objectives, must see himself as embarked on the world's
greatest talent search, with jobs of immense power and prestige going to America's finest as rewards.

Whether they come from academia, Wall Street, or
Madison Avenue, those who are assembled to help run the
country are in a unique but perilous position. Most never ran
for public office. Many, including some in the most powerful
positions (McGeorge Bundy, Walt Rostow, Henry Kissinger
prior to September 1973), completely escape the congressional
confirmation and committee hearing process which constitute
a key part of Congress' constitutional responsibilities. Already
successful in their chosen fields, they come to Washington
drawn by the power that only government can offer. They
come either at the direct invitation of the President or of
someone close to the President. Some, but by no means all, are
personally loyal to the President. Some are party loyalists, who
may have served a rival politician in the battle for the Presidential nomination (Kissinger for Rockefeller, George Ball for
Stevenson). Some are academics or lawyers who are quite
willing to serve any President of either party, if called. A few

are technically career officials, but with personal ties to the new President which will elevate them out of the career system. (General Vernon Walters and General Cushman, for example, both became Deputy Directors of the CIA.) Some go into the Cabinet, others into key sub-Cabinet jobs, still others to the White House.

They have come down very different paths to meet not as a close-working team, but as individuals or small groups, unsure of their future role or how they will fare. They don't usually intend to stay at the level at which they arrive; most seek more power. They learn quickly—if they did not already know—that their future will be determined by their loyalty to the President, their success in his eyes, and a great deal of luck. They obviously don't have the responsibility of a President, nor the tenure of the bureaucrat. They are in a position of maximum risk or gain.

The first thing many of them do is turn on each other. The worst battles within any government are usually among President's men. This is understandable and predictable, although in its recent excessiveness, highly lamentable. Some Presidents, like FDR and LBJ, seem to enjoy the spectacle and deliberately pair off feuding aides in the belief that competition and rivalry produce better results. This theory, better suited to the legislature than the executive, is unfortunately widely believed. Generally, it is a mark of a weak leader, one who feels more comfortable manipulating and dividing people than leading and uniting them. Today, government is filled with men of intelligence who lack character, and it is precisely this sort of individual who is most likely to substitute clever manipulation for strong leadership.

Yet the President must rely on his men to protect him and to make the government run. Among their crucial responsibilities:

- They must filter information and opinions as they come up through the bureaucracies to make sure the President receives the best, most accurate, and useful information available.
- They must present the President with the full im-

plications of courses of action that are recommended by
the permanent government, warn him of hidden booby
traps and biases, and alert him to hidden opportunities
—in short, *protect him.*
  • They must work out detailed plans and programs
designed to achieve his objectives and plans which make
full use of the resources of the government.
  • They must make sure that the bureaucracies carry
out the established policies efficiently.

What a short and simple list, filled with clichés! But look
again. On Vietnam, three sets of President's men failed badly
to meet even a minimum standard in every one of these areas.
Their failures outweighed their successes, and the costs of
failure were immense.

The three elements I have described—President, President's
men, and bureaucrats—view each other with a mixture of
suspicion and cynicism. The President looks at the bureaucracies with alarm and contempt, fearing that they will thwart
his desires and knowing that they will outlast him. Yet he
needs them and he knows it. The President looks at his own
men with a different feeling, wondering who among them he
can really trust, who will offer the best advice. The bureaucrats
will watch the President warily, for in the short run he can
order them to the far ends of the earth, but in the long run he
will be gone and they will survive. To bureaucrats the President is a mixed blessing, someone who relieves them of ultimate responsibility for decisions, but who thinks in short-run
political terms. Bureaucrats react more selectively to the President's men. Some are potential allies; some are enemies.
Each bureau makes its own determination, based on self-
interest. While the prevailing cliché is that political appointees are just political fat cats getting a reward, in fact the
permanent government distinguishes quickly between a party
hack who is getting a pay-off and a serious Presidential appointee who can play a significant policy-making role. Sometimes an individual may slip over the line, becoming more
professional than political, as was the case with Ellsworth
Bunker and David Bruce. These two Democrats came to gov-

ernment through politics, stayed on to serve Republicans, and the Foreign Service came to regard them as two of their own.

Each of the President's men is in the middle of a complex set of interrelationships. Above and around him are other President's men (often rivals) and the President himself. All around are the bureaucrats and military officers of the permanent government. In time some will become allies, if he is sympathetic to their problems; most he will distrust. Around many influential appointees a few careerists cluster, hoping to gain influence and power through the association. Washington is filled with career officers who are rising rapidly as some political appointee's "Special Assistant" (protégé); General Haig is only the most spectacular example. The route is no longer unusual or strange; risky, certainly (if one chooses the wrong man), but increasingly common.

Presidents, President's men, and bureaucrats—together, in a constantly changing set of relationships, they hammer out policies, strategies, and tactics. They react to a vast array of outside pressures as they go about their business; they perceive and weigh these pressures quite differently. Congressional pressures look different from every vantage point. Press criticism brushed aside by one man may leave another in a rage. Public demonstrations will be ignored by some while others tremble and plan counterattacks. Impending elections produce obvious changes in Presidential priorities, and bureaucrats often object to this biennial intrusion of democracy into their "professional" world, but they can do little about it.

These outside pressures are, in the final analysis, essential to an appreciation of the way policy is put together and carried out. The more important the issue—or, at least, the more press attention an issue gets—the more important outside pressures become. Much recent analysis of how the government works has focused excessive attention on the inner workings of the bureaucracy, while failing to place the discussion within the proper political framework. Thus, we may read a learned and even fascinating description of what one division of the Pentagon did to another, or how the institutional biases of the State Department and the CIA predetermined the positions that they were bound to take in a dispute over tactics—the scholar trying to tell us that *this* is what really matters: bureaucratic politics as a major guide to explain great events.

Understanding the hows and whys and whens of the government is indeed important; but while such discussion can illuminate many aspects of policy, it rarely can explain the policy itself. In order to do that, we must examine policy by looking not at the bureaucrats—the so-called players in a dreadful but currently fashionable phrase—but at the "levels of importance of policy." In briefly examining American policy in Vietnam at four different levels, ranging from the initial level of commitment and objective down to the levels of tactics and of assessments, one can see how growing opposition to the war forced each Administration to change its strategy—but not its objective.

II

"The South Did Not Lose, and the North Did Not Win"

1. *Commitment and Objective.* The basic objective remained unchanged through six Presidents and more than twenty years: *To Keep South Vietnam out of Communist Hands.* Even two years after the signing of the Paris cease-fire agreements, when most Americans thought that we were out of the war, the Ford Administration was in fact pursuing a modified version of the same objective, limited only by the crucial congressional cut-off of American military involvement in Indochina that took effect August 15, 1973. Only after the final collapse of that policy in April 1975 did it become unmistakably clear to everyone that we had not changed our objectives in 1973.

Of course, most Presidents hoped for more than the minimal objective: they hoped to get the Communists to cease their endless efforts to pull down the Saigon government. But if the United States kept Saigon non-Communist until 1975, it never came very close to its larger objective. North Vietnam was determined and ruthless—and relentless.

2. *Strategy and Policy.* But while each President personally signed up for a renewal of the basic commitment, each Administration designed a new grand strategy or policy to meet changing circumstances in Indochina and changing political problems at home. For Truman, who first set the commitment in 1950 as an integral part of the cold war ("We were seeing a pattern in Indochina and Tibet timed to coincide with the attack in Korea as a challenge to the Western World," he would write later [3]), the strategy was relatively simple: aid, both military and economic, filtered through the French colonial regime. It was at best a stop-gap strategy, but years later Dean Acheson admitted: "While we may have tried to muddle through and were certainly not successful, I could not think then or later of a better course." [4]

Eisenhower inherited the problem; the first strategy he followed was essentially an increase in aid to the French. But when the critical moment came and the French stood at the precipice, their garrison at Dien Bien Phu surrounded and their only hope American intervention, Eisenhower, after testing the desire in Congress and in London for military intervention, overruled his Vice-President, his Secretary of State, and the Chairman of the Joint Chiefs and let the first Indochina War end without direct American military involvement, an important exception to the historical pattern before and since. In the second phase of his Indochina policy, after some initial confusion in 1954 and 1955, Eisenhower settled upon the strategy of economic and military assistance to the new, shaky, undemocratic government of Ngo Dinh Diem. And while that regime wobbled, with massive American support and a small number of military advisers it survived into the Kennedy Administration, a sick client with a poor prognosis, alive but worrisome. Kennedy would have to work out a new strategy, or else abandon the commitment.

There is no evidence that Kennedy hesitated over whether the commitment would be maintained. The key question was how, and through a series of high-level trips and task forces the issue was fought out. The answer was the advisory war strategy, which in Kennedy's Thousand Days built up our military advisory effort from a few hundred to almost 20,000; created a Military Assistance Command Vietnam (MACV) under a singularly ill-chosen four-star general, Paul D. Harkins; created the largest and most omnipresent economic advisory effort in our history; and poured hundreds at millions of dollars into the South Vietnamese economy to keep it afloat. But fewer than one hundred Americans died for this strategy. Diem thereby survived the initial wave of the Vietcong movement, but barely—and Diem's growing isolation led to his downfall and assassination in November 1963.

Lyndon Johnson was thus confronted with a problem of staggering proportions. His response turned the war into the longest and most divisive in American history. For him, the objective was never in doubt. The strategy his Administration devised to meet the commitment it had inherited is a searing part of our national memory: Air war north and ground troops south—over four years, against an enemy which never won, but never stopped coming. It was the tragic high point of American involvement in Vietnam.

Inheriting the stalemated war in 1969, Richard Nixon devised a new and clever strategy. At home, dissent over the war had reached new heights and helped bring him back from the political dead to the White House; in Vietnam the end of the war could not be seen. Yet above all Richard Nixon did not want to abandon the commitment. To solve this extraordinarily difficult problem, he and his advisers, particularly Kissinger and Laird, devised a strategy which included Vietnamization, or the gradual scaling-down of U.S. force levels, primarily in response to U.S. domestic pressures, not to battlefield realities. He also pursued negotiations, at first in secret, and, when he needed the boost it would give him politically, in public. Many believed that he was looking for an "elegant bug-out," what Stewart Alsop called a "fig leaf," but in fact, it now seems clear that he was unyielding on the basic commitment and was willing at every critical juncture in the war to take major military steps: Cambodia, 1970; Laos, 1970; Haiphong, 1972; Hanoi, 1972; and Cambodia, 1973. Nixon never had any intention of being "the first President to lose a war," and, by his definition, he wasn't.

3. *Tactics*. Below the level of grand strategy lies something which can be called "tactics." By tactics I do not mean merely the specific details of a specific campaign. Rather, in the present context, tactics include such major operational questions as whether to adopt the "enclave strategy" or send American troops out into the jungles and up against the Cambodian border; how much emphasis to give to pacification; whether to press the South Vietnamese government for far-ranging reforms or let it be corrupt; how far north to send the bombers; and how forthcoming and ready to negotiate to appear in public and private.

This was the stuff of daily headlines. These were the issues of greatest internecine warfare within the government, as bureaucrats and political appointees clashed over every aspect of how to fight the war or negotiate the peace. (Some confusion can be avoided here by understanding that to the principals then engaged in such debates, these would have been considered "strategic" issues; only in hindsight can we see that they were more tactical than strategic, for they were generally fought out within the larger strategy that had already evolved.) The list of these debates is almost endless. Most of the disputes eventually reached the public; but public opinion, even informed public opinion, played only a *negative role*: what would "wash" with the public was always a factor in the final decisions.

4. *Assessments*. But how we were doing? Everyone wanted a "report card" on the war, and everyone participated in writing it—or rewriting it. Nothing that we actually *did* in Vietnam was as fiercely debated within the government and with the press as the question of *how well* we were doing.

Thus the assessments—a fourth level of activity that permeated attitudes toward commitment, strategy, and tactics—a level which eventually became a major political issue of its own, with a devastating catch-phrase to describe it—"credibility gap."

The assessments flowed in daily from every corner of Vietnam in what eventually became the most elaborate reporting system in the history of warfare. They were matched by the most extensive, if not comprehensive, coverage any war ever received from journalism—nightly in living color in America's living rooms and daily in the press. The assessments involved everyone, from the President and his closest advisers down to captains advising district chiefs. Everyone sought to affect the reporting, since it was everyone's report card—to the bureaucrats, it was their status report with the President and President's men on *tactics*; to President's men it measured the rightness of their strategic advice; to the President it was his public report card to the people on the success of the commitment—a vital political fact.

Yet from the outset, the situation was in hot dispute both inside and outside the government, and the dispute has not ended even with the departure of our troops.

Dissent on facts was often the starting point of one's doubts: If our leaders believed the official assessments, they were deceiving themselves; a policy based on such false assessments was built on quicksand; we were lying to the public and to ourselves; where would a policy based on these so-called facts lead?

Facts are elusive in Vietnam, but today we can see that the assessments were based on dangerously self-promoting report cards. A pyramid of self-deception was created. When it collapsed and the domestic reaction set in, Johnson in 1968 had to switch strategy and Nixon in 1969 had to devise a new one. Yet neither man changed objectives. The "report card" they kept issuing stayed determinedly upbeat, for political and bureaucratic reasons.

To the end, the situation was always in dispute. Were we winning? How long could they take the pressure? Could the South Vietnamese hold together? Who controlled the people? How firm was that control? And finally, when the POWs left Hanoi, the question they all asked as soon as they got on the plane: Who won the war? To this the official military escorts gave the prepared reply: "The South did not lose and the North did not win." For twenty-five years of involvement, hundreds of billions of dollars and 55,000 American lives, it was not much of an achievement. And within thirty months, even that was lost in the final agony of the collapse of the Thieu regime.

III

Who made the decisions at each level? We have seen the levels of decision on Vietnam—commitment, strategy, tactics, assessment—and the different forces in the executive branch which play roles in policy—the President, the President's men, and the bureaucrats. When we match them up, a revealing pattern begins to emerge which sheds light on how the President and the bureaucracy share responsibility for the formulation and implementation of policy.

1. *Commitment and Objective.* The reasons why five Presidents maintained the commitment lie in the domestic political climate that each President perceived, as well as the personal values and intellectual baggage that he brought with him to the White House. Each President was reacting to Vietnam within the larger context of international relations—for Truman and Eisenhower, the classic dark days of the cold war; for Kennedy, the need to show personal strength in 1961, the year of his defeat at the Bay of Pigs and challenge in Laos, the Congo, Berlin, and the Vienna summit; for Johnson, a belief that our word would be universally worthless if we failed to live up to our commitments in Vietnam, and that this would encourage Moscow and Peking; for Nixon, a belief that strength in Vietnam was essential to negotiations with Moscow and Peking; for Ford, a sense that, as an accidental President and a long-time congressional supporter of the war effort, he could not be the one to change course.

The *commitment*, therefore, was "Presidential." Many others got into the act; the Joint Chiefs of Staff pointed out military dangers if Vietnam slipped away; so did Secretaries of State and congressional leaders. But the big decision was Presidential and made within a political context.

2. *Strategy and Policy.* In the sense that I have previously used this term, strategy was also primarily a Presidential decision. Its implications were political, and the issues being decided could never be resolved without Presidential direction. But the President's men played crucial roles in the formulation of strategy, and some senior bureaucrats and mil-

itary officers were also deeply involved, the latter usually on behalf of traditional service positions.

In 1954, for example, in the great debate over whether or not to intervene to save the French at Dien Bien Phu, the line-up arguing the case for intervention included the Vice-President, the Secretary of State, and the Chairman of the Joint Chiefs, then Admiral Radford. Opposed, among others, was the Army Chief of Staff, General Ridgeway, as well as most of the congressional leaders consulted, and in London, Anthony Eden. Later, it was the Dulles brothers, who played key roles in the strategy to aid Diem.

In the early 1960s, under Kennedy, the President's men engaged in a bitter dispute over how to contain the growing guerrilla insurgency (note that with only the barest exceptions the debate was not over *whether,* but *how*). Men like McNamara and Taylor, Hilsman and Lansdale, Rostow, Harriman, Rusk, Robert Kennedy, Paul Nitze, McGeorge and William Bundy, debated the best way to fight the war. Listening to their various proposals, President Kennedy chose a middle course, the advisory build-up and stuck to it through his brief administration, rejecting suggestions for air strikes in the North or ground troops in the South (although this was perhaps because the situation did not yet seem desperate).

The bureaucracies had great stakes in these decisions, but their direct participation and influence was fairly restricted. The assessments on which decisions were based came in part from them, and senior career officials participated in important meetings and discussions. The U.S. Army, in particular, played an important role, partly because its former Chief of Staff, Maxwell Taylor, an influential President's man and later also Chairman of the JCS (a rare combination) was in a good position to advance his theories of "flexible response," theories which provided for an important Army role in Vietnam. The State Department showed little inclination to take a strong position, although a few officials did raise some disturbing questions about the future of the Saigon regime.

In the Johnson years, again, the great strategic decisions were made by the President. His advisers were consulted frequently. By this time the pressures for air attacks against the

North and U.S. troops in the South had mounted, and Johnson felt continual pressure from the Pentagon, pressure to which he yielded inch by inch as time went on. But this pressure was more over tactics, force levels, and bombing targets, once the basic decisions had been made in 1965. In that initial set of decisions—the most fateful in the history of the war—the military gave their suggestions along fairly predictable lines, which played an important part in determining the outcome. But the battle within the government was fought out primarily by the President's men, most of them inherited from Kennedy, but now bending to the new wind they discerned at the White House.

Under Nixon, the role of the bureaucracies in formulating strategy was significantly reduced. In fact, even the number of President's men involved in decisions dropped off sharply. Kissinger and Haig, surely; and Laird, the key architect of Vietnamization, can be credited with important roles in the formulation of strategy. Beyond that, the evidence available at present suggests that Ellsworth Bunker and later Graham Martin, fighting for a client in Saigon, continued to play his single note with great effect, as he had under Johnson. And beyond that? So far, the rest is silence.

3. *Tactics.* Once the strategy has begun to evolve, what then? If we are going to support South Vietnam with advisers, who does what to whom? Who's in charge? If we are sending planes north, whose planes are they? What targets should they hit? If ground troops are going in, how many? Where? Marine or Army? What are the rules of engagement? What is the mission?

If we are trying to build up the South Vietnamese government, which American agencies are in charge of what parts of the effort? How much money is available for the task? What is our plan—to broaden the base of the government or to improve its repressive efficiency? Are we for or against land reform? Bombing rural areas to create refugees? How much emphasis on pacification? And what is pacification, anyway? Who is in charge of it?

The list is as long as the war. It was the stuff of daily battles, in provincial and regional advisory offices, in the U.S. Mission in Saigon, in the magnificent mid-ocean headquarters of CINCPAC, in countless interagency meetings in Washington, and in the National Security Council itself.

Here were issues which *really* mattered to the bureaucracies. They could accept more easily a complete reversal of objectives or grand strategic design than a revision of their own roles. Personnel, staffing, budgets, bureaucratic prerogatives, and careers were at stake, and the confrontation was often fierce. My own memories of battles in the field, in Saigon, and in Washington over the endless jurisdictional disputes is still vivid: a three-star general and a CIA station chief both resorting to openly dishonest statements to gain control of a new program; "back-channel" messages and private letters from each Saigon participant to his Washington backstop to alert him that an issue could not be resolved in Saigon, and please carry on the good fight back home; instructions from Washington officials to their Saigon representatives to take a certain position on an issue regardless of what seemed correct in Saigon—"the situation in Washington is complex and we need your support"; the bitter accusations of misconduct if someone made a field visit and bypassed some echelon in the chain of command; the rigid rules set up to assure that cables in normal channels were fully cleared with everyone (which in turn made the creation of the back channels inevitable); the endless hostility and suspicion; the constant tension, with senior officials in Vietnam knowing that their predecessors had not always left with honor; and the restrictions on information.[5]

I do not want to make too much of these tactical disagreements. They are rarely as historic or momentous or interesting as students of "bureaucratic politics" would have us believe. Because they involve huge organizations and vast amounts of money, because they engage not only bureaucrats but also President's men, because they get leaked to the newspapers as dramatic confrontations, and because they sometimes overlap larger issues, they have recently become a fashionable subject for academicians.

But much can be learned from a study of these disputes. They are costly and hurt smooth implementation of policy

—any policy. They are usually against the interests of the President and his policy. They are wasteful, time-consuming, and often stupid. But a few of them can be important. The decision to send U.S. troops out on search-and-destroy missions, for example, was essentially left to the senior levels of the U.S. Army to decide, with only slight involvement by others. To most civilians, this was a military decision. To most military outside of the war zone, this was something that should properly be left to the field commander under time-honored concepts of the integrity of command. And so General Westmoreland and his staff made one of the most fateful tactical decisions of the war (a strategic decision, of course, to him) which led to costs and casualties unforeseen in Washington, to domestic upheavals that shook the United States, and finally, in the aftermath of the Tet offensive in 1968, to a profound upheaval in American political life. And afterwards, it turned out that we also had My Lai as a result, but of course no one could have foreseen that at the time.[6]

There is a strange apparent contradiction here. While it is hard for the President himself to get involved in most of these issues, on occasion every President does. The temptation to play Desk Officer and actually direct some specific action is very great, as JFK discovered in the Cuban missile crisis when he personally directed the ships; as LBJ demonstrated repeatedly (he used to follow the price of pork in Saigon closely, for example, and blame his staff when it went up); and as Nixon did in such escapades as the unsuccessful Son Tay prison raid.

Kennedy's personal intervention in the missile crisis was understandable and proper. But Presidential interventions are often based on considerations of press reaction rather than policy implications. Why did Lyndon Johnson try to run the air war in the North personally, picking targets and waiting for the BDA's (bomb damage assessments), while paying less attention to the more important ground war in the South? In large part, I think it was because the bombing seemed a bigger political issue for a long time; because the press gave bombing so much attention; and because Hanoi made the bombing a focal point for world protest. Also, because the level of bombing was viewed as a "bargaining chip" for negotiations, it needed "fine tuning" (as JFK felt about the Soviet ships off Cuba). But the irony was that fine tuning backfired, and bombing ended up taking place when it wasn't desirable anyway, as during the disputed "Marigold" peace feeler of 1965. Meanwhile, Westmoreland and his Chief of Operations, General William DePuy, devised a strategy for fighting a ground war in jungles, swamps, and Vietnamese villages, using American firepower and American infantrymen. Why wasn't it debated, and its policy implications understood, earlier?

Presidential intervention, no matter how frequent, still can only touch a fraction of the vast efforts of the operating bureaucracies. It is therefore vital to recognize that some tactical decisions—the ones which really engage the bureaucrats and in which they play the greatest role—can have important political consequences. The failures of General Westmoreland's strategy, we can see with the benefit of hindsight, hurt President Johnson politically more than anything else—and certainly far more than the issue of the commitment itself, which polls until late in the war showed still had great support among the public. Con Thien, Khe Sanh, Hamburger Hill, Hill 881 —these battles, all sought by U.S. commanders, left the President weakened at home.

The role of the President's men in the formulation of tactical decisions varies, of course, but by and large they are deeply involved in most such decisions. The most important exception, again, would be military strategy—an area which, tragically, was virtually left alone until 1969. But there was involvement by President's men in most other areas. Often the President's men would take sides with elements in the bureaucracy to gain additional power or position for themselves.

The President's men should have forged the essential link between strategy and tactics. They were the movable forces within the government who participated in making grand policy (strategy) and also oversaw the bureaucracies who were working out detailed operational plans. Men, like McNamara and Rusk, Helms and Gaud, Rostow and Komer, Lodge and Taylor and Bunker, all had a vital role to play—if policy implementation was to be effective. What went wrong?

4. *Assessment.* The answer leads us back to that elusive

question: How do we measure our progress in the war? For years this question was as hotly debated in the government as in the press. Yet there never was a clear-cut answer. The battle lines were sharply drawn. The optimists saw growing strength in the South Vietnamese forces and signs of weakness—even collapses—in the enemy ranks. Statistics were compiled to prove each point of view. The official American assessment was usually on the upbeat side, often outrageously so. But there was always disagreement down the line, and in the press.

A strange and troublesome process took place. It has been described by many observers and denied by some participants. But it seems unmistakable to me: Down the chain of command, and emanating from highly placed Presidential men, came a repressive thrust which gradually eliminated negative reporting on the progress of the war. The message slowly got through: Make the reporting more positive. Those who did not go along usually found themselves eased out, or else, like John Paul Vann in 1964,[7] they quit in disgust. Because the U.S. Mission in Vietnam was so large, and the turnover so rapid, there were always people in the system who saw things differently from the official assessments. Discouraged and prevented from making their views felt through the chain of command, they became sources for the press. It was as if one took a garden hose with the tap running and covered its end; the water started leaking out the sides at lower levels. But the prevailing view within the government was shaped by the public posture; the credibility gap really originated in official reporting.

There were always individuals of integrity and courage in the system, reporting an unwelcome picture of the situation. Many people today tend to think of the bureaucracies as completely faceless machines which never produced any dissent on Vietnam, but this is not true. (In the State Department, for example, the Bureau of Intelligence and Research regularly sounded the alarm.) In every agency, there were men who were ready to question and to oppose if given any encouragement, or any sign that their careers would not be hurt if they stood up. Those signs were not forthcoming; on the contrary, dissent took unusual courage, and so gradually it was suppressed except among the rare men of strength. A few of them come to mind: John Paul Vann in his early Army days; Frank Scotton of USIA throughout the entire war; George Allen of the CIA; Paul Kattenberg and Lou Sarris of the State Department. There were others, at lower levels, but they risked far less in career terms. There could have been more, with encouragement from above.

The process of suppression of the dissenter began not in the bureaucracies, as is commonly supposed, but with the President and the President's men. They knew what they wanted to hear, and they took steps which squeezed other points of view out of the reporting system. Among the President's men, the hard-liners edged out the doubters, obviously with Presidential encouragement. As the press repeatedly made clear, there was another way of assessing events in Vietnam. That this view did not reach the President is evidence of the fierce trap the President and his advisers had created for themselves. They were all writing their own report cards, and trying to eliminate the others, for fear it would affect public opinion.

IV

Throughout the war there was a constant confusion over what the domestic debate was about. Were critics of the Administration opposing the commitment to keep South Vietnam non-Communist? Or was the debate over whether or not to bomb Hanoi or mine Haiphong? Or was it over the reporting of the war, the credibility gap? Or was it over the cost of the war and its length?

This confusion extended to the heart of the government. Senior officials regarded a disagreement over an assessment as a frontal attack on the commitment and, in so doing, helped turn hawks into doves.

The inability to distinguish between different levels of dissent was serious indeed: by failing to encourage debate over assessments and tactics, the government lost repeated opportunities to strengthen its own hand in pursuit of its objective. The strategic and political implications of "tactical" decisions—particularly those involving military operations and political support to the Saigon regime—were not adequately brought out.

By failing to insist on honest assessments *inside* the system, the government rewarded self-promotion and devised new tactics on a base of quicksand. Bureaucracies made short-run gains but paid for them eventually, as their predictions proved unreliable and their positions declined. By failing to point out the strategic implications of tactical decisions, the bureaucracies often failed to warn the Administration of risks ahead. By not debating large strategic issues often enough, the bureaucracies missed opportunities to protect the President. (The JCS probably raised these issues more than anyone else, but their rigid position was discounted in advance by everyone else.)

By failing to search for more accurate assessments, Presidential advisers were easily led, or misled, into advocating poor tactics and strategy. They failed to protect their President. And Presidents were led into public statements which were costly politically.

By failing to realize the importance of certain tactical issues, Presidents and their advisers allowed some major decisions to be made without their involvement, and later found that they were saddled with political and strategic problems they had not foreseen.

By deluding themselves on the chances for success for their latest strategy, Presidents failed to foresee the full costs of their strategies. By misleading the American public, Presidents created even greater political problems for themselves. And the vicious circle led back to assessments, public and private: Try to convince everyone that things were going to be fine, in just a little while. . . . Meanwhile, devise new tactics, new strategies. . . .

How would it end? Not, surely, with the signing of a cease-fire agreement in Paris, televised live to a Saturday-morning national audience in the United States. More than 50,000 Vietnamese were killed in the first year after that signing ceremony and American treasure continued to flow into Saigon, Vientiane, and Phnom Penh—in violation, according to some observers—of the cease-fire agreements themselves. The answer came, unforgettably, in the spring of 1975.

Would anything have been learned? It is possible that some bureaucrats would have found greater courage, that some President's men would have learned that they must perform differently in their special roles, that a President would perceive the next set of problems differently. Possible, but not certain. The war was so confused in every way, and so many people now wanted to forget about it. So, too, was the understanding of it confused. Myths—"no more Vietnams" or "next time we'll do it right"—will carry more force than the elusive facts.

In the final analysis, the lesson of Vietnam will not be forged within the government at all, but in the public, political arena. How the American people assimilate the experience will determine how future bureaucrats, future President's men, and future Presidents—including some who may have participated in antiwar demonstrations in their youth—react the next time they face such a supreme test.

Notes

1. Perhaps one result of Watergate and its aftermath will be a decline in the aura of infallibility which has grown up around the Presidency. This would be all to the good; Presidents are also human, and it would help everyone, including themselves, if their subordinates treated them as such.
2. See Leslie H. Gelb, "Vietnam: The System Worked," *Foreign Policy,* 3, Summer, 1971, for the most important and original analysis of this question.
3. Harry S. Truman, *Memoirs. Volume Two: Years of Trial and Hope* (Garden City, N.Y.: Doubleday, 1956), p. 380.
4. Dean Acheson, *Present at the Creation: My Ten Years in the State Department* (New York: Norton, 1969), pp. 672-73.
5. These were all memories of the middle and late 1960s, and I was assured that things were better in Vietnam in more recent years. But when I was there briefly in late 1972, shortly before the cease-fire, things did not seem too different. To be sure, there was more of a feeling of weariness, and many of the earlier, bitter battles had finally been resolved in one way or another. Some

senior officials, including Ambassador Bunker, had been there so long that they had succeeded in removing many of the points of friction. But the result was still not a smooth and unified mission. In fact, when I was there a serious battle was shaping up over who would be in charge of the American efforts after the cease-fire, and this dispute was, predictably, mirrored in Washington.

6. Or could they? On February 22, 1965, in arguing that we should move very slowly before sending in large numbers of American combat troops, Ambassador Taylor cabled the President as one of several objections that "there would be ever present question of how a foreign soldier would distinguish between a VC and friendly Vietnamese farmer." (EMBTEL 3384) The cable was ignored. "Having crossed the Rubicon on February 7, [the President] was now off to Rome on the double," Taylor wrote later. *Swords and Plowshares* (New York: Norton, 1972), p. 341.
7. See David Halberstam, *The Making of a Quagmire* (New York: Random House, 1965), for a vivid portrait of Vann at this time.

Vietnam and the Press:
Limited War and an Open Society

PHILIP GEYELIN

The Nature of the War

On Thursday, April 1st, the President made the following decisions with respect to Vietnam:

5. The President approved an 18-20,000 man increase in U.S. military support forces to fill out existing units and supply needed logistic personnel.

6. The President approved the deployment of two additional Marine battalions and one Marine air squadron and associated headquarters and support elements.

7. The President approved a change of mission for all Marine battalions deployed to Vietnam to permit their more active use under conditions to be established and approved by the Secretary of Defense in consultation with the Secretary of State. . . .

11. The President desires that with respect to the actions in paragraphs 5 through 7, premature publicity be avoided by all possible precautions. The actions themselves should be taken as rapidly as practicable, but in ways that should minimize any appearance of sudden

changes in policy, and official statements on these troop movements will be made only with the direct approval of the Secretary of Defense, in consultation with the Secretary of State. The President's desire is that these movements and changes should be understood as being gradual and wholly consistent with existing policy.

—From National Security Action Memorandum 328, April 6, 1965, signed by McGeorge Bundy and addressed to the Secretary of State, the Secretary of Defense, and the Director of Central Intelligence.

There, in one brief excerpt from the famous Pentagon Papers, you have the essence of what was fundamentally wrong with American policy and strategy over the ten or so most tortured years of our heaviest involvement in the Indochina war. And there, by extension, you also have a large part of the explanation for what it was that so confounded and distorted the performance of the press in its efforts to report the war. For what this memorandum did was to convey to three senior officials of the government a secret order from the President of the United States to expand American participation in combat in South Vietnam. And with these orders came another order to conceal this expansion of the American combat role not only from the public at large but also, by implication, from the Congress and indeed from large parts of the government itself. You can get some idea of the spirit of concealment behind McGeorge Bundy's directive by reading the transcript of a press conference conducted by President Lyndon Johnson on April 1, 1965—the very day that he had made his decisions to expand the American military effort in Vietnam in three quite specific ways. Repeatedly, President Johnson was given opportunities by the reporters to confirm reports of a widening American war effort, and each time the President was at pains to convery the impression that nothing out of keeping with the current public perception of our Vietnam policy was contemplated.

In other words, the President and a handful of close advisers were setting out in the spring of 1965 to change the minds of the rulers of North Vietnam by applying graduated military pressure in an effort to project a readiness and willingness to conduct an open-ended escalation of the American effort. Their hope was that this prospect would persuade the government in Hanoi to abandon its support of the insurgency in the South long before the escalatory process had reached anything like the level it was ultimately to reach. Inherent in this strategy was a desire *not* to engage the American public in the policy-making process so as not to raise hard questions about declarations of war or other conventional means of dealing with a state of hostilities that was increasingly involving the use of American forces. For this was to be an open-ended conflict of unpredictable dimensions and duration—a *limited* war, in other words, for a *limited* purpose, conducted with *limited* means. That is to say, for the United States to "win," it was not contemplated that the enemy had to be destroyed or conquered or forced to surrender as in World War II. Up to a point, some precedent could perhaps be found in the Korean War, for in that conflict the objective was also to persuade the "other side to stop doing what it was doing," in Dean Rusk's litany. But in Korea the conflict was conventional, at least to the extent that there were front lines; progress or lack of it was plainly measurable in territorial terms. The public, accordingly, could see pretty much for itself how well or badly things were going and deduce from this what further efforts and sacrifices might have to be made. In Vietnam, by contrast, military force was to be applied in carefully controlled increments, and not necessarily to its best effect, in a conflict with no front lines. Consequently, there was no easy way to measure failure or success. Instead of territory won or lost, "progress" was something to be determined arbitrarily by the government. It was measured in body counts (always of dubious reliability, and also of questionable relevance when one had to weigh the relative readiness of either side to sustain and to replenish losses); or in Hamlet Evaluation Surveys (equally controversial when what you are evaluating is a state of heart or mind); or in the developing capability of the South Vietnamese to defend themselves (a criteria beyond calculation for as long as the United States was compulsively taking on more, rather than less, of the job).

And yet the government could not at any stage along the way publicly offer an impression of anything other than progress, for it could at no time afford to confront the American public with the essential open-endedness of the undertaking. To do that would have invited at a much earlier date the sharp questions and open debate and ultimate division which the government had to try to forestall at all cost and for as long as possible if it were even to succeed in conveying to the North Vietnamese the necessary impression of unending American capacity and resolve.

All this is by way of establishing the essential background for any assessment of the way the news media covered the Vietnam war. Inevitably, as confusion and disillusionment set in, it became fashionable to blame the press for not alerting the American public sooner to what was going on. Or, alternatively, it became routine for the government to blame the press for telling too much about what was going on—or about what was going wrong—for this, quite naturally, had the effect of undermining the whole strategy of "graduated response." Or so the government argued. (An excellent case can be made that the whole premise was wrong: that North Vietnam's policy and objectives were determined without much regard for anything so transitory, or perhaps even inscrutable, as American public opinion. But that is not the issue here.) The point is that American policy-makers believed they could transform Hanoi's perceptions and ultimately influence its performance simply by projecting the right impression about U.S. intentions. And this quite naturally put a high premium on appearances. Thus, it was considered distinctly unhelpful, if not actually destructive of American interests, for the press to suggest that U.S. strategy wasn't working as advertised or that the war effort was failing, for this could only invite public questioning. And it was the conventional government wisdom that this, in turn, could only invite questions in Hanoi about American staying power.

Some idea of the problem this presented to the government as well as to the press is indicated by the way thoughtful and committed officials wrestled with it. On one occasion, in a press conference on November 5, 1965, Secretary of State

Dean Rusk was asked, "are you at all afraid that the anti-Vietnam demonstrations would give a wrong kind of signal to Hanoi, as to the backing of the American people for the President's policy in Vietnam?" His struggle to answer that question is worth setting down in full:

Well, there is a certain dilemma on a matter of this sort for a vigorous and thriving democracy such as ours. We must have debate and an opportunity for dissent and the use of our constitutional processes for expressing opinions and views. I think it would be wrong for government to try to restrict those opportunities in any way. It is true that in a situation of this sort, that evidences of dissent are used by Hanoi and by Peiping, and undoubtedly these evidences bolster their morale, lead them into perhaps some miscalculations and misjudgments.

So we have a real dilemma here. And I certainly feel very strongly that government should not interfere with the normal processes of democratic discussion in our system. Those who engage in such discussion should be aware of and take some responsibility for the fact that what they have in mind may be frustrated by the way in which they go about it. If they want peace in Southeast Asia, then it is very important that Hanoi and Peiping not be misled about the determination of the American people and the American government to meet our commitments—because we have had a number of occasions in the past where such miscalculations have reduced the chances of peace, have invited the aggressor to keep going, and have increased the appetites of those who would use force to invade their neighbors or to bring about solutions by violent means.

So it is a complicated problem. I don't think that, quite frankly, I could give a simple and clear answer, except that we must maintain our own institutions and our own great structure of democracy, the processes of free discussion, and hope that those who take part in it would recognize that when these voices travel beyond our borders, they sometimes have effects which are not intended by those who give voice to them.

There it was, in a not entirely coherent nutshell: We must maintain our free and open system, but we must not use it freely and openly because by doing so we reduced the chances of peace and prolong the war.

The Record of the Press

To say that this placed the press between a rock and a hard place—damned if it reported the war and damned if it didn't —is not to suggest that the record of the press was exemplary, or even exceptionally good. It was sometimes irresponsible, misleading or unfair—as it generally is—and it was also, by the nature of things, incomplete. For obvious, practical reasons it was not easy for American correspondents to report at first hand on the "enemy" until the final stages of the war. For different reasons, having to do in part with a natural inclination to deal with any war in terms of battle reports and with this particular war in terms of the American participation in it, insufficient attention was undoubtedly given to reporting even about the real nature and true state of our South Vietnamese "allies." In short, a case can be made that too little effort was made to report on, or even to understand, the Vietnamese on both sides of the struggle. But it is not the purpose here to present a complete accounting of every aspect of the performance of the press, or even of that part of its performance which I was able to observe during two separate month-long tours of South Vietnam and a much more extensive and intensive exposure to the war as it was conducted from Washington. What can be said with certainly is that the performance of the press, in general, got better as the war went along, and that in the end the press coverage had a considerable impact on the course of events. Or perhaps a better way to put it is that events themselves—in the form of developments adverse to the U.S. cause—finally could not longer be rationalized or suppressed or distorted by "progress reports." In any case, the word was gotten around that the war was not being won and probably wasn't winnable on the terms American policy-makers were talking about, and this had a powerful effect on the American war effort. Whether one thinks that this effect, on balance, was for the good or to the detriment of the national interest is, of course, another question, of no particular relevance to an assessment of the performance of the press. What is relevant to a discussion of the work of the press is simply that in this instance it must be judged in the context of a new kind of international conflict and a unique experience in the conduct of American foreign policy.

It may be helpful to begin by attempting to define what the press's proper role should be. For if it is thought to be the responsibility of the press to hold up a mirror to the publicly revealed, official view of things, then you would have to conclude that for far too long the press did its job all too admirably. If, on the other hand, one is foolish enough to believe that the press is engaged in an endless quest for some abstraction called the Truth, then any analysis breaks down over the problem of determining what the Turth was at any given time, and in any given place, in Vietnam. It might be safer and sounder to accept at the outset some variation of Walter Lippmann's view that news and Truth are not the same thing and that in the rush of its daily activities the press is incapable of coming to terms with anything so absolute as Truth. As Lippmann put it: "The press . . . is like the beam of a searchlight that moves restlessly about, bringing one episode and then another out of the darkness into vision." He was careful to add that "men cannot do the work of the world by this light alone."

Nevertheless, this light has its uses, and it can be said fairly that in the end the press did bring "one episode and then another out of the darkness into vision" and in a way which ultimately had a crucial, not to say conclusive, impact upon the course and the conduct of this country's involvement in the Vietnam war. The trouble, of course, was that it took so long. But the main reason for this, in my view, does not reflect nearly as badly on the press as it reflects on the government. For what was distinctive about the interplay between the press and the government during the Vietnam years was not in the first instance the performance of the press, which was, by and large, not much better and not much worse than usual. What was distinctive was the performance of the government—and the impact that this had on the press and on its confidence in the reliability of what it was being told by the government.

By way of elaboration, one could do worse than look for analogy to the matter that came to be called Watergate. In the age of Watergate, which directly followed the era of Vietnam, there was a temptation to find a Watergate connection to everything—to read lessons into Watergate for application to whatever it may be that seems to ail our system or our society. So it is important, in any such analogies, to separate that part of Watergate that is essentially Nixonian—the excessive fearfulness and suspicion and combativeness and secrecy, the extraordinary lack of confidence in the ordinary processes of government and politics. That done, there remains an analogy between Watergate and Vietnam, for there runs through both dark chapters in our national life a common thread of secret conspiracy—a conspiracy, that is to say, in restraint of public participation in public events and in suppression of legitimate dissent, all in the sacred name of National Security.

Watergate worked, or at least was gotten away with for a time, because enough people in the White House and even a few outside of it in government and elsewhere were prepared to conspire against the public; to deceive and to cover up; to exploit the established institutions; to break the law or at least to violate ordinary perceptions of public trust; to engage in conduct that if it had become known and, once known, fully comprehended, would have instantly and overwhelmingly been found to be if not illegal at least improper; if not immoral, at least unethical; and if none of the above, at least unworkable if not profoundly imcompatible to our system of government.

In the same sense, Vietnam worked long enough to bring about a massive American entanglement in a war without an accompanying public support because enough officials had managed not only to accept its rationale as essential to the national interest but had also persuaded themselves that it was perfectly acceptable to deceive and to mislead in the name of this higher morality. So that at the outset, and for a prolonged period, an unknowing and unsuspecting public gave at least an adequate, if increasingly grudging, measure of support.

And both conspiracies collapsed, each in its own way and in its own time, because somebody somewhere within the government—some who had participated and some who were charged with investigating or revealing or reappraising the matter—refused to continue to conspire. Eventually, with their help, and with the critical assistance of events beyond the government's control, the press got hold of some loose ends of the truth and tugged long enough and hard enough to unravel still more. In Watergate it was the investigators and the prosecutors and lower-level and often peripheral participants who began to talk; in Vietnam it was officials and military men, again in the lower echelons, who did most at the beginning to help reveal the true bankruptcy of the policy. In various episodes of Watergate, J. Edgar Hoover and the leadership of the CIA as well as the top men in the Justice Department simply refused at crucial moments to go along. In Vietnam, retired elder statesmen, second-level civilian officials, and those outside of the war councils whose interests began to be severely damaged—the economists and the budget-makers—suddenly began to make their influence felt when the Joint Chiefs of Staff and the senior civilian war managers wanted to go on, and on, and on. In both instances, events, unpredictably and uncontrollably, played decisive roles. The 1968 Tet offensive in Vietnam had the shattering impact it had on the Administration's overstated progress reports. The Saturday Night Massacre had the same sort of impact on the Watergate case. If these events were sometimes overplayed by the press, it is probably fair to say that this was more than compensated for by the fact that too many members of the media were never nearly as diligent as a distinguished few about the business of examining and exposing the conspiracies.

The Power of the Government

The frailties of the press are one reason why it took so long. But the main reason is nothing other than the enormous inherent capacity of government to deceive. To this must be added the inherent vulnerability of our communications system to deception. One would not want to labor the analogy much longer, but Vietnam and Watergate, each in its own way, make roughly the same point: When the government, for good reasons or bad, wishes to influence opinion by concealing something damaging to its interest or by promulgating a self-serving point of view, its powers in these respects far outweigh those of the media to break down the barriers of secrecy. This is most obviously the case when we are dealing with a short-lived crisis—Soviet missles in Cuba or the Bay of Pigs—when the need for secrecy is not sustained over a long period of time and the argument for national security can be made in urgent and compelling terms. Thus, President Kennedy could briefly talk the *New York Times* out of revealing what it knew of his plan to launch an invasion by Cuban exiles to overthrow Fidel Castro. And thus President Nixon and Henry Kissinger could contain for an even longer period their closely held plan for rapprochement with Communist China. Concealment is easier, of course, when only a very few men have access to the secret.

But there is a further explanation for the extraordinary ability of the government to make its version of events believable for many months—even when there is at least some persuasive evidence to the contrary—and it has to do with the nature of the news media in America. For all the talk of their awesome power and irresponsibility, our news-gatherers are remarkably pliable. The initial impulse, at least, is to accept a responsibility to report for the record and more or less at face value not only what the government says it is doing but what the government says are the results of what it is doing.

Consider, for example, that hallowed institution known as the "background" press conference where large numbers of reporters are assembled and spoon-fed a government line for attribution to nothing more authentic than "official sources" or simply "it was learned." In theory, it is a nice trade-off, the backgrounders have the sense of getting the inside, in-depth account of things too sensitive for open disclosure; often this ritual takes place in congenial surroundings with a glass of spirits for all hands. As for the government officials conducting the briefing, they are freed of accountability to the public for the validity or even the veracity of what is said. Again in theory, the reporters are free to mull over what they have learned, check it with other sources, and present whatever their best judgment leads them to believe is an accurate, balanced account. But in practice, the assembled group is subject to fierce competitive pressures; wire services and radio and television are quick to fasten onto the hardest news and get it on the wires or on the air, on the natural assumption that everybody else will be doing the same thing. To hold something back for further checking is to risk being "beaten," which results in a "call-back" from editors. Although their pace is more leisurely, the newspapers usually follow along, for what is news in the minds of their editors is often going to be defined by what is moving on the wire services or on the air. Besides, there is that escape clause tacked on to every declarative sentence of consequence—the fine print that reads: ". . . informed sources said yesterday." In this fashion, skilled officials at the White House, the State Department, the Pentagon, and the U.S. Mission in Saigon were able for too long a time, but with gradually diminishing effect, to propagate their own version of how the war was going in Vietnam.

In time, of course, skepticism hardened and doubts set in. But it needs to be remembered that the backgrounder operates under cover of a resounding barrage of public pronouncements from the most respected high officials, reinforced in ordinary times by at least an initial public presumption that people in high authority actually speak authoritatively, and that on matters of great moment they are entitled to be believed.

Moreover, the government is in a position to deliver its message directly in critical situations, without the filter of a newspaper account or a summary on the evening news. Thus, most of the crucial statements about the war in Vietnam came to us resoundingly and overwhelmingly from the President on nationwide television on all three networks. It came to us in an address from General William C. Westmoreland to a joint session of Congress or in the drumbeat of daily briefings by White House spokesmen. It came to us in a carefully orchestrated crescendo of public statements by the highest officials of government and by the government's surrogates in Congress. It came to us in White House Papers and in handsomely bound official progress reports. It came to us in the evening briefings in Saigon and at the noon briefings at the State Department in Washington and in the chart-and-pointer, spit-and-polish presentations of the generals and the admirals at the Pentagon, on TV, in living color. And then, it was relentlessly reinforced by the interview graciously extended by an otherwise inaccessible and close-mouthed high official.

What is an only moderately trusting reporter to think, for instance, when Walt W. Rostow, the President's most intimate adviser on National Security affairs, speaking earnestly and confidentially from across his desk in the plush, inner recesses of his White House office, promises to "empty his pockets" and proceeds with charts and statistics and other suddenly declassified material to demonstrate beyond a doubt that we are "winning the war"? And what is one to think when, a week or so later, Robert Komer, freshly returned from his post as chief of the Saigon pacification effort, hunches across a table in a fine French restaurant in Washington and says: "So, okay, the hamlet evaluation stuff is a lot of crap"; but that we are nevertheless "winning the war" by the sheer weight of the resources we are bringing to bear. "This is a wasteful, inefficient effort," he argues, disarmingly (how can so candid a man be wrong, you ask yourself), "but that is the way we have won most of our wars—this is what we are good at, simply pouring on overwhelming weight."

Eventually, more and more reporters and their editors accepted the utter necessity of basing their coverage and their conclusions on what they could see for themselves. This required more than just a brief exposure to shot and shell and more than the once-over-lightly battlefield tour by helicopter. For there was so much more to the underlying struggle than the indecisive but always dramatic battles and skirmishes of a conventional kind. Somehow a way had to be found to measure the much more significantly inconclusive struggle for the lasting allegiance of hamlets and villages and district towns. You had to have been in Dak To in 1965 or Hoi An in 1966, when both were rated relatively secure at least by day, to see the significance of subsequent news dispatches a year or two years or five years later that fighting of one sort or another in those areas was still going on.

In short, you had to find some way to provide the perspective that could only come with time and with the continuing, demonstrable "unwinnability" of the war. That's one reason it took so long; it was a matter of proving a negative. Another reason, of course, is that a developing stalemate is by its nature hard to document in the face of a pervasive government propaganda blitz. And it is still harder to dramatize. That may really be the nub of why, in practical news terms, it took so long. The official line is published as an obligation, and also because of the force with which it can be delivered and the splash it makes. But .the other, unfashionable side of the argument—the hard-won analysis, interpretation, rebuttal, and refutation—comes to us like Sandburg's fog on the little cat feet of anonymous sources, sometimes not even American sources or certainly not high-ranking sources and almost never for attribution. And so, when news come to us in this form, it winds up, not in the banner headline of a Presidential report to the people on national television, but somewhere inside the paper, or in a Sunday "interpretive," or in the dispatches of syndicated columnists, or in television documentaries rather than on the evening news. It comes in the form of anecdotes, or bits and pieces of evidence, or generalized analysis without the pounding impact of a Presidential declaration from on high. This is not to suggest that the TV film clip from the war front did not have a powerful effect on public opinion. But this, in a way, is no more than a measure of the unevenness of the contest, for there was no way by which Walter Cronkite or Eric Severeid, for all the resources at their command, could speak with the authority of a President, with all the weight of government and all the intelligence resources at his command, in conveying to the American public their own version of how the war was going and of why we should or shouldn't be there and of what awful consequence might ensue if we attempted a different approach.

So when you ask yourself why it took so long, the answer has to begin with the elementary fact that in the matters of molding and controlling public opinion, the press may be free to the point of irresponsibility with the advent of television, and it may be powerful beyond the dreams of the founding fathers. But large elements of it, at least, are also remarkably dutiful, the more so when they are under attack for bias, distortion, and a chronic disinterest in reporting the good news. The net result is that in any given situation, the government or a particular political figure at least starts out holding the high ground.

Consider by way of illustration the McGeorge Bundy memorandum already alluded to, for it bears directly on a crucial moment in the American involvement in the Vietnam war. It nicely points up the inordinate capacity of the government to present events in a way most favorable to its interests, and also in a way most inimicable to an honest public perception of what in fact is going on. In March 1965, the first organized American combat troops had been landed in South Vietnam. Some 3,500 Marines went ashore near Danang, and both the Secretaries of State and of Defense, Dean Rusk and Robert McNamara, were emphatic and explicit about what they were there for. They were to provide "close-in" security for air bases from which American fighters and bombers were operating; they were not supposed to tangle with the Vietcong. On the contrary, they were supposed to free South Vietnamese army units for combat against the enemy, partly on the theory that American infantry could provide more reliable protection for American air units. In short, we were told that this was in no way a change of policy, in no way an alteration of the American role.

And this, of course, remained the official public line well past the date of the Bundy memorandum, which clearly shows that the role of the Marines—those who had first landed and those who had followed—had been changed materially, if indeed it had ever been what it was publicly and officially purported to be. But the public was not to know. Later that spring, sounder heads in the State Department, aware that American units were indeed fighting far from the air bases and suffering casualties, attempted somewhat surreptitiously to get the word out so as to prepare the American public for the reality. First, there was a background briefing in Saigon and a spate of speculative stories about a wider American combat role. As expected, this brought questions at the State Department noon briefing, and the briefing officer for the first time gave some hint of the widening mission of our forces. The repercussions very nearly ended the career of the briefing officer; President Johnson's rage was towering and the White House promptly fired back with a pronouncement of its own: there had been no, repeat no, change in policy. Not until July, with American forces now on hand in growing numbers and the military demanding still larger numbers, did the President reveal the true nature of our deepened involvement. And he did it, of course, only out of necessity; he had felt obliged to send another 50,000 American troops to Vietnam, and an escalation on this scale could no longer conceivably be disguised or concealed. Even before publication of the Pentagon Papers, there was some reason to believe that what McGeorge Bundy said in his memo had been the truth of the matter all along—that there had always been an option available to the South Vietnamese to call upon our forces for "combat support" and General Westmoreland had always had authority in his hand to accede to that request. As it was once explained to me by an official in a position to know, Westmoreland had miscalculated; the need for U.S. "combat support" had come far sooner than expected; had it not, the deception practiced by Dean Rusk and Robert McNamara would not have been exposed as such so blatantly and so soon after the fact. That is the nub of it; all along there had been hints of the real facts, but as long as the documents remained hidden and the proof was unavailable, the facts would never have the impact of a public statement by the Secretaries of State and of Defense. The American public would not comprehend that this country was being irretrievably committed to an ever widening combat role in South Vietnam until it was too late for the public to participate.

This, it should be said, was not so much a matter of calculated deceit by craven leaders as it was the first imperative of limited war: the public was to be told no more than the government thought it needed to know for the purpose of the message that the government was trying to convey at any given time to Hanoi. This meant, in the government's view, that there should be the least possible public dissent. And this in turn meant that the press must be made at least an unwitting, if not willing, accomplice.

Nowhere was this principle put more effectively into practice than in an earlier episode in our involvement in force in Vietnam: the famous Tonkin Gulf incident, which may have been the most crucial development of the war, in terms of American entanglement and of the American public's bamboozlement. No one yet knows precisely what happened in the series of sea skirmishes between the U.S. destroyers, *Maddox* and *Turner Joy*, on the one hand, and a pitiful handful of North Vietnamese torpedo boats in August 1964. It is still not clear to what extent junior naval officers misled senior naval officers, or to what extent the senior men misled the civilian leaders, and with what design in mind. But for Lyndon B. Johnson and the men closest around him it became Trafalgar revisited, a golden opportunity to mobilize the nation and to secure from Congress, under the duress of national emergency, a blank-check endorsement of whatever the Administration might choose to do in the future in Vietnam, and with it, in effect, an open-ended bank draft on American resources of money and manpower. The government spoke with one voice —that of Lyndon Johnson. And, whatever their misgivings, so did the members of Congress, with only a handful of notable exceptions—Senators Morse of Oregon and Gruening of Alaska, who cast the sole votes in either house against the measure, and the men such as Cooper of Kentucky and Nelson of Wisconsin, who bravely challenged it on the floor. That many reporters had misgivings and suspicions is a matter of record. That they were obliged to report dutifully and fully what they could plainly see and hear in the absence of clear and incontrovertible evidence to the contrary is not open to questioning. So the country was awash in the Munich analogies and in the old stereotypes about North Vietnamese aggression and the need to honor commitments and the urgency to demonstrate American good faith and resolve. The towering fact of the matter, looming over everything else, was the overwhelming congressional vote. Doubts were raised, by Nelson, Brewster of Maryland, Morton as well as Cooper of Kentucky. "My question," said Brewster at one point, "is whether there is anything in the resolution which would authorize or recommend or approve the landing of large American armies in Vietnam or in China." And Morton added: "If we make that clear, we will avoid war and not have to land vast armies on the shores of Asia. In that connection I share the apprehension of my friend, the Senator from Maryland."

But Senator Fulbright, loyally floor-managing the measure for the Administration, was persuasive in his reassurances: "Speaking for my own Committee," he said, "everyone I have heard has said the last thing we want to do is to become involved in a land war in Asia; that our power is sea and air, that this is what we hope will deter the Chinese Communists and the North Vietnamese from spreading the war. That is what is now contemplated."

And that, in turn, is what the American public believed, not because there were some doubts expressed and faithfully recorded, but because the government held the high ground.

When Senator Nelson kept hammering away for an amendment to the Tonkin Gulf Resolution, which would have made it crystal clear that the Congress was not authorizing or recommending a "change in our mission" in Vietnam, he was pacified by Fulbright in the following words: "I do not interpret the joint Resolution in that way at all. It strikes me, as I understand it, that the joint Resolution is quite consistent with our existing mission and our understanding of what we have been doing in South Vietnam for the last ten years."

No change in the mission—those were the tranquilizing words as we moved on, step by inexorable step to the assault on an American installation at Bien Hoa, which was almost certainly provoked by the emplacement there of six American bombers as a demonstration of this country's capacity to repeat the Tonkin Gulf reprisals if necessary. The Johnson Administration did not take up the challenge on that occasion, because it was three days before the November election and it did not seem a proper time to go to war. The Administration did not take up a similar challenge in similar circumstances at Christmas-time, when an American billet was bombed in Saigon, because for a number of reasons it did not seem the appropriate time to go to war. Finally, in February, the challenge was accepted—and vigorously reacted to—when yet another military installation was (by then almost predictably) attacked at Pleiku. Once again, as with the Tonkin Gulf Resolution, as the American bombers roared north, we were told about aggression, and invasion, and the horrors of appeasement. The impression was that the United States had suddenly been intolerably provoked; not until much later did it became apparent that long before Pleiku, even long before Bien Hoa and perhaps even before Tonkin, the contingency plans were being laid for a wider war. "Pleikus are like streetcars," McGeorge Bundy told me much later, meaning that if that particular pretext for reprisal had not fit the Administration's timetable, another one would have come along, for the North Vietnamese were thought to be clearly embarked on a systematic campaign of provocative acts against the American presence in the South. Still later, the Pentagon Papers confirmed the contingency planning for postelection escalation of the U.S. war effort—planning which was taking place in the middle of an election campaign in which Lyndon Johnson the Peace-maker was seeking to demolish Barry Goldwater the War-maker, with repeated assurances that he wasn't going to send American boys to fight wars that Asian boys ought to fight for themselves.

By March of 1965, with a long White Paper on Vietnam, the Johnson Administration began cautiously to prepare a public opinion for a drawn-out struggle to save South Vietnam from North Vietnamese aggression. But there was no real hint of what was in the works, no suggestion that a week after the report was published the first contingent of U.S. Marines would be landing south of Danang. The North Vietnamese are setting out "deliberately to conquer a sovereign people," the White Paper said with all the authority of the government behind it; and who in the press was to say, with anything like the same persuasion, that this was not the case, or that there was not a larger, global national security concern which obliged the United States to act.

It would be unfair to suggest that the technique of deception and dissembling was practiced exclusively by the Johnson Administration. For the same imperatives of limited war in an open society imposed upon both President Kennedy and President Nixon the same need to manipulate public opinion according to their own estimate of what was required both to stifle dissent and to convey the proper message to the North Vietnamese. Thus, Secretary of Defense McNamara was holding out one of those long series of bright visions of light at the end of the tunnel in October 1963 of a predictable moment when American troops could withdraw, even as the American mission was maneuvering in Saigon to bring some fundamental changes in the policies of the Diem government—if not necessarily or predictably the downfall of that government—in a way which did not suggest then, and still less suggests now, that all was going well.

And much later, of course, President Nixon was plotting deeper American involvements—in the Cambodian incursion and the Laotian invasion and ultimately the mining of Haiphong and the bombing of downtown Hanoi—even while he was promising us that he was ending the war and progressively disengaging American forces. Perhaps the best example of this was what the Nixon Administration had to say, by way of heading off congressional restraints on American action in Cambodia, about what would follow the "incursion" there. There would be no further American combat, no further use of American troops on the ground, and by clear implication no use of American air power in support of the Lon Nol government. American air power was to be used only in support of the action against the sanctuaries, and then only for so long as that operation was in progress. Secretary of State Rogers said as much, and the President certainly implied as much. These reassurances, once again, were dutifully reported until it became obvious many months later—not only obvious, but frankly acknowledged—that American bombers were working over the suburbs of Pnom Penh for no other conceivable purpose than the salvation of the Lon Nol government.

It is not as though the right questions were not asked at the time of the original Cambodian "incursion." In an extended exchange at a press conference on June 7, 1970, Secretary of State William P. Rogers insisted that American interest in Cambodia was limited to the use of the Cambodian "sanctuaries" by the Communists in a way that would endanger American forces—and disrupt the American withdrawal—in South Vietnam. Asked if Communist control of all of Cambodia would be considered "intolerable" by the U.S. government, Rogers replied: "Well, there is no doubt ... that obviously if the government of Cambodia came into Communist hands, it would be an unfavorable development. We would hope that doesn't happen. Pressed as to whether it would be "unacceptable," Rogers answered:

No, not unacceptable in the sense that would we use American forces to support the government. Now, that is a decision that the President made when he entered into Cambodia. And there has never been any deviation from that. ... Now, South Vietnamese forces may return; the President said we may use air interdiction to protect our forces. But we will not use American forces in Cambodia. If we did, it would enlarge the war, and it might mean that we'd be there on a semi-permanent basis, and we're not going to do that.

Not, it is true, that the word "forces" was loosely used in this exchange in a way which technically might not preclude the use of American air power. But it is also undeniable that the Secretary's remarks would lead no reasonable person to anticipate that three years later, in the spring of 1973, President Nixon would be begging Congress not to deny him authority to continue using American bombers for no other purpose than to support Cambodian forces and thus to shore up the Lon Nol government—without respect to any concern for protecting American ground forces whose total withdrawal from Indochina combat had been negotiated several months earlier in the Paris Accords of January 1973.

As it was in the process of escalation, so it was all through the agonizing process of de-escalation, and right up to the final disengagement from the war. It did not seem to matter who was President—Johnson, Nixon or Ford—in this period of active conventional combat involvement, for the need to deceive was inherent in the nature of limited war. Thus it became abundantly clear, in the spring of 1975, that President Nixon had made secret commitments to President Thieu as to the possible resumption of the use of American force in the war if Saigon's fortunes took a bad turn, even though Secretary Kissinger had given public assurances at the time of announcement of the Paris Accords that "there are no secret understandings." The explanation for this deceit was even plausible—in the context of limited war. It was that Thieu would not sign the accords without Nixon's secret assurances; that North Vietnam would not have signed the accords if the promise of American reinvolvement had been openly given; and the United States felt the need to keep open the possibility of re-involvement as part of the pressure it thought was necessary to deter violations of the cease-fire by Hanoi. And so, for these reasons, a secret pledge was made on behalf of an unwitting and unforewarned American public to recommit American military force to the Vietnam war.

Ultimately it fell to President Ford to compound a decade or more of dissembling with his spurious, eleventh-hour request to Congress for a ludicrously high level of emergency military aid for South Vietnam at a time when Congress had already made clear it was no longer ready to continue even a modest amount of arms aid to Saigon. Again there was a certain method to the madness: the last-minute evacuation of American citizens, together with as many loyal South Vietnamese as possible, was the urgent objective of U.S. policy. The great threat to an orderly evacuation was demoralization and panic among the South Vietnamese; so it was deemed necessary for the sake of morale and a measure of stability in Saigon to conduct the charade of a solemn request for military-aid-as-usual as a smokescreen behind which desperate evacuation planning could proceed.

Piercing the Veil

It is important to note that almost all along the way, very little of the government's dissembling and deception was entirely successful. Thanks to several generations of Dave Halberstams, Neil Sheehans, Malcolm Brownes and Peter Arnetts, the word got out and around that the war was not being won and that the American public was not being told the truth. But it was uphill work, for the loudest and most pervasive voice—if not always the most persuasive—was that of the government. One striking example of this was the so-called "secret bombing" of Cambodia which preceded the "incursion" by American troops. That this was not even a secret at the time, in the strictest sense, is well documented in newspaper morgues. In May 1969, William Beecher of the *New York Times* reported that American B-52 bombers had been raiding Vietcong and North Vietnamese supply dumps and base camps in Cambodia, with the tacit approval of the Cambodian government, and despite President Nixon's bland assurances that the United States was strictly respecting Cambodian neutrality at the time. Later in the year, the Associated Press had the same reports from "allied officials" in Saigon. In fact, there were even pro forma protests by the Cambodians in the United Nations, and the matter was sufficiently a public issue for Senator Mansfield to be raising questions about it on the Senate floor in November 1969. But the Nixon Administration was, if not denying it, not acknowledging it; it was ignoring it. The stories about it were one-column headlines tucked away on inside pages because the sources were anonymous, by and large, or at least not official, identifiable, responsible Administration spokesmen speaking plainly for the record. Much the same can be said in the case of President Nixon's secret commitments to President Thieu. On January 28, 1973, three days after the Paris Accords were announced, Sylvan Fox wrote in the *New York Times* that Nixon had given Thieu secret, written promises of continued military aid and of a willingness to return to the use of force (i.e., bombing) if the North Vietnamese violated the agreements. The story was attributed to anonymous South Vietnamese sources. It was datelined Saigon. It appeared on page 23 of the *Times*. And so it did not come forcibly to public attention until two years later, when Senator Henry Jackson, in his role as an early candidate for President, raised the "secret agreements" as a political issue long after they had any practical relevancy to the Vietnam War.

That was, more often than not, the way it worked. The government's deceptions succeeded in part because the refutations did not come in attributable, official, convincing form and in part—there is more than a little irony in this—because the government was able to exploit exactly the opposite characteristics of the American press from those that were being attributed to the press at the time. Even while public figures were assailing the press for its abuse of awesome power, the government, in fact, was profiting from the all-too-easy acquiescence of the press to the official government line and its virtuous sense of responsibility to record in good faith the spoken word from on high.

It is interesting to note in this connection that when the Pentagon Papers were revealed and the government went to court to restrain their publication, the newspapers argued with some persuasion and considerable documentation that there was very little genuine news in them. Highly classified as they were, most of what they said had been alluded to somewhere along the line; there had been hints and suggestions and you could look it up and find it all. But you couldn't find it in black headlines, and you could rarely find it on Page One because it had been said by "official sources in Saigon" or an "administration official in Washington"; but never had it been said forthrightly and for attribution by the President or the Secretary of State for they were otherwise occupied, vigorously denying that it was so.

A case can be made that this was the only way that this war could be waged. In the view of those in charge of planning and conducting the war effort, to confront the American public with the real potential consequences of our involvement would have been to ask the public to comprehend an enormously sophisticated concept—and to accept the possibility of five or ten or fifteen years of open-ended warfare, always depending on the will and the resources of the North Vietnamese. And it would have invited a resort to conventional military reflexes, already quite sufficiently rampant at the Pentagon. It would have raised the issue of a declaration of war and of an all-out war effort, at enormous risk of involvement with the Russians and the Chinese. That was how the war planners saw it. So the gamble was made on "graduated response," with no more to be said than was necessary for fear of stirring debate and dissent and thereby transmitting a message of weakness to Hanoi.

But the result was, of course, that none of the fundamental contradictions ever were resolved. For example, the military was never reconciled, deep down, to giving less than its best effort, and this also contributed to distortions in press coverage. For it led to continuing speculation about the next escalatory move, and it encouraged inflated reporting of military successes in conventional terms, while seriously exaggerating their significance. The pacifiers' reports were couched inevitably in terms of "progress." (For those reports which filtered through the Naval Command in Honolulu, the operative word was "headway.") Anything less than progress or headway, naturally, would give heart to the enemy and ammunition to the war critics at home and thus ostensibly prolong the war.

Another contributing factor in the distortion of press coverage of the Vietnam war was the relatively brief time that the average American military man or civilian official actually spent in Vietnam. Short tours of duty and the consequent high turnover rate robbed the participants of the perspective that comes with long service and put a high premium on a show of success. The pressure for progress was intense, and careers could be quickly formed—or damaged—in the crucible of Vietnam. A young Army officer, assigned to what might be the only combat command of his career, was not inclined to dwell heavily in his battle reports on the setbacks suffered or on the intrinsic hopelessness of the mission. AID officials similarly did not stress the monumental wastefulness inherent in their work, if for no other reason that the adverse effect this would have on next year's budget requests.

That the press undoubtedly overstated American progress out of perhaps an overdeveloped sense of responsibility to report the government line was somewhat compensated for by the fact that the press also often exaggerated the enemy's military victories. The Tet offensive is perhaps a case in point—although there was a sort of poetic justice at work in this instance because the adverse impact of Tet on the United States government and its policies would never have been as serious as it was if the Johnson Administration had not spent the better part of the preceding fall in a massive propaganda campaign to raise the level of American support by the war with a flood of reports and public appearances by General Westmoreland, Ambassador Bunker, and others. Thus, to say that the press was responsible for the impact of the Tet offensive is to overlook the role of the government iself in building up, with an endless string of confident predictions and rosy reports, a towering structure of false hopes and overblown expectations. That it took time for this structure to come tumbling down is hardly surprising. For it takes time when the most reliable accounts of a great national venture must come, not from the top in official, public declarations but from anonymous sources or from careful cultivation of the most junior and least influential officials at the very bottom of the bureaucratic pyramid: the provincial representatives, the company commanders and platoon leaders, the AID and USIA operatives in the field. These were the people who knew firsthand how the war was going, but who had little or nothing to do with the decision-making at the top. Ultimately, their version of events filtered into news stories and began to influence editors and television producers as well. Eventually, these necessarily faceless and nameless informants had a profound impact on the way the war was covered. The tragedy, of course, was that it took so long.

The Remedy

In having begun with McGeorge Bundy, there may be a certain symmetry to ending with reference to some of his later

reflections about the Vietnam war. That he signed a memorandum in April 1965 which confirms a conspiracy to hide the
true nature of the undertaking from the public takes nothing
away from his retrospective conclusions in a speech he delivered to the St. Louis Council on World Affairs in October
1973. For there was a certain logic in the argument that concealment and some degree of dissembling and duplicity are
part of the inevitable price of trying to conduct a limited war
in a "free society." The proper lesson to be drawn from that, of
course, may well be that limited wars won't work under our
system. Indeed, the lesson McGeorge Bundy seems to have
drawn from his own White House experience as a principal
Vietnam adviser, as he propounded it in 1973, was that excessive secrecy for whatever purpose is inimical to the conduct of
just about any large foreign policy venture when operating
within a political system which requires a good measure of
public support for the effective conduct of the business of
government. With particular respect to the exposition of U.S.
policy toward the Middle East in the fall of 1973, Bundy
observed:

> Cryptic press conferences and back-channel conversa-
> tions with journalists will no longer do the job . . . my
> point is not . . . that I know just what should be said or
> just when. My point is rather that quite a lot needs to be
> said, to us and to the world, and that no policy which
> requires public support can be sustained without such
> exposition. . . .

To this, a working newsman can only say amen. That the
press can do better, goes without saying, just as it is self-evident that the press in its coverage of Vietnam fell victim to
just about all the sins and weaknesses which characterize its
coverage of other events. But press coverage depends heavily
upon the willingness of the government to speak forthrightly
about what it is doing.

It does not necessarily follow from Bundy's second thoughts
on the efficacy of secrecy in the conduct of foreign policy that
a forthright exposition of what the policy-makers were up to or
how well they were doing would have improved the chances of

success in the early days of our developing entanglement in Vietnam. It might merely have turned the public decisively against the enterprise, and at who can say what gain or loss. Nor does it absolutely follow that a limited war cannot under any circumstances be conducted within the ground rules governing an open society. "If it were done when 'tis done," Macbeth said of an earlier exercise in incremental homicide, "then twere well / It were done quickly . . ." It is entirely possible that if the North Vietnamese could have been quickly bullied, threatened, or frightened into "leaving their neighbors alone" (in Dean Rusk's litany), then the secrecy and the manipulation of public opinion and the exploitation of the press would have as quickly been forgiven and forgotten as it was, let us say, in the Cuban missile crisis. Success exonerates.

But surely the lesson of Vietnam upholds Bundy's general thesis that a successful foreign policy cannot be sustained for any prolonged period without public support, founded on public understanding of what really is going on. For when this is absent, all the processes break down, all the fundamental and continuing relationships are threatened: those between President and Congress, government and people, press and government. That is what happened in Vietnam. Out of the sundering disillusionment of Tet came the New Hampshire primary and the fresh wave of antiwar protest and the fall of Lyndon Johnson. Out of an inordinate need for extreme secrecy came an extreme sensitivity to press leaks, and out of that came the creation of the "plumbers" and an atmosphere and a way of life that eventually destroyed the Nixon Administration. Out of the developing war protest came excesses that twisted and strained the traditional relationship between the people and the press and the government and produced a Daniel Ellsberg, who produced the most monumental breach of security in this country's history in the release of the Pentagon Papers. The breach was made all the more shattering by the extraordinary amount of effort and space which the *New York Times* gave to raw documents and files, reprinted in full text. Even an Administration more sophisticated and secure and less suspicious and fearful by nature than Nixon's would have been shaken. For Nixon it was a signal to redouble his repression of the press and a rationale, however warped, for sending his "plumbers" into Ellsberg's psychiatrist's office.

Along the way, in this process of disintegration, all sorts of people, and a rich variety of events beyond anybody's control, contributed to the excesses which brought about the breakdown of the traditional relationships. But a reasonable argument can be made that the original catalyst was the manner in which the government conducted the public relations of the Vietnam war. It was this that caused the collapse of public trust upon which our system of government is based. You can blame it in part on the press for being slow at getting onto the truth; but you have to begin by blaming it on the government for making the truth so hard to get at. Any assessment of the role of the press in Vietnam must end with the conclusion that when all was said and done, it was the press which had more than anything to do with saving the government from itself.

In the end everybody lost; two Presidents lost their mandates and their capacity to govern; the people lost in terms of lives and treasure and effective government. And the press as well, for it was one of the first of the established institutions to suffer a crippling loss of public confidence—with no end of help, it must be added, from the government. A recent poll revealed that the news media ranked appreciably below trash collectors in the public trust. And so it may. But if this is indeed the case, there is at least a certain poetic justice in the press' fall from grace. For it derives in large measure from the fact that what the press gives out, dutifully and day after day, is determined to a large extent by what it gets openly or in carefully calculated, thoroughly managed "background" official briefings for supposedly faithful delivery to the public. And more often than not, and for far too long, what the press was getting from the government over the long, agonized, tormenting years of Vietnam was—not to put too fine a point upon it—trash.

Congress and Vietnam: The Fruits of Anguish

ALTON FRYE AND JACK SULLIVAN

As a symbol of the hazards of executive dominance of American foreign policy, Vietnam is unparalleled in the nation's history. Yet most members of Congress acknowledge that the horrors of the years from 1964 to 1973 owe as much to legislative failure as to executive misjudgment. This sense of institutional as well as national failure has bred an incipient determination to make Congress' constitutional authority more effective across a broad range of national security issues —issues which global war and cold war had drawn more and more into the almost exclusive purview of the President and the bureaucracy.

There is room for argument about whether it is wise or feasible for such a pluralistic body as Congress to assert a larger role in these delicate and dangerous matters. But that argument should take account of what Congress actually has been attempting in the wake of Vietnam. Congress is not out to destroy the Presidency as the principal U.S. agent in world affairs. Nor is it on the verge of some breakthrough in the wiser management of the country's foreign policy. Instead, Congress has been groping for a judicious application of its power, both as partner and as overseer of the executive branch.

This movement rests less on the premise that "the President cannot be trusted" than on the more complex insight that "the President can best be trusted when Congress meets its responsibility to share the burden of decision on questions of preparedness and peace-keeping." In practical terms this means that the President and Congress must reconstruct the institutional alliance which Vietnam damaged so severely. But the alliance cannot be rebuilt on the old foundations of cold war suspicion and exaggerated deference for executive leadership in international affairs, which are themselves prime casualties of recent history. The task is to find bases for legislative-executive harmony in a world in which the nation no longer enjoys the simplifying luxury of a monolithic adversary or the reassuring presumption of superior Presidential competence.

Congress has begun to address this task, tentatively but in general constructively. Without projecting onto a ramshackle process more order than it exhibits, the broad trend of congressional behavior may be characterized as combining a gradually increasing assertiveness regarding specific current policies, including those affecting Southeast Asia, with an historic if halting effort to strengthen the institutional arrangements for molding future policies. Both elements are essential to the long-range goal of reviving the nation's self-confidence in foreign policy: the first, to demonstrate that Congress has the will and capacity to resolve complicated issues in this realm; the second, to guarantee that there are procedures to facilitate congressional action, rather than evasion, in future instances of imperative national decision-making.

Circumstance necessitates what the Constitution mandates: The rejuvenation of the checks and balances which had grown moribund through the modern acceptance by Congress of Presidential dominance in foreign affairs. The President, as well as Congress, has an overriding interest in a vigorous legislative role in foreign policy. Because of the increasing constituent pressures under which it operates, Congress can no longer afford to appear as a mere lackey in such matters. But neither can the President afford such an impression, if he is to

regain that vital presumption of approbation which the
country has given its foreign policy for many years. Once
persuaded that an active Congress is insisting on thorough and
scrupulous evaluation of executive proposals, the country will
again have a rational basis for vesting trust in its foreign policy.
A substantive consensus must await a procedural consensus.

This is the implicit principle which informs many of the
initiatives Congress has taken since 1968. Ranging far beyond
the conflict in Southeast Asia, these initiatives have touched
the level and composition of the defense budget, intimate
questions of diplomatic practice, strategic weapons policy and
arms control, international trade issues, and a host of other
topics. Central to these efforts, however, and illustrative of
both its caution and its ambition, have been the attempts of
Congress to define ground rules for the use of American armed
forces abroad.

Toward a Fail-Safe System

On May 10, 1973, the House of Representatives affirmed its
conviction in three separate votes that the bombing of Cambodia—that "last lingering corner" of America's participation
in the Indochina war—should halt. The votes were significant,
marking the first time since the United States became involved in Southeast Asia that the House had gone on record in
opposition to continued U.S. military activity there. The Senate had done so in varying ways. In addition to anticipating
legislative-executive negotiation of an ultimate bombing halt,
the actions of May 10 meant that the Congress had completed
its movement away from the Tonkin Gulf Resolution of 1964.
Both houses now were willing to deny the President a foreign
policy instrument he clearly wanted, and to take the potential
responsibility for "losing" Cambodia to Communist insurgency.

To many citizens the prolonged and arduous process by
which a reluctant Congress finally acted to constrain Presidential war-making in Southeast Asia confirmed the debase-
ment of American politics. While numerous members of both
houses were in the vanguard of critics who stressed the moral
and political disproportion of the U.S. role, survey data and

editorial commentary suggested that the majority of congressmen trailed their constituents in concluding that the violence and costs of the war exceeded genuine American interest. Yet the political pressures at work during the war were notoriously varied and contradictory. Public opinion was never homogeneous, and until well after 1968, few members had a clear signal from their constituents which could guide their action on specific votes. Most members faced acute dilemmas in seeking to weigh both what they thought their constituents wanted them to do about the war and what they judged to be in the best interest of the nation.

Politics, like statesmanship and other assessments, lies in the eye of the beholder. For several years the balance of personal and national calculus persuaded most congressmen and senators that they should not flatly oppose the President, even while they were pressing him to expedite an end to hostilities. Just as the lengthy period of deference to the President stemmed from mixed motives—respect for executive leadership, fear of executive displeasure, reluctance to accept the onus of undercutting the country's designated agents, and basic agreement with the stated policy—so the eventual rejection of the White House's proposed bombing operations in Cambodia flowed from a number of dissonant factors. These included moral repugnance at the continuation of U.S. military engagement, anger at executive arrogance, vehement sentiments among constituents, political opportunism in striking at a weakened President, and the considered opinion that the imbalance of institutional power demanded reassertion of congressional prerogatives.

On August 3, 1973, in a bitter letter to the congressional leadership, the President warned of the "hazards that lie in the path chosen by Congress." This abandonment of a friend, he said, would have a profound impact on other countries, and he wanted the Congress "to be fully aware of the consequences of its action." As Nixon seemed to be setting the stage for blaming future setbacks in Indochina on Congress, voices of conciliation also were heard. Meeting with the press a few weeks later, upon his nomination for Secretary of State, Henry Kissinger pledged to "bring the Congress into a close partnership in the development, planning, and execution of our foreign policy."

These developments were in marked contrast to the pattern of legislative-executive relations that evolved during and after World War II. Congress had been generally content with a junior-partner role in foreign policy, and dissent was an unaccustomed phenomenon. There were, to be sure, exceptions: the Bricker amendments, Senator Taft's critique of an undeclared Korean War, and the "Great Debate" over sending American troops to Europe under NATO. In the main, however, these were rear-guard actions, fought by a relatively small number of unreconstructed members. For a generation, Presidents, Secretaries of State, and Secretaries of Defense got what they wanted on Capitol Hill, usually with little trouble. The Senate, which had built a reputation for extended debate, voted United States participation in the United Nations after less than a week of discussion. Foreign Relations Committee hearings on the SEATO treaty lasted two days; only one hostile witness—a retired isolationist congressman—testified. In 1955, a defense commitment to the Republic of China on Taiwan won overwhelming endorsement by Congress after one day of hearings and one day of debate in the House, and two days of hearings and three days of debate in the Senate. Congress sometimes gave the Commander-in-Chief more authority than he thought of asking for. When President Kennedy sought a "fight-if-we-must resolution" on Cuba in 1962, Congress passed it and ten days later approved a similar expression on Berlin, even though the Berlin crisis of 1961 had faded nearly a full year before.

The apex of this phenomenon was passage of the Tonkin Gulf Resolution. Within two days after Lyndon Johnson's request, the House by a 414 to 0 vote and the Senate by an 88 to 2 vote passed a joint resolution authorizing the President "to take all necessary steps, including the use of armed force" to prevent North Vietnam from taking over South Vietnam. Retrospective claims that things might have been different had the Congress been adequately informed about the dubious nature of the Tonkin Gulf incidents cannot stand scrutiny. Numbed by the practice of its responsibilities and confirmed in the rightness of American intervention, Congress would have given the President whatever he said he needed, almost without regard to circumstances. All but a few members of Congress were, in the words of Senator Fulbright, "caught up in what we must now recognize as the shortsighted cult of presidential predominance in foreign policy."

The cult might still be flourishing had not President Johnson found it necessary to cash his Tonkin Gulf blank check again and again for ever-mounting totals of men and resources. From the moment that the first combat Marines waded ashore near Danang in March 1965, disintegration in the national consensus on foreign policy began. Congress stirred. At first, dissent came from isolated individuals—Senator Morse and Senator Gruening. With the seeming success of the Communist Tet offensive in 1968 and no clear prospects for the war's termination, the Senate Foreign Relations Committee opened a remarkable series of hearings—remarkable because for the first time since Pearl Harbor members of Congress, including members of the President's own party, questioned high Administration officials in depth about the basic premises of American foreign policy. Televised nationally, the Fulbright hearings helped crystallize opposition to the Indochina war among an informed public, which in turn encouraged war critics on Capitol Hill to intensify their rhetorical and legislative attacks.

The road back from Tonkin Gulf proved to be a slow and tortuous one. From July 1966 through July 1973, Congress took 113 recorded votes on measures related to the Indochina war.[1] Of these, the great bulk (94) were taken after President Nixon assumed office. Some 86 votes were taken in the Senate, 62 on measures limiting or cutting off funds for military activities in Indochina, and 14 on proposals to curtail military operations or set policies on troop withdrawals. Significantly, fewer votes occurred in the more hawkish House: 26 votes on limiting or cutting off funds and 6 limiting military operations or withdrawing forces.

The great majority of these votes were lost by antiwar forces in the House and Senate. Efforts to use the "power of the purse" to cut off the war entirely were unsuccessful, as many senators and representatives proved reluctant to face accusations that they had denied adequate funds to the fighting men in the field. In 1969, however, Congress for the first time voted to restrict American military activities in Laos and Thailand to support local forces; it prohibited actual engagement of U.S. forces in these countries. In June 1970, following the Cambodian invasion, 58 senators approved the Cooper-Church amendment to bar funds for direct U.S. military operations in Cambodia after July 1 and obliged the House and the Administration to accept a modified ban which exempted air support.

Gambits by congressional doves on Vietnam policy similarly were frustrated. The Tonkin Gulf Resolution was repealed in January 1971, but with no opposition from the Nixon Administration. The President claimed sufficient powers of his own to carry on the conflict. Two Mansfield amendments setting a specific deadline for the withdrawal of troops, pending the return of prisoners-of-war, were adopted on the Senate floor in 1971. In each case the House removed the deadlines and otherwise weakened the language, permitting the President to ignore them or claim that he was carrying out the specified policy. In August 1972, the Committee on Foreign Affairs by a one-vote margin sent a Vietnam cut-off proposal to the House floor as an amendment to the foreign military aid authorization bill. It drew the largest number of representatives ever to vote against the war up to then, 177, but the opposition had 229 votes and killed the antiwar language.

Not until the last American combat soldier had left Vietnam and the prisoners-of-war were returned was a majority of the Congress willing to vote an end to direct American involvement in the Indochina war. For four years the "grunts" and POWs were the President's trump cards. When, after the Paris Agreements, they could no longer be played, Mr. Nixon found that other time-honored arguments about the Communist menace, abandonment of friends, and disturbance to delicate ongoing negotiations no longer sufficed. For many in Congress, the deteriorating situation in Cambodia in 1973 had a *déjà vu* quality: Vietnam in 1964 and the tunnel at the end of the light. Unwilling to make new American prisoners-of-war or otherwise to risk further involvements in Southeast Asian conflict, Congress called a halt to the Cambodian bombing. National opinion polls showed roughly 80 per cent of the American people agreed.

If the sum of direct congressional action on ending the war seems very little and done very late, the total experience has had an intense and possibly enduring effect on legislative-executive relations. Congressmen at all points of the ideological compass have come to want a larger voice in foreign policy formation. For some, putting a curb on the President's power had been a surrogate for voting against his war policy. For others, the Indochina war was but the most noxious result of a general malaise stemming from an arrogation of power in matters of foreign policy and national security by a succession of recent Presidents.

An early manifestation of the new mood in Congress came on the issue of "national commitments." Because military action in Indochina frequently was justified on the grounds that it was necessary to fulfill alleged commitments, debate arose on what constitutes a national commitment and how it is made. A resolution introduced in the Senate in 1967 sought to clarify those questions, as well as to reassert senatorial prerogatives. As finally passed in 1968, it defined a national commitment as:

> . . . The use of the Armed Forces of the United States on foreign territory, or a promise to assist a foreign country, government, or people by the use of the Armed Forces or financial resources of the United States, either immediately or upon the happening of certain events.

Such a commitment, the resolution continued, could only be effected by a specific treaty, statute, or concurrent resolution of both houses of Congress.

The national commitments resolution represented a naïve and futile congressional effort to regain lost power. Opposed by the Johnson and Nixon Administrations, the resolution was utterly ignored by the White House when it made decisions to invade Cambodia, to provide aid to the Lon Nol government, and to order the incursion into Laos. When asked in 1971 about the impact of the resolution, Senator Fulbright replied frankly that it had no effect at all.

The debate, however, did set in motion other activities which proved influential. In 1969, Chairman Fulbright appointed Senator Stuart Symington to head a special subcommittee to investigate the extent of U.S. security agreements and commitments abroad. As a result, the Congress and the American public became aware of the breadth of the nation's overseas involvements, particularly in the affairs of Southeast Asia. Revealed were costly agreements with Asian allies to induce their direct participation as "free world forces" with the United Sates in Vietnam. The disclosures stripped away the trappings of idealized collective security. Some agreements had been deliberately kept secret from the Congress: with Ethiopia in 1960, Laos in 1963, Thailand in 1964 and 1967, South Korea in 1966, and in classified annexes to the Spanish Bases Agreement of 1953.

In response to these disclosures, Congress in 1972 passed a bill requiring that all executive agreements be transmitted to Congress within sixty days of their signing. Secret pacts were to be restricted to the Committees on Foreign Affairs and on Foreign Relations. Introduced by Senator Clifford Case, the bill initially was opposed by the Nixon Administration. Following its passage in the Senate by an 81 to 0 margin, the White House capitulated. The House subsequently passed the bill, and the President signed it without expressing reservations about its blanket application, as he had been expected to do. Although a modest achievement, passage of the Case bill represented the first—and for some time, the only—victory which could be claimed by those seeking an enhanced role for Congress in foreign policy formulation.

On a related front, the campaign for war powers legislation was triggered by the Cambodian incursion of May 1970. Memories of the cavalier treatment accorded Congress on that occasion still chafe on Capitol Hill. The President had informed foreign governments but had not entrusted such information to Congress. Within a few days after President

Nixon's televised announcement of the invasion, several members had introduced war powers measures.

In the House, extensive hearings by a House Foreign Affairs subcommittee chaired by Representative Clement J. Zablocki led to a measure which directed only that the President report to Congress whenever he committed American forces to combat without prior congressional approval. Acceptable to the Administration, the resolution three times passed the House by enormous margins during the 91st and 92nd Congresses. Meanwhile in the Senate, a broad coalition led by Jacob Javits, John Stennis, and Thomas Eagleton formed behind a much more restrictive bill. After extended floor debate, the Javits bill was approved 68 to 16 in 1972, despite strong White House opposition.

Because of interbody rivalries, parliamentary snarls, and the conceptual gulf between the House and Senate measures, no serious attempt was made to reconcile the two in 1972. In the 93rd Congress, the House, stung by continued Administration intransigence on issues like the Cambodian bombing, approved much stronger legislation. The conferees forged a workable and attractive compromise measure. When the President carried out his threat to veto it, both Houses marshaled the necessary votes to override the veto on November 7, 1973. The confrontation produced the first reversal of a Presidential veto in the 93rd Congress. Some commentators attributed this to President Nixon's weakened political position in the festering Watergate scandals, but few congressional observers agreed. Those revelations no doubt gave congressmen a greater sense of latitude in challenging the President, who could no longer "wrap himself in the flag" with impunity. But enactment of war powers legislation stemmed from lengthy and thoroughgoing deliberations which convinced large majorities of the need for such a measure.

To the end, the President disputed both the constitutionality and practicality of the statute. But the Chief Executive's attempt to ward off the law by offers of improved consultation and cooperation with Congress rang hollow. The actual consequences of the measure must be distinguished from those feared by its vocal critics. The War Powers Act does not prohibit Presidential use of force in emergency situations. Beyond the requirement that the President report promptly to Congress any introduction of American forces into ongoing or imminent hostilities—a requirement to which the President did not object—the remainder of the legislation is designed not to constrain the President's responsibilities but to insure that Congress meets its own.

The statute's principal mechanisms provide for expeditious consideration and decision by Congress of whether military action should be sustained beyond an initial sixty-day period. Congress will thus be forced by its own rules to reach a collective judgment on a particular case; the impact of that judgment will be more political than constitutional. Even if the President were to contend that Congress had no authority to terminate his use of force by the concurrent resolution provided in the law, there is no doubt that, once such a resolution were enacted, Congress could govern the use of American forces through its control of appropriations. In most cases the President will be under greater compulsion to consult with congressional leaders, lest he involve the nation in hostilities which Congress would not support. Having proceeded on the basis of extensive consultation, however, the President will know that Congress must promptly and publicly confront the question of sustaining any hostilities which occur, thus relieving the White House of the unsupportable burden of conducting undeclared wars in the twilight zone of Presidential authority.

The apprehensions of Senator Thomas Eagleton and others who came to oppose the legislation after supporting initial versions of it turn on whether the procedures represent a true reassertion of legislative control, or an invitation to even more sweeping interpretations of Presidential authority. Without a relatively precise enumeration in the bill of those instances in which the executive can use force prior to congressional authorization, Senator Eagleton feared that the Chief Executive could assert the right to use force as he deemed fit and that, once American personnel were committed to combat, Congress would be boxed into approving support for the men in the field. To former Senator Fulbright and leading members of the House, however, this type of enumeration of executive powers would create the presumption that the President had acted constitutionally in such circumstances. The latter view prevailed, and the act as passed obliges the President to demonstrate the constitutional grounds for any use of force undertaken without prior congressional authorization. The wisdom of this choice can only be tested by the vigor with which future Congresses employ the authority reclaimed by the measure's procedural innovations.

Some opponents likened the war powers bill to the constitutional amendment restricting Presidents to two terms: just as the one was Republican retribution for a deceased President's four terms, so the other is portrayed as a vendetta against the war policies of Kennedy, Johnson, and Nixon. Although members drafted legislation with the events of the past decade clearly in mind, the drive for congressional war powers represents more than revenge. Most members recognize that the Congress already has sufficient powers to call a halt to ill-advised Presidential military ventures, if it will use them. Keenly aware of executive branch claims of virtually unlimited war-making powers and past abjectness in Congress, proponents deem it vital that the legislative branch again declare and assume its own responsibilities. Then, given specified procedures, it will have to exercise them in future situations.

Congress found the writing of war powers legislation an extraordinarily difficult task. While most members of Congress agreed on the need for belling the Presidential cat, there was no agreement on how to proceed. Language which to some seemed adequately restrictive of the President appeared to others as freehand grants of new authority to the Chief Executive. Under other circumstances the lack of any clear consensus would probably have doomed the war powers drive to futility. Obduracy on the part of the Administration, however, led significant numbers of legislators to abandon past positions and to embrace legislation which seemed necessary to correct the imbalance between the executive and legislative branches.

The efficacy of the War Powers Resolution remained untested for sixteen months, until the spring of 1975, when the collapse of several states in Indochina resulted in no less than four Presidential uses of U.S. armed forces reportable under the resolution. The incidents were the evacuation of Vietnamese refugees from Danang, the evacuation of Americans and Cambodians from Phnom Penh, the evacuation from Saigon, and the recovery of the *Mayaguez* from its Cambodian captors.

In each case the President adhered to the resolution by reporting to the Congress within forty-eight hours what he had done. Again in each case, by the time the report had been received the operation had been concluded and American forces had withdrawn. As a result, mechanisms by which Congress could approve or disapprove the actions never came into play. Critical attention, therefore, centered on alleged failures of the President properly to consult with Congress before launching an engagement, as requested—but not mandated —by the War Powers Resolution. In one or two instances, the criticism seemed justified; in others, less so. Senator Eagleton introduced an amendment to the resolution aimed at making the consultation provision more specific.

In the main, however, the resolution had proved a useful instrument in bringing Congress and its constitutional war powers into the flow of events. Presidential usurpations like the Cambodian invasion of 1970 seemed to belong to a departed era.

Less successful have been efforts to require that overseas-bases agreements be submitted as treaties to the Senate for its advice and consent. Although ultimately pressured by Congress to submit the Okinawa reversion agreement, the Administration refused similar action on base agreements with Spain, Bahrain, and Portugal, the last regarding facilities in the Azores. In March 1972 the Senate passed a resolution by 50 to 6 calling on the executive branch to submit the Bahrain and Portugal agreements to the Senate for advice and consent. When the Administration refused, the Senate amended the Foreign Assistance Act of 1972, prohibiting any spending to implement the Azores bases agreement until it had been submitted as a treaty; the measure also required that all future agreements relating to overseas military installations be subject to Senate ratification. A deadlock with House conferees over those amendments ultimately doomed that foreign aid bill. Another attempt in 1973 was foiled when a conservative coalition in the House succeeded in defeating a similar provision which had been added as a "rider" to the State Department authorization. Concurrently, a proposal to permit Congress to veto executive agreements by majority vote within sixty days of their signing stalled, as its sponsor, Senator Sam Ervin, was preoccupied with Watergate. Nevertheless, the growing demand for Congress to be kept informed promised there would be steady pressure to curtail perceived abuses.

In the 94th Congress, Chairman Thomas Morgan of the House Foreign Affairs Committee, together with Zablocki, startled the Administration by introducing his own executive agreements proposal. Early in the first session, the Senate began to stir on the question as Senator Abourezk led his Separation of Powers subcommittee into hearings on a variety of proposals to curtail use of executive agreements.

As a practical matter, foreign powers are on notice that executive commitments without congressional concurrence could well prove ephemeral, a point driven home by the revelations of unwarranted secret undertakings made by President Nixon in his dealings wth Nguyen Van Thieu.

Inconclusive, too, have been efforts to increase congressional access to information on foreign affairs. Although such disputes go back to George Washington and the Jay Treaty, the Indochina war escalated the struggle to new intensity. As belated revelations about U.S. bombing in Cambodia have shown, the executive branch was willing to take extraordinary measures to keep facts from Congress. Members justifiably charge that through three Presidencies, they were denied full, accurate information about the course of the war and American war policy.

Congressmen, for their part, were often all too willing to be kept in the dark or even deceived. Years of reliance on the bureaucracies for information left Congress woefully dependent. Moreover, it had grown too accustomed to Administration manipulation of executive privilege and secrecy to keep friends on Captiol Hill in the know and to keep non-sympathizers ignorant.

Despite greater awareness of the importance of information for its functioning, Congress has yet to conceive a coordinated strategy for obtaining the facts it wants when the executive is unwilling to volunteer them. Battles over executive privilege have frequently had a whiff of parochialism about them. Generally, only those members or committees directly involved care deeply enough about the denial of information.

Efforts initiated by the Senate Foreign Relations Committee to force disclosures by foreign affairs agencies consistently have failed to obtain congressional approval. In 1973, however, both houses did pass a requirement that the United States Information Agency provide information requested by a majority of either the Foreign Affairs or the Foreign Relations Committees or face a funding cut-off. The provision resulted in a veto of the USIA authorization, a veto which Congress was unable to override. The Senate also has given serious consideration to legislation which would require any employee of the executive branch to come before the committee to which he was summoned and there, in person rather than in absentia, invoke any claim of executive privilege. At that point a special panel of senators could be convened to determine whether the claim was legitimate; and if it was found not to be, an order could follow which, if ignored, might be punished as contempt of Congress.

Congressional divisions on executive privilege could be laid in part to a view by some that no legislation should recognize any authority of Presidents to withhold any information from Congress. In its 1974 decision in the *United States v. Nixon*, the Supreme Court established the right, though not the scope, of executive privilege in areas of "military, diplomatic, or sensitive national security secrets." With that issue evidently settled, the 94th Congress may well move on relevant legislation.

Other proposals would provide CIA intelligence briefings on a regular basis to congressmen, make the National Security Adviser to the President subject to Senate confirmation, and establish legislative guidelines for the classification of information. The fate of such proposals remains in doubt, given the reluctance of Congress, particularly the House, to make a determined assault on the Chief Executive's right to withhold information. Nevertheless, the successful battle for war powers legislation may be a portent. Continued Administration intransigence, including former Attorney General Kleindienst's testimony that the President can keep anything he wishes from Congress subject only to impeachment, may yet elicit legislative action to extract needed information.

While concentrating on methods to improve its own standing and capability to deal with foreign affairs, Congress is also heading toward reconsideration of the extravagant grants of discretionary authority which it has made to the President. Since 1933 the Congress had enacted at least 580 separate sections of the United States Code delegating extraordinary powers to the President in time of war or national emergency. Moreover, flexibility amounting to enormous "loopholes," as critics say, has been built into such legislation as the foreign economic and military aid bills. They permitted the President to do virtually what he pleases with the money authorized, regardless of congressional intentions.

Congress had an inkling of the results of its liberality after the assault on the Cambodian sanctuaries, when President Nixon took military aid funds which Congress had approved for Taiwan, Indonesia, and Turkey to buy guns and ammunition for Cambodia without seeking congressional permission. When President Nixon did finally come to Congress, his request for supplemental funds emphasized reimbursement of the other countries. Thus was he able to avoid a direct congressional debate and decision on the wisdom of aiding Cambodia until months after aid had been given. The President could also have used another discretionary clause in the military aid legislation permitting him to take military items from regular defense stocks for grants to other nations.

A bipartisan Joint Committee on the National Emergency held extensive hearings on emergency power statutes and reported a bill repealing many of them. With lukewarm executive branch concurrence, the Senate approved the bill in the fall of 1974. The House was unable to act before the end of the 93rd Congress, and the bill died. The drive to repeal many emergency powers, however, did not die.

Successful attempts to end or limit executive discretion in implementing foreign aid programs highlighted both Senate and House committee consideration of the Foreign Assistance Act of 1974. Transfer authorities were curtailed. Aid ceilings were imposed on countries like Korea, Vietnam, Cambodia, Chile, and India. The Act also included provisions permitting Congress to negate Presidential intentions by passing "veto-proof" concurrent resolutions.

So restrictive did the Senate foreign aid bill become that the Administration came to oppose it, and it was recommitted from the Senate floor to the Foreign Relations Committee.

Almost immediately, however, the new Ford Administration became embroiled in a legislative-executive dispute over U.S. assistance to Turkey. By sizable majorities Congress sought to cut off military aid to Turkey against the wishes of the President and Secretary of State. Before the conflict had ended—at least temporarily—there were two Presidential vetoes, a delayed pre-election recess, and a revolt of rank-and-file Democrats against more conciliatory leadership in both houses. Although a compromise, the final language signaled a congressional victory—perhaps a dubious one. By May 1975 the Senate was having second thoughts. By a margin of 41 to 40, it voted to lift the ban on military aid to Turkey. The House, on the other hand, appeared adamant.

Some Conclusions and Prognoses

This discussion of congressional attempts to devise procedures and acquire the information essential to a responsible role in foreign policy, particularly on issues of war and peace, is only a fragmentary sketch of a historic phenomenon. Few observers would have predicted the resurgence of congressional interest and power in the area of national security and foreign policy. It would be premature to judge the positive and negative consequences of that resurgence, or even to assert that it will persist. But it is not too early to note that some of the changes flowing from the Vietnam ordeal are likely to endure. In addition to the statutory procedures set forth in the war powers legislation, perhaps the most fundamental changes are the shifts in congressional attitudes and habits which have emerged in the last few years.

Foremost among these shifts is one of perspective: claims of national security no longer go unchallenged in the halls of Congress. Closely paralleling the development of popular sentiment that defense spending has been too high, as first reflected in the Gallup Poll of 1969, Congress has come to subject the military budget to intensive scrutiny. The annual debate over the defense budget, which formerly sped through Congress in a few hours, now consumes many days on the floor and many months in committee. For several years now Congress has regularly reduced by billions of dollars the proposed levels of defense spending. Among these reductions have been major cuts for specific weapons systems—the antiballistic missile system, the Manned Orbiting Laboratory, the Cheyenne helicopter system, the C-5A aircraft, and the Trident submarine, to mention just a few. These decisions typify the more informed and discriminating judgments which Congress is bringing to bear on military proposals. Even in such arcane fields as strategic weapons policy, Congress has come to exercise an affirmative influence. Having pressed for an early start on ABM deployment during the mid-1960s, congressional reconsideration of the destabilizing implications of such weapons generated pressure to slow the proposed deployments in both the Johnson and Nixon Administrations. The eventual conclusion of a low-level limit on ABM deployment undoubtedly owed much to the restraint displayed by the Congress. Had it speeded approval of the proposed twelve-site nationwide system contemplated in 1968, it is questionable whether diplomacy would have had the time and the opportunity to negotiate the arrangements concluded in the Strategic Arms Limitations Talks in 1972 and 1974. Similarly, had members of Congress routinely yielded to Pentagon requests for a hard-target counterforce MIRV system, the United States would have been well on its way to more destabilizing technology before the negotiators ever had an opportunity to seek mutually agreed controls.

In many respects of defense procurement a more attentive Congress has added a welcome tautness to military programs. Recent congressional inquiries have underscored the costly and debilitating practices of "gold-plating" in the design and acquisition of military hardware. They have elicited badly needed reforms in procurement methods aimed at simplifying and enhancing system reliability. In areas like tactical air support, it is the Congress that has insisted on choices among competing systems rather than acquisition of several intended for the same mission.

These developments both reflect and reinforce the basic alteration in the pattern of congressional participation in national security policy. Not only between Congress and the executive, but within Congress itself, recent years have seen a shift from a relatively closed to a relatively open system of decision-making. No longer are vital decisions reserved for the hushed cubicles of the Armed Services and Appropriations Committees of the two houses. Because of the wide ramifications of decisions on these issues, there is now active competition in many quarters to take part in shaping them. Individual members of Congress, even without positions on committees of jurisdiction, have asserted a legitimate claim to speak and work on national security issues. A productive tension has developed between the Foreign Affairs and Armed Services Committees of the two houses, and members of many other committees—Ways and Means, Finance, Banking, the Joint Economic Committee, Commerce, the Joint Committee on Atomic Energy, and Government Operations—have achieved solid bases from which to address important international issues. The result is that Congress is not only examining the executive branch more diligently but is keeping a better eye on its own agents in these fields. The multiplication of participants in the national security policy network in Congress has been accompanied by measurable improvement in the performance of the prime committees, energized no doubt by the knowledge that their peers are in the audience. Formerly inaccessible chambers of the responsible congressional committees are now more frequently open to receive independent testimony from private authorities in addition to the execu-

tive commentary on which these committees have traditionally relied.

As these trends unfold, Congress has begun once more to
show a keen institutional self-consciousness. Within limits,
this new psychology must be welcomed as in keeping with the
constitutional traditions which predated the cold war, and as
prerequisite to healthy legislative behavior in any era. Respect
for the duties and prerogatives of the President must never
become contempt for those of Congress if the legislators are to
function positively and conscientiously. Though the distinct
proclivities of the House and Senate will continue to spawn
fierce disagreements between them, the shared sense of congressional responsibility to oversee executive conduct of foreign affairs augurs well for improved relations between the
two bodies. It should be increasingly difficult for a manipulative executive to resort to ploys designed to divide and conquer the members of Congress.

To a considerable extent the durability of these new patterns of behavior depends upon public opinion. Attentiveness
to American foreign policies has expanded markedly during
the Vietnam imbroglio, and the public disposition toward the
several branches of government has changed considerably. As
confidence in the President has waned, concerned citizens
increasingly have come to look upon Congress not with dis-
dain but with expectation. In assuming a larger role in American foreign policy, Congress is thus complying with a felt need
in the nation. No one perceives Congress as a savior, but many
demand that it be a safeguard against executive mistakes and
excesses. While great international crises will surely invite
public sentiment to rally around the President, it is reasonable
to assume that the larger political context in which both
Congress and the President function will continue to demand
an alert legislative posture in foreign policy. A growing fraction of members has won election by appeals to this very
demand and, by contrast with previous decades, many congressmen now have a vested interest in demonstrating their
active involvement in foreign affairs.

A great deal hinges, of course, on the complementary evolution of executive attitudes. So long as the President and the

President's men view Congress as a hostile presence, to be fended off or manipulated in the interest of an executive conception of the national interest, the prospects for meaningful collaboration between the branches are dim. The cooperative relationship between Congress and the President contemplated by the Constitution cannot survive condescension on the part of either partner. If the President and the bureaucracy lack a sense of their own fallibility and some appreciation of the values inherent in a genuine legislative-executive alliance, the nation is in deep trouble. A Congress treated as an adversary may well behave as one.

With the succession of Gerald Ford to the Presidency in August 1974, this perspective gained essential strength in the executive branch. At the same time, there was spreading disillusionment in some sectors of Congress with the continued personalization of foreign policy by Secretary Kissinger. His standing with Congress remained high, but skepticism about the consuming secrecy of his style and doubts about détente and other policy emphases placed Kissinger increasingly on the defensive. Perhaps the most remarkable illustration of this trend was the intense triangular negotiation among the Administration, the Soviet government, and Senator Henry Jackson regarding the latter's proposal to deny most-favored-nation treatment to the Russians until they relaxed their restrictions on Jewish emigration. Vital trade legislation remained hostage to the Jackson plan until, in an astonishing reversal of form, the Soviets quietly committed themselves to allow expanded emigration to Israel—a development immediately publicized by Senator Jackson in a press conference held in the White House itself. The Jackson amendment symbolized both the hopes and the hazards of a revived congressional role in foreign policy. It undoubtedly enhanced diplomacy in a difficult area of human rights, but it also threatened mutual paralysis of the two branches. When the Soviet Union ultimately repudiated the agreement, the Secretary of State was not slow in pointing out the hazards of congressional foreign policy-making.

Neither branch expects Congress to cope with the innumerable facets of daily diplomacy and policy, but both must understand that the function of the legislature is to insure broad-ranging debate of executive proposals and performance. This is the central lesson Vietnam has etched in the minds of congressmen. It is surely true that the two branches approach such debate with distinct political perspective and requirements, since an Administration may rise or fall according to its success in international affairs. Legislators, however, are seldom accountable to their electorates primarily in terms of foreign policy. Nevertheless, congressional review of foreign policy would be no more than a charade unless the President remains open to compromise and to rational adjustment of his plans in light of legislative expressions or preference or advice. The assumption of Olympian grandeur has no place in the conduct of democratic foreign policy.

Not long ago a former Assistant Secretary of State, lauding the effort by Congress to reclaim its role in foreign policy, complained that the legislators were fighting the right battles but that they never won. That is precisely the wrong approach, we submit, to the relationship between Congress and the President. That relationship is not a zero-sum game in which one side's loss is the other side's gain. Both sides can win or lose in proportion to the degree they recognize that they are *not* two sides but integral elements of the same government, elected to pursue the common interests of the American people. The turmoil between the branches, so evident of late, is likely to linger until both branches regain a proper respect for their interdependence. That respect cannot flourish either in the siege mentality of a beleaguered President or in the inferiority complex of an impotent Congress.

In moving to rejuvenate its powers, Congress has not thrown down the gauntlet. In most instances, it has extended a helping hand. On the President's acceptance or evasion of this proffered alliance hang the future harmony and effectiveness of American foreign policy.

Notes

1. According to *Congressional Quarterly* statistics.

The War and the American Military *

ADAM YARMOLINSKY

The most important fact about the war in Southeast Asia, for the U.S. military establishment, is that, despite military success with subordinate objectives, despite Presidential rhetoric to the contrary, and despite the fact that the war continued, we lost. The military is not accustomed to losing wars; the United States had not lost a war for 160 years, and this is the first American war in which necessary political constraints made it impossible to win.

It is a fundamental tenet of the military ethos that failure to accomplish an assigned task is an indication of personal (or organizational) inadequacy. The ingrained response of the professional soldier is: "Can do, sir." When he discovers that he cannot do, he is at first incredulous, then profoundly frustrated, and, in a major assignment, overcome with guilt and anger—in part because his second ingrained response is: "No excuse, sir."

* The author wishes to acknowledge, even where he departed from it, the very helpful advice and counsel of William W. Kaufmann and Colonel John W. Seigle.

216

All these feelings were exacerbated in the Vietnam situation by four circumstances: the enormous size and visibility of the military establishment; the obvious one-sidedness of a conflict between a small underdeveloped nation and the richest superpower; the political constraints imposed on the military; and the lack of general support for the war, even among those who were not part of the vigorous opposition to it. It was a war subject to two kinds of major constraints: external ones on tactics, territory, and rules of engagement; and internal ones on mobilization of reserves and deployment of forces. And it was a war fought in the absence of any general popular acceptance of the relevance of the war aims, however stated, to vital national interests. The initial public willingness to go along with a small war was increasingly dissipated just as public support became more important to the military. The constraints and the lack of general support might have relieved some of the military's guilt and frustration. Yet because of the "no excuse" philosophy, they only made them worse.

Feelings of guilt and frustration have been further exacerbated by the fact that in the post-Vietnam world, while the need for some kind of nonnuclear force (in addition to a nuclear deterrent) is generally acknowledged, there is very little agreement on what we need it for. Military men today cannot get their civilian leaders to tell them what they are supposed to be prepared to do.

Before speculating about postwar consequences, we need to examine what happened to the military during the war, internally and in its relations with other elements in government and society. And in order to understand the wartime changes, we need to go back even further, to the beginning of the 1960s, when military morale and military prestige were at their zenith. John Kennedy had come into office after a campaign in which he had attacked neglect of the military, warned of a developing missile gap, and condemned the previous Administration's reduction of nonnuclear capabilities. Abandonment of the doctrine of massive retaliation irked the Strategic Air Command and its partisans, but the successor McNamara Doctrine of flexible response gave new hope to all the other components of the military. The rhetoric of the Kennedy inaugural ("Let every nation know . . .") gave a major role to the military, and the first Kennedy budget amendments increased the means available to fill that role. Secretary McNamara's budgetary instructions from the President, to determine the budget necessary for military security without regard to arbitrary or predetermined ceilings, increased their sense of confidence—no other Cabinet officer received such instructions. The green beret of the Special Forces became almost as much a symbol of the New Frontier as the Peace Corps.

Then came the involvement in Vietnam, gradually deepening despite some initial military resistance, and alienating an increasing fraction of American and world public opinion. Because, unlike the situation in other wars, every step was taken with reluctance by the political authorities, inevitable conflicts developed in the mid- to late 1960s over the adequacy of military resources in Vietnam. And because this reluctance was accompanied by a general shift of priorities away from military spending (fed by disillusion with the war itself), resentment within the military establishment also deepened.

While the military might at least have been reconciled to a declining peacetime budget, its frustration over a war it could not win infected the general attitude toward what it saw as reduced budgets outside Vietnam. At the same time, what amounted to a crisis of confidence developed within the Army over the discovery that the Provost Marshal General had been misappropriating confiscated weapons, that there was a major scandal in the administration of service clubs and post exchanges, that troops were refusing to go into combat and were attacking their own officers with grenades, and that atrocities like My Lai were being concealed or ignored by senior officers who chose to conduct their private wars without bothering to inform the central command. All four services were caught in a wave of racial violence and in the rapid spread of the drug culture in the late 1960s. And all these things were projected on the family television screen, in the first modern war to be fought without formal censorship.

While the principal internal effect of Vietnam on the military has been sheer frustration at not being allowed to move unimpeded toward the goals publicly stated by at least two Presidents, an interesting side-effect is what Major Warren Clarke has characterized as "goal transference." In the absence of national goals from which military objectives could properly be derived, professional military men tended to rely on personal goals: career advancement, "ticket-punching," and experiencing the personal challenge of combat. But these limited goals necessarily tended to be subversive of larger group loyalties and of the spirit that holds military organizations together. "Duty, honor, country," is a triad in which all the pieces have to fit.

A secondary internal effect was to provide the physical and temporal setting for a significant breakdown of traditional behavioral standards in the enlisted ranks. Army "fraggings," primarily in Vietnam, rose from 0.4 per 1,000 in 1969 to 1.8 in 1971. In that year drug abuse reached epidemic proportions and racial conflict in the armed forces was prevalent.[1] Without more specific evidence, the incidence of drug abuse and race riots must be attributed as much to problems and changes in domestic society in the United States as to the war in Vietnam. Episodes of mass murder, rape, and killing of prisoners are endemic to a war involving enemy guerrilla forces and a population often unsympathetic to its presumed defenders, with whom it shares neither a common language nor a common racial identity. For the victims, the horror is permanent; for the institution that harbored the perpetrators, the unhappy consequences are also lasting.

It might be argued that there was some countervailing positive effect on military morale flowing from the fact that at least the military was doing the job for which it was trained. Clearly, the military bureaucracy gave weight, actually too much weight, to this fact when it adopted policies to maximize the opportunities for career officers to take Vietnam assignments, even at the expense, in some cases, of combat effectiveness. Clearly, also, Vietnam was a learning situation for the military, even if most of the lessons were negative: e.g., strategic bombing does not stop the guerrilla war machine of a less developed country; the traditional divisional structure is inappropriate for ground combat in such a war, etc.

The war was regarded by many professional military men as an occasion for the application and refinement of professional skills. But so pervasive was the disparity in military power between the United States and the Vietnamese (both North and South) and public concern about the justification for military action that the day-to-day conduct of the war was, from the military viewpoint, relentlessly politicized, much to the detriment of analytical professional attitudes. Conflict between U.S. military authorities interested in maximizing purely military objectives and U.S. civilian authorities committed to the "pacification" strategy (described, with unconscious irony, as "winning the hearts and minds of the Vietnamese people") was never resolved. Extravagant techniques were adopted, like saturation bombing with B-52s, or proposed, like the electronic fence (an alternative to the bombing only remotely possible but, if achievable, politically and perhaps morally preferable) out of an apparent sense of desperation. Despite the congenital expressions of optimism that emanated from the military, the Vietnam experience must have seemed almost as much a morass to them as it did to civilian society in the United States.

The important difference is that the military services were face to face with the enemy (when they saw him at all), and with the enormous disparity between the means of destruction available on each side. Reconnaissance by fire (using weapons fire rather than scouts to explore for the presence of enemy forces) may have been barred by the rules of engagement. But the fact remained that our side had the fire power to do it, and the other side, by and large, did not. A sledgehammer is a poor weapon to use against a fly; the more the flies swarm, the more frustrating it is for the wielder of the sledgehammer. And too often the military came to see their antagonists as more like flies than human beings.

The principal effect of Vietnam on the military's relations with society was to lower its prestige, at the same time that its size and potential influence were significantly increased. Nobody talked about a military-industrial complex in World War II or in the Korean War, and the phrase coined by General Eisenhower at the very end of his Administration only acquired general currency as the Vietnam crisis deepened.

The general identification of the military-industrial complex as a major factor in American society coincided with the development of an increasingly critical attitude toward the military, even within the congressional committees that had been the military's principal defenders. The criticism became skepticism and doubt, extending from the Vietnam involvement to the wisdom of particular military research and development efforts.[2] On college and university campuses, recruiters for military services and for civilian employment with military contractors were excluded; ROTC members learned not to wear their uniforms on the way to and from class; and the total number of participants in all three ROTC programs declined precipitously from 212,400 in 1968 to about 75,000 in 1973.[3]

A secondary effect on the military's relations with society is the extraordinary defensiveness of their spokesmen toward civilian audiences. Their rhetoric about the U.S. military may be the same as the rhetoric of the 1960s, but the tone is different. Criticism is anticipated even when it is not forthcoming. Even with an Administration that is significantly less critical of the military than were the Kennedy or Johnson Administrations (which sharply attacked organizational practices and procedures even while increasing military budgets), the defensiveness has been intensified. It is as if military leaders see themselves being held responsible for all the shortcomings of American society.

When one turns to the most important consequences of these events for the future, surely the first on the list must be the end of the draft. While this event might have occurred without Vietnam, the unpopularity of the war gave added emphasis to the drive to end conscription. The effect of the end of the draft, when coupled with the expected reduction (within the next five years) of the eighteen-year-old cohort and the increasing popularity of life-styles wholly at odds with military service, can be expected to make manpower ceilings rather than overall budget ceilings the determinative factor in the size and shape of the military establishment. Maintaining the present manpower levels may require greater pay and hence greater manpower budget increases than the Congress is willing to allow.[4]

Despite the temporary beneficial effects on recruiting of recession and very high youth unemployment, there are long-run concerns about significant shortfalls in recruiting[5] and renewed fears that quality standards may be compromised. Not only is the active military establishment likely to be substantially smaller, but it will probably include fewer and smaller active reserve units than could be maintained under the stimulus of selective service.[6] The National Guard will presumably remain as the major reserve resource. But even the Guard will be less and less capable of attracting and holding volunteers in a society that is increasingly mobile and atomized and where intensely local institutions like the Guard have a diminishing drawing power. It is perhaps paradoxical that one of Robert McNamara's few unsuccessful organizational efforts was to cut the reserves down to manageable units, so as to have a few high-priority units available for rapid mobilization instead of many low-priority units in a low state of readiness.

The military properly anticipates a significant reduction in manpower over the remainder of the decade—and perhaps some reduction in the quality of available manpower. It also fears a significant reduction in the pace of development of new weapons systems as a result of the shift in national priorities. Military attitudes here are the reverse of the attitudes of traditional liberals in civilian society. While liberals deplore the continued high levels of military spending, the military sees significant reductions as imminent. While liberals are concerned that under the cloak of ambiguous policy declarations, such as the Nixon Doctrine, an aggressive military presence will be maintained in the Third World, the military are worried that force structures will no longer be adequate to support even somewhat reduced United States commitments around the world.

Reduced purchasing power is a fixed consideration, and a major one, in military thinking about the post-Vietnam era as a period of contraction. Military spending has increased in absolute dollars over the past decade from $50.8 billion in fiscal 1964 (the last pre-Vietnam year) to $81.9 billion in fiscal 1975. If the 1975 figure were adjusted for the effects of inflation on military pay and price levels, however, it amounts to only $46.5 billion. Put another way, if you priced the 1964 force structure at 1975 prices and pay levels, it would cost $93.6 billion, or about $7 billion more than is expected to be available in fiscal 1975.[7] The reduction in purchasing power has resulted not only from the general effects of inflation, but also from the considerable cost of achieving pay comparability with the civilian economy, a policy initiated in 1964. The volunteer army continues to put additional pressure on pay levels, if force structures are to be maintained. Further, we are just entering the period when major existing weapons systems are beginning to wear out, and present plans call for replacement with more complex and expensive models. Unless they can squeeze out more budget dollars or learn to simplify as they modernize—and they show no signs of doing so—military planners see themselves as having to make do with fewer weapons. Lastly, a currently overofficered force sees manpower and budgetary stringencies producing a tidal wave of forced retirements.

Reactions within the military are varied. Some are reverting to the overt interservice rivalry of the 1950s. When the size of the pie seems to be fixed, it matters more how it is sliced. With the Secretary of Defense holding a looser rein, each separate service is shaping its strategies and its budget proposals with a view to maximum reliance—and maximum spending—on its own weapons and forces. It can be argued that the services never stopped pressing their parochial interests, but there was almost a decade in which they were primarily concerned with meeting the needs of actual conflict or were on the defensive because they were preoccupied with responding to questions and challenges of the Secretary of Defense and his staff. Changes in the budgetary process within the military establishment over the last four years have significantly increased the influence of the military services, and reduced proportionately the role of the Office of Secretary of Defense and particularly that of the Assistant Secretary for Systems Analysis, whose rank has now been reduced to a Director—a less prestigious position.

The prospect of scarcer resources has also sharpened internal conflict between the nuclear and nonnuclear force components. Expanding the number of nuclear warheads and "modernization" of strategic retaliatory forces have been given new life by the bargaining-counter theory of negotiation at the SALT talks, and by a certain restlessness within the Nixon and Ford Administrations with mere nuclear sufficiency and old-fashioned deterrence. This restlessness has expressed itself not in any specifically articulated alternative strategies, but rather in a generalized concern that the President should continue to have other (unspecified) options than responding to a nuclear attack by destroying the attacker's cities.

Higher costs and lower manpower ceilings revive the nuclear will-o'-the-wisp of "more bang for the buck," and elicit warnings from military spokesmen about the possibility of having to lower the nuclear threshhold—as if the threshhold at which the nation would be willing to invoke nuclear Armagedon could be consciously lowered by contingency planning—although changes in the structure and armament of the nuclear force can increase the likelihood of accidental or unplanned nuclear war. While contingency plans can be changed to call for earlier use of nuclear weapons, it is at least questionable whether changing them would have any practical effect in a situation in which the President had to decide whether and when to begin a nuclear war. The President's calculation of vital national interest is likely to be determinative, rather than any predetermined plan.

But spending for nuclear weapons can be increased, and here the Air Force is still pressing for a new strategic bomber and for placing MIRVs on all Minutemen, while the Navy is moving ahead on development of a new nuclear submarine fleet. And the Army is continuing to ask for, and to get, substantial research and development funding for the ABM.

At the same time, on the nonnuclear side of the ledger, the Air Force is pressing for new deep interdiction and air superiority aircraft, the Navy for more modern carrier task forces, and the Army for the R & D and the equipment for a more fully automated battlefield in the next limited war. Since the nonnuclear roles and missions involve a higher ratio of manpower to equipment, they are likely to be at some disadvantage in these debates. But their proponents can and do argue that there is an enormous range of contingencies in which nuclear forces are clearly irrelevant. The automated battlefield concept, still very much in the drawing-board stage, is particularly appealing to Defense Department planners because it involves limited (if highly skilled) manpower resources.

Another difference in military reactions to the post-Vietnam situation, particularly in the Army, is between those who seek a wider role and a broader justification for military spending in so-called domestic civic action (e.g., using engineer battalions to build roads in Appalachia, or helicopters to ferry automobile accident victims to the hospital), and those who are worried about dissipating energies required for military readiness. For soldiers concerned about the shift in priorities from national security to domestic problems, it is natural to ask why the military cannot play a broader domestic role, as it did in the Civilian Conservation Corps of the 1930s, and as it was originally intended to do in the Poverty Job Corps Program. But the military did not in fact get to play the role in the Job Corps that it played in the CCC, and for several good reasons: There was not that much military manpower to spare, and there was a good deal more popular resistance to the idea of military involvement with its way of doing things in any civilian activity—even before the Vietnam issue had mobilized antimilitary sentiment. Domestic civic action does not seem a way out of the military dilemma.

It seems reasonable to suppose that internal struggles over the allocation of relatively fixed budgets will be accompanied by a greater concern with internal matters generally, which cannot help but decrease the responsiveness of the military to foreign policy needs. A military worried about "roles and missions" will have less time and energy to think about its overall foreign policy mission. This introspection is the more likely as there are fewer "outsiders" in uniform, fewer men who are serving involuntarily. (The involuntary veterans of Vietnam would say that the "lifers" are taking over.) Many of the reforms instituted by Admiral Zumwalt in the Navy and General Forsythe in the Army to eliminate unnecessary and irksome "Mickey Mouse" discipline may survive. But a general tightening of discipline seems likely in the wake of the turbulence that characterized the Vietnam period and its immediate aftermath.

Racial conflicts, particularly acute in the military establishments of the late 1960s and early 1970s, may be abating since military service for blacks has become more truly voluntary. But the percentage of enlisted blacks in the basic military rank and file is likely to increase more than in the specialist and officer corps, as better qualified blacks find more attractive opportunities in civilian society.[8] In fact, a major problem may develop—and already has developed to some extent—in attracting and holding high quality officer and NCO/specialist manpower. Opportunities for advancement are diminishing visibly, and length of time in grade will stretch out inexorably along with the increasing prospects for forced retirement at mid-career.

The breakdown of discipline at all levels as a result of the Vietnam experience was inevitable. Men fighting a war that did not make sense to them or to a large and growing segment of world opinion would be particularly reluctant to risk injury or death. Yet the rules of engagement prescribed by the political circumstances of the war (and by moral imperatives as well) called on American soldiers to search a village instead of setting fire to it, to scout an area instead of saturating it with weapons fire, and not to molest prisoners even to get essential information out of them. When discipline is sporadically broken, enforcement becomes more rigid and more resented. Then there are fraggings, and some men or units turn their resentment against innocent bystanders, as in the My Lai incident. At the same time, senior officers who cannot reconcile their civilian superiors' public prononuncements with their orders take matters into their own hands, and we have private wars like General Lavelle's. When the war is over, the military reacts to the unhappy memory of all these events by turning to tighter, more formal discipline as a kind of reassurance that basic military values can be regenerated.

The military career may become less attractive also for the career officer in politico-military issues. The military establishment is not likely to remain an unchallenged champion in interdepartmental warfare. The Pentagon of the 1960s built a redoubtable reputation for getting there fastest with the mostest in the battles of the memorandum and the staff paper. That reputation will be severely tested in the years to come, even though the Pentagon will continue as by far the largest organization in the national security business, and the financial constraints that press on it are likely to press at least as heavily on the other national security agencies.

It remains to be seen how much of the policy role of the Secretary of Defense the NSC staff will assume, and particularly whether the Office of International Security Affairs, very much in eclipse during the first Nixon Administration, will be restored to anything like the position of influence it enjoyed during the 1960s. Paradoxically, that office conducted a more lively debate with the Joint Staff on politico-military issues than did its opposite numbers in the Kennedy and Johnson Department of State—but the nature of its competence tended to keep the focus in interdepartmental discussions on military issues and military solutions. The fusion of the jobs of Secretary of State and Assistant to the President for National Security Affairs—which may or may not survive the present incumbent—adds another unknown to the equation.

Still, the existence of an organization spending several tens of billions of dollars to maintain approximately 2 million men under arms is a formidable fact. The problem, for the next decade at least, is how that institution can contribute most usefully to American foreign policy as it emerges from the trauma of a minimally camouflaged defeat, in a war fought under political and military conditions that made conventional victory impossible.

The military has good grounds to resent its treatment by its civilian masters through the Vietnam years. It sinned as much as it was sinned against, in overoptimistic estimates of what it could accomplish (in strategic bombing, for example), in systematic underestimates of enemy strength, and in seemingly willful blindness to the political consequences of the military courses of action it recommended. Both military and civilian leaders need to remember the lessons of Vietnam, but they need also to put that experience behind them.

Yet the military can rightfully ask for better direction than it ever got in Vietnam—or than it seems likely to get in the near future. In some areas, the mission of the U.S. nuclear forces remains fairly simple to define, although there continues to be a good deal of argument about how to prepare for it. The NATO nonnuclear mission in Western Europe is relatively clear, if extremely improbable and not wholly believable to our European allies. In the rest of the world, however, it is unclear what military response, if any, the United States will make in a developing crisis.

In this situation, the military can legitimately ask: "How do you expect us to tell you what we need, when you can't tell us what we need it for? How do you expect us to have a sense of purpose, when we don't know what you want us to do? How can we be prepared to give you military advice, if you don't give us some policy direction? There are no easy answers to these questions. The first requirement for our civilian leadership is to admit that our present need for a nonnuclear military establishment (apart from NATO requirements) is based on uncertainty as to what may develop in the world, and how we may be called upon to use military force. Although the NATO requirements will probably drive the force structure for some time to come, they do not provide a rationale for possible military action in the Middle East, in Africa, or in Latin America.

After the civilian leadership has leveled with the military about its uncertainties, it needs to provide some reassurance that it is developing a clear and consistent philosophy for the use of military power. The best way to provide that reassurance is to be seen to be engaged in the task, and to consult with the military along the way.

The last requirement is that civilian leadership address promptly the question of structuring the military establishment in ways that make it as easy as possible to live with uncertainty. And that is not easy for an enormous, bureaucratic organization.

There are at least four ways in which the post-Vietnam military establishment can be made to work more effectively within the context of a United States foreign policy that is a good deal less sure of itself and a good deal less clear on its direction than it was in the 1960s: it must emphasize the maximum flexibility in the structure of the military establishment's nonnuclear component; it must further refine and strengthen civilian control; it must broaden the base of the professional and leadership corps within the military; and it must renew the resources of civilian scholarship that fed the mainstream of thinking about strategy and force structure in the 1960s.

The natural tendencies of organizations, at every level, is to get bigger and more complicated. The military is the biggest organization of all, and this tendency is already deeply ingrained. To reverse it will require enormous but essential effort. The effort was barely begun in the McNamara years, with an emphasis on readiness, mobility, and flexibility, on fewer and simpler weapons systems, on the Special Forces and the Strike Command. But in those years the United States still thought of itself as a global policeman, still maintained specialized forces oriented toward different parts of the world, still preserved (and still preserves today) elaborate divisional structures with enormous logistical tails, still duplicated (and still duplicates today) a wide range of civilian services in the military. The military must reexamine the relationship between current quality measures and actual job requirements;[9] and it must make a radical reassessment of the role of women in the armed forces and the range of job opportunities available to them. The process of simplification and rationalization needs to be carried a good deal further, and it will require close supervision by civilian leadership to ensure that it happens.

Civilian control is a function of vigorous political leadership, informed by a comprehensive and sophisticated management information system that surfaces the key issues for decision. These issues include not only the key budgetary decisions discussed above, but also questions of force structure and the planning and control of military operations. A good deal of the machinery developed for this purpose in the McNamara years has been rusting through disuse or has been dismantled. And that machinery was never fully adapted to exercising even the lesser degree of civilian supervision that is appropriate to operational decisions in the field, as distinguished from development and procurement decisions at home. The system worked reasonably well only for operations in crises of intense but limited duration like the Cuban missile crisis or a U.S.-Soviet confrontation on the Berlin *autobahn*. A better system would not have changed the result in Vietnam. It might have compelled earlier acceptance by civilian leadership of what was actually happening. It should help to reduce frustration within the military by ensuring that civilian political authorities and military professionals work from a common factual base. But without vigorous civilian leadership, the information will not reverse major decisions.

Persuasion is a key to increased civilian control. A military career has long been a career open to talent and a ladder for social mobility in the United States. Yet the pressures of the career itself have tended to isolate professional soldiers from the mainstream of American life. Students of military society in recent years have noted a tendency toward convergence between military and civilian life styles and attitudes. Military men tend to work in offices instead of command posts, and to live off the post in housing developments alongside civilian professionals. It has been pointed out that to a degree this convergence makes it more difficult for civilians to control an institution that will still pursue its own bureaucratic imperatives.

If the military is isolated from the rest of society, it can more easily be controlled by direct regulation (what Samuel Huntington refers to as "objective control").[10] But if military men work side by side with civilians in spelling out and carrying out sophisticated policy directions, civilian control rests much more on mutual understanding, and particularly on giving the military the civilian policy perspectives which, in our society, must ultimately be the determining ones. Particularly in

Vietnam, but generally throughout the world, military policy cannot be separated from its political and economic consequences. The civilian policy premises cannot all be spelled out in explicit detail (as the Eisenhower Administration attempted to do in the massive Basic National Security Policy, which the Kennedy Administration never rewrote but simply revoked). Military leaders need to have some implicit grasp of the policy intentions of their civilian masters, as the civilians need to understand the natural bent of the military bureaucracy.

To the extent that the tendency of the post-Vietnam military is to turn inward for mutual support, it must be countered by measures designed to broaden the perspectives of military professionals.

A number of measures would help. The ROTC units that have been phased out of colleges and universities, particularly the academically stronger institutions, should be reactivated. At a minimum, such institutions should participate in the creation and support of off-campus options, such as the network of Regional Officer Training Centers proposed by Professor Lawrence Radway. Concessions will undoubtedly be required on both sides, but, given reasonable good will, they can be managed.[11] The military academies should not be further expanded,[12] but their recruiting net should be thrown even more widely.

Promotion lists for flag officers should include nonacademy graduates on much the same basis that civilian promotion lists include disadvantaged minorities. New kinds of sabbatical and educational tours should be devised for officers at all levels. Unless war college curricula can be drastically revamped, more senior officers should be sent to civilian institutions for the equivalent of the war college year—a move that would involve a reversal of present directions.

The possibility of lateral entry for specialists into the officer corps should be seriously examined. The proposition is gradually being accepted that the military needs to open up more career lines to staff specialists who do not aspire to or qualify for combat command assignments. It is a logical corollary of this proposition that some of these staff specialists need not make their entire career in the military, and that they can as well make a later part of their career in uniform, as an earlier part.

None of these measures will be effective, however, unless pursued in a spirit of genuine concern for the welfare and morale of the uniformed establishment. Its members cannot respect the views of the civilian authorities unless they have a feeling of self-respect for their own institutions. This self-respect is not inconsistent with civilian control. If members of the military know that they are respected and valued for what they can do, then they can live with the principle that others should determine when and where they do it.

The structure of ideas with which the military moved into the age of nuclear weapons was largely put together by civilian strategists. The conceptual limitations on the usefulness of nuclear weapons are primarily a product of civilian thinking. The basic managerial concepts for budgeting and planning in very large organizations are similarly a civilian product. Many of the men who formulated the concepts had an opportunity to try them out in practice in the Pentagon of the 1960s (although the effectiveness of their development and procurement concepts is still very much in doubt). But the succeeding generations of civilian analysts have been focusing their efforts primarily on domestic problems, and there is far too little civilian scholarship dealing with basic military strategy for the 1970s and 1980s.

This gap is being filled to some extent by scholars in uniform, an increasing number of whom are producing doctoral dissertations and learned articles. But it is extraordinarily difficult for a man who is making his career in the military to achieve the perspective of a person whose career is in scholarship itself.[13] The questions facing the military and its civilian masters have no easy answers. They are just not amenable to technological or organizational quick fixes. To figure out what it means for the military that its nonnuclear role will be primarily constabulary, or primarily deterrent—or primarily unpredictable—is a task worthy of the best imaginations of our generation.

Notes

1. A follow-up study of Army drug users in Vietnam in 1972 found that nearly one-half of the enlisted veterans (aged twenty-eight and under), who had served during the peak of the heroin epidemic of 1971 (for which no official estimates are available) had tried narcotics at least once. (Lee Robins, "A Follow-up of Vietnam Drug Users," quoted in testimony by Assistant Secretary of Defense Richard Wilbur before the Subcommittee for Special Studies, Committee on Government Operations, June 28, 1973, p. 17.) Drug and alcohol addiction and race riots were not limited to or concentrated in U.S. forces stationed in Southeast Asia. According to the testimony of Assistant Secretary of Defense Richard Wilbur before the Subcommittee on Drug Abuse in the Military Services (September 20, 1973), Germany was considered a high-risk drug area, and in the month of October 1972, the percentage of identified drug abusers in Europe was slightly higher than in Vietnam, although both were under 3 per cent at that time.

2. A Gallup Poll survey (September 21-24, 1973) indicated that nearly half the Americans questioned felt that "too much" is being spent for defense, while 13 per cent responded "too little" and 30 per cent felt that spending was about right. Among those with college backgrounds, 51 per cent said that "too much" was spent, which was significantly higher than those respondents with less than college level education.

3. The number of institutions offering ROTC, however, was actually larger (291 in 1973) than it was during the period of peak enrollment (256 institutions in 1967), although a number of prestige institutions were still out of the program.

4. A recent report of The Brookings Institution estimated that average military pay will have increased by about 113 per cent during the period from FY 1968 to FY 1974. Nearly 70 per cent of this estimated increase was due to comparability pay legislation which preceded the inception of the volunteer army, while only 18 per cent was attributed to incentive pay for the volunteer service.

5. On the other hand, it should be noted that during the period of transition to an all-volunteer army, between 1970 and 1973, an

intensified recruitment campaign was initiated. From January 1971 to December 1972, there was a dramatic growth in "true volunteer" enlistments due in large measure to the special recruiting programs. Even in the most difficult recruiting area—ground combat forces—the average number of "true volunteers" increased from 1,200 per month in 1971 (January-June) to over 3,500 per month in 1972 (June-December). Total male enlistments between fiscal years 1971-73 (estimated) increased from 368,000 to nearly 420,000 respectively. ("All-Volunteer Armed Forces: Progress, Problems and Prospects," Martin Binkin and John D. Johnson, The Brookings Institution, May 1973, pp. 9, 10, 20.)

6. A large proportion of initial accessions volunteered for reserve forces in order to avoid conscription into active service. According to The Brookings Institute report, an estimated 70 per cent of the reserve recruits were draft-motivated in FY 1972. Along with the declining draft pressures in 1972, the number of applicants for enlistment into, for example, the Army National Guard, diminished from 100,000 in December 1969 to approximately 5,000 by December 1971. The total projected shortfall for FY 1974 is approximately 90,000, representing about 10 per cent of the needed reserve forces. (Binkin and Johnson, cited, pp. 29-30.)

7. I am indebted to Professor William Kaufmann for these calculations.

8. In the Army, for example, the percentage of blacks among the July 1973 recruits was 36.4 (the highest monthly percentage since the end of the draft); in August, 29.7. The August percentage is 16 per cent higher than the proportion of the U.S. male population between eighteen and thirty-five years of age represented by blacks, and 12 per cent higher than the black percentage of enlistees and draftees in the Army during the period from June to August 1972. It should be noted, however, that of the thirty-five educational institutions which, in the last six years, have established new ROTC programs, seven are predominantly black campuses. This reflects, in part, the intensive effort by the Pentagon to recruit black officers for the volunteer Army. (*New York Times*, October 25, 1973, p. 36.)

9. Further analysis may reveal that financial incentives to attract

men who score higher on some specific quality measures could be buying more quality than is necessary, and that concerns about shortfalls in certain skills may be satisfied by establishing more precise correlations between job performance and quality standards. (See further, Binkin and Johnson, cited, pp. 2-4, 27-29.)

10. Samuel P. Huntington, *The Soldier and the State* (Cambridge: Harvard University Press, Belknap Press, 1957), pp. 80-97.

11. Of the fourteen major campuses (including Harvard, Columbia, and Stanford) which terminated their ROTC programs because of faculty and student opposition in 1969, only Boston University has requested the reactivation of ROTC. It is interesting to note that the University of Massachusetts reversed its decision to withdraw academic credit for ROTC.

12. According to the National Association of State Universities and Land Grant Colleges, the "cost to taxpayers is at least six times more to commission an officer at the service academies than through ROTC programs at institutions of higher education." (National Association of State Universities, *Circular Letter No. 16*, Oct. 26, 1973, from Office of Executive Director, p. 7.)

13. But see further the radical proposals of Colonel Richard F. Rosser, USAF Ret., in *Foreign Policy*, no. 12 (Fall, 1973), pp. 156-75.

PART III

U.S. Policies and Practices Abroad

U.S. Security Policies

This section is on the substance of American policies in Indochina and elsewhere. The first three essays concern the security concepts that got us into Vietnam, and some concepts which might guide our security policies in the future.

Senator John Tower writes that it was an oversimplified and overly restrictive view of the basically sound concept of containment that led the United States into Vietnam and then to fight only a limited war. By believing that containment required reaction to any challenge anywhere, the United States became embroiled in Indochina. And by believing that containment should not mean creating instability in Communist areas, but merely preservation of the status quo, Washington adopted a restricted, gradualistic approach to the war that ruled out victory. But this does not mean, in Tower's view, that the basic idea of containment is wrong. He argues for a strong American sense of responsibility, and strong forces to back it up. "Containment should consist," he writes, "not only of a wall of allied nations circling our Communist competitors to prevent overt conventional military aggression, but also a willingness to compete economically, politically, and, if necessary, militarily in countries behind this wall to prevent subversion."

Earl Ravenal draws contrasting conclusions from the war. Dissecting the various "lessons" that seem to have been drawn from the war, he finds them all lacking. Given the "stickiness" of interventions when they have failed to achieve their purposes, he suggests that what is needed is a policy of "strategic disengagement." His argument is based on a "strategic" critique of the war that leads to "consistent nonintervention" except in rare, transcending cases. We should not cherish the illusion that we can continue to defend peripheral interests at less cost; rather, we should maintain a force structure (which he describes) designed only to protect our essential national security.

Ravenal's essay primarily concerns national interests and security goals; the argument of the next essay turns mainly on politics—bureaucratic and national, domestic and foreign. Reviewing likely and unlikely military threats to American interests, Ernest May writes that "the temptation is to regard the United States as relatively free from serious threats to its national security, and hence to conclude that military forces should have comparatively low priority in the allocation of resources." But, he suggests, political pressures in both the United States and the Soviet Union make strong reliance on arms control agreements as a future means of cutting defense expenditures unsound. And, in any case, "a prudent military policy involves sustained preparedness; anything less presents the danger that the people and the Congress will at some later date see the nation as having been left naked." This could set off "a massive new wave of weapons-buying. We all would be the poorer for it," May concludes.

Senator John Tower (R., Texas) is Chairman of the Senate Republican Policy Committee and a member of the Senate Armed Services Committee. He was chairman of the Platform Subcommittee on National Security and Foreign Policy at the Republican National Convention in 1972. He taught political science and government for nine years at Midwestern University, Wichita Falls, Texas. Senator Tower is in his third term in the Senate.

Earl C. Ravenal was Director of the Asian Division (Systems Analysis) in the Office of the Secretary of Defense from 1967 to 1969, was a Fellow of the Woodrow Wilson International Center for Scholars and the Institute for Policy Studies, and is now Adjunct Professor at The Johns Hopkins School of Advanced International Studies. He is coauthor and editor of *Peace with China? U.S. Decisions for Asia*, and author of the forthcoming book, *Beyond the Balance of Power: Foreign Policy and International Order*.

Ernest R. May is a Professor of History at Harvard University. He was Dean of Harvard College from 1969 to 1971, and Director of the Institute of Politics, from 1971 to 1974. His most recent book is *"Lessons" of the Past: The Use and Misuse of History in American Foreign Policy*.

Foreign Policy for the Seventies

JOHN G. TOWER

The war in Indochina was but a violent manifestation of the policies of containment and balance of power that guided Soviet-American relations throughout the 1950s and 1960s. Several factors influenced the American foreign policy that produced Vietnam.

Principal among these factors was the disassembly, after World War II, of the great colonial empires of France and Great Britain. Weakened by the war, these central governments could no longer maintain power over their colonies. Faced by growing nationalism in the colonies, England saw the future and slowly retreated. France, plagued with growing restiveness and revolution, fought in Algeria and in Vietnam to restore the grandeur that was once hers. But her struggle was futile, and it seemed to some that the war not only had crushed Nazi Germany but also dealt a mortal blow to the crumbling "free world."

Only a disarmed America stood in the path of the Communist onslaught. Our eyes and compassion turned toward Europe. With the Marshall Plan the United States began to rebuild the destruction of war and to strengthen its allies in the struggle against communism. We aided Greece, which was threatened by Communists in a bloody civil war. But as we built the European wall of containment, the Pacific fell apart. Our ally China was lost to the Communists. South Korea threw back a Communist invasion only with the efforts of the United States and its allies. The Communists' war in Indochina divided Vietnam and laid Laos under siege. Indonesia, wooed by the East, turned its back on us.

American, rearmed because of the Korean War, recognized that only through its efforts could the Red tide be turned. The United States shouldered the burden that had bowed England and France. It was clear that the Communists were intent upon ruling the world and that the path they had chosen to that throne lay through the underdeveloped nations of Asia. America looked from Europe to the Far East.

Several concepts guided the formulation of American foreign policy in the post-World War II period, and a basic understanding of the differences among them is essential for the more detailed discussion to follow. The most important concept is containment. As it came to be enunciated, containment meant prevention of the expansion of Communist influence, though a broader interpretation could have included the active attempt to throw back Communists in the world struggle. Containment is a general philosophy; war, diplomacy, or economic pressures can be used in its support.

Another concept important to understanding American foreign policy is limited war. All wars, thus far, have to a certain extent been limited. But some have been more limited than others. So the concept is really a continuous rather than a discrete one. The limitations of limited war are both on the types of weaponry used and on the geographic expanse over which the conflict is waged.

A different way of categorizing war is by the use of the concepts of guerrilla, conventional, and nuclear war. These concepts are more discrete than that of limited war, but there is nevertheless a gray area between the weaponry used in guerrilla and that used in conventional war. The distinctions among guerrilla, conventional, and nuclear wars are mainly ones of weaponry and tactics, but not necessarily geographic expanse.

A final concept necessary for discussing American foreign

policy is gradualism. It deals simply with the speed at which the fighting is escalated or de-escalated. Essentially, gradualism describes how quickly a limited war becomes less limited.

It should be understood that these are all truly separate and distinct concepts. There have been limited wars of containment (Korea, Vietnam), but there can also be limited wars of aggression. War is but one tool of containment; that goal can also be attained through diplomatic or economic pressure. While we normally think of limited war as nonnuclear, it is possible to have limited nuclear war, both geographically and in the sense that only certain types or sizes of nuclear weapons are used.

The main principle that had guided American national security policy through the twentieth century was that the defense of the United States must take place as far from our shores as possible. It mattered not that the Communists lacked the ability and perhaps the desire to invade our country. In the minds of most Americans, the threat was as real as if the Chinese, Koreans, and Vietnamese were wading ashore in California.

The policy of containment is basically a sound one. If a war must be fought, it would, in self-interest, better be fought on foreign soil and best on enemy soil. Also, to relinquish lands would be to relinquish resources—men and matériel that would sorely be needed in the struggle against Soviet Sputnik technology and Chinese Communist hordes. But the concept of containment was oversimplified. Every nation in the "free world" was a vital link in the chain around communism. Every nation in that chain was worth fighting over. The idea that there might be a price too high to pay, a burden too great to bear was foreign to our concept of containment; for, in its oversimplified form, to lose one link in the chain was to lose the chain itself. The dam would break, we would all drown in the flood of communism that would burst forth. It was, in fact, this oversimplification of the principle of containment that, when combined with a restrictive interpretation of that concept, governed our involvement in Vietnam.

This restrictive interpretation of containment, in essence, meant a prevention of Communist expansion, which in turn was taken to mean maintenance of stability, the status quo. Creation of instability in Communist countries was perceived as outside the realm of our policy and as dangerous; thus, active measures to regain more territory than was lost, i.e., in Korea or Vietnam, or in Hungary or Poland, was deemed undesirable. In its quest to paint Communists as bent upon world domination, America passed by opportunities to throw back communism—opportunities which certainly her enemies would not have overlooked.

This narrow interpretation of the policy of containment had its effect, in time, upon the military strategies that were chosen in violent confrontations with the Communists. In the Korean War, U.S. troops were allowed to strike back into North Korea, but military action against the Chinese Communist homeland was prohibited. In Vietnam, even the opportunity to carry the war on the ground to North Vietnam was denied, though it was eventually recognized by the civilian hierarchy that prosecution of the conflict in Cambodian and Laotian sanctuaries would save friendly lives and possibly the future of the Republic of Vietnam as well.

Some have compared, inaccurately, this narrow interpretation of containment with the concept of limited war. However, there is a difference between the two. In essence, the limitations imposed by the theory of containment rule out the aggressive use of military power, particularly to gain new lands or nations for the "free world." The limitations imposed by the concept of limited war, on the other hand, include the type of weaponry to be utilized and the geographic expanse of the fighting. It would be possible, therefore, to have a limited war of aggression.

The oversimplification of the theory of containment contributed in significant measure to our deepening involvement in the Vietnam war because the importance of Vietnam to the worldwide struggle was overemphasized. And a narrow interpretation of containment prevented the invasion of North Vietnam, which in all probability would have ended the war favorably. However, there are other factors to consider. First among these was the choice of limited war, which in this case meant restricting the spectrum of weaponry to be utilized.

The policy of gradualism also guided both our entry into and exit from Indochina.

The concept of limited war, as it was used by those leaders making decisions early in the Vietnam conflict, was basically a nonnuclear, conventional military war of containment. It did not allow for striking at the North Vietnamese homeland, except by air. This exception was possibly due more to the strong insistence by the Air Force that it could make a significant contribution to the effort through selected application of strategic conventional bombing than to any real belief on the part of civilian decision-makers that such bombing would indeed be useful. In fact, the bombing was the first bargaining chip to be tossed in, to get negotiations under way. There was, undoubtedly, the philosophy of "guns and butter" running through the early decisions on the war, so if there was a little waste in such a *limited* strategic bombing campaign, it could be excused. At least, they thought so.

As important as the fact that Vietnam was a limited war of containment is the fact that it was a *conventional* war of containment. It could have been a limited nuclear war. Or, more importantly, our leaders could have, and should have, recognized earlier the significance of political and economic factors to our eventual victory.

It has been argued by some that through the use of nuclear weapons the war would have been over within a matter of days. Of course, no one can know for sure, but that is probably not an accurate assessment of the situation. True, Hanoi, Haiphong, other cities and choke points on the lines of communications could easily have been destroyed. But without destroying the will of the enemy to fight, the war could have gone on. After all, Vietnam was, with the exception of the Tet offensive and the North Vietnamese invasions of 1972 and 1975, basically a guerrilla war, utilizing small arms, requiring only the support of the people and local food supplies. Nuclear war would have destroyed North Vietnamese industry; but without either destroying their will to fight or annihilating the population (which would have required the massive use of nuclear weapons on what was essentially a rural society), such a war would likely have been a futile effort and a dangerous precedent.

Instead of escalating the war, greater economies, i.e., a more "cost-effective" war, could have been achieved through selected use of conventional military power coupled with responses to the political and economic wars being waged by the Vietcong and North Vietnamese. It is clear that the significant gains made in pacification came after we began placing greater emphasis, in 1965 and again in 1969, on improvement of the rural and popular forces. Though it was necessary to push VC /NVA main force elements back into unpopulated areas for this growth of progovernment militia to take root, it is nevertheless true that the weakening of those main force units was due not to the large-scale sweeps and massive use of air power on search-and-destroy missions, but rather to the costly failure of the Tet offensive in 1968. Obviously, it was that same conventional firepower that broke the Communist's back in the Tet offensive and in the spring offensive in 1972. But the difference between those operations and search-and-destroy missions was that in the Tet offensive we knew where the enemy was and he stayed there. It seemed as though in the jungle we could seldom find the enemy, or, once found, he could never be forced to stay and fight, thus subjecting himself to that terrific firepower.

It is true that toward the end of the war the United States improved the technology to overcome some of these deficiencies—lasar-guided bombs for pinpoint targets, electronic sensors to find the enemy, and gunships to haunt him even at night on the Ho Chi Minh Trail. But the point remains that the thinking of our national leaders, military and civilian, led us into a conventional war against guerrilla fighters. And this choice meant that we were to mark time for nearly four years after massive involvement of American forces before making any significant advances in pacification.

The policy of containment spurred our original involvement in Indochina. Our interpretation of that policy and the concept of limited war guided our military actions there. But once there, additional reasons for our staying in Vietnam appeared or were created. Probably the most important—at least in terms of persuading wavering supporters of U.S. policy—was the effect a precipitous withdrawal would have on our allies. Clearly, this consideration had no influence on our initial involvement in Indochina, for in those years it was unthinkable that America would willingly relinquish territory to the Communists. But as some began to think the unthinkable, it became necessary to point out that the rest of the world, allies as well as enemies, were watching the American performance in Vietnam.

Cable traffic not made public as well as recent public statements by Asian leaders support the contention that our allies were concerned that the United States might make such a precipitous withdrawal. Certainly the impact of our actions has been watched most closely in Southeast Asia, but there is no doubt that the ripples have been felt in Europe and the rest of Asia. The fear exists that a growing neo-isolationism in America will result in commitments of questionable reliability all over the globe. The credibility of our commitments to other nations has therefore been compromised by congressional nonsupport of South Vietnam and Cambodia.

Some observers thought our performance in Vietnam would have little effect on other countries. But the long history of American involvement produced a reverse domino effect. Indonesia overthrew its pro-Communist regime as it became clear that the United States was still going to maintain an interest in Southeast Asia. Had South Vietnam fallen earlier to the Communists, it is improbable that the overthrow of Sukarno would have taken place. As America deepened its commitment to and involvement in Vietnam, Cambodia remained "neutral" despite strong pressures to support openly the Communists. But as events unfolded, the Cambodians finally deposed Sihanouk and moved against the Vietcong and North Vietnamese. Now, with South Vietnam taken by the Communists, we will see the dominoes begin to fall back toward us. Thailand has already asked that American troops be withdrawn. The Philippine President has openly questioned the wisdom of allowing U.S. bases to continue in operation there. Naturally, these actions do not necessarily mean that Thailand or the Philippines are going to go Communist. But they do mean a perceptible shift away from our camp.

Thus, the role which we played in the Vietnam problem has been judged by world leaders. To those who realized the importance of maintaining our alliances, this became a persuasive argument indeed for patience and care in *how* we ended our participation in the war, and for continued levels of military assistance sufficient to meet Communist pressure.

Yet the basic policies of containment, limited war and gradualism, that marked American involvement have all fallen into some disrepute. Since the beginning of Vietnam, Cuba has gone Communist; Egypt and now Syria have flirted with the Soviet camp; and Third World nations ally themselves with Chinese Communists. That the policy of containment has lost its popularity has probably been more a result of détente and weariness with the cold war than of Vietnam.

This is unfortunate, for in a very broad sense the policy of containment is a sound one. But rather than thinking of containment as simply a wall of allies built around the Communists, it should mean the denial of all resources in the long-term, worldwide struggle. To believe that détente means an end to the competition for people's minds is to ignore the fact that the struggle is multifaceted, that we are currently in an economic competition against the Soviets. To ignore the economic and political challenges presented us by the Soviets over the next years would make futile the sacrifices we have made over the last two decades in defense of the "free world."

Containment should consist, then, not only of a wall of allied nations circling our Communist competitors to prevent overt conventional military aggression, but also a willingness to compete economically, politically, and, if necessary, militarily in countries behind this wall to prevent subversion.

At the time of our entry into Indochina, the concepts of limited war and gradualism already had opponents, both in uniform and in the more conservative members of Congress. Remembering Korea, they supported the use of nuclear weapons, the invasion of North Vietnam, and an immediate overwhelming application of military power. It seems as though no matter what step the United States took, it was too little or too late. In the end, a massive bombing campaign in the heartland of North Vietnam finally forced the signature of a "peace agreement," but what would the same bombing have gotten us eight years earlier? Would the Ho Chi Minh Trail have even mattered, much less grown larger, if the United States had invaded North Vietnam in 1965?

Of course, such speculation is problematical. Would the North Vietnamese have conducted a guerrilla war on their own ground had we invaded? Would the Soviet Union or Communist China have responded with nuclear weapons if we had initiated such use? Could the South Vietnamese have held out against the Vietcong while the United States was occupied in a North Vietnamese invasion? Despite these unanswerable questions, the vast portion of American military experts and the majority of conservative elected officials have become disenchanted with the concept of both limited war and gradualism.

Perhaps a more publicized foreign policy change that came from the Vietnam war is the Nixon Doctrine. In brief, the Doctrine states that American ground troops will no longer fight another country's wars. The United States will continue to provide a strategic umbrella as protection against nuclear blackmail. It will continue to provide resources, matériel, and the training to utilize weapons, but no significant numbers of troops. In certain cases, the United States will provide sophisticated weaponry and the troops to man it. Regional alliances are encouraged under the Doctrine, presumably to allow countries in a region to send troops to their allies under attack so that the United States would not have to. But America is no longer to be the world's policeman.

Still, there is one important caveat to the Nixon Doctrine. It does not apply to Europe. We continue to furnish ground troops to NATO; about a third of our divisions are stationed there. Air and naval units are likewise devoted to Europe. This exception is a recognition that vital American interests are integrally linked to Western European security, that a slippage of those countries into the Soviet camp would be so disastrous as to warrant direct American involvement there.

The Doctrine guided our actions in the latter part of the war. Its implementation was the Vietnamization program, in which the South Vietnamese forces, particularly the militia, were expanded, retrained, and equipped with modern weapons. The American bombing program was simply the provision of sophisticated weaponry that our South Vietnamese allies lacked the technically qualified personnel to run. Such bombing was well within the concept of the Nixon Doctrine.

The war can be divided into two basic periods, each characterized by different perceptions of the world, each managed by different strategies. Our leadership through the late 1960s was guided by a perception of the Communist world as overtly aggressive, intent upon world domination by military force. The policy of containment was the reason for American entry into Vietnam. The concepts of limited conventional war and gradualism guided our military actions there through the 1960s.

But our perceptions of the Communist world slowly changed throughout the war, that change culminating in the Nixon Doctrine. We began to view the Communists as fragmented, but nevertheless saw the fragments as being potentially hostile. We recognized that Communist adventurism was as likely to take the form of economic, political or guerrilla action against the "free world" as overt attack. And perhaps, most importantly, we realized the pitfalls that exist when we fight for an ally who lacks the motivation to defend himself. These changed perceptions of the enemy and of our allies were reflected in the Vietnamization program that guided our military activities toward the end of the war.

Future American Foreign Policy

Foreign policy is nearly always an imperfect response to the reality of international relations. It is imperfect not only because human beings make it, but also because policy is nearly always less flexible, and therefore less current, than the real world.

Vietnam crystallized the evolution of foreign-policy thinking that had been going on through the latter half of the 1960s. But the changes in the world that brought about that metamorphosis of foreign policy are still occurring, and new ones have surfaced which have even broader implications for the future of America's relations with its allies and adversaries.

Principal among these changes is the growth of two new power centers, Europe and Japan, and the possible emergence of a fifth one, the People's Republic of China. In the 1950s, our policy was containment through collective security agreements and heavy reliance upon American military forces rather than indigenous forces. Europe and Japan were still recovering from the devastation of World War II. They had little money to devote to defense and the case of Japan little desire as well.

But both Western Europe and Japan have emerged as industrial giants. The American dollar has been devalued, and jokes about cheap Japanese goods have lost their humor as American companies battle a flood of Japanese automobiles, television sets, and other quality products. While the United States contributes somewhere between $8 billion and $17 billion a year to defend its interests in Europe, the Europeans pay about $35 billion. (The $8 billion figure represents those forces actually in Europe; the $17 billion is for all forces earmarked for NATO defense, many of which are U.S.-based.) The economic balance has obviously changed; the United States no longer possesses an economy that is technologically superior or more vibrant. Since a nation's ability to support a military force can be measured in large part by its economy, this means that Western Europe and Japan must be reckoned with, by any prudent defense planner, as potential major military powers in the late 1970s and beyond.

The United States continues to possess the major nuclear arsenal in the "free world." It will probably not be challenged by either Western Europe or Japan for that predominance, though Britain has a handful of POLARIS-type submarines and France is developing a modest, domestically produced, nuclear strike force. This means that throughout the 1970s both Western Europe and Japan will probably continue to have to rely upon the American nuclear shield against a strategic threat from the Communist world. But rocket-rattling seems to occur more often nowadays across the Sino-

Soviet border than over the polar cap, and it is not yet clear what effect détente will have upon our allies' perceptions of the Communist threat. It is possible, then, that at least one element of the Nixon Doctrine can be applied to our relations with the two new superpowers: that the United States will continue to provide nuclear protection against intimidation by hostile nuclear nations.

However, for the time being at least, it is difficult to predict whether American troops will continue to be deployed in Europe and in support of our Asian strategy. Further congressional action seems likely, but the precise form of such action is unpredictable.

This raises another major effect Vietnam will apparently have on our foreign relations. The deep schism that developed between Congress and the executive branch as a result of the war fostered a desire on the part of the former, particularly the Senate, to take legislative action in what is essentially the purview of the executive. This willingness to interfere with the President's conduct of foreign policy will probably persist throughout the 1970s and could easily force an unwise application to Europe of that element of the Nixon Doctrine dealing with troop withdrawal. Such troop withdrawals would probably result in force-level reductions since withdrawals alone would not save money. This could happen in spite of the fact that the current manpower levels are the lowest since the Korean War. Troop-level reductions, without mutual, balanced reductions by the Soviets, would seriously endanger, if not neutralize, our conventional deterrent, and return us to the trip-wire strategy of the 1950s. It should be obvious that in a period of growing American strategic nuclear inferiority such a strategy is simply not credible.

Yet, the appeal of the Doctrine is very strong: Let these two emerging superpowers, Europe and Japan, furnish the manpower for their own defense, while we furnish sophisticated combat support and nuclear protection. The temptation will exist even among cooler minds to forget that American troops are deployed to Europe and American vessels ply the oceans not out of pure altruism, but to protect American interests.

A third major element of the Nixon Doctrine, in addition to

guidelines on nuclear protection and ground troops, is the provision of sophisticated combat support to allies. The support includes advanced aircraft, such as the F-111, tactical nuclear weapons, electronic sensors and communications equipment, and other technologically superior matériel, upon which the United States holds the lead. It is unlikely that within the next several years either Western Europe or Japan will attempt to become self-sufficient in this kind of weaponry, though this is probably more due to desire than to a lack of the necessary technological base. But should Congress take precipitous action against our existing commitments with NATO and Japan, these allies would be forced either to make separate accommodations with the Communist world or begin to produce on their own the expensive technologically advanced combat support that is essential to modern armies.

The Nixon Doctrine was not promulgated with Europe in mind. It was to be essentially an Asian doctrine. But because it touches so many nerve endings grown increasinly sensitive in the 1960s, the danger exists that Congress, knowingly or unknowingly, will force its application to Europe. Vietnam would have then left its most damaging mark on American foreign policy for the 1970s—a kiss of death for our national security.

The Communist monolith no longer exists. Nevertheless, the desire on the part of both the Soviet Union and the People's Republic of China is still the aggressive expansion of their influence. This may come through overt military aggression, political propaganda, armed subversion, or economic pressure. But the United States, as long as it continues to value freedom and independence, must be prepared to meet those threats wherever they arise. Détente does not solve the differences that exist between the Communists and the "free world." It will not end the struggle between these two ideologies. Nor does the existence of two competing forms of the Communist ideology, with the potential emergence of the Chinese Communists as a superpower, negate this threat.

The presence of the United Nations in the world is not a deterrent to Communist expansion. That body is powerless to prevent aggression or subversion by superpowers such as the

Soviet Union. The grand hopes which we held for the United Nations at its beginning have crumbled under the weight of its powerlessness. And it will continue to be crippled by its impotence until some as yet unknown disaster forces mankind toward a more collective effort in the solution of its problems. We can, therefore, count on no aid from this body in our effort to prevent the conquest of mankind by aggression and subversion.

This responsibility, then, must remain on our shoulders and those of our allies. To force Western Europe and Japan to go their own way in defense would be to invite the fragmentation that would weaken the "free world" and facilitate, even encourage, Communist expansionist efforts. We must, of course, ask our friends to bear an increasing share of the defense of freedom as their economies grow stronger, but we must never forget that the economy of the United States and the welfare of the American worker are integrally related to the security of American interests overseas—to markets and to sources of raw materials processed by its industries.

The more vocal elements of American public opinion and congressional representation of those elements are likely to be the major constraints on the fulfillment of our commitments overseas. Rising costs for manpower, procurement of weapons and equipment, and research will pose momentary problems for defense planners, but they are not insurmountable. Only as rising costs contribute to the arguments of isolationists for withdrawal will they hinder protection of American interests. Those arguments will span a variety of issues, many of marginal relevance. We can only hope that the traditional strength of the American system will sustain the military posture that has kept the world peace and deterred major aggression over the past quarter-century.

The Strategic Lessons of Vietnam

EARL C. RAVENAL

Five Types of Lesson

Reflections on the American experience in Vietnam have precipitated a more general examination of the nation's posture of military intervention. We can distinguish and formulate the various kinds of "lessons" of Vietnam—lessons *from*, not just about, Vietnam—that figure in the debate about the role of the United States in the world.

If the lessons of Vietnam were obvious, they would have been settled long ago, with much greater economy of means and words, and with a good deal less heat. The extent and irresolution of the debate indicate that there must be something about the structure of the problem that is not entirely simple. In fact, it involves some elusive and disputed points that run very deep in the analysis of historical cases: the "meaning" of history; and the nature of strategic choice. I intend to confront both problems in order to explicate the strategic lessons of American intervention in Vietnam. I will propose some "lessons about lessons," attempting to say some generally meaningful and immediately relevant things about the use of historical analogy.

If lessons were only a matter of coming up with a few criteria for improving effectiveness, restricting intervention, limiting defense expenditures, or practicing morality, then the task could be simply an exercise of opinion, apology, or sheer preference. But what matters more is how the Vietnam experience has actually affected the attitudes of the American people, certain key groups, and the national leadership; and what Vietnam demonstrates about the environment in which these attitudes will be exercised in the future. This implies an understanding—a model—of the policy *process*: a scheme of determinants, intermediate terms, and ultimate effects that will support some conclusions about the adaptation of the nation's security structures, the metamorphosis of the civil-military relationship, and the evolution of foreign policy.

There are five types of critiques that could be made of Vietnam. The first four have in fact been made and characterize and inform the thinking of certain groups of Americans. I arrange and label them as follows: the instrumental, the consequential, the fundamental, and the proportional. I intend here to criticize each of these critiques as misleading, inadequate, or merely partial and incomplete.

Of course, no classification has more than a transient and relative validity. These lessons are really constructs—syndromes of attitudes held by various groupings. Nor are they even mutually exclusive. For example, the same individual critic can harbor "fundamental" objections to the tendencies of American diplomacy, along with the elements of a naïve "consequential" critique (that savings from the defense budget translate automatically into commitments to domestic welfare). Or one could subscribe to the "proportional" thesis, that the nation's interests in Southeast Asia were not worth (so) much, and at the same time to the "instrumental" conclusion, that, if the job could have been done with a few divisions in a couple of months (as Robert Kennedy once impatiently suggested in the early 1960s), then such an excursion might be validly made. But the classification is "operational": that is, it represents the various criticisms of Vietnam, intervention, and the American military posture in terms that imply *differences* in alternative or corrective policies.

The fifth kind of critique would be my preferred prescription. I propose the notion of "strategic" lessons—the kind which, in their structural depth and appropriate generality, *ought* to be drawn from the American experience in Vietnam. In connection with the strategic lessons of Vietnam, I will suggest the need for a set of noninterventionist "presumptions" and a restricted definition of the requisites of national security, and will sketch an illustrative force structure to implement these requisites. The revised force structure itself could be seen as a tangible lesson of Vietnam. But that would not be valid. After all, the tendency of the Nixon Doctrine has been toward a lower conventional force structure. But in the light of our continuing commitments, it is a pseudo-strategic shift that might simply change the modalities or even prejudice the success of future interventions, which remain just as likely. It is in this respect that strategic lessons differ from merely "instrumental" lessons, including the Nixon Doctrine, which might have already resulted from retrospection on Vietnam. Strategic lessons would go to the heart of the policy process; they would represent a reorientation so pervasive that our likely response to future strategic challenges, as well as to those present instrumentalities—alliances, commitments— that obligate or dispose us to future interventions, would be quite different. This strategic adjustment, if ever achieved, might be the result of a long, patient diplomatic journey. But only when we, as a nation, had achieved it, might we say that we had truly learned the lessons of Vietnam.

Lessons About Lessons

Many observers fear that the experience of Vietnam has been so pre-emptive that America might have lost its capacity to wage an active, responsible foreign policy. But this fear is misplaced. Rather, I would judge that most of the conclusions drawn from the Vietnam experience have been so qualified and so particularized that they amount to the unexceptionable resolution that we should not fight Vietnam over again. Indeed, it is ironic that some of those observers who are most articulate in condemning Vietnam are also most reluctant to draw sufficiently general conclusions from that experience. So it is worth taking some time to analyze the notion of lessons. If lessons are to be useful and reliable, if they are not to be simply discrete point *judgments* about a single unreplicable past event or series of events, then they must meet certain requirements: (a) They must be *projective*—forward-looking, with the future as their time reference. (b) They must be *general*, or more accurately, generic. An event (such as Vietnam) is an instance of some more general principle; thus, its lessons will have a certain scope of application. Furthermore, (c) it is important that lessons be applicable to *collectives*—that they imply actions that a complex entity such as a nation-state can structure itself to do, rather reliably or consistently, as matters of policy. And (d) lessons must be *appropriate* to the activity that gave rise to them. In the present case they must be "strategic," in two senses: they must apply to defense preparations, security commitments, intervention, and war; and they must focus on the process of strategic choice. Finally, (e) lessons are not lessons unless they are *learned*. This is far from an obvious proposition. The learning of a collective, such as a nation, is very different from the learning of an individual. This implies that lessons must be internalized or institutionalized in some enduring, objective, and therefore predictable way.

If we look at lessons in this rather complex and structured way, it is apparent that the lessons of Vietnam are far from settled. There are several reasons for this: One is that the coalition—or coalescence—that brought pressures on our government to move toward a quicker termination of the war, whether by negotiation, coercive escalation, or unilateral withdrawal, was not a true consensus. It was a patchwork of motives, perceptions, and values. The pressures of this diverse and unstable anti-Vietnam coalition foreclosed certain options to our government and forced an indecisive and thus inconclusive end to the war. Moreover, this temporary and fragile coalition has already been fractured. Consequently, its impact on future national strategic choices is not clear; in fact, the various meanings of "no more Vietnams," in future circumstances, might even be contradictory in their implications.

The second reason for the indeterminacy of the lessons of Vietnam is that the war endured so long that several sets of rationales, or premises, were literally shot out from under the same ongoing action: (a) we may have initiated our intervention in a last attempt at implementing *collective security*; (b) the war evolved into an exercise in *bipolar confrontation* where the "real" adversary was China, operating through the proxies of North Vietnam and the Vietcong; (c) with the accession of Nixon and Kissinger, the war became something else: an exercise in the *balance of power*. This rationale requires a less definitive conclusion than the previous ones; even a tenuous stalemate, a perpetual equilibrium, based on continuing contention, would "successfully" implement this mode of international political conduct. A final settlement would not be necessary. Moreover, in the balance-of-power reading of Vietnam, the "real" adversary became, once again (though in a different sense), a major Communist power, the Soviet Union—not simply because the Soviets happened to be the bankers of the last North Vietnamese offensive of April 1973, but because the Soviets were the only significant "objective" challengers, the captive and impressionable pupils of a decisive American response, or the inescapable beneficiaries of a local failure on our part. By frustrating various challengers and implicit beneficiaries, we teach them, as well as all bystanders, the rules of the new international political-military game. And in this *sense*, it could be argued that we achieved a degree of success in Vietnam, whatever might eventually happen to the elusive truce, to the government in Saigon, to the other nations of Indochina, and to the general situation in Southeast Asia.

The Nature of Policy Choice

Meanwhile, a new mythology has begun to take shape. I refer to the emerging mythology of the loyal but critical liberal center—those who early supported the main thrust of the United States effort in Indochina, later dissenting in midstream on relative points of efficiency or morality. This myth is that the war was a "mistake." The critics diverge somewhat as to the clarity and profundity of the error, but to all the error was circumstantial: Either (1) the executive authorities responsible for the crucial decisions to intervene and escalate (that is, Presidents Kennedy and Johnson and their immediate advisors) ignored, at certain critical junctures, the specific analysis and advice that might have indicated and urged a different course. Or (2) the cast of mind—the prevailing views and shared beliefs—of the entire government was generally mistaken about the character of the conflict and the nature of the enemy. A variant of this view is that the war *became* a mistake—at least an "objective" mistake—as the Sino-Soviet split developed, and as the diplomacy of Nixon and Kissinger partially defused China's support for North Vietnam and isolated Hanoi diplomatically.

But the "mistake" theory begs the essential question that would differentiate judgments from lessons: It *assumes* that, had the "true" facts that were presented or revealed been believed and accepted, the "right" conclusions and actions would have followed. It ignores the live possibility—and the plausible interpretation—that, even if the decision-makers had appreciated the intelligence and advice to which they were exposed, they would still have acted as they did and set the United States on the course of intervention and escalation in Vietnam. In other words, there were not mistakes, but *choices*: arrays of substantive alternatives and acts of choice; the course that was chosen and the courses that were not chosen, and the costs and consequences of each. The "mistake" theory puts the whole matter on the wrong basis: Only judgments proceed from the attribution of error; lessons proceed only from the analysis of choice.

Some Constraints and Adjustments

What, then, are the adjustments—the empirical or "existential" lessons—occasioned by Vietnam, in terms of the institutional constraints and pressures, the force structures, budget limits, and decision-making rules, and the new civil-military and foreign policy dispensations? Perhaps the most important of these is that the American voting public will no longer tolerate either a long, costly conflict or a large peacetime force structure that appears to have only limited utility in solving the country's external problems. Of course, the American economy can absorb several times the expense of such efforts, under conditions of mobilization of the economy and the emotional support of the nation. But it would appear a more obvious and central threat to the country's security to allow such a degree of mobilization. So the practical emergent constraint is, in most circumstances, the denial of mobilization. The judgment of the national leadership would be that the public cannot be taxed or mobilized to fight an indecisive peripheral war or provide large peacetime conventional forces.

A second general influence on the future structure of the nation's military system is the change in public attitudes toward the profession of arms. Whether it is independently cyclical, or a lagged reaction to war or a certain kind of war, or a continuously evolving public sentiment—or some overlay of several or all of these factors—a drift of antimilitary feeling became evident during the long involvement in Vietnam.

A third major determinant of a profoundly altered American military and foreign policy position is the increasing intractability of the world political-military environment. It has become clear that American conventional military power will be exercised successfully only in those areas that are uncontested by large powers—perhaps only in policing our own sphere. In this reading, the few "successful" uses of American power were the cases of Taiwan in 1958 and Cuba in 1962, in which big-power confrontations were resolved by nuclear threats; and the cases of Lebanon in 1958 and the Dominican Republic in 1965, in which small-power situations were smothered by sudden, overwhelming mobile interventions, unopposed by major adversaries.

These pressures and constraints are the significant determinants of the size and nature of American forces and the strategies planned for their employment; in turn they became important influences on civil-military relationships and foreign policies.

The "Instrumental" Critique: Quick Fixes and Trade-offs

The first of the four reaction syndromes—instrumentalism—is a partial response to the contradictions between foreign policy objectives and the new constraints and pressures. The instrumentalist critics adhere to the the purposes and main themes of American diplomacy but search for more efficient means to project U.S. power. Therefore, their proposed solution characteristically take the form of "quick fixes" or comprehensible trade-offs: fiscal, technological, organizational, and doctrinal. Even the "policy" changes they propose are less true policy changes—in the sense of orientations to situations—than trade-offs of means (though these may have serious policy *implications*).

The first of the new constraints and pressures, which has expressed itself primarily in the form of budgetary stringency, has occasioned a series of instrumental changes: a smaller, relatively cheaper force structure; a more controlled scope—a quicker termination, or determination—of future American military actions; possibly a more tightly managed procurement and operation of weapons systems and forces; and even an acceptance of some cost-compelled deficiencies in military capabilities—a compromise between budget cuts and the desire of the senior military to keep intact the organizational sinews of their services. There is also a preference for greater military, rather than economic, assistance to other nations.

The physical expression of this thrust is more technological and more mobile forces, many of the specific innovations being results of product-testing in the laboratory of Vietnam: close air support, tactical mobility, gadgetry such as night vision, "smart bombs," and particularly the "automated battlefield."

Another technological orientation is a renewed interest in the domestication and packaging of small-yield nuclear explosions, or tactical nuclear weapons, with efforts to invent appropriate applications and tactical doctrine. For such an impression little hard evidence is forthcoming; there are some revealing suggestions in the strategic literature, both inside and outside the military services. In any case, an interest in tactical nuclear weapons is consistent with America's presumed comparative advantage in capital-intensive, high-technology war-making.

Other consequences of budgetary constraints are a leaner base structure, both within the continental United States and abroad; the further development of intertheater mobility

—i.e., getting centrally located forces mobilized, transported overseas, and deployed; and possibly the devising of less conspicuous and less dislocating forms of partial mobilization that may allow the President to project American power in the world without provoking domestic crisis and congressional obstruction.

The second major influence, antimilitary feeling, has had some early consequences. One is a defensive reaction of the professionals who embody the standards and determine the conduct and the structure of the military organizations. The likely effects will be: a smaller, more reliable cadre; a narrower conception of professionalism; a psychological deflection of criticism from outside—in some ways a justified response to misdirected hostility from civilian society, which has attempted to narrow and redefine its unmanageable frustrations and fasten them on those to whom it had delegated the dirty tasks.

Another effect is more cleverly managed military organizations—staffed and run by systems-oriented men (such as Nixon's first appointment as Chief of Naval Operations, Admiral Zumwalt), who are familiar with the analytic vocabulary in which a case must now be dressed in order to be credible.

The advent of the all-volunteer Army—the ultimate success of which depends on sufficiently high military pay-scales, sufficiently low manpower quotas, and perhaps sufficiently high unemployment levels in the civilian economy to effect the necessary recruitment and retention—completes the professionalization of the Services. (It is far from certain that all these conditions will be met.) Such an organization might, remotely, acquire some of the characteristics and the role of a praetorian guard, the more ready to do a President's bidding efficiently abroad in exchange for a certain organizational immunity and even autonomy at home.

The third empirical lesson of Vietnam—the basic intractability of the world to U.S. intervention—has not been thoroughly absorbed by the policy- and strategy-making establishment. But a limited lesson has been learned. And there has been a corresponding instrumental change in the nature of our foreign policy—toward a Byzantine model: more mature, more sophisticated, less ideological; premised on our ability to engineer allied contributions on the marches of empire (the Nixon Doctrine itself); manipulative of ally and adversary alike (balance-of-power diplomacy); articulating subtle threats rather than squandering actual strength. Support for intervention will be sought less fervently by American Presidents. But our policy might still depend on interventions, where possible—though sharper, more competent, more overwhelming—in short, more decisive.

Since the future American military establishment will be conservative, in the sense that it will impinge little on the ordinary life of the nation, we can expect—and perhaps we are already seeing—the return to a civil-military relationship characterized by tacit public toleration of the military establishment. A new concordat may be established, particularly if a "low profile" foreign policy and a volunteer Army are installed and sustained. Also, the civilian national security bureaucracy will probably become more complaisant toward the military —even though the overt influences of the Services and the Joint Chiefs of Staff in the decision process seem to be at a low ebb. For one thing, the relatively neutral decision processes favored by the move to "fiscal guidance" budgeting in the first Nixon Administration may prove to be agnostic toward the strategic concepts of the military organizations.

In return, the defense structure will be less dependent on the maintenance of public enthusiasm for the military virtues, or on the generation of public apprehension of external threat. Overall defense budgets—though in absolute dollars they have bottomed out and have begun to climb—will be relatively less burdensome in terms of their share of the national income. The military will be more withdrawn in its public expressions, more discreet in its currying of congressional favor, and more concealed in its rendering of advice in the councils of government.

Thus the dominant policy adjustment, amounting to a new American consensual posture, will be the instrumental one: a smaller force establishment, but the maintenance of the essentials of order abroad through proxy military forces, sharp selective interventions, and large implied threats.

The "Consequential" Critique: Priorities

The "consequential" critics have been genuinely hostile to
the American posture toward Vietnam, and toward the cold
war in general, but *because of the consequences*—the distortions of society and the economy, particularly the burgeoning
of the "military-industrial complex." Their emphasis has been
on the pathology in American life and consciousness that has
resulted from the pressures and deprivations of a global posture of intervention. Their watchword, now ubiquitous as a
popular rallying point, is "priorities." But the consequentialist
critique, which centers on perceptions of the quality of domestic life, could be neutralized by a different structuring
and application of American force—for example, the Nixon
Doctrine—with alleviated impact on the domestic system.
Unlike the argument of the fundamentalists, the consequentialists' talk of priorities is not particularly moral. It could lend
itself to a reordering of material allocations, without much
effect on the nature of America's role in the world. Priorities
could mask the continuing exercise and enforcement of
American privilege abroad, as long as it was cheap, successful,
and domestically invisible, and as long as it contributed to the
preferential enhancement of American life.

The consequentialist critics of the military-political-social
complex also have a mistaken macro-model of the basic
trade-offs. They pitch their complaint on the ground that the
defense budget is related to domestic expenditures in some
tight logical and fiscal framework and that, therefore, adjust-
ing priorities will acheive in one blow (1) a moderation of
defense spending, (2) a diversion of the savings to domestic
needs, and (3) restraint in our foreign policy. But reduction of
the military budget is more likely to produce (1) a total federal
budget that is lower than otherwise, and (2) national strategies
for managing our foreign interests that are more efficient, but
not necessarily safe or good.

More technically, the model of the consequentialists
implies symmetry of economic reactions to higher or lower
levels of defense spending. In doing this, it misconceives the
determinants of the allocative process. In particular, it con-

fuses two manifestations of constraints. A constraint will "feel" and function differently, and consequently have a different meaning, depending on whether it is being approached as a limit on *increasing* activity, or is being backed away from, by *decreasing* activity—roughly the difference between pulling and pushing on a string. The consequentialists' confused treatment of constraints becomes evident when defense spending is to be *decreased*. This is the case of distributing the "dividend" that should accrue through a decision to wind down a war. The dividend produced by reductions in Vietnam war expenditures at best was merely *available* for other uses. It might also have been simultaneously pre-empted by other defense projects. Or the dividend might have been partially aborted through total-demand-reducing economic strategies designed to counter war-stimulated inflation (the course actually taken by the Nixon Administration in its first economic "game plan").

Decisions on defense spending and on domestic programs are independent, especially when defense spending is being reduced. Perhaps domestic programs should be enhanced; *and* perhaps defense programs should be cut—but not "because"; and by no means "only if." The consequential critique, implying a grand and automatic trade-off between military and domestic expenditures, provides too indirect, aggregate, and neutral an approach to the motives and objects of defense spending. In short, it does not challenge interventions and defense projects for the right reasons.

The "Fundamental" Critique: Morality and Institutional Change

The "fundamental" critics view American policy and actions in the world with the perspective—if not the objectivity—that comes from renouncing allegiance to the "national interest." They contend that destructive intervention is immoral—not warranted at all, on any grounds, even if probably successful, and even if within limits. They sense that the common denominator of the *other* positions is the perception and the moral datum that a demonstrated American interest is validly defensible anywhere in the world, even in despite of the more natural interests of the people who exist and subsist there—so long as the means are effective or proportional or domestically tolerable. Fundamentalist critics fear that, once the validity of U.S. interests abroad is granted, then the question of intervention becomes only a matter of style. The answer will not be found, they sense, until the American government understands revolution, not to subvert or subordinate it, but to tolerate it, and indeed (in Richard Barnet's phrase) to "make the world safe for revolution."

Not to be confused with the consequential critique, which rests on "priorities" (domestic reform enabled by national security revisions), the fundamental critique of America's role and behavior in the world insists that we (1) reform our security posture, but that we can do this way only by (2) restructuring our system—bureaucratic, economic, social, and political. The fundamentalists begin to ask the right questions, and in depth—something that may not be true of other kinds of critics (instrumentalist, consequentialist, and proportionalist), whose analysis may be shallow as to causes and therefore not efficacious in foreclosing dissimilar but analogous future interventionist disasters. The fundamentalists have, perhaps, the opposite problem: their analysis is *too* deep. It entails nothing less than a total change in the structure of institutions and the pattern of incentives in the domestic and international system.

But the critical question is: What if this change cannot be accomplished, at home or in the world? Even one who sympathizes with the fundamentalist position must realize that it neglects the political-military consequences of the rigid and complete nonintervention that it implies. Two problems arise, which are interrelated: (1) Surely there must be *some* minimum strategic requisites—a baseline for any nation's foreign policy outputs—generated by the very notion of a responsible national government that can take moral positions and exercise restraint. These requisites might cut across the ability of a state to abstain from exercises of force to preserve its security. And (2) there must be some realization that the international system inhibits—or penalizes—the unilateral exercise of moral restraint by an individual nation in its external actions.

So the issues become: How—under what conditions of the international system—can a nation afford the moral position of the fundamentalists? And how—under what set of policy presumptions—can a nation consistently carry out a moral course of action, based on nonintervention? When the moral critique of the fundamentalists is seen this way, it will lead to a *strategic* critique; and it will invite us to draw strategic lessons from the Vietnam war, and from the situation of the United States in the world as it emerges from the shadow of Vietnam.

The "Proportional" Critique: Limits and Exits

The "proportionalist" critics of Vietnam share some of the emotive judgments of the fundamentalists but are unwilling to pursue their implications. They include some of the more philosophical former public servants, as well as liberal-realist academics. Some originally supported the stand in Southeast Asia on strategic or ideological grounds but, as the war ground on, criticized it on the basis that the costs and the destruction had become disproportionate to the actual and probable results and the value of the objectives. This position offers a logical—and respectable—way to climb down from previous support while reaffirming the feasibility of future interventions, the necessity and morality of limited war, or the balance of power as a criterion for involvement.

The proportional critique entails that Vietnam be seen as peripheral and irrelevant to the global or regional balance of power, and also unique and not replicable—in short, not an instance of the type of situation in which we need to intervene. Furthermore, the uniqueness, the peculiar character, of the Vietnam situation and conflict is posited as the reason for the futility of our intervention.

The logical problem of this group of critics is how to preserve the premise of intervention when necessary, but distinguish and repudiate the case of Vietnam. The solution is to see our intervention in Vietnam as a "mistake"—the mistake, precisely, of *failing to recognize* the unique features of the situation. Ironically, the sensitivity of the proportionalists in defining the Vietnam war leads to a *failure* to generalize usefully from that situation, to draw conclusions of sufficient amplitude to provide guidance in future situations that will vary in certain respects and degrees.

Wars are escalated or extended because they cannot be won at the existing level or intensity or scope of violence, or within the calculated period of time. In making the decision to escalate or extend, the value of the original stake is only one factor. More salient, at that juncture, is a calculation that the additional (marginal) increment—whether of numbers, force, technique, scope, or simply duration—will be efficacious, and that the additional costs and risks can at least be managed. To question the value of the stakes at that point is either to accept an adverse outcome and write off the entire investment, or to postulate the existence of some satisfactory third solution between winning and losing—some "political solution" (a postulation that, indeed, George Ball made in his distinguished internal dissent of October 5, 1964), with the implication that it is there for the taking and somehow has been blindly overlooked or negligently discarded. But, if this third solution is not available, the doctrine of proportion merely increases the likelihood of defeat after expending the effort. It invites intervention, but frustrates it by imposing limits just at the critical point.

Furthermore, particularly in revolutionary wars, proportion is an unreliable principle even to curb escalation. In fact, in these conditions, proportion almost guarantees the worst situation: It (1) limits the effort to a point just inferior to that required for success, while (2) allowing the adversary to set that point and make it continually more remote. Stalemate, but at ever higher levels of escalation, is almost a logical deduction from these premises.

The insoluble dilemma of limited war—how to win without indefinite escalation—leads a proportionalist to the elusive problem: how to quit if not winning. It is not surprising, then, that George Ball, for example, turns to the question of "minimiz[ing] the costs of extrication." [1] But in Vietnam we did not lack the wit to find a smooth and diplomatic way out (though we might have lacked some grace to accept defeat); probably none was available, since the other side (and our own ally) never was willing to accord us any. Our extrication, after the general unwisdom of entry, would always have been a tough decision, with bad withdrawal symptoms and bad after-effects. The choices were always more stark than the proportionalists were willing to entertain.

The proportionalists fail to generalize from historical experience broadly enough to formulate a presumption against intervention that will shape our decision even—especially—where at first the odds look good and the effort looks reasonable. The lesson is not how to extricate—whether with honor or otherwise—but how not to intervene in the first place.

The "Strategic" Critique: Consistent Nonintervention

The strategic critique takes Vietnam as exemplifying a set of circumstances that constitute serious constraints on the future ability of the United States to undertake limited wars. Also, contrary to the proportional critique, it sees Vietnam as an object lesson, representing a more general category of intervention; as an instance that *ought* to be broadened into a more general rule or a set of strategic presumptions. The ultimate lessons of Vietnam should be, then, a set of strategic orientations, construed and applied with sufficient generality and consistency to have a constructive effect in the relevant range of future cases. Though these strategic orientations are not tangible and specific prescriptions, it should nevertheless be possible to deduce from them a set of national objectives, an illustrative force structure, a doctrine for employing the forces, and a rough estimate of a defense budget.

Strategic lessons do not indicate a case-by-case limitation of the exercise of American power, nor a calculus of the costs and benefits of given or contemplated interventions. These considerations are more appropriate to a "national-interest" approach, which is a kind of slide rule of realism applied to foreign policy. But such a finely tuned policy could lead to unprincipled discrete decisions, with unreliable consequences and inconsistent implications for future situations. In particular, a national-interest approach could lend itself as much to the extension as to the limitation of objects of intervention. It would not constitute the kind of strategic lessons that should be learned from Vietnam. Furthermore, the problem with any degree of intervention is that it is too "sticky," its entailments and its consequences too unpredictable. Situations are unclear, in their own nature or as instances of certain proscribed or allowable intervention, until well after the commitments must be made—if at all—and it is too late to adjust to double-takes.

A thorough set of strategic lessons would require us to abandon the illusion that we can purchase safety or advantage by regulating and controlling our political environment—that is, dominating the will or orchestrating the behavior of other nations, whether through the pursuit of a balance of power, or the construction of an international organization. In short, strategic lessons are not another redefinition of American interests, another prescription of means, or another arbitrary or wishful reduction of the "threat." Rather, they are a reorientation to challenges and a conclusion that we might have to adjust to the contingent loss of American interests, rather than continue to prepare to protect them in cases such as Vietnam represents.

To install a strategy of disengagement, rather than intervention, would require a new set of presumptions—antipresumptions, in fact—that would make intervention improbable, even in the face of the profound disturbances that are likely in the world. All the specific antipresumptions would add up to a strong orientation of nonintervention—a skepticism of exercising control of the international order. It is an orientation against exercises of deliberate violence to prevent or pre-empt future danger, to anticipate future disadvantages, to wage long-range defense, to reinforce credibility in large matters by intervening in small ones. Thus, a set of antipresumptions that establish a structured bias against intervention would result in a profound change in the direction of our foreign policy.

In calling this set of principles presumptions, I also mean that there might be transcendent cases—not "exceptions," since these are not "rules"—in which intervention might be chosen. There are two kinds of cases: (1) defensive, or self-protective, action in situations of palpable, irrevocable, and mortal danger to the identity and physical existence of *one's own* national community; (2) sympathetic response to insure the survival and well-being of *another* state or community, when these are threatened.

Such acts of transcendence are not trade-offs of our consistent strategic presumptions and moral principles against the imperatives of a single compelling instance. Nor are the presumptions altered or negated by the actions. They are simply and literally transcended. Normally, we must prefer the steadier, if dimmer, light of logical and consistent principle. Transcendence of the logic of nonintervention must not be common, or casual, or, for that matter, calculated. It should occur, if at all, far down the path of the policy-determining process—not easily and immediately in some mindless act, facile rationalization, or unprincipled scheme.

The Requisites of National Security

A policy of strategic disengagement would not foreclose the pursuit of national security; indeed, it would take as its essential point of reference the requisites of national security. But it is false to treat security as an independent goal of the system, as if there were any sense in maximizing it. Rather, security is a *condition* of the system, in the sense of a minimum set of constraints or relationships that must be observed or fulfilled.

It is possible to indicate the general purpose (conventional) force structure, the military manpower, and the overall defense budget to which the country could return by the end of a decade if it were to adopt strict noninterventionist foreign policy premises. Such a force structure would provide the following general purpose forces: 8 land divisions (6 Army and 2 Marine), 19 tactical air wing equivalents (11 Air Force, 2 Marine which are equal to 4, and 4 Navy), with 6 carrier task forces to sustain 2 forward. With the addition of "sufficient" strategic nuclear deterrent forces (a diad of alert bombers with stand-off weapons, and invulnerable missile submarines), it would require fewer than 1,350,000 men (Army under 420,000, Air Force under 420,000, Navy under 370,000, Marine Corps under 140,000).[2] The total defense budget would be about $50 billion a year (in 1975 dollars). This level of defense spending would be about 3.5 per cent of a projected gross national product of about $1.5 trillion—consistent with many mature nations. The fact that we have been spending more than twice this percentage for twenty-five years is not evidence of "fat" or incompetent procurement (though there may well have been such) but rather testimony that the United States, since the end of the 1940s, has undertaken to provide for much more than its own national security.

In other words, the United States has been spending at least half of its defense resources on protecting allies and friends against local external and internal challenges, establishing "procedural" rules regarding discontinuous military and political change, maintaining access for our commerce and general influence, and insuring the health of our institutions (as opposed to their essential integrity) by fostering a certain political and moral climate in sufficiently large portions of the rest of the world. These are milieu goals, which we hold for the shape and character of the international system, disguised as, or assimilated to, more immediate—even vital—security interests. ("Vital" must be reserved for those truly supreme interests that derive so strictly from our identity as a nation that they could not credibly be alienated, even by some official expression.)

Most contemporary attacks on inflated defense spending implicitly assert that we can protect and preserve these sometimes important, but not always essential, national interests, but with sharply reduced, more efficient, "leaner" forces. Though impressive savings can always be made, most of those analyses and contentions are illusory, however comforting and perhaps politically judicious. The important point about a drastically reduced defense budget is that it must proceed from—and at least strongly implies—the fact that we will have to *give up* some of the penumbra of national interests, if they are seriously challenged. We must abandon the illusion that they can be protected at dramatically lower cost.

General purpose forces are derived from (at least indirectly), or justified by (at least ultimately), the requirements of various possible theaters of operation. A noninterventionist force structure would entail a mid-Pacific posture—not the redundant construction of bases in the Pacific Trust Territories to hedge against the denial of Western Pacific bases and to maintain the capability of intervention in East Asia. It would mean no American forces or bases west of Guam. It would mean no military assistance to Asian clients. It would mean phasing out all military alliances and defense commitments —to be replaced, in some cases, with nonmilitary treaties establishing various forms of cooperation and formulas of mutual trust. It would mean the end of declaratory statements of policy that commit us to intervention or the threat of intervention in the defense of asserted interests in East Asia. We would not attempt to replace the American presence by devolving nuclear or other arms upon presumed proxy states, particularly Japan. Nor would we invest American diplomatic effort or national prestige in the establishment of regional defense associations. If such evolve, we might look benignly upon them, or ignore them; we would not acquire a stake in their creation or orientation. We would, in short, allow an indigenous "balance" to establish itself among the great territorial powers in this region, China, Japan, and the Soviet Union, and stand clear of the determination of their competitive and collaborative struggles and schemes, seeking no political or military advantage.

Of course, such moves would be accomplished in an orderly and phased manner. At the end of a half-decade of adjustment, total forces maintained in the active force structure with some nominal orientation to Asia might be: 2 land divisions (1 Army and 1 Marine), and 6 tactical air wing equivalents (2 Air Force, 2 Marine which are equal to 4, and 2 Navy carrier wings operating from 3 carrier task forces, 1 forward, 1 rearward, and 1 in overhaul).

There might also be a considerable deletion of forces kept in our active force structure primarily for a contingency in Europe. At present we provide, in Europe and the Mediterranean, 4-1/3 divisions (all Army;), 9 tactical air wing equivalents, and 2 carrier task forces, with a full complement of headquarters and support forces; and, in and around the United States, earmarked for Europe, an additional 4-2/3 divisions (3-2/3 Army and 1 Marine), 6 tactical air wing equivalents, and 4 carrier task forces to back up the 2 forward. At the end of a decade of adjustment, there might remain in Europe no American forces, and in and around the United States, in some sense oriented to Europe and the Mediterranean, 3-1/3 divisions (3 Army and a Marine brigade), 7-2/3 tactical air wing equivalents (5 Air Force, 1/3 Marine which is equal to 2/3, and 2 Navy), and 3 carrier task forces.

In addition to the forces loosely oriented to Asia and Europe, this illustrative force structure would include an active strategic reserve of 2-2/3 divisions (2 Army and 2/3 Marine and 5-1/3 tactical air wing equivalents (4 Air Force and 2/3 Marine which is equal to 1-1/3).

With the shrinking of overseas forces and overseas military objectives, there would also be a diminished function for our surface Navy, our attack submarines, and our antisubmarine aircraft—all dedicated to keeping open the military sea lanes to conduct the forward defense of foreign countries.

Conclusion

The strategic lessons of Vietnam do not consist of a revised—even drastically reduced—force structure. Revisions and reductions might happen in any case, and for a variety of reasons: either as responses to economic or political constraints (as the Nixon Doctrine), or as results of tight management, or shrewd fiscal measures, or virtuoso technological trade-offs, or radical doctrinal changes (as the New Look of the 1950s).

Such changes might be no more than extensions of the "instrumental" critique of Vietnam, described earlier. They would not constitute strategic lessons, unless they reached the operational terms of intervention: where, when, why, how, and, above all, for what? The ultimate lessons of Vietnam lie in these conceptual shifts in national strategy, and in the profound changes in the "categories" through which, and in terms of which, we recognize and interpret events in the international system that constitute strategic challenges to which we "must," as a nation, respond.

It might be said that only the learning of such lessons would guarantee against a repetition of Vietnam, in some other—

perhaps not recognizably similar—circumstances. But if we are truly to learn these strategic lessons, we must also realize that, in purging ourselves of Vietnam, and in avoiding future Vietnams, we will be abjuring, as well, many other objects of our foreign policy.

Notes

1. "The Lessons of Vietnam: Have We Learned, or Only Failed?" *New York Times Magazine*, April 1, 1973.
2. This noninterventionist force structure and defense budget is far lower than that for Fiscal Year 1975: 16-1/3 land divisions and 42 tactical air wing equivalents, 2,152,000 men, and expected total defense outlays of $85.8 billion. It is even considerably lower than that of most of the administration's critics (including the well-known "McGovern defense budget" of 1972, which required 12 land divisions and 28 tactical air wings, 1,735,000 men, and was undercosted, optimistically, at $54.8 billion, in 1975 dollars).

American Security Interests After Vietnam

ERNEST R. MAY

The last dozen years have seen the beginning of a transformation in American beliefs. Until sometime in the 1960s, most of us assumed democracy to be in peril. The Soviet Union, we thought, lusted to impose its ideology and totalitarian political system on all the world. Controlling all Communist governments and parties, it would use military force or subversion to take over any vulnerable non-Communist country. Each success would make it stronger. If we did nothing, the United States would eventually be an island in a Communist world. We would ourselves face conquest and have to choose between surrender and war.

So it seemed logical that the choice not be put off. The United States should take a firm stand while it yet had allies. With Soviet leaders deterred, all those who cherished freedom would remain safe and the calamity of a new world war would be averted.

Now, fewer of us accept these premises. Many Americans suspect that Soviet ambition for a Communist world is millennial, resembling more the dreams of Paul VI for Catholicism than those of, say, Mohammed for Islam or Hitler for

Nazism. Communist governments and parties seem fragmented, and for the most part are no more instruments of the
Soviet Politburo than non-Communist governments or parties
are instruments of Washington. Thus, there seems far less
cause for supporting non-Communist regimes, or for maintaining powerful military forces and displaying the determination to use them, if challenged.

The principal reason for this change is simply the passage of
time. In World War II totalitarianism seemed actually about
to engulf the world. Those who lived through it were convinced that the democracies should have resisted sooner.
Judging the Soviet Union of Stalin and Khrushchev to be like
the Germany of Hitler, Americans had little doubt that the
right course of action was to do what had not been done in the
1930s.

With the Soviet-Chinese rupture and other developments,
the seeming analogy between Communists and Nazis has lost
most of its force. And the crucial memories have dimmed. An
increasing proportion of the American public knows World
War II only as the setting for old movies on television. Large
numbers do not even remember the early cold war. The
American of median age was scarcely born at the start of the
Korean conflict and only thirteen during the Cuban missile
crisis. For many, both old and young, the Vietnam war has
taken the place of World War II and the cold war as the
experience that shapes thinking about the future. Its seeming
lesson is that the United States should be cautious about
commitments to foreign governments and stay out of wars
which might provoke significant dissent at home.

These American attitudes do not necessarily betoken a relapse into isolationism. At least in the foreseeable future, the
majority of informed Americans are unlikely to assume that
we have no vital interest outside the Western Hemisphere and
hence little need for ready military power. For few persons can
ignore the progress in technology which has made the planet
so small, and life on it so precarious. Nevertheless, Americans
are bound to ask with increasing insistence whether there exist
threats to their vital interests which require continued investment in defense on the scale of the 1950s and 1960s.

It then seemed sensible to remain prepared for nuclear attack, a major nonnuclear war in Europe or Asia comparable to World War II, and a limited war like that in Korea. Now, all of these contingencies seem unlikely.

Although the Soviet Union has succeeded in matching or even surpassing the United States in most categories of nuclear weaponry, Soviet leaders seem to recognize that the United States has the second-strike capacity to make the initiation of nuclear war a suicidal act. Chinese nuclear missiles cannot yet reach us. While it is possible that Japan may develop strategic nuclear forces, and just faintly possible that a united Europe might do likewise, it takes considerable strain to imagine Japan or Europe threatening the United States with nuclear attack.

The possibility of a large-scale nonnuclear war seems even more remote. With some exercise of fantasy, scenarios can be conjured up. A conflict involving Yugoslavia or Israel could build into an East-West war, or an American effort to assist India or Brazil might grow into a super-Vietnam. At present, however, all such contingencies seem chimeras.

As long as "no more Vietnams" remains a watchword, it is hard also to envision the United States once more becoming locked in a major limited war. A treaty might be invoked as a result of, say, a North Korean attack on South Korea, a Chinese invasion of Taiwan, or the landing of a Cuban expeditionary force somewhere in the Caribbean. In such event, however, the most likely American response would be to send supplies—not troops. Naval and air support would probably be denied if there seemed any danger that it might lead to a ground force engagement.

In short, the temptation is to regard the United States as relatively free from serious threats to its national security, and hence to conclude that military forces should have comparatively low priority in the allocation of resources. As a result, the following policies are likely to find public favor. To diminish even further the risk of nuclear war, it will be argued, the United States should pursue strategic arms limitation talks (SALT), seeking agreements with the Soviets to reduce arsenals on both sides and halt or limit development of new weapons systems. In the meantime, the United States should maintain a second-strike capability, but do so at minimum cost. Specifically, the government should arrest or slow down such expensive qualitative improvements in the nuclear arsenal as MARVing (or tipping missiles with warheads that can maneuver as they approach their targets), equipping submarines with longer-range, more accurate POSEIDON or ULMS-1 missiles, and developing the higher capability TRIDENT submarine or the B-1 bomber. The Chinese and Europeans should be brought into SALT arrangements, and Japan and others should be induced to sign the nuclear nonproliferation treaty.

With either a large nonnuclear war or a major limited war apparently so improbable, one can also foresee increasing public demand for withdrawal of American troops from Europe and elsewhere. And while the public may well approve of maintaining enough ready force to carry out rescue operations in case of a mortal threat to Israel, a localized war in the Middle East threatening U.S. oil supplies, or a hostile seizure of the Panama Canal, it is apt to frown on the maintenance of general purpose forces at their current size. In short, the national security policy most likely to find public favor during the next eight to ten years will probably have as its principal elements arms limitation negotiations, a standstill in strategic force development, and rollbacks in other forces.

Since these policies were advocated by McGovernites in 1972 and McGovern was badly beaten, it may seem odd to make such a prediction. But the policy has been advocated by Democrats in Congress who were not closely identified with McGovern and by left-of-center Republicans. And Americans whom pollsters find leaning toward such a policy are those who ordinarily lead public opinion. These groups will probably shape an antipreparedness consensus in the late 1970s, just as their counterparts shaped a propreparedness consensus in the early 1950s.

Those leading us into the new consensus feel certain that the previous generation exaggerated perils, passed up real opportunities for negotiation, and spent so much on defense that the economy and the political system suffered a distorting militarization. They may well be right. Looking ahead, however, one can reasonably fear that these new opinion leaders will appear equally or more mistaken in the eyes of the generation that follows. They may be judged to have underestimated dangers, exaggerated the potentialities of diplomacy, and prepared too little for war.

Consider first the case for dealing with the danger of nuclear war primarily through SALT negotiations and the suspension of strategic force development. It depends on an assumption that the United States and the Soviet Union have a common interest in ending the nuclear arms race. Both nations have come to recognize, it is argued, that their conflicts of interest are subject to compromise. Each is aware that the other has more than enough power to cripple its society even after suffering a devastating first blow. And each is faced with mounting costs of military hardware and pressure to spend relatively more for domestic purposes. It should follow that the two powers will eventually come to terms and that the United States can assist progress by not wasting money on new weapons which would spur further competition.

Underlying such optimism, however, is the assumption that American-Soviet negotiations can progress as if conducted by omnipotent bargainers. Nothing in recent history encourages this assumption, for the steps taken thus far have been only those that were relatively easy for both sides. The limited test-ban treaty of 1963 helped leaders in each country deal with domestic pressure to do something about radioactivity in the atmosphere. The first SALT agreement was preceded by intense debate and doubt about the potential effectiveness of any feasible ABM network. Curbing ABM development by international agreement was for President Nixon probably the simplest solution to a troublesome domestic problem. Though evidence is lacking, this may also have been true for Brezhnev.

It is by no means evident that American and Soviet leaders will find it equally easy to continue progress toward an agreed standstill or reduction in strategic weapons competition. MIRVs (or missiles with independently targetable multiple warheads) menaced the strategic balance at least as much as major ABM deployments, yet President Nixon obviously judged it prudent not to halt our MIRVing program either by fiat or by international accord. He apparently believed that U.S. security interests required MIRVs. Possibly, however, he would have taken the same position even if skeptical about them. For, if he reversed himself, he would risk a fight with powerful elements in the bureaucracy, Congress, and the business world—and he could not afford to alienate the few allies he had in Washington.

The same rule holds for possible subjects of future arms limitation negotiations. At present, our most credible second-strike system is that composed of submarine-mounted missiles. American confidence in the strategic balance would be severely shaken if the Soviets developed new locating devices and significantly improved their attack submarine forces. Abstractly, therefore, it would be in the American interest to negotiate limitations on the development of new weapons for antisubmarine warfare. Yet few Chief Executives would wish to campaign for such limitations. To do so would involve battle with Admiral Rickover and others in the Navy who champion the attack submarine, powerful Congressmen who have traditionally been Rickover's supporters, and a host of local interests, engineering firms, contractors, and the like whose prosperity is involved. At most, a President is likely to slow the pace of progress in undersea weaponry.

Whether the Soviet leadership is similarly constrained cannot easily be judged. The fact that an increasing proportion of the Soviet defense budget has gone to attack submarines suggests similar circumstances. Certainly, at least some strategic force projects in the Soviet Union have behind them interests which Brezhnev and his associates are disinclined to challenge.

It follows that both Americans and Russians would be ill-advised to count on negotiation as the sole or even chief means of preserving a strategic balance. Indeed, keeping a close eye on the politics of defense policy in the U.S.S.R., Americans should try to detect developments which Soviet political leaders are apt to have difficulty controlling. If any show signs of progressing to a breakthrough which might threaten our second-strike capability, the United States should promptly spend money on countermeasures.

To make this recommendation is not to argue against continued negotiations. At some point, SALT agreements may become independent forces in American and Soviet politics. The naval limitations treaties in the 1920s suggest what may occur. Even had there been no treaties, a halt in battleship construction might well have been brought about by pressures for economy, fear that the battleship was obsolete, and other factors. But the fact that a halt had been agreed upon contributed to a sense of security, even complacency, which for a decade influenced defense policy in all the major maritime nations. Contrary to popular myth, the Japanese cut back as much as did the Americans or British on contruction of most types of warships. SALT-II or SALT-III might help create a similar sense of safety. But this has not yet occurred; and unless and until it takes place in *both* Moscow and Washington, security against nuclear war will continue to depend on a strategic balance resulting from controlled and deliberate competition in the development of new weapons systems.

Although the peril of nuclear attack from some other source cannot be ignored altogether, the possible eventual threat from China, and the imaginable threats from other sources are not contingencies which demand much attention. For the foreseeable future, China's nuclear forces will be targeted on the Soviet Union. As for Japan and other nations, the United States can influence their debates over offensive strategic forces by offering reassurance against Soviet or Chinese nuclear blackmail and by abjuring efforts to extort advantages from its own nuclear superiority; but it can have only modest effects on decisions which will be largely products of their own national politics.

With regard to general purpose forces, it is harder to build a case against retrenchment. The Soviet Army is less fully manned than was earlier feared; in fact, Russian and Warsaw Pact forces positioned for a possible invasion of Europe are apparently little larger than the American and NATO forces positioned to resist them. Controversies between the Russians and their East European clients make it questionable whether, in any case, the full strength of the Warsaw Pact could be mobilized for an offensive. Although the Russians could conceivably effect a build-up by transferring forces from Asia, the state of their relations with China makes this most unlikely. In short, the prospect of a massive Russian attack on Europe has come to seem more a nightmare of the past than a contingency requiring constant readiness.

For the same reasons, a Russian ground offensive against Turkey or Iran has come to seem improbable. The one plausible scenario that can be written for the Middle East commences with Soviet support for a new, successful Arab attack on Israel and subsequent American intervention leading to direct American-Soviet combat. Such a scenario becomes more unlikely, however, as it envisions either the Soviets or the Americans dispatching ground forces to the area.

Although Japanese defense plans necessarily consider it, a sudden Soviet invasion of Japan hardly seems probable. As for other parts of the world, it is reasonable to assume that the United states simply will not soon get itself into a situation inviting any significant commitment of ground forces.

In their analysis of the 1974 budget, Charles Schultze and his colleagues at The Brookings Institution outline three possible policies which might correspond more closely to probable needs as envisioned in current public thinking about general purpose forces. One policy would leave as they are the forces earmarked for possible war in Europe but cut back those elsewhere. All that would be left in Asia would be the minimum necessary for guarding Korea and giving Japan a sense of confidence in America's defense commitment. A second policy would encompass these steps and some reduction in forces for Europe. Abandoning the assumption that the United States must be ready not only for a short, sharp contest with the Soviets but also for a long war involving a struggle to keep open the sea lanes, supply allies, and build up a large expeditionary force, this policy would provide only for a war of approximately ninety days. A third policy would pare back all general purpose forces, retaining a token division in Europe but otherwise maintaining preparedness only for minor contingencies. The underlying assumption would be that the danger of escalation into nuclear war would be adequate to deter potential enemies. Schultze and his associates estimate the alternative force requirements and their average annual costs as follows:

	Current Plans	Alternative I (lower profile in Asia)	Alternative II * (lower profile in Asia and Europe)	Alternative III (primary reliance on nuclear deterrance)
Army and Marine Division	16	14	12	6
Tactical Air Wings	38	27	27	6-7
Carrier Task Forces	12-15	9	9	6
Average Annual Cost, 1974-80 ($ billion)	56.2	52.0	45.7	30.0

* Also involves altered procurement of tactical aircraft and of antisubmarine warfare vessels.
Source: Edward R. Fried, Alice M. Rivlin, Charles L. Schultze, and Nancy H. Teeters, Setting National Priorities: The 1974 Budget (Washington, D.C.: The Brookings Institution, 1973).

Arguments for the first alternative, or something like it, seem compelling, for polls suggest that most Americans would be reluctant now to commit forces in defense of even Korea or Japan. In a survey by Louis Harris reported in *Time* as long ago as May 2, 1969, only 33 per cent indicated willingness to fight for South Korea. It would seem only realistic to dismantle our contingents in Southeast Asia, since public opinion precludes their use.

Arguments for going on to the second alternative also seem powerful, in view of the fact that professional military opinion, at least in the Army and Air Force, has been steadily swinging toward the opinion that no war in Europe is likely to last more than three months. If neither side has won by that time, it is argued, one or the other will either make peace or resort to nuclear warfare. And it seems likely that arguments for moving toward the third alternative will seem more and more convincing as the decade wears on.

To prevent it, however, a significant change in thinking will be required, both outside and inside the military establishment. It is often assumed that both strategic and general purpose forces should have the most sophisticated weaponry and equipment that technology can devise. To some extent, it is also assumed that both categories of forces need to be trained, manned, and positioned to cope with surprise attacks involving all of the enemy's strength. As argued, the first assumption, and perhaps the second, must continue to hold for strategic forces. But it is by no means clear that either assumption must or should govern thinking about general purpose forces.

To tailor general purpose forces to currently foreseeable contingencies could, however, be most unwise. In the first place, events that now seem unlikely might become less improbable if the United States were clearly unprepared to react to them effectively. Major cutbacks in U.S. conventional forces would not automatically produce more adventurous Soviet policies. But in Moscow or some other capital advocates of military action might be much stronger if they could argue that the United States was too weak to put up opposition. One can speculate that in 1950, the Russians would have been more hesitant about the North Korean invasion of South Korea if they had thought the United States was prepared to intervene. If U.S. forces are reduced to what may now seem realistic levels, the danger could increase of, say, a Soviet incursion into Yugoslavia or Iran or a new North Korean offensive.

In the second place, a force posture fitted to American perceptions of national interest in the mid-1970s might come to appear pitifully insufficient even without any dramatic changes elsewhere in the world. It is not unrealistic, for example, to anticipate wrenching civil wars in Thailand, Argentina, or Chile. At present, most Americans would take the position that, if so, these would be strictly Thai or Argentinian or Chilean problems. In the 1980s, however, when memories of U.S. troops in Vietnam are ten years old, the public and

Congress may join a President in finding reasons to help one side against the other. After all, during the Cuban war for independence in the 1870s there was little disposition in the United States to intervene. When a similar war came in the 1890s, the public proved to be passionately for intervention. The immediate aftermath of Korea saw strong public and congressional opposition to military involvement in Indochina; a decade later, our Presidents were able to build powerful, if temporary, support for such a policy.

If American general purpose forces are so reduced in strength that the government does not at that point have open the option of military action, there could be several unhappy consequences. One is panic about the state of the nation's defenses and pell-mell spending for preparedness—the pattern during World War I, World War II, and the Korean conflict. Of course, an emergency military build-up at some later time might be less expensive than constant preparedness in the interval. As the earlier table indicated, tailoring defense outlays to currently foreseeable contingencies could save $40 billion to $260 billion in the decade 1975-85; a crisis in 1985 would probably not require a sudden spending of such sums.

But the significant costs would not necessarily be reckonable in money. If the past is any guide, our political system could be disturbed. Leaders of opinion who could be blamed for the country's military unreadiness might be discredited, as were Bryanites and Progressives in World War I, isolationists in World War II, and both left-wing Democrats and Taft Republicans during the height of the cold war. For some period of time, authority could be monopolized by a segment of the élite largely indifferent to domestic problems which we cannot afford to ignore.

Thus, in view of the unpredictable nature of change in the world or in the American mood, and the costs which could be entailed if the nation suddenly decided it was dangerously ill-prepared, levels of general purpose forces should not be adjusted wholly to foreseeable contingencies.

Yet such cuts in our forces are implied not only by trends in congressional and public opinion but by trends within the military establishment itself. The services seem now to assume that there will not be large increases in federal taxes, that domestic programs will make increasing claims for money, and that defense may well have a declining share of the budget. Their own internal costs are shooting upward. Especially in view of the shift to a volunteer army, the services will increasingly be forced to choose between hardware and manpower. Their most probable course will be to buy new weapons systems and strip general purpose forces below the levels prescribed by current contingency planning. Meanwhile, defense spokesmen will begin to warn that a niggardly President and Congress are denying the nation the wherewithal to respond to a threat. This is what happened after World War II and again at the end of the 1950s; it is important that it not recur in the 1970s and 1980s.

On the contrary, in many categories of weapons for non-nuclear warfare, quality may be much less important than quantity. The new Air Force F-15 has marginally greater maneuverability and firepower than the F-4, but it costs more than three times as much. Surely, in actual battle, fifteen squadrons of F-4s would count for more than five squadrons of F-15s. In the eyes of both Americans and foreigners, the United States would seem better prepared for war with a large number of F-4s than with a third as many F-15s. The same rule holds true for most pieces of equipment, down to and including rifles for infantrymen. And maintenance of a large inventory of serviceable weapons rather than a small inventory of advanced weapons would facilitate sharing them with allies or making fast transfers of equipment, as in the Arab-Israeli war of 1973.

Similarly, in hedging against the most plausible contingencies of nonnuclear war, the number of mobilizable troops may be more important than their state of training or location. The obvious question is how to maintain large general purpose forces when Congress and the public want to spend less for defense. Since it would be unrealistic to advocate either cancellation of pay raises or reinstitution on a large scale of the draft, there seems but one possible answer—greater reliance on reserves recruited by some system of incentives.

One can imagine methods of developing a large reserve

force at relatively low cost. For example, high school graduates could be offered college scholarships in return for enlistment in the reserve. Those selected could undergo basic training in the summer before entering college, receive some more advanced training in each subsequent summer or during other periods, and upon graduation choose some combination of active duty and participation in an active reserve unit either in enlisted status or, if qualified, as an officer. While the costs would be far from negligible, some of them would represent aid to education rather than an outlay for defense per se. The current military pay scale would apply only during periods of active duty, and the program itself would entail no retirement benefits. In all probability the pool of applicants would be large and of relatively high quality. There is almost no question that the services could, if necessary, develop systems for training and feeding reservists into and out of units both here and overseas, so as to maintain ample effective forces.

If the United States is to remain militarily prepared for crises which might arise in the future—and if the American people are to be spared a recurrence of panic about national security—the nation should change its criteria for general purpose forces. The quantity and serviceability of weapons should take precedence over ever-newer technology. For manpower, numbers of mobilizable and movable reserves should substitute for numbers of active duty professionals.

Because of the trends in congressional and public opinion, I doubt that this prescription will be adopted. I even have some doubt that we will pursue the different set of policies which seem to me essential to preservation of a strategic balance.

Nevertheless, I adhere to the view that the "right" national security policy would be one based on two uncomfortable assumptions. First, that the military posture of the United States and other nations is governed more by internal politics than by strategic calculations. From this assumption it follows that our estimates of the behavior of other governments should be grounded less on assessment of what their presumed interests dictate than of what their political processes are likely to produce. It follows more specifically that we should be skeptical about negotiation as the chief safeguard against nuclear war. The second assumption is that the United States itself has no permanent security interests. Instead, the American people and their leaders have perceptions of interests which change from time to time. From this it follows that a prudent military policy involves sustained preparedness; anything less presents the danger that the people and the Congress will at some later date see the nation as having been left naked. Defense spending will certainly be limited in the foreseeable future. If these limits are too tight, a future crisis could set us off on a massive new wave of weapons-buying. We all would be the poorer for it.

Negotiating Strategies

Negotiations involve more than the give and take at the bargaining table. They also include the complex interplay among the terms offered at the table and the situation on the ground, perceptions of what the future situation may be, the potential and real force available to each side, the actual minimum each will accept and the perception or guess of the other side as to what that minimum is, the time pressures on each side to make a deal, and many other factors.

In what President Nixon called an "era of negotiations," the relationship between force and diplomacy—between our general posture and our efforts to negotiate many different issues with the Soviet Union and others—is extremely important. In the following essays, Maxwell Taylor and Paul Warnke draw some lessons from the long history of the Indochina negotiations that led to the agreements of early 1973.

Taylor believes that on Vietnam, as elsewhere, the United States should have negotiated from strength, giving nothing away simply for the sake of negotiating—as President Johnson mistakenly did in 1968. The model, rather, should be something more like the performance of President Nixon and Dr.

Kissinger in 1972-73: When the conditions were right, "Nixon's uncompromising military measures against Hanoi . . . overcame any residual reluctance to accept the inevitable." Among other key elements that Taylor cites were the cooling of anitwar sentiment in the United States and the skill of the President and his National Security Staff in avoiding harmful publicity.

The Communists in Korea and Vietnam, Taylor concludes, saw "war as an extension of politics . . . and negotiations as an extension of war by diplomatic, political, and psychological means." We must learn, he argues, "to harness our politico-diplomatic resources with all other forms of national power in pursuing our negotiating objectives."

While Taylor concentrates on the importance of power, Paul Warnke concentrates on the importance of the terms and objectives of the two sides. The United States, he believes, was never willing to concede enough to gain Hanoi's agreement until 1972-73. In effect, we finally agreed to withdraw without resolving the continuing struggle. The basic problem for the United States was not disparity in force—which favored us—but the disparity in goals:

> An uncompromising approach has, of course, worked in the past. It will again, when ours is the greater strength and when the end-result is perceived as integral to our national security. But it apt to be fruitless, regardless of our edge in power, when what is at stake is more important to our adversary than it is to us. This was our plight in Vietnam.

Successful negotiations, in Warnke's view, tend to be on issues in which the status quo can be ratified. They should not be carried out in too much secrecy, lest their results be greeted with suspicion by an uninformed Congress and public. And, he argues, while the strength of one's posture is important, negotiating opportunities can be lost "if either side tries to accumulate more bargaining chips in the hope of making a better deal." Thus, with regard to strategic arms, "negotiations that

become an occasion for military build-up, rather than reciprocal restraint, are worse than none at all."

General Maxwell D. Taylor (Rtd.) was Chief of Staff, U.S.
Army, 1955-59; Chairman of the Joint Chiefs of Staff, 1962-64;
and the American Ambassador in Vietnam, 1964-65. He is the
author of *Swords into Plowshares*.

Paul C, Warnke, a Washington attorney, was General
Counsel for the Department of Defense 1966-67, and Assistant Secretary of Defense (International Security Affairs),
1967-69.

Waging Negotiations—A Vietnam Study

MAXWELL TAYLOR

It is no doubt a good thing to conquer on the field of battle but it needs a greater wisdom and a greater skill to make use of victory.

Polyibus

My first exposure to the difficulties of negotiating with Communists occurred in 1953 when I assumed command of the Eighth Army in Korea. The armistice talks had been suspended but were resumed shortly after my arrival in February. My initial interest in the talks arose primarily from the obvious ties between the negotiations and the military behavior of the Sino-Korean enemy facing the Eighth Army. Subsequently, I came to view them within broader aspects as a demonstration of Communist skill in coordinating and synchronizing negotiations with military operations, which should have provided guidance in our later experience in Vietnam.

When the armistice talks had begun in 1951, their principal military effect was to stop the advance of our army into North Korea. Since the initial progress of the talks raised hopes in Washington and in the United Nations that a cease-fire was at hand, the Eighth Army was ordered in November 1951 to cease offensive operations and to assume a passive defense along a line largely in North Korean territory. It was the beginning of the military stalemate that lasted until shortly after my arrival.

Sometime early in 1953 the Communist leaders apparently decided that it was in their interest to agree to an armistice despite indications that thousands of their prisoners in our hands would refuse to return voluntarily to North Korea or China. At the same time, they sought to cover their diplomatic retreat by a resumption of offensive military operations in the hope that, if the latter were successful, the result would support a claim of final victory.

From May until the armistice in July, the Communists gave us an impressive demonstration of the talk-fight technique which our diplomats were to encounter later in the Vietnam negotiations. While the conferees in Panmunjom were arguing about the eventual cease-fire line, enemy military commanders began a series of probing attacks of mounting intensity, culminating on July 13 in the largest coordinated attack of the war. While it gained a few miles of mountainous terrain, it cost the enemy over 100,000 casualties. Nevertheless, on the morning following the armistice Communist soldiers were posing on hilltops, waving propaganda banners prepared long in advance, and singing paeans of victory.

During this period of intense activity, I received frequent tips of enemy intentions from the discussion at Panmunjom. Whenever the Communists claimed territory they did not hold, I could expect an attack in that vicinity and usually got it. The correlation of the state of the battlefield with the state of the negotiations was clear and immediate. In determining the outcome at the table, the logic and eloquence of our spokesmen were as nothing compared to the location of the infantry front line.

Like most of my contemporaries in Korea, I carried into the Vietnam conflict a deep feeling of the essentiality of avoiding a repetition of the obvious mistakes made in the Panmunjom negotiations. Many American participants had stressed, in official reports and published writings, the importance both of keeping all forms of pressure on the enemy to prevent stalling and of being willing to break off talks when progress became impossible. They also emphasized the point that a negotiated settlement with Communists can be no more favorable to us than the power relationship existing between the two sides at the moment of signing.

Despite having participated since 1961 in deliberations on our Southeast Asian policy, I never participated in serious consideration of the problem of terminating our involvement in Vietnam until I arrived in Saigon as ambassador in 1964. The first formal document on the subject of which I am aware was a cable to Washington from our embassy in January 1965. Largely the work of Deputy Ambassador U. Alexis Johnson, it raised for consideration many of the persistent issues which were to engage the attention of our negotiation planners in coming years.

Among the views expressed in the cable was a preference for basing the overall American position on a return to the 1954 and 1962 Geneva accords, with participation in the discussions initially limited, if possible, to the United States and North Vietnam. While we in the embassy recognized the overriding interest of South Vietnam in any settlement, we wanted to bypass at the outset the question of Vietcong participation, a thorny issue which any South Vietnamese presence in discussions are sure to raise.

In addition, the cable discussed briefly the possible play of the so-called blue chips: those counters we had to barter for the things we wanted. Our list of blue chips was fairly long—a progressive reduction of U.S. military personnel in South Vietnam; amnesty and civil rights for the Vietcong; safe passage to North Vietnam for those who wanted to go there; a normalization of trade relations between North and South; and an American-sponsored economic development program for all Indochina.

Washington seemed to like the cable and authorized us to broach selected parts with the Saigon government. However, by the time I left Saigon for Washington in late 1965, we had made only limited progress in exploring local views.

Back in Washington, I immediately became involved in pursuing these matters, and remained so until the end of the Johnson Administration. Throughout most of this period, it often appeared that our government was more interested in getting negotiations started than in creating conditions favorable to their success prior to initiating them. When in early 1965 President Johnson made the difficult decision to introduce American ground forces into South Vietnam and to begin air attacks against North Vietnam, he matched the military effort with a diplomatic effort to engage Hanoi in negotiations. He liked to call attention to the Seal of the United States, on which the American eagle grips the arrows of war in one talon and the olive branch in the other. This symbolized what he wanted to do, Johnson said: strike hard at the enemy with the arrows while simultaneously offering the olive branch. He therefore launched his peace offensive, enlisting in the cause not only his own high officials but friendly and neutral governments, as well as the Secretary General of the United Nations, Pope Paul, and all the sundry other helpers likely to join forces with him. His general theme was unconditional discussions anywhere, at any time, with a cease-fire as a first order of business.

I must confess that, from the start, I considered the peace offensive premature and a likely disservice to the cause of true peace. From 1965 to the end of 1967, there was nothing in the power relationship between the two sides which offered hope of successful negotiations, even if we got them started. Also, there was a strong probability that the enemy would interpret our perfervid efforts to "stop the shooting and start talking" as signs of weakness and lack of confidence. Such a misreading, I feared, would make genuine negotiation on a basis of reciprocal concession highly unlikely.

A final reservation was my conviction that our leaders were not ready for opening negotiations. There were always unsettled internal arguments in official Washington regarding negotiating objectives and tactics. Many lasted at least until the very opening of talks in Paris in 1968. While everyone was generally in agreement that our overall objective was an independent South Vietnam free from attack, there was a great deal of uncertainty over how to reach that goal via the negotiating route.

Most of the uncertainties clustered around three points: the preferred modalities for negotiations, arrangements for a satisfactory cease-fire, and the play of the blue chips. The first involved such matters as the location, participants, auspices, and agenda for negotiations. As to the site, we considered meeting in several neutral cities, on a neutral ship at sea, or in a tent in the Demilitarized Zone. The participants, all agreed, should include the United States and the three Vietnamese elements—South Vietnam, North Vietnam, and the Viet-cong—but we recognized the difficulty of getting all three to sit down together in a cooperative mood. We would have liked the talks conducted under auspices of the United Nations, although it was quite clear by that time that the United Nations wanted no part of the task and, in any case, would be rejected by the Communist side.

Discussion of the cease-fire appeared in various contexts. It was a key issue, involving some fundamental choices. Most Washington officials favored separating military from political items on the conference agenda, and addressing military matters first. I favored either dealing with the political first or treating the two packages simultaneously by separate groups of conferees. My reason was the inordinate complexity of the arrangements for a genuine cease-fire under the conditions existing in Vietnam, which would require the expenditure of as much time as a political settlement. The latter, if achieved first or concurrently, would vastly simplify the cease-fire problem as both sides would know the outcome on the vital political issues before putting down their arms. Furthermore, we needed to continue military operations while negotiating to avoid repeating our mistake in Korea. We should not, I thought, forego military pressure as a means of including prompt and substantive discussions—an argument often advanced.

Although I peppered my associates with memoranda on the subject and although the President never rejected my argument, I made few converts. Interoffice papers were constantly appearing which assumed the practical impossibility of continuing vigorous military operations during negotiations, and for a cease-fire as the first order of business.

While opposing this view, I had to admit to myself that very little had been done to prepare American public opinion for a hard negotiating stance—if our representative decided to take one. A early as July 1966, I appealed to President Johnson to rally public support behind a policy that would refuse to pay a price to the enemy for entering upon negotiations or to accept a protracted stalemate on the Panmunjom model. The President seemed to agree in principle but never directed positive or persistent action to influence public opinion.

As to the play of the blue chips, the question was always what we should give for what we would get in return. After 1965, it was fairly clear what the enemy wanted from us: cessation of the bombing of North Vietnam above all, a halt in the American build-up in South Vietnam, the eventual withdrawal of all American forces, an end to our support of our South Vietnamese allies, and probably economic aid for North Vietnam (although Hanoi had shown no interest in the matter when President Johnson first suggested it in 1965). For our part, we wanted the enemy to stop all military and terrorist acts in South Vietnam, to end further infiltration, to withdraw North Vietnamese forces in the South, and to dissolve or withdraw Vietcong units.

The biggest debate always arose over what to get in exchange for a cessation of the bombing of North Vietnam. Most of my colleagues were inclined to equate it with a cessation of infiltration. I was opposed to such a deal, because we could never be sure whether enemy infiltration had really stopped, whereas the whole world would know whether our planes were bombing North Vietnamese targets. Instead, I favored lumping our offensive ground operations in South Vietnam with our bombing of the North, and agreeing to stop both if the enemy stopped their acts of violence in the South. The advantage of such a deal was that all parts of it could be roughly verified. We kept daily charts recording incidents of Vietcong terror and guerrilla warfare, by which we could check the ebb and flow within broad limits. Conceivably, we could adjust the number of our bombing sorties to the fluctuations in the number of these incidents. If they subsided completely, we could stop all bombing and there would in effect be a cease-fire based on mutual restraint.

This kind of drill, inconclusive though it always was, demonstrated the importance of not giving away any of our blue chips as a prepayment for the negotiations since it was obvious that to get the chips we wanted from the enemy we had to husband every one of our own. But such prudential considerations were discarded in the climactic year of 1968.

While these internal debates of 1965-68 dragged on, the military situation was slowly improving. Our counteroffensive made possible by the introduction of American ground forces in 1965 began to bear fruit in 1966; by 1967 it had forced the main enemy units back to the frontiers and into the Laotian and Cambodian sanctuaries. Sometime toward the latter part of 1967, Hanoi leaders appear to have decided upon a drastic change in military strategy. They abandoned the protracted war tactics followed since 1965 in favor of an all-out drive for victory in early 1968: the Tet offensive.

This offensive was a disastrous military defeat for Hanoi: over 30,000 men killed in the first two weeks of the fighting, and some 120,000 lives lost in the first six months of the year. Nevertheless, the enemy scored a psychological victory in the United States and abroad, made possible largely by the defeatist reporting of events by American reporters in Vietnam and by the pessimistic reaction to these reports in the United States. The effects of lowered national morale were far-reaching, and undoubtedly influenced President Johnson's dramatic decision at the end of March to withdraw from the Presidential campaign and to constrict the bombing of North Vietnam. Unfortunately, the latter action constituted an unrequired de-escalation which was, in effect, a down payment for the privilege of negotiating—something we had promised ourselves never to do.

The President's announcement of March 31 was followed by further efforts to get Hanoi to negotiate, but the leaders there continued to play hard to get. When they did consent to talk, it was only about "the unconditional cessation of the bombing and all other acts of war" by the United States against North Vietnam. So when our envoys, Averell Harriman and Cyrus Vance, opened the Paris negotiations in May, they were immediately confronted with a refusal by the North Vietnamese representative, Xuan Thuy, and his associates to discuss reciprocal concessions. They insisted that we stop all bombing without imposing any conditions whatsoever.

The impasse was not broken until President Johnson accepted a gambit recommended by his Paris representatives: the so-called "understandings." The proposition was that Harriman and Vance would indicate to their counterparts that we were about to cease all bombing of North Vietnam, but with the understanding (which we did not ask them to confirm) that substantive negotiations would promptly follow, that the government of South Vietnam would participate, and that during the talks the enemy would respect the Demilitarized Zone, would abstain from attacks on the principal South Vietnamese cities, and would not fire on our unarmed reconnaissance planes over North Vietnam.

When these understandings were explained to the Communist delegates, they neither accepted nor rejected our proposition. Nevertheless, with the concurrence of his principal subordinates and despite his personal reservations, the President on October 31 announced a halt to all American attacks on North Vietnam by air, sea, and artillery, and an expansion of the Paris talks to include South Vietnam and the Vietcong. Unable to refer directly to the "understandings," he justified his change of position by reference to unspecified developments in the Paris talks and by his conviction that the United States could henceforth expect productive negotiations "in an atmosphere conducive to progress."

It was soon apaprent that he and his advisers had been misled. When the so-called plenary sessions finally got under way, the Communists showed no intention of cooperating in productive negotiations. They boldly denied that there had been any "understandings," insisted that the Americans had stopped the bombing unconditionally, and proceeded during the ensuing months and years intermittently to violate the Demilitarized Zone, attack South Vietnamese cities, and fire on reconnaissance flights over North Vietnam.

The stalemate of the public meetings which followed extended throughout the final days of the Johnson Administration and well into President Nixon's Administration. President Johnson's advisers suggested numerous ways of breaking the impasse, which amounted to additional unilateral concessions: the withdrawal of some American forces from South Vietnam to demonstrate our pacific intentions or a de-escalation of our military activities in South Vietnam in hope of generating a corresponding restraint on the other side. I favored an opposite course. In view of the heavy casualties inflicted on the enemy in the first half of 1968, I thought General Abrams should now smite them hip and thigh, to the extent permitted by his current troop strength. Military experience had convinced me that short, intensive fighting causes fewer casualties in the long run than prolonged campaigns of attrition, and offers far greater hope of a prompt termination.

Another fallacy, in my view, was the opinion occasionally voiced by some officials that our side should never suggest publicly that we might resume bombing North Vietnam. I thought it in our interest to keep Hanoi always conscious of that possibility and to squelch any hope that the President had lost his option because of fear of public reaction. Hence my repeated argument that the government should prepare American public opinion for this contingency.

The advent of the Nixon Administration ended my participation in these intramural debates over the conduct of negotiations. However, as an interested bystander during the ensuing years, I was gratified to see how the new President proceeded to shake up the situation in Paris and South Vietnam. It is true that his early indication of intention to proceed with the unilateral withdrawal of some American ground forces disturbed me. While some reduction of our forces had been made possible by the progress of the Vietnamization program and would have some effect in moderating antiwar sentiment at home, I was afraid that Saigon and Hanoi would interpret the action as the beginning of a retreat. However, Hanoi, always aware of the importance of the role of American public opinion, correctly anticipated the adverse effects from their point of view of a reduction in American casualty lists. Therefore, they claimed that our troop withdrawals were a fraud.

If I was cold to this first initiative of the new President, I heartily applauded most of what he did subsequently to stimulate progress toward his goal of an honorable negotiated settlement. When Ambassador Lodge resigned as head of the United States delegation in Paris at the end of 1969, I liked the way the President refused to play along with a continuation of the propaganda show and delayed the appointment of Lodge's successor while pressing for the extended use of secret bilateral talks.

On the military front, at the President's bidding, the armed forces kept pressure on the enemy, who suffered an annual average of over 100,000 men killed in action during 1969-72. As the number of American combat forces declined, it was the South Vietnamese forces which inflicted most of these losses, ominous evidence to Hanoi of the success of Vietnamization.

Also to his credit, President Nixon ruthlessly discarded many of the dogmas of the final Johnson years about what we should or could not do—that we could not afford to break off the Paris negotiations, that we could never resume the bombing of North Vietnam or attack the enemy troop sanctuaries in Cambodia and Laos. He did all these things and more. Antiwar sentiment was sometimes inflamed, but resentment died quickly as the success of these actions became evident. By a series of diplomatic and military moves he succeeded, in Clausewitz's words, "in putting the enemy in a situation more disadvantageous than the sacrifice we demanded of him." After all, the immediate sacrifice demanded was not great, merely to join with us in a serious attempt to reach a negotiated settlement.

However, it took heroic efforts by President Nixon and Dr. Kissinger at the end of 1972 to bring about this culmination. Many factors contributed to their eventual success. Added to enemy troop losses, the obvious success of Vietnamization, and the cooling of Moscow and Peking toward a continuation of the war, Nixon's landslide reelection and the cooling antiwar sentiment in the United States imposed a change of policy. Nixon's uncompromising military measures against Hanoi, starting with the closing of Haiphong harbor in May and ending in the intensive bombing of military targets in the Hanoi area in December, overcame any residual reluctance to accept the inevitable. After some five years of futile pseudo-negotiations which had accomplished virtually nothing, the time was finally right. Within three months, the contending parties formulated and signed an agreement which was generally consistent with the national goals for Vietnam pursued by American policy since 1954. However, the continued pressure of North Vietnamese forces in South Vietnam discouraged any hope of enduring peace.

II

Whatever one's attitude toward the many controversial aspects of our Vietnam involvement, it should be hard to disagree about the need to profit from its lessons. They fall into many categories—diplomatic, political, military, economic, and psychological. This essay focuses attention primarily on lessons to be derived from the negotiations which began in the summer of 1968 and ended with the cease-fire of January 1973.

We need to profit from this aspect of the Vietnam experience because the record shows, unhappily, that we learned little from the parallel experience at Panmunjom. In spite of the recorded warnings of our representatives in Korea regarding the Communist approach to negotiations, most American political leaders in 1968 viewed the Paris conference as a forum in which to establish our case before the world—not, as the Communists regarded it, as another hostile front in extension of the battlefield. In their view, the contest on this new front was to be waged with the same fervor, tenacity, and implacability as that shown by their soldiers and guerrillas. As modern disciples of Clausewitz, they regarded war as an extension of politics by military, paramilitary, and terrorist means and negotiations as an extension of war by diplomatic, political, and psychological means.

Acting on this concept, our adversaries displayed great skill in coordinating their actions on the battlefield, in Hanoi and in Paris, and in keeping their objectives all aligned on a single target: the will of the American leadership, which they wished to bend to their political purpose. Recognizing that in a democracy, leaders are necessarily responsive to the will of the people, they bombarded our domestic opinion with continuing propaganda from Paris and Hanoi, often using for that purpose the "free world" media.

On our side, there was no such clear conception of the nature of negotiations in general or of the objectives of these particular negotiations. There was much talk in Washington about the need to "stop the shooting and start the talking" or to move the conflict from the battlefield to the conference table, but little agreement prior to opening discussions on the specific positions to be taken on specific issues. Many thought that we should remain flexible on most points until the adversary took a position. This desire for flexibility often concealed a vagueness of purpose or a lack of commitment to a desired outcome.

Some of this indecisiveness could have been avoided, I believe, had our negotiating team been designated early in the war and then been required to think through the coming battle of wits and wills in much the same way as military leaders prepare for an important campaign. I suggested a war-gaming procedure as a device for testing the advantages and disadvantages of different negotiation tactics—producing only amusement, I suspect, over this aberration of the rigid military mind.

During the negotiations, Presidents Johnson and Nixon were often publicly criticized for their alleged efforts to create a position of strength from which to negotiate. Some critics apparently felt that there was something immoral in such efforts, particularly if they resulted in military actions such as the invasion of the Laotian and Cambodian sanctuaries and the final intensified bombing of the North just prior to the cease-fire in January 1973.

As I understand the expression, "negotiating from a position of strength" describes at least two cases. The first is the kind of situation which confronted the Japanese representatives when they faced the American victors on the deck of the battleship *Missouri*. Their side of the negotiation amounted merely to recognizing formally a state of total defeat. The second is a situation in which neither side has triumphed decisively, but one has unused strength available which could be invoked to overcome further resistance at the conference table. This was, roughly, the situation facing the German leadership in 1918.

Since the objective of total victory by military means was rejected from the outset, it was a situation of the second kind which most American leaders wished to establish in the Vietnam negotiations. They always had the potential to increase the military pressure—if not restrained by concern for possible Sino-Soviet reaction and by public opinion at home. Such restraint had been effective in the Johnson Administration and also in the early years under President Nixon, so that Hanoi had grown to hope that, through stubborn persistence on their part, aided by American antiwar sentiment, they could prevail in Paris. The President's tough response to the spring offensive in 1972, and to the October hedging by Hanoi's representatives on private understandings reached with Dr. Kissinger, put an end to these hopes. In my opinion, the result was further proof of the essentiality of negotiating from strength when dealing with an adversary who rejects reciprocal concessions and will yield only to superior coercive strength.

Without having established a clear plan for the conduct of the negotiations, it was always easy for American officials to lose sight of the primary objective at the conference table—to establish an independent South Vietnam free from aggression. But there was often a tendency to deviate from this objective and to substitute some changeling purpose such as peace, a cease-fire, or merely negotiations as an end in themselves. Obviously, if peace without qualification had been our goal, we should never have taken up arms in the first place. If our costly efforts were to be justified, it would be by establishing a better *post bellum* situation in Vietnam than would have existed had we not resorted to arms. Such a situation could not be obtained through negotiations so long as Hanoi's hopes were high for a collapse of American will.

Another factor which created difficulties was the American

impatience for quick results, first in getting talks started, then in achieving a prompt settlement. President Johnson had set the pace with his multiple peace initiatives (*The Vantage Point* lists seventy-two during 1964-68) and the sixteen bombing pauses. These efforts culminated in the unilateral concessions implicit in the "understandings" of 1968. These overtures, made with the best intentions, whetted Hanoi's appetite for further concessions and dimmed the chances of an early settlement at the conference table until President Nixon finally convinced Hanoi's leaders that no further unilateral concessions would be forthcoming.

Not surprisingly, the negotiations raised many problems in our relations with our South Vietnamese ally. Hanoi's leaders were keenly aware that the conference offered potential trouble between Saigon and Washington, and they made repeated efforts to exploit the opportunity. Unfortunately, Americans sometimes made the task easier by gratuitous affronts to Vietnamese sensibilities. From at least 1961 onward, the South Vietnamese found many occasions to be suspicious of American intentions, always fearful that despite our repeated professions of fidelity, sometime, somehow, we would abandon them. Over the years, these fears have been fed by the Laotian Accord of 1962, by American involvement in the overthrow of Diem in 1963, and by the campaign of defamation directed at the Diem and Thieu governments by the liberal American press.

On our side, the political turbulence in Saigon after the fall of Diem had raised serious doubts that there could be an effective South Vietnamese government just as defeats of South Vietnamese troops caused concern over the ability of the country to defend itself. President Thieu's uncooperative conduct aroused American resentment when, in the last days of the Johnson Administration, he delayed joining the Paris talks. In 1972, his objections to the text of the final settlement were even more irritating to Americans eager to be immediately rid of the war. But all things considered, our relationship with Saigon probably survived with fewer scars than one might have expected. In any case, our disagreements and difficulties with the South Vietnamese government should be a reminder that an alliance often does not entail a gain in aggregate strength or represent an unalloyed advantage. Inevitably, both parties sacrifice some degree of freedom of action, a loss which is particularly irksome in the final stages of a long, exhausting struggle.

Most of the problems which I have mentioned were illustrative of the difficulties which a democracy encounters in conducting a negotiation with a tough, well-trained opponent. There are others which should be noted. In the course of a conflict waged without the domestic constraints and inhibitions imposed by a declared state of war, many public figures in the United States felt free to give public airing to their views on the Vietnam situation—views which were often contrary to those of the government. The media felt no obligation to moderate criticism of Vietnam policy any more than of domestic policy. To arouse popular support for the war, a commodity always in short supply, government spokesmen often had to indulge in prolonged public explanations, in the course of which they inevitably gave indications of future intentions and in some degree exposed their hand to the enemy. In deference to the Wilsonian vision of open covenants openly arrived at, the Paris negotiations were conducted in a goldfish bowl of garish publicity with klieg lights ablaze and TV cameras rolling—to the gratification of Hanoi propagandists. The conclusion is inescapable that our adherence to traditional democratic practices appropriate for times of peace made it very difficult for our side to compete on an equal footing with our totalitarian adversaries in the settlement of an undeclared limited war.

One suspects that it was a desire to nullify some of those disadvantages which led President Nixon quickly to press for secret discussions in parallel with the public sideshow in Paris. In any case, the covenant eventually agreed to in 1973 was certainly not openly arrived at; rather, it was produced with a secrecy in the best tradition of Metternich or Talleyrand. An obvious question is whether this is a change in American diplomatic style that is likely to remain or whether it is a transitory phenomenon, the result of the concurrence of two unusual personalities, the President and Dr. Kissinger. At any rate, the working methods of this redoubtable team not only in Paris, but in Peking and Moscow as well, have provided an interesting solution to many of the problems which have plagued our diplomacy in the past. Their success thus far permits the hope that they have found a way to correct some of the inherent weaknesses which de Tocqueville noted in a democracy in "combining its measure with secrecy and awaiting their consequences with patience."

In an era in which President Nixon hoped to replace international confrontation with negotiation, we need to reflect on the growing use of blackmail in negotiations as a coercive method short of military force. In our diplomatic bout with Hanoi, our adversaries used the American prisoners-of-war in this manner, who, as hostages, represented a blue chip of enormous value for bargaining purposes. Unfortunately, we had exposed our weakness to such pressures in paying ransom to Castro for the captives of the Cuban Brigade after the Bay of Pigs affair and in obtaining the liberation of the *Pueblo* crew from the North Koreans in 1968 by a quasi-confession of guilt. These episodes were not missed by the North Vietnamese, who probably decided early in the war to exploit our prisoners for all they were worth. We confirmed them in this course by showing premature concern for their return, expressed most conspicuously by unofficial American emissaries of various persuasions and motivations who journeyed to the enemy capital to plead for their release.

As the negotiations drew to a close, the prisoner-of-war issue was an albatross about the necks of Dr. Kissinger and his associates. Without the prisoners to consider, we could have ignored Hanoi, withdrawn our combat forces, carried out the full Vietnamization program as planned, and continued our bombing attacks until North Vietnam withdrew its major units from the South. As it was, uncertain about getting our prisoners back and always fearing reprisals against them while in captivity, we felt obliged to seek a signed agreement covering their release and to make concessions for it which included conniving at the continued presence of North Vietnamese army units left in South Vietnam.

The prisoner issues raises a serious question. How does a reasonably humane Western power deal with a cold-blooded, calculating adversary whose capacity for inhumanity to captured enemy soldiers is matched only by an indifference about what happened to his own? Appeals to the Geneva Convention on the treatment of prisoners-of-war are of no avail; no more than were appeals to world opinion which, during the Vietnam war, showed little interest in the barbarities of our Communist opponents. The payment of a price for our prisoners—i.e., overlooking the presence of North Vietnamese soldiers in South Vietnam—sets another precedent which will encourage a repetition of this kind of blackmail.

The foregoing discussions highlight some of our negotiating experiences in Vietnam which may provide guidance for the future. As they are limited to my personal impressions, the study is of necessity subjective. But it does, I hope, focus attention on the need for a thorough examination of the diplomatic activities of our government during this period. We must learn not only to improve our negotiating tactics and techniques, but also to harness our politico-diplomatic resources with all other forms of national power in pursuing our negotiating objectives. This need for a fuller integration of power applies in particular to the mutually supporting roles of the political and military arms of our government. Our military leaders learned long ago the importance of maintaining an elaborate school system to train professionals in the conduct of war by means of case studies of past experience. I would hope that our political leaders, mindful of the sentiments of Polybius quoted at the start of this essay, would devote similar efforts to acquire "greater wisdom and a greater skill to make use of victory," by whatever means achieved.

The Search for Peace—Vietnam Negotiations

PAUL WARNKE

As negotiators, our self-image is a somewhat muddled one. On the one hand, we recall with affectionate pride the Yankee trader of folklore and perhaps of fact—a shrewd bargainer who typically got the better of the bargain, or thought he did. But the Yankee trader knew that for a deal to be reached and held, there had to be something in it for both sides. He had to have a live horse to sell and he had to receive something of real value in return.

But this "David Harum" image doesn't match our traditional view of negotiations on the international scene. There, in dealing with either present or potential adversaries, we have come to be wary of the processes of give-and-take. Our self-image stereotype is that of the innocent abroad—the honest American whose integrity leaves him ill-equipped to deal with the callous cynics of the old world. Accordingly, the stand on principle has been admired, and the flexible position despised. Perhaps this moralistic stance is in part the product of the relative geographic isolation which enabled us, for the first century and a quarter of our national existence, discriminately to select instances in which we would deal with foreign adversaries. And then our real bargaining secret was first to win on the battlefield.

Whatever the reason, we have tended to view negotiations with foreign rivals (and at times even with allies) as a conflict between good and evil and hence not susceptible of genuine compromise. Such sorry episodes as Neville Chamberlain's "peace in our time" confirmed our view that you could not "do business with Hitler." Yalta, Potsdam, and the subsequent failure of the Soviet Union to behave as we thought a wartime ally should, provided further evidence of the perfidy of foreigners and the dangers any accommodation might pose to our national security.

The relative rarity, magnitude, and importance of our international conflicts led us to expect and to demand unconditional surrender. Not dependent upon empire, we were, until quite recently, spared the vexation of the imperialist's minor foreign quarrels, where the tranquillity of the empire often required that the other party be at least minimally satisfied with the results.

An uncompromising approach has, of course, worked in the past. It will again, when ours is the greater strength and when the end-result is perceived as integral to our national security. But it is apt to be fruitless, regardless of our edge in power, when what is at stake is more important to our adversary than it is to us. This was our plight in Vietnam.

From the start of the major American intervention in 1965, President Johnson spoke repeatedly about his search for peace. At the same time, however, he stated consistently his conviction that our own security was at stake in the successful resistance to North Vietnam's ambition. In his speech at Johns Hopkins University on April 7, 1965, Johnson called for a peaceful settlement in Vietnam and offered the promise of a billion-dollar American investment for a development effort in which North Vietnam would be a beneficiary. But he argued that any peaceful settlement demanded "an independent South Vietnam." And he insisted that only "in a world where every country can shape its own destiny . . . will our own freedom be finally secure."

In pursuing his Vietnam policy, President Johnson faced a

double-barrelled problem. The steady increase in American participation in the struggle did not seem to discourage the leaders in Hanoi and the National Liberation Front. But this growth in the intensity and the cost of our Indochinese adventure did evoke a steadily rising tempo of dissent in the United States. President Johnson's problem was to hold his public while plunging deeper into what many critics increasingly characterized as a morass without real meaning for American interests.

His constant call for negotiations was thus addressed as much to his domestic audience as it was to his foreign adversaries. He voiced repeatedly his willingness to go any place in the world to meet with the other side for full and frank discussions of a negotiated settlement.

In Vietnam, the rationale for the massive American involvement was consistent only in its elusiveness. Four Presidents attested to the necessity of our presence there. Each of their attempted explanations scaled higher in emotion than in analytical content. And the imprecise articulation of our goals compounded the difficulty of achieving them by the negotiating route.

I have referred to the negotiator's need to have something he can offer to his rival. In Vietnam, all that Hanoi wanted was all of Vietnam. Whatever our negotiators might from time to time have regarded as the real reason for our involvement, they always knew that this was something they could not give. The "Fourteen Points for Peace in Southeast Asia," released by the State Department on January 7, 1966, asserted that we would "welcome negotiations without preconditions" and announced support for "free elections in South Vietnam to give the South Vietnamese a government of their own choice." But these same fourteen points included one which tied the removal of U.S. troops in South Vietnam to the cessation of North Vietnamese hostilities.

As for free elections, a theme sounded consistently in the years that followed, they appealed more to American sentiment than to Vietnamese reality. East Asian experience suggests that elections there serve largely to record a political decision already reached. President Thieu's electoral charades were not atypical.

Perhaps the most forthcoming proposal advanced by the United States during the period of American build-up was embodied in a cryptic phrase from the Manila Summit Conference of October 25, 1966. It was noted that the allied forces would be withdrawn from South Vietnam "as the other side withdraws its forces to the North, ceases infiltration, and the level of violence thus subsides." The time limit for withdrawal of those forces was set as "not later than six months after the above conditions have been fulfilled."

Contemporary evidence indicates that this language was intended to convey the thought that American and other forces supporting the Saigon government would withdraw if the North Vietnamese did so, and even though the Vietcong continued to fight on in their opposition to the Saigon regime. The subsidence in the level of violence sufficient to bring about American disengagement was meant to be that which would ensue automatically from the removal of Hanoi's military forces. The residual level of violence occasioned by indigenous rebels would not postpone the return home of American and other foreign troops.

The ambiguity of the Manila communiqué, however it might have translated into Vietnamese, may be sufficient to explain North Vietnam's failure to respond. Perhaps, however, even total comprehension might not have moved Hanoi because the communiqué embodied the principle of mutual troop withdrawal. At no point was North Vietnam ever willing to accept the description of its forces as foreign in any part of Vietnam, or to equate its withdrawal with ours.

President Johnson's calls for peaceful settlement were, in my opinion, entirely sincere. Dramatic corroboration of his sincerity was evident when in March 1968, in an effort to precipitate talks, he ceased all bombing north of the Nineteenth Parallel and, even more compelling, when he announced at the same time that he would leave public life when his term ended in ten months.

These actions were, in fact, a partial implementation of the offer made to Hanoi in the President's San Antonio speech of September 19, 1967. And the March moves suffered from the same inherent limitation as the San Antonio formula: neither sketched even a bare outline of what we would be able to propose as a remotely feasible political settlement.

Instead, what the San Antonio formula offered was a concession designed simply to bring about negotiations, without any promise as to what these negotiations might produce. President Johnson said in September:

> The United States is willing to stop all aerial and naval bombardment of North Vietnam when this will lead promptly to productive discussions. We, of course, assume that while discussions proceed, North Vietnam would not take advantage of the bombing cessation or limitation.

In making this offer, the President asserted that this was something "we have told Hanoi time and time and time again." It did resemble earlier formulations, but in fact it had new elements carefully designed to get around certain sensitivities of the North Vietnamese. To achieve an end to the bombing, they were not to be required to withdraw their forces from South Vietnam. Under the San Antonio formula, they needed only to indicate that a bombing halt would "lead promptly to productive discussion." Of equal importance, they were no longer asked, as a precondition, to provide assurances that they would not take advantage of a halt in the American bombing. Instead, this was something we would "assume" while the discussions proceeded. And, as subsequently made more explicit by Clark Clifford in hearings in January 1968 on his confirmation as Secretary of Defense, North Vietnam would not be regarded as taking advantage if the infiltration of men and supplies continued but did not increase over what had existed during the bombing.

The San Antonio approach, partially implemented in March 1968, was sufficient to bring Hanoi to the bargaining table. The complete cessation of American attacks on North

Vietnam in October of that year, again based on our assumption that Hanoi would not exploit this forbearance, enabled the talks to move on to substantive matters.

But in moving the conflict from the battlefield to the bargaining table, we chose no easier game. In war, we had the power to destroy and conquer North Vietnam, although sound considerations restrained our hand—both the risks of Russian or Chinese retaliation and a "decent respect to the opinions of mankind." These, and mounting domestic pressures, prevented such measures as an invasion of the North or an attack on its people that could end Hanoi's physical capacity to achieve by force the reunification of Vietnam.

Thus when the preliminary talks began in May 1968, it was increasingly clear that we had little left to threaten and even less to promise. Our trump card was our ability to withdraw, and we saw no way to make a graceful exit. What we were prepared to offer was of little appeal to the Vietnamese on the other side of the table, however desirable it might be to their giant Communist allies. The latter proved no more skillful than we in coping with a small nation fighting for what it regarded as its national existence.

There is reason to feel that President Nixon took office confident that the key to peace in Vietnam, on terms he could accept, would be found in relations and bargaining between the United States and the two Communist giants. In these relations, there was obviously much that we could offer of interest and of unquestioned value—but not to the North Vietnamese. The inducements within our dispensation were designed for other parties. To the Soviet Union and the People's Republic of China, we could hold out the hope of greater security for each and a relationship with the West that could advance their diplomatic and economic aims. We could ease China's readmission as a respected member of the family of nations. We could provide the Soviet Union with the feedstuffs and the technology that its leaders coveted. But neither China nor the Soviet Union could buy off the North Vietnamese and the Vietcong. They could not give them what we were keeping from them—control over Vietnamese territory they claimed as their own. Whatever may have been the virtues of Administration calls for linkage among international issues, here they were directed to the wrong addressee.

President Nixon's problem was no less complex than that of his predecessor. He, like President Johnson, had to address himself to the audience in Hanoi and the audience here at home. In the United States, the domestic pressures which had earlier foreclosed any real consideration of the all-out military measures that might perhaps have proved decisive were eased by the Nixon program for withdrawal of ground troops and the very existence of the peace talks. Indeed, the asserted need to protect our withdrawing forces and to strengthen our bargaining hand served to rationalize such actions as the extension of the hostilities into Cambodia and Laos and the renewed bombing of North Vietnam. But not all the critics were stilled, and strong sentiment in Congress favored a much more rapid termination of our active military role in Indochina.

These domestic pressures had no real impact, however, on the course of negotiations. The fact that the American presence in Vietnam was steadily reduced bought time for President Nixon to pursue his efforts at settlement with Moscow and with Peking, as well as with the North Vietnamese and NLF in Paris. The country waited and hoped and the war went on.

No amount of time, however, was enough to permit any genuine peace settlement to be formulated. Needed instead was recognition that the goals for which we had intervened in Vietnam could not be achieved by negotiation. We had already learned that they could not be won in limited war.

The intractable fact was that neither Hanoi nor Washington could compromise its position without in effect admitting defeat. The goals were fundamentally irreconcilable because of conflicting perceptions of the political and moral issues involved. The conditions for a true compromise settlement never in fact existed.

For Hanoi, the issue was the right of the nationalist forces inspired by Ho Chi Minh to secure the unification of Vietnam under native control. For us, the issue was the prevention of Communist aggression directed against neighboring states—

aggression we believed would lead to regional Communist hegemony and threaten ultimately the peace of the world. For us, the enemy was international communism. To them, it was Western colonialism.

For Hanoi, to "compromise" and end its military pressure against Saigon would be to capitulate and accept the defeat of an idea that had motivated its leadership since World War II. For the United States, to "compromise" and permit the indigenous forces in Vietnam to work their own way would be to condone the demise of the anti-Communist regime we had supported in Saigon for twenty years.

We wanted our way in Vietnam too much to quit, but not enough to do what proved to be necessary to win a military victory. As the level of our commitment had increased under President Johnson, so did the difficulty of allowing Hanoi to claim the triumph it both craved and expected. President Nixon had changed the nature of our military activity, but not the definition of our security stake in Indochina. A negotiated complete American withdrawal, on terms that risked extending Hanoi's rule throughout Vietnam, was perhaps even harder to accept than unilateral American withdrawal without any agreement. We were always prepared to accept in Paris a pledge by North Vietnam that it would, as Secretary Rusk so often demanded, stop its aggression and "leave its neighbors alone." But Hanoi regarded the South Vietnamese not as neighbors, rather as part of its own family.

Either Vietnam was one, and should be united under the strongest political party, or it was two separate countries, each of which was entitled to live in peace and independence. North Vietnam viewed the first proposition as unassailable truth. The United States regarded the second as historical fact, and one which was intrinsic to world order. It was almost impossible even to join issue on real substance, let alone to conduct useful debate.

Efforts were made repeatedly to separate the military and political issues. Kissinger expounded this "two-track" approach in his *Foreign Affairs* article of January 1969, just before he assumed official responsibilities. But the utter lack of common ground not only blocked the political track, it also meant that the weaker side dare not strike a military deal for fear that the other's political design would then be stamped indelibly on Vietnam.

The negotiating difficulties which the Nixon Administration faced were thus enormous. For Hanoi and the NLF, the stakes were as high as ever. For us, the reasons had almost disappeared. It had become harder and harder to detect any security interest in a war that had already brought down one President. We had serious international business to do, but not with Hanoi and none of it involving Indochina.

But the negotiations rapidly became an end in themselves. The asserted need to win a "peace with honor" precluded adoption of the course urged by many that President Nixon propose to Hanoi the simple solution of a safe withdrawal of American forces and the safe return of our prisoners-of-war.

Instead, President Nixon continued for at least the first three years of his Administration to insist on mutual withdrawal as a prerequisite to settlement. On July 5, 1970, in his television interview with the three network anchormen, Chancellor of NBC, Sevareid of CBS, and Smith of ABC, he said: "We are prepared by negotiation to bring out all of our forces and have no forces at all in South Vietnam if the enemy will negotiate, if they will withdraw theirs." The following year, in an appearance before the American Society of Newspaper Editors on April 17, 1971, he reiterated that "we will have a total withdrawal in 12 months if they would be willing to mutually withdraw their forces." We have since been told that this unyielding stance was changed within the next six weeks. Kissinger informed a press conference on January 26, 1972:

On May 31st, we proposed a withdrawal of American forces. We were prepared to set a deadline for the withdrawal of American forces and the exchange of prisoners. This was the first time that the United States had indicated that it was prepared to do so unilaterally; that is to say, without an equivalent assurance of withdrawal from the other side.

This proposal of May 31, 1971, was not, however, the simple offer to withdraw troops in exchange for American prisoners. A precondition was North Vietnam's agreement to a winner-take-all Presidential election to be held in South Vietnam within six months. Moreover, President Thieu was to continue in office until one month before election, at which time a member of his Saigon government would nominally assume the Presidency. Nor does it appear that the failure to require an "equivalent assurance of withdrawal from the other side" meant that North Vietnamese troops were to be free to remain in South Vietnam. Inasmuch as the proposed settlement would provide that "there will be no further infiltration of outside forces into any of the countries of Indo-China," normal attrition could not be offset even by one-for-one replacement; hence, piecemeal elimination of a North Vietnamese presence would be inevitable. Indeed, this proposal, as phrased by President Nixon on January 25, 1972, envisioned that mutual withdrawal should occur. It specified: "Among the problems that will be settled is the implementation of the principle that all armed forces of the countries of Indo-China must remain within their national frontiers." Under the terms, Hanoi would have had to accept the existence of two Vietnams, with the DMZ transformed from the military demarcation line of the 1954 Geneva Accords into a national boundary.

The insistence on mutual withdrawal seems to have been the principal sticking point in the negotiations from 1969 until late in 1972. The hundreds of thousands of American troops in Vietnam when President Nixon took office gave him a powerful bargaining tool, had he chosen to use it. On a number of occasions, the North Vietnamese hinted strongly that they would respond favorably to a proposal for withdrawal of these forces in return for the repatriation of American prisoners-of-war. Among such overtures were that of Ha Van Lau, North Vietnam's second-ranking man in Paris, on December 18, 1969. Both U.S. Congressman Leggett of California and Chalmers Roberts of the *Washington Post* were told by Hanoi's negotiating team, in June of 1971, that if the

United States would set a date for withdrawal, the release of the prisoners could be negotiated, without any requirement that President Thieu be removed from power in Saigon.

The settlement of January 1973 was, in essence, based on this combination of American troop withdrawal and return of American prisoners. These were the objectives which we shared with the other side. Both we and they wanted our men out of Vietnam and, with the American military presence eliminated, Hanoi had no further use for our prisoners-of-war. Under the agreement, North Vietnam maintained its own forces in the South.

The political differences, which remained as intractable as ever, were submerged under the murky cover of present ambiguities and future improbabilities. Reconciliations, elections, supervised cease-fire, and peaceful reconciliation were woven into a curtain that did nothing to hide the continuing political and military struggle. For over two years the Vietnamese continued to kill one another in battle. For the same period, we supported the Saigon government in its refusal to seek accommodation with competing political forces. Our combat forces were finally out of Vietnam and, through an act of congressional will, out of the entire Indochinese conflict. But all we achieved in four years of negotiations, while 20,000 Americans died and tens of thousands more were wounded, was the right to leave and to take our prisoners with us.

The record of other and more successful negotiations may shed some light on why the Vietnam talks went so badly. Two of the most important in recent years are the strategic arms limitation talks between the United States and the Soviet Union, which yielded the treaty restricting antiballistic missile deployments, known as SALT I, and the deals struck in Europe, primarily the treaties reached by the Federal Republic of Germany with Russia and Poland. The common and controlling feature in both negotiations is that settlement involved basically the acceptance of the status quo. Probably the optimum climate for agreement exists when those concerned are reasonably content with things the way they are. They then are dealing with a known quantity and on terms that can readily be defined. They do not have to commit themselves to drastic action. The bargain that can be struck is to let well enough alone.

For years the nuclear arms race raged on while the Soviet Union and the United States struggled for strategic superiority. The objective each sought was the traditional one of achieving the military power that could destroy the enemy and leave him powerless to retaliate. In the nuclear field, however, this traditional goal proved to be a meaningless anachronism. Neither country could gain a first-strike capability unless the other were prepared to hold still for it. No known or foreseeable technology could protect the respective populations from devastation from the missiles and bombs that would still be available for retaliation even after an all-out surprise attack.

Our fear of an illusory "missile gap" drove us in the early 1960s to achieve an appreciable numerical edge in ICBMs. Fear of antiballistic missile deployments that might eliminate our assured retaliatory capability led to the development of the Multiple Independently Targetable Re-entry Vehicles (MIRVs) that allow one missile to attack several targets.

For some time the Soviet Union turned a deaf ear to overtures to begin negotiations to control the further growth of nuclear arsenals. It now seems evident that the Russians would not negotiate because they dared not do so when we were ahead of them by every standard across the spectrum of strategic nuclear power. By the beginning of the 1970s, however, any meaningful advantage had been eliminated. Indeed, the Soviet inventory contained more missile launchers, although the United States still had, because of its MIRVs, many more individual warheads.

But on any significant military basis, a state of parity had been reached. It was possible for each country to accept and to preserve the status quo. If there were to be agreement, moreover, the opportunity had to be seized before some major new program or further development destabilized the balance in apparent nuclear strength.

SALT I, in May 1972, did not go as far as it should have to freeze the existing nuclear situation. It did, however, by strict limitations on antiballistic missile defenses, render further accretion of offensive weapons palpably unnecessary. The number of warheads each country can now deliver on the other's soil without effective interference is greater than the number of available targets. Despite the many difficulties that must be resolved in agreeing on a permanent treaty limiting offensive weapons, this ratification of the status quo gave good reason to hope for effective qualitative as well as quantitative controls.

This hope has dimmed with the dubious results thus far in the follow-up of SALT negotiations and the efforts of each side to improve its negotiating position. Much has been made of the argument that new strategic weapon starts are needed by us as "bargaining chips." But experience and logic show that the Soviet Union would insist on offsetting any meaningful improvement in our nuclear arms before fruitful negotiations could proceed. A new weapon that didn't disturb the strategic balance would be, of course, only wasteful. In any case, negotiations that became an occasion for military build-up, rather than reciprocal restraint, are worse than none at all.

Despite the intense interest of other nations, the basic issues of nuclear arms control can only be resolved in bilateral negotiations between the two superpowers. The current agreements to recognize and accept the existing situation in Europe have had a more complex history. With the political and economic reconstruction of Western Europe, a state of affairs was brought into being which should have been satisfactory both to the Soviet Union and to the United States. From our standpoint, the threat of Soviet control over the people and the resources of Western Europe had been averted. The suppression of the Hungarian Freedom Fighters, and the inability of the United States and its NATO allies to do more than lament their fate, confirmed the Soviet buffer in Eastern Europe. Berlin remained as an irritant, but not so severe a one as to provoke a crisis if the other vexing issues of borders and hegemony could be accepted.

It was, for sound political reasons, impossible here for the United States to take the lead. A definition of Germany, agreed upon by Soviet and U.S. negotiators, as being permanently west of the Oder-Neisse line and divided into two states for the indefinite future would, at the very least, have been resented deeply. It might have provoked a mood of extreme German nationalism that could have tightened tensions and increased the risks of major war. Until the Federal Republic found it feasible to take the initiative itself, we therefore could not be seen to settle for the European status quo.

Chancellor Brandt's *Ostpolitik* did the job we could not do ourselves. But our somewhat schizoid attitude toward genuine international compromise was shown again by the reluctance and apprehension with which we greeted Chancellor Brandt's earlier moves. Some dedicated Europeanists in this country saw his Soviet and Polish treaties as risks to NATO solidarity and even as harbingers of a "mad rush to Moscow."

In the climate that developed, however, the four powers (France, the United Kingdom, the United States, and the U.S.S.R.) were able to achieve arrangements that helped soothe the Berlin sore. The political and popular support in West Germany for Chancellor Brandt's policies allowed further progress toward normal relations between the Federal Republic and its East European neighbors. The prospects for multinational agreements to ease tensions and improve security were enhanced.

The sudden exit of Brandt did not divert the process of accommodation. Under Chancellor Schmidt, even the international recognition of East Germany has been accepted with relative equanimity.

Success in international negotiations need not be confined, of course, to instances where the status quo can be confirmed. These are, I believe, the prime candidates for fruitful agreement. But adjustments can also be negotiated where they offer something of value to all the negotiating parties.

In the Middle East, for example, negotiations directed toward ratification of the status quo would obviously be unavailing. To the Arabs, even a new military disaster was preferable. Indeed, the ambiguous results of the Yom Kippur war of 1973, with new losses of Arab land, had enough elements of Arab success to facilitate negotiations.

In helping to bring about the cease-fires, Kissinger was able to trade on Israel's objective of security and the desire of Arab states to regain their lost land. A more comprehensive and durable settlement will require a sensitive balance of territorial adjustment and security guarantees.

It seems doubtful at best that any lasting resolution of Arab/Israeli differences could or should be imposed by any combination of outside powers. But a concurrent negotiated agreement between the U.S.S.R. and the United States could create a climate more conducive to settlement by the local adversaries. We and the Soviets should agree that neither will use military force to affect the situation in the Middle East and that each will limit drastically the nature and quantity of arms flow into the area. Israel, freed of the specter of Soviet intervention, might then feel secure enough to compromise. Deprived of any prospect of overt Soviet support, the Arab countries might conclude that compromise is inevitable. If, however, a Middle East settlement comes to be viewed instead as a part of the superpowers' negotiating agenda, no compromise on either side seems likely.

In much of the rest of the world the status quo itself is unstable or intolerable. These are, however, areas where our national security stake is nonexistent. The risk of more Vietnams is, in essence, the risk that we may see unrest, insurgency, and local conflict as somehow a threat to our own national interests.

In the postwar years, when we could not bring ourselves to accept formally a situation in Europe that was stable, if imperfect, we tried unsuccessfully to confirm in Southeast Asia one that was unnatural. In Vietnam, the status quo we were prepared to ratify was to Hanoi a silly and pernicious fiction. No adjustment we were prepared to consider would satisfy its minimum requirements. Our own recognition of the situation's fragility led to our frantic efforts at nation-building and at winning the hearts and minds of an Asian people for an exotic regime of Western design.

A true negotiated settlement could not have been achieved by different negotiators or more inspired tactics. Vietnam thus holds no negotiating lessons. It shows only that, where the case is weak, the bargaining table is no more productive than innovative counterinsurgency or massive use of American firepower.

The basic lesson learned, therefore, should be to avoid a contest where we have little to gain and the other side has everything to lose. Nothing short of a genuine threat to national security is likely to make the American public support a war for very long. And when time runs out for military action, you can't expect to take away in a negotiated settlement the prize for which the other party is prepared to fight and die.

A settlement might yet have been possible in Vietnam. Had the Thieu government not been encouraged to perpetuate the political polarization, a situation might have been created which the Vietnamese parties could have regarded either as acceptable or one that could be made so by bargained adjustments.

With a United States announcement in 1973 that it expected such a settlement, and would condition its aid on visible steps toward its achievement, and with the tacit agreement of the U.S.S.R. and the People's Republic of China on a policy of great power abstention, the true parties in interest might have been moved to resolve their differences. No such negotiations ensued. The Thieu government went down with its guns silent but its rhetoric undaunted.

In my opinion, the major risk today is not that we will fall into the trap of more Vietnams. Surely the good sense of those who formulate our foreign policy will protect us against a return to the stale and discredited notion that we must continue to take action in Indochina or elsewhere to put down every insurgency led by Communists.

The real risk, I am afraid, is that our Vietnam experience may reinforce our distaste for genuine international bargaining. Because the Vietnam agreement turned out badly, because the Vietnamese continued to kill one another, and because a Hanoi-sponsored regime came to sit in the Independence Palace in Saigon, nevertheless this was not the outcome because we were misled or out-traded. It should not be taken as proof that we should have persevered in a military solution. It does not show that we can afford to negotiate only from a position of unquestioned superiority and on the basis of inflexible principles.

In Vietnam we were trying to reach a deal on a matter that was really none of our business and with a party to whom we had nothing to offer. In terms of relative military strength, our position could not have been stronger. But this made no difference in the real bargaining equation.

In the near term, our major negotiations will be with our principal rival, the Soviet Union, with our major allies, Western Europe and Japan, and with the developing nations, particularly those that are resource-rich. In the former case, we can achieve more progress in arms control from a position of relative equality than we could ever hope to gain from a position of clear, but necessarily transient, military superiority. The experience of the strategic arms limitation talks shows that neither the Soviet Union nor the United States will bargain from a position of weakness. When the two greatest military powers find themselves momentarily in positions acceptable to both, the opportunity should not be lost. It will be lost if either side tries to accumulate more bargaining chips in the hope of making a better deal.

The opportunity for useful understandings with the Soviet Union will also be forfeited if we set as the price of agreement the abandonment of internal policies which we regard as unjust and immoral. We should not, of course, enter into any arrangement which perpetuates or compounds injustice and immorality. But we substitute unwise counsels of perfection for sound progress toward a better and more peaceful world if we forego pragmatic negotiation either because we lack confidence in our own bargaining ability or because we dislike many elements of Russian policy.

Much of our dealing with the Soviet Union will be outside the usual field of national security. The international crises of the future are far more likely to involve common problems of food and energy, trade, environmental protection, and resource development. Such negotiations will be more fruitful if the context is cooperative rather than adversary.

On these nondefense matters, on which our true national security is no less dependent, we will also find ourselves engaged in hard bargaining with our friends, particularly the European Economic Community and Japan. The tensions in these latter instances may not be markedly less, despite the common background as cold war allies.

Indeed, our evolving relations with the Soviet Union, and to a lesser extent with the People's Republic of China, may strain the ties with established friends. This will certainly occur unless we are sensitive to the impact of "superpower" deals on the hopes and fears of those with fewer troops but equally vital interests.

The continuing conferences on European security and cooperation and mutual reduction of European forces will therefore pose a real test for our negotiating sophistication. An awareness of the acute security concerns of the West Europeans is essential.

On the other extreme, however, we will guarantee failure in these conferences if we grant to our allies the degree of control over our initiatives that we allowed the Saigon leaders in the Vietnam peace talks—the "tyranny of the weak." An unflattering, and accurate, estimate of the strength of the Thieu regime may explain the solicitude we showed for South Vietnamese concurrence with any promising initiative. The record contrasts strangely with our callousness toward Japan's reaction to the Peking surprise and the economic shocks of 1971. Japan and Western Europe will endure. In the negotiations involving European and Asian security we need not fear that realistic American adjustments will lead either to their alienation or flabby accommodation. But their strength and friendship makes them our greatest international asset, and we cannot afford to take them for granted.

Finally, our international negotiating process would be improved by broader participation. Even the best deal made in private, with rigid insistence on executive prerogative, will be highly suspect. The heavy premium put on security and secrecy in the past may well have been misplaced. Surely the other side knows what we are proposing. The American Congress and public need not be kept in the dark. A process of extensive and continuing consultation with Congress may deprive the eventual agreement of an element of surprise. But the lack of suspense may be more than offset by broader public understanding and support.

The growing interdependence of nations makes the process of international negotiation too important to leave to a few inside experts. Wider participation can improve both the end-result and its acceptance. We may even find that the traditional skill of the Yankee trader is neither a myth nor a memory.

American Involvement in Foreign Societies

Fifteen years ago, there was a near consensus on the wisdom of America's deep involvement in the "development" of the new nations just gaining their independence. It seemed right morally, economically and strategically—good for them, good for us, and bad for the Communists who would seek to subvert them. Now, after Vietnam, the assumptions behind that view are being strongly challenged.

Some, like Richard Barnet in the first essay in this section, criticize the underlying concept behind the American approach to the Southern Hemisphere in recent years. Although President Nixon's moves towards Moscow inevitably softened the cold war context in which Washington had approached the developing nations, our policy remains one of building and preserving a peaceful status quo. But Barnet asks whether a global system based on peace without justice can survive? "The United States," he concludes, "cannot make the world safe for America by seeking to shape the political and economic development of other countries to its own short-term interests, for the attempt will exhaust both our treasure and our spirit."

Barnet proposes the elimination or reform of a number of American policies and practices, including military and para-military or covert intervention, military assistance to dicta-torial regimes, the use of economic pressure to induce political changes abroad, our approach to violations of human rights, the practices of U.S.-based corporations operating overseas, and our domestic consumption patterns. In the course of his discussion, Barnet also suggest that the current criteria for American aid be "stood on their head": our assistance would be given only to those governments prepared to undertake structural reform for the benefit of a majority of their populations.

In a following essay, Senatory Hubert Humphrey seems more hopeful about our ability to get the benefits of our aid to the poor majorities in nations not noted in the past for their progressive policies. He suggests that there are some kinds of aid which can benefit the poor even in such countries; that we should avoid too close an identification with such regimes while seeking to get assistance to the most needy in those countries; and that, while eschewing use of aid as a political lever, we should still impose conditions on our assistance, insisting that recipients "make tough political-economic deci-sions, such as those relating to equitable tax structures, land reform, family planning or price and wage controls." In cases where the Senator believes we must, for the sake of our own security interests, give military assistance to governments that are violating the rights of their citizens, he suggests we be less timid in criticizing those violations.

Particularly noteworthy is the Senator's review of our ex-perience in Vietnam, in which he shows that our deepening economic involvement there followed rather than preceded our military commitments. Thus, he argues, Vietnam does *not* show that American civilian assistance abroad need entrap us in deepening, even military, interventions. Indeed, he says, by becoming so heavily involved in Vietnamese affairs, we stifled the development of both civilian and military leadership and "undermined the self-respect and integrity of those whom we meant to assist . . ."

In the third essay, Lucian Pye makes a different argument.

While there were failures in the American aid program in Vietnam, he writes, and while its purposes seemed confused and its pace too sudden, there *were* successful projects. These "were generally those in which American specialists could work with Vietnamese who had a personal or social interest in . . . the endeavor." Frequently, the lower the level at which Americans were working, "the more likely it was that motivated Vietnamese could be tapped and mobilized." The same, he suggests, holds true for other nations: American involvement should go deeper than the national government level. Americans should work with "those who are the most anxious for change."

Pye traces an erosion of support in the United States for foreign aid which would have occurred even without Vietnam. The conceptual confusion about its purposes has flowed from an essential American ambivalence: on the one hand, most Americans recognize an "imperative of helpfulness." On the other, there is a growing sense of cultural relativism and recognition of "the principle of not meddling."

But, Pye writes, "there needs to be greater public awareness of the importance of the developing world for America," not least for the sake of our view of ourselves. After describing an "entirely new world economic situation," Pye suggests different types of aid for different categories of developing countries.

Richard Barnet is a co-founder and co-director of the Institute for Policy Studies. He is the co-author of *Global Reach: The Power of the Multinational Corporations.*

Hubert Humphrey is United States Senator from Minnesota and a former Vice-President of the United States.

Lucian Pye, Professor of International Studies at the Massachusetts Institute of Technology, has written extensively on nation-building, political development, and Chinese politics.

Lessons Learned and Unlearned

RICHARD BARNET

The lessons of Vietnam have been incorporated into a new official U.S. map of the world that bears little resemblance to the one that used to hang in the White House of Lyndon Johnson. In the Nixon-Kissinger projection of the world, the face of the Soviet Union has changed. There is a revised picture of the Third World, and a new analysis of the inter-action of foreign and domestic policy. The chief virtue of the new official map is that it is much closer to reality than the old one. The chief defect is that it is a guide to neither development nor peace.

Barely five years ago the J. Edgar Hoover view of the Soviet Union still dominated the Administration. The view that the Soviet Union was more international conspiracy than nation-state, more interested in "scavenging" abroad than in its own national security and "great power" status, and more concerned with mounting a worldwide challenge to the "American will" than in solving its own domestic problems colored all official pronouncements from Washington. This analysis, and the rhetoric that flowed from it, has been radically revised, in large measure because it offered no hope of extrication from the Indochina war. The Kremlin, although still made up of essentially the same people, is now seen as a group of pragmatic managers far more interested in securing national borders, developing its own consumer economy, and controlling its own population than in making revolution anywhere—including Russia. There is a new sophistication about the relationship of the Soviet Union to guerrilla movements. Nationalist leaders in the Third World, contrary to the classic Hoover view, are not puppets on a long string from Moscow, even when they call themselves Communists. Much as Henry Wallace proposed almost thirty years ago, the Soviet Union is to be treated as a great power and by means of moderate treatment, respectful rhetoric, and economic concessions, given an incentive to cooperate in building "a generation of peace." In effect, the Russian Revolution of 1917 has been recognized and the dreams of the "roll back" of Soviet power in Eastern Eruope or the "mellowing" of the Soviet regime into a liberal, democratic, capitalist state have been abandoned.

The new relaxed view of the Soviet Union, which is quite consistent with an intensified arms race that serves political interests in both countries, has led to a more moderate and less hysterical view of political change in Asia, Africa, and Latin America. The Third World, a more flattering but hardly more descriptive designation for what used to be called the "grey areas" in the global U.S.-Soviet confrontation, is now seen in perspective. The 2 billion or more people who live in Asia, Africa, and Latin America are not, Ché Guevara and Lyndon Johnson notwithstanding, about to rise up and take America's wealth.

They are hungry, divided, and vulnerable, and all the more so because the U.S.-Soviet détente makes it harder for small countries to play one giant off against the other. Most Asian, African, and Latin American governments are in the hands of military dictatorships, rightist regimes, or technocratic modernizers, all eager for U.S. military aid, loans, and private capital, despite their growing insistence on better terms. Many of the "romantic" and "unstable" revolutionary leaders who so upset Walt Rostow and Dean Rusk—Sukharno, Nasser,

Nkhrumah—are gone, replaced by men more willing to serve as pillars for Nixon's "structure of peace." The two revolutionary triumphs of the 1960s—Cuba and Vietnam—now appear to be unique historical cases rather than models for export throughout the formerly colonial world.

The Nixon-Kissinger Doctrine also reflects a new understanding about the ways in which domestic politics determine the limits of foreign policy. The Vietnam war made it clear that the President did not have unlimited freedom to employ military power abroad even in support of goals on which a domestic political consensus existed. Thus, while most Americans in the mid-1960s accepted anticommunism as a legitimate and necessary goal of U.S. foreign policy, first a large and vocal minority, and finally a majority, came to believe that the political, economic, and social costs of producing a military victory in Indochina were unacceptable. The "low profile" strategy—letting "Asians fight Asians," to use John Foster Dulles's earlier formulation, assigning primary responsibility for maintaining the status quo to such deputy peace-keepers as Brazil and Iran, and releasing American voters from conscription—had as its primary purpose the disentanglement of foreign policy from domestic politics. The Watergate revelations dramatized the extraordinary concern in the White House that the "emotionalism" engendered by the war would be mobilized by hostile domestic forces to tie the President's hands in the conduct of future foreign policy. Thus, the activities of the United States abroad, particularly in the Third World where most Americans have no ties, had to be arranged in such a way as to keep them out of the headlines and beyond popular consciousness. For the purposes it was designed to serve, the "low-profile" strategy was a considerable success. The antiwar movement collapsed, and only a tiny fraction of the American people remain interested as to whether the national interest is being served by the explicit Nixon-Kissinger policy of dependence on repressive military dictatorships around the world.

The most significant lesson so far to be learned from the war is that a successful foreign policy for a great status quo power such as the United States must be based on conservative, not liberal, rhetoric. Like many writers on U.S. foreign policy, including Tocqueville, the Secretary of State has worried since he was a graduate student about the difficulties of reconciling great imperial tasks with the hopes, fears, and prejudices of a democratic people. From Franklin Roosevelt to Lyndon Johnson, the rhetorical theme of foreign policy was liberation. Cynical and absurd as it often was, the consistent use of the rhetoric of the "free world," the anti-Communist crusade against "slave economies," and the sacrifice for "democracy" in Southeast Asia created a certain set of expectations in the American people which, it turned out, complicated the task of maintaining a modern empire. Kissinger, the student of Metternich, has understood that when nations profess morality, some people at least expect them to adhere to it. The rhetoric of moral crusade, which permeated American postwar foreign policy until Kissinger, leads to the potentially explosive contradictions of defending "democracy" in Greece and "freedom" in South Vietnam.

The rhetoric of peace in a world convulsed by three generations of war, revolution, and confrontation is more powerful than the rhetoric of justice. John Foster Dulles used to speak of "peace with justice" but Kissinger clearly believes that there is a necessity for choice, a theme embodied in one of his book titles. The appeal for a new foreign policy consensus to take the place of the one that fell apart in the late 1960s is based on the assumption that most people are prepared to ignore justice in return for a "structure of peace." Kissinger's vision of a world restored (to use the title of another of his books) is a Westphalian system in which each sovereign is free to profess what he wishes within his own territory, except an ideology such as national liberation or revolutionary socialism which threatens to undermine the system as a whole. Once a regime is in firm control of its territory, there is no need to apologize for the brutality with which it treats its citizens or the repression with which it resists social change. Indeed, strengthening the "structure of peace" requires that the United States support such efforts. Revolutionary governments, such as the Soviet Union and China, that are firmly in power are accorded Westphalian treatment; revolutionary movements struggling for power in the Third World are to be isolated from revolutionary powers and are to be denied legitimacy.

The new official understanding of Soviet motives, of the relationship between the Soviet Union and national liberation movements, and of the isolationist impulses of the American people is much closer to the truth than the old analysis was. Much of the acclaim for the Kissinger-Nixon policy was based on sheer relief that the age of the "eyeball-to-eyeball" confrontation appears to be receding, and that a number of stubborn conflicts that have dominated the headlines of the past generation (though fewer than are claimed) are being settled or defused. Obviously, these are not negligible accomplishments. But the crucial question remains: Can a global system based on peace without justice survive?

Before we can approach the normative questions about what questions we *should* have learned from the American experience in Indochina, we must make some predictions about what the "generation of peace" will look like. Here are three crucial factors that will affect the environment in which United States foreign policy will be operating in the next two decades: First, drought, the cumulative effects of soil erosion, overpopulation, and increasing maldistribution of income due to widespread unemployment and a growing concentration of wealth with the rich in poor countries are creating the threat of escalating famine. (The number of deaths due to starvation in 1973 has been estimated at more than 3 million.)

The second factor is "monkeywrench politics." The power of the powerless to make life unpleasant for the beneficiaries of the status quo by hijackings, kidnappings, and, conceivably, nuclear threats, is increasing. In the face of a frozen and totally unacceptable status quo, groups like Latin American guerrilla movements or the Palestinians have strong motives to play the politics of desperation. As the world economy becomes more interdependent and complex, this new form of warfare will have increasingly crippling effects—not enough, perhaps, to effect political change but certainly enough to maintain a high level of tension and insecurity. One consequence will be the continued rise in domestic repression in all countries, including the United States.

The third factor is the intensified struggle among advanced industrial countries for scarce raw materials, most of which are located in the Third World. The shift from the ideological confrontation of the cold war to the geopolitics of survival in Kissinger's five-power world is another shift in the direction of realism, but conflicts over material things are not always less dangerous than conflicts over symbols. The temptations to offset with military power the increased bargaining power of the poor countries with respect to the terms on which they sell their raw materials and labor to the rich were openly expressed in the "energy crisis" of 1974. U.S. military officers continue to base their requests for appropriations on the need for the United States to develop "low-level violence" capabilities to support negotiations on resources.

Despite these new types of conflicts which Kissinger-style diplomacy does nothing to resolve, the United States has concluded from the Vietnam experience that the world can be made safe enough for the United States if the levels of international violence are held down. Peace with honor was stipulated in Indochina and redefined to mean continuing low-level war until the rout of April 1975. The great expectations of global reform which the United States fostered in the first postwar generation when this country had more ambitious notions about "organizing the peace" are gone.

Given the new realities of the 1970s, the official lessons of Vietnam which now dominate our policy are no more likely to lead to an acceptable peace than did the official lessons of Munich. At the very moment when it is becoming clear that there can be no peace without development, the United States appears to be abandoning even its rhetorical commitment to the alleviation of mass poverty and misery in the world. More important, the United States is lending its financial support and its prestige to the familiar fascist model of "development." South Vietnam, Brazil, Chile, Iran, and, almost without exception, America's other "good friends" around the world all follow the same basic strategy of rule: stimulation of the economy through foreign investment, fierce repression of dissent, tight control of labor and wages, and terrorizing of any potential opposition. Through training, financial aid, and, most important, legitimation, the United States helps to maintain these regimes. While it is true that most of these dictatorships are able to maintain an uneasy peace on their territory by means of modern police and communications techniques largely supplied by the United States, and some have enjoyed impressive growth rates in their gross national products, there are more than what are sometimes dismissed as "moral or aesthetic reasons" to be opposed to them. The three great interrelated world problems of the late twentieth century are mass misery for an increasing majority of the world's population, unemployment and uselessness, and the gross disparities between rich and poor. The fascist model of development has proved unable to solve any of these problems and indeed aggravates them. The principal problem with these dictatorships is that their clientele is extremely small. They cannot—and they know they cannot— run the country in such a way as to benefit a majority of the population, and so they are prepared to face a continuing low-level civil war with any part of that population that resists.

The "moral and aesthetic reasons" for opposing the spread of torture and the condemnation of millions of people are compelling enough. But a foreign policy that counts on building a generation of peace on so unstable a foundation rests not only on bad morals, but on bad politics. If we assume that the preservation of American democracy and freedom for Americans is the fundamental purpose of a national security policy, then the systematic promotion of fascism abroad is extremely short-sighted. The Watergate crisis is instructive. The Nixon Administration's attack on our system was accomplished with the same methods and some of the same people that have been used to undermine other countries officially declared to be "threats" to our security, such as Cuba and North Vietnam. It is not possible to base a national security policy on legitimizing and encouraging repressive regimes abroad without risking free institutions at home. The statement sounds rhetorical, but there is much historical evidence to support it. The habits of mind, the bureaucratic structures, and the official fantasies needed to rationalize and defend antidemocratic governments around the world cannot be kept isolated from our own domestic politics. The United States cannot escape the complex boomerang effects at home of the policies it pursues abroad.

The United States is still the most influential country on earth in shaping the international political climate, which in turn shapes the possibilities for American development. That is what it means to live in "an interdependent world." Henry Kissinger has correctly noted that the spirit of a nation is a crucial component of its strength in its international dealings, and he worries publicly about the flagging of the American spirit. But just as the reformist appeal to build an American Century was too pretentious and too self-contradictory to inspire a genuine internationalism, so a "structure of peace" based on the repression of the world's poor is too mean a vision to call forth the constructive energies of our people.

The United States is deeply involved in the Third World, and inevitably so. The issue is not whether the United States should seek to exert an influence over the development process, but what kind of influence and by what means. Americans "intervene" in a practical, if not a juridicial, sense in an underdeveloped country whenever they undertake such purely domestic activities as inventing synthetics to replace some primary product on which some poor country depends for its economic survival. Much of the discussion of intervention has a scholastic quality because it mixes up legal obligations and political and economic realities that are so closely allied in an interdependent world. But the difficulty of distinguishing permissible intervention cannot relieve us of the obligation to make the attempt.

A new international system which offers the possibility of rescuing a majority of the world's population from escalating misery is clearly beyond the capacity of any single nation to achieve. To overcome the huge gaps in world development, a global transformation involving the cooperation of all the great powers and the Third World countries themselves is required. This process of transformation would include far-reaching institutional reform in the world system of food production and distribution, in the monetary system, and in the international security system. The most important contribution to that process any nation can make is to discontinue those policies and practices which exacerbate the present plight of the Third World and which complicate the prospects for global reform. This is especially true of the nation that commands greater power and influence than all the others. However elusive the positive policies for creating an alternative international system remain, we can, if we are willing to examine recent history, speak with considerable assurance about the negative effects of certain policies and practices. If the United States, for its part, were to end them, it would be an indispensable first step toward the creation of a rational and just world order and a major contribution to peace.

1. *The United States should not engage in military intervention.* Not only is the use of military force on the territory of underdeveloped countries which pose no security threat to the United States an act of aggression within the meaning of the United Nations Charter, but it also undermines the possibility of development and the foundation for a stable peace. The social dislocation and ecological destruction brought about by the advanced lethal technology of the United States in Indochina has solved nothing but has helped to destroy the social fabric on which the possiblity of peace rests. The continued development of the technology of intervention—supersonic bombers, transport planes, landing craft, and sophisticated counterinsurgency weaponry—creates expectations and increases probabilities that they will be used. U.S. military intervention cannot solve the domestic political problems of Third World countries. The most it can do is to submerge or conceal them under various forms of martial law and to promote a "stability" that favors the few at the expense of the many. The cost of fighting colonial wars in the postcolonial era—in money, natural resources, world prestige, and domestic dislocation—is so great, as the Indochina war showed, that military interventionism can no longer be defended on traditional "national security" grounds. But while the new consensus on "no more Vietnams" has been incorporated into the Kissinger Doctrine, the danger remains that the "low-level violence" and "low-profile operations" contemplated under the new strategy will escalate.

2. *The United States should not engage in paramilitary or covert intelligence operations.* The use of bribery, assassination, fomenting of strikes and demonstrations, and other methods of promoting social dislocation on the territory of any other country, irrespective of ideology, should not be ruled out. The very reason why it is relatively easy to manipulate the internal politics of poor countries suggests why it should not be done. The only hope of development in such countries is for them to build strong governmental institutions capable of addressing their own massive problems. That cannot happen so long as such institutions are subject to the clandestine influence of an outside power. The consistent pattern in the cases where clandestine operations have occurred—Guatemala, Iran, Brazil, Chile, among others—is that the governmental changes effected have thereby favored a small class at the expense of the poverty-striken majority who are worse off than before. (As a result of the recent Chilean coup, which the United States has admitted supporting, substantial parts of the middle class that by and large welcomed the overthrow of Allende are doing less well than under the *Unidad Popular.*) The clandestine collection of intelligence in poor countries can be politically disruptive and undermine the nation's own capacity to govern and organize the society. Moreover, covert operations for intelligence collection have no national security justification other than the support of clandestine paramilitary operations. There is nothing that the United States needs to know about the Third World for its legitimate security purposes that cannot be obtained by overt means. If the United States were to abandon its efforts to control internal political developments in Third World countries, it would have a much more modest and less intrusive itelligence system. The result would be healthier political development, both in the Third World and in the United States.

3. *The United States should not provide military or paramilitary/police aid to governments for use against their own population.* U.S. aid in many parts of the world makes the crucial difference in whether a military dictatorship stands or falls. Without such aid, a government must seek political

accommodation with domestic dissident forces as an alternative to repression. It should be U.S. policy to encourage this accommodation, not to frustrate it, as in South Vietnam. It should be U.S. policy to discourage the governments of poor countries from spending scarce resources on military hardware and large standing armies. The demilitarization of the Third World is a prerequisite of development. The traditional argument, of course, is that if the United States did not supply arms, other nations would. But the point, while true in a number of cases, hardly disposes of the issue. The United States, which has been and remains the leader in the shipment of weapons to the Third World, supplies the principal energy to the international arms race. Were it to make demilitarization of the Third World a major policy goal and to press hard for a world agreement in arms traffic, the other arms-pushers would find it difficult not to participate. It is becoming clearer that the influence the great powers buy with their arms sales to poor countries is not worth much. (All the millions in Soviet military aid to Egypt did not prevent the Egyptian government from imprisoning local Communists and ejecting the Soviet advisers.) But political leaders in the Third World will probably resist efforts to limit arms flows to poor countries unless the big powers also renounce military and paramilitary intervention in the Third World and curb the arms race among themselves.

4. *The United States should not engage in economic pressure to induce internal political changes within other societies.* When we move from military and paramilitary activities to economic activities, distinctions between what a great power should not do and what it cannot avoid doing become hazier. A good deal of the economic activity of rich nations can have unfortunate consequences for poor countries irrespective of the political motivations behind such activity. The chief characteristic of the present international order—that the rich keep getting richer at the expense of the poor—is to a considerable extent the "natural" consequence of the distribution of power in the contemporary world. As long as our legal and political conventions provide that the United States and, say, Ghana are each to be treated as equivalent actors in

the same international economic and political system, irrespective of the historical and geographic factors that have
made one rich and the other poor, the "vicious circles" that
Gunnar Myrdal and others have noted will continue to operate, and the gaps between the privileged and the condemned
will widen. The problem of world poverty is of such colossal
dimension that only far-reaching constitutional changes in the
international system promise hope of solution.

Even so, the United States could make a major contribution
by abandoning policies that smack of economic warfare and
complicate the life of poor countries trying to develop. Two
examples are the economic blockade of Cuba and the denial of
credits to Chile under Allende. Both were attempts to squeeze
a government the United States did not like by creating intolerable economic conditions within the country. One failed
and the other succeeded. (I am not saying, of course, that the
U.S. economic pressure on Chile was the sole, or even the most
important, cause of the crisis that led to Allende's downfall;
only that it was an important factor in preventing the *Unidad
Popular* from succeeding in its development planning.) As
long as the United States deliberately complicates the life of
Third World governments that are seeking to effect a far-
reaching redistribution of wealth within their societies (however ineptly we think they may be doing it or however much
we may dislike their methods), it can never be a force for
development. The evidence of the Decade of Development is
now in, and it is clear that the United States does not have a
model of development that works. Growth spurts in the gross
national product of poor countries leave the most urgent and
tragic human problems of the Third World untouched, and
often worse than before. No one else has the definitive answer
to development—not Cuba, nor China, nor Tanzania, nor
Mexico. (Various models appear to work in some places and
not others.) For this reason it is essential to encourage a variety
of experiments around the world aimed at the three problems
that overshadow all the others: mass misery and hunger, unemployment, and grossly unequal distribution of wealth and
power. The crushing of any such experiment is a cruel blow for
all poor countries whose chief need is political know-how and

experience to confront their massive problems. When the United States engages in economic warfare against such experiments, it encourages totalitarian tendencies—leaders invoke "capitilist encirclement" to justify ruling with a heavy hand—and it increases the likelihood that U.S. policies will fail.

The United States need to reexamine the basis for its opposition to nationalist or socialist regimes in the Third World which are committed to attacking the real problems that stand in the way of development. Too sophisticated to believe that socialist regimes in the Third World should be counted as military assets of the Soviet Union, the United States still considers the spread of revolutionary government to be against our national interests. Why should this be so? There are two plausible reasons: (1) such regimes nationalize the property of U.S.-based corporations and offer an inhospitable climate for doing business; (2) such regimes drive a harder bargain on the terms by which they will provide vital raw materials to the United States.

The United States must choose whether to attach a higher priority to promoting development or to the protection of the interests of particular U.S.-based corporations in underdeveloped countries. In many cases there is a clear conflict between the development goals of poor countries and the profit-maximization strategies of foreign corporations on their territory. The U.S. national interest is usually equated with the interests of ITT or Kennecott or some other corporation in conflict with the local government. If the power of the United States at the service of such corporations is used to punish the government for exercising its sovereign prerogatives, i.e., if it is thereby forced to pay a price for company assets without due regard to the return the company has derived over the years from those assets, then the possibilities of capital accumulation and the mobilization of the local economy are frustrated. The United States should publicly recognize that there are many cases where its national interest in the promotion of development is closer to the local government's interests than it is to those of the U.S. company.

The old argument that leftist or revolutionary governments

will not trade with the United States is no longer plausible in the light of the strong Soviet interest in East-West trade. It is true that a politically independent government is likely to bargain harder than a dependent government over the terms of trade. But once again we cannot have it both ways. The development of stronger bargaining power vis-à-vis the rich nations is a hopeful development if we are really concerned with "narrowing the poverty gap." If poor nations are able to develop the power to get better prices from the rich, then the rich will pay more. No one likes to pay more, to be sure, but one cannot oppose it in a time when the terms of trade for many Third World countries have steadily deteriorated, and still claim to be for a reversal of present world economic trends. The increase in bargaining power of raw-material-producing nations and the labor-supplying "export platforms" of the Third World offer the most hopeful prospect for poor countries in many years. Moreover, the new consciousness about bargaining power transcends ideologies. The fiercely anti-Communist Saudi Arabians have been leaders in the movement, and we can anticipate that all countries, the Brazils as well as the Chinas, will try to exact the best possible terms in their negotiations with the United States. Using political or military power to control the access to raw materials in poor countries is likely to prove less and less effective for preserving the economic advantages U.S. corporations have traditionally enjoyed around the world. The United States should be welcoming the successes of Cuba, Tanzania, China, and others in providing a more equitable distribution of food, health care, and basic education, not trying to compound their failures.

What then are the practical implications of such an analysis? With respect to foreign aid of a nonmilitary nature, the United States should develop certain explicit criteria. Poor countries that are prepared to make structural changes in their societies to improve the prospects of a majority of their populations (i.e., land reform, mass literacy, public health, sanitation, income distribution, and employment programs) should receive support, provided they are not carrying out these programs with repressive methods. Thus, practically speaking, present aid criteria would be stood on their head: no money to support the stability of a status quo regime unwilling or unable to address the problems of poverty; support for regimes prepared to experiment with structural reform even at the risk of instability.

Is this not imperialism in a new form? Certainly it is an effort to reinforce certain values in the Third World and to discourage others. How is such a policy more defensible than the interventionism I have just been attacking? It must be said that in a world of nominally sovereign but absurdly unequal states the problem of interventionism can never be entirely solved at the level of logic. The interdependent world is already here. The United States, even by what it does on its own territory, influences the direction of development in the Third World. Even a policy of total isolationism from the development process—an impossibility in view of the involvement of U.S.-based corporations around the world—would not solve the dilemma. The United States has disproportionate power over what happens in poor countries. The question is, why is it more legitimate to use that power in the way suggested here rather than in the way it is now used?

The answer is that there is an emerging international consensus which defines development in terms of progress on the related problems of poverty, unemployment, and inequality rather than by growth rates, stability, and industrial activity. This consensus is to be found in resolutions of the United Nations General Assembly, UNCTAD, and other international bodies, in which the poor majority of the world is now represented. To support that international movement by new explicit U.S. aid criteria is not interventionist in the classic sense because it is not narrowly self-serving. (Indeed, such a reorientation of aid criteria would run counter to U.S. interests as they have been traditionally defined; the new policy could never be adopted without a redefinition of U.S. interests in the Third World.) Ultimately, the solution to the "aid as imperialism" problem can only be solved by creating strong multilateral organizations capable of formulating global development criteria independent of the short-term political interests of any single nation.

Clear-cut rules with respect to trade are also difficult for many of the same reasons. As a general proposition, it is desirable to trade with all nations, irrespective of their internal policies. Certainly trade implies less approval than does aid. No nation should be excluded from the trading community in order to force internal changes. The problem becomes more difficult when the issues of credits and trade concessions arise. There are no general rules to apply. The careful application of political judgment in accordance with global development criteria cannot be avoided. Where the withholding of credits cannot effect a serious change of internal policy, as I believe is the case in the Soviet Union, then the advantages to encouraging United States-U.S.S.R. trade relations for détente and peace outweigh the moral distaste in dealing with a repressive regime. Where, on the other hand, the supplying of credits appears crucial to the economic development plans of a regime seeking to hold onto power by terrorism and assassinations, then the responsibility, it seems to me, is to deny the credits. It may be fairly said that under such a rule big countries can get away with more than small countries and that is true. But the problem cannot be solved until there are international criteria for the development and administration of economic sanctions. It should be a priority of U.S. policy to develop those criteria, and where in fact they are adopted, as in the Rhodesian case, they should be observed.

5. *The United States should oppose the violations of human rights everywhere but should not use such violations as a pretext for forcing other changes in other social systems.* American diplomacy with respect to the protection of human rights has been quixotic, to say the least. It has been traditional in the cold war until now to express continuing official sympathy for the victims of Communist oppression (protests over the treatment of dissidents in Eastern Europe and millions of dollars for the resettlement of anti-Castro Cubans) and to keep silent about torture, political murder, and mass executions that take place in the "free world" (Indonesia, Greece, South Vietnam, South Korea, Iran, Brazil, Portugal, Chile, among others). So selective has the United States been in noticing violence around the world that while the im-

prisonment of poets by our cold war enemies have on occasion been rightfully condemned by the State Department, the colonial massacres by the French in Algeria and Indochina, the mass executions in post-Allende Chile, and the tens of thousands of political prisoners still held in Jakarta and Saigon jails have escaped official attention. The failure of the United States to condemn the terrorist regimes it supports with financial and military aid effectively destroys the moral force of any professed concern with the violation of human rights. The Kissinger policy of avoiding the condemnation of inhuman policies, whether practiced by Communists or anti-Communists, has at least the virtue of consistency. But it represents a tragic failure of leadership. Just as the overriding world economic problem is hunger, so the overriding political problem is totalitarianism. The continuance of relatively favorable conditions for the protection of human rights in the United States cannot be assured if the trends toward totalitarianism in other parts of the world continue.

The protection of human rights should therefore be a paramount policy goal in itself. The issue should not be used to score points in diplomatic skirmishes. This means that the United States should speak out officially whenever violations of human rights become apparent and should take the lead in developing international machinery—investigating teams, conventions on prisoners, prisons and the use of torture—to curb the present alarming worldwide trends toward rule by institutionalized violence. The violation of human rights should not be used as a pretext for overthrowing governments or for violating sovereign rights. But a finding that rights are being violated should lead to international condemnation. The United States should take the initiative in trying to establish norms of international law on genocide and the treatment of political dissent. As a matter of unilateral policy, it should protest inhuman treatment and, particularly with respect to countries that are dependent on its support, withhold economic concessions. The argument that it should have concerned itself more with violations of human rights in Saigon than in Moscow, a position I would support, is not based on the ideological character of the two governments but on the reality that the United States had much more influence with the former and much more responsibility for having brought it to power.

An absolutist position—cutting off all diplomatic and commerical relations to punish governments that violate the rights of their citizens—is not practical in a world where the maintenance of contact is necessary to avoid nuclear war. But there is a range of lesser actions that could be taken which would communicate the fact that protection of human rights was a real, not merely theoretical, concern of the United States. These lesser actions should be related to the extent of the violation of human rights. Mass torture, imprisonment, terrorism, and deliberate deprivation of the means of livelihood or food for large numbers of people are of a somewhat different order in comparison to censuring poets for what they write, limiting novelists to small printings, discriminating against members of a religious faith, and voluntary or forced exile—all of which are deplorable. The international community cannot be involved with every injustice committed in a single country. Yet there are violations of human rights of such a character and of such a scale that cannot be ignored. As a minimal first step the United States should call for a United Nations conference on the worldwide human rights crisis at which evidence of torture and mistreatment from around the world could be officially presented and the development of international criteria on the responsibility of the international community for the protection of human rights within national borders be further defined.

6. *The United States should impose legal obligations on U.S.-based corporations operating overseas to compel them to cease antisocial or exploitative practices in the Third World.* There is mounting evidence that global corporations have been consistently undervaluing imports from Third World countries and overvaluing exports to them, particularly technology. Price manipulation (transfer pricing) obviously compounds the capital and foreign-exchange problems of poor countries and should not be permitted. The United States ought to take the lead in proposing an international convention on accounting practices to set international standards on

disclosure, pricing, etc., and to seek harmonization of national legislation among all the industrialized countries with respect to taxation, environmental impact, and labor standards for controlling multinational corporations. Unless the industrialized countries take an active role in curbing the antisocial overseas practices of their home-based corporations, the possibilities that these corporations can play a constructive role in the development process will be negligible since the poor countries do not have the power by themselves to institute adequate controls.

7. *The United States should reassess its current and projected consumption patterns and revise domestic growth policies so as to reduce its disproportionate demand for increasingly scarce resources.* In order to decrease the likelihood of severe geopolitical confrontations that threaten the remaining decades of this century the United States must consume less. Instead of boasting about the fact that 6 per cent of the world's population consumes about 30 per cent of its exhaustible resources, as President Nixon did on more than one occasion, we should recognize that the huge disparity between the U.S. standard of living and that of most of the rest of the world is a major global problem. The energy and resource requirements of the other industrial countries are growing at a much faster rate than the U.S. rate of increase. Countries like Japan are far more dependent on outside energy sources than is the United States. Unless there is national and global planning for more equitable and more rational resource distribution, the United States will be under irresistible pressures to preserve its lead in consumption by continuing to pursue economic and military policies harmful to the Third World.

The lessons of the 1960s which have yet to be learned in the 1970s could be reduced to two propositions: (1) The United States cannot make the world safe for America by seeking to shape the political and economic development of other countries to its own short-term interests, for the attempt will exhaust both our treasure and our spirit. (2) There can be no security and no stability for the United States except in the context of a global system based on justice.

Building on the Past:
Lessons for a Future Foreign Policy

HUBERT HUMPHREY

Although the war ended only a short while ago, Vietnam has faded from our political consciousness like the image from a television screen. Many of us, for many different reasons, might prefer to erase from our memories the American experience in Indochina. But the cost was so great in terms of lives, the wounded, opportunities lost, and billions of dollars expended that we cannot forget. Moreover, Vietnam has profoundly affected many of our political attitudes. This is particularly true with respect to what we have come to refer to as "American involvements overseas." The very invocation of the phrase is tantamount to raising a warning flag.

Thus, despite our apparent desire to forget, we seem to have learned at least some lessons in Vietnam. Many of them are particularly relevant to our relations with the nations of the developing world to whom we give aid. Some of these lessons are apt and could serve us well; others are erroneous and should be unlearned.

Perhaps the most misleading impression which we have carried away from Vietnam is the notion that the United

States government is neither sincerely interested in nor, indeed, capable of truly unselfish assistance to other nations. If unchecked, this misperception could undermine public support, as well as the imagination and innovation which are so necessary if there are to be successful U.S. programs of assistance to the developing world. It is not simply a question of the war having made us cynical about our leaders' purposes: we have also begun to lose faith in our ability to do good works. In addition, many Americans, including many of those who steadfastly supported the war, have now concluded that we will inevitably be taken advantage of by those whom we seek to assist. We seem afflicted with syndromes of self-condemnation over our past mistakes and self-pity over what we perceive as a lack of appreciation.

At the heart of some of our doubts and fears about foreign involvement is an erroneous concept of the sequence through which U.S. military involvement in Vietnam came about. The slow stages by which Americans became aware of what was going on in Vietnam have given rise to the notion that our involvement there began in a small way with economic aid to civilian programs and gradually ballooned into a full-blown military involvement. This clearly was not the case for, as the record shows, the intensification of our civilian involvement came *after* we were fully committed militarily and then as an almost desperate response to a deteriorating battlefield situation. Similarly, in Laos and in Cambodia, civilian programs followed an original commitment to military support.

The notion that our military intervention in Vietnam somehow grew out of initial nonmilitary ties is widespread. It is often cited as an argument against foreign assistance generally and against efforts to exert any manner of influence on the affairs of others. Because this and other related, but equally mistaken, notions about our involvement in Vietnam serve to undercut public support for new economic development initiatives, it would be well to review certain aspects of the Vietnam experience.

From the outset of our Vietnam experience, U.S. attention focused not on Vietnam itself, but on its relationship to our security interests elsewhere in Asia and the world. During World War II, President Roosevelt decided to assist the Vietnamese Communist forces as a means of aiding China against Japan. President Truman, whose initial views on Vietnam's future were ambiguous, promptly lifted the embargo on arms to the French in Indochina following the outbreak of the Korean War. During the two remaining Truman years and in President Eisenhower's first two years, the United States poured billions of dollars into France's futile effort to hold on to Indochina. Although Eisenhower, due possibly to the strong opposition of key Congressional leaders, declined to intervene at Dien Bien Phu, he had Ngo Dinh Diem recruited as South Vietnam's Premier and set him up with promises of American economic and financial aid. Throughout this process it was clear that our motives were primarily military and security-oriented. If there is any doubt of this, one has only to examine the rationale for aid to Indochina presented to the Congress during these years and the NSC policy papers of the time. One of these described Vietnam as, "of great strategic importance in the general international interest rather than in the purely French interest, and as essential to the security of the free world, not only in the Far East but in the Middle East and Europe as well."

But for purposes of studying the immediate past, we might begin in 1965. Between June 1965 and March 1966, U.S. troop strength in Vietnam increased from 70,000 to 215,000. U.S. air strikes against North Vietnam were begun during this period. It was also during this period that the kaleidoscopic rotation of government which had followed Diem's removal was halted and Nguyen Cao Ky installed as Premier, marking what was to be a decade of outward stability of leadership in Saigon.

Yet, as the year 1966 began, it was evident that the war was going very poorly. With the failure of various peace initiatives over the 1965 Christmas season, American public sensitivity to our involvement in Vietnam quickened. In early January 1966, Majority Leader Mike Mansfield and other members of the Senate Foreign Relations Committee returned from a visit to Vietnam and reported that "a rapid solution to the conflict in Vietnam is not an immediate prospect."

The Administration found itself particularly on the defensive regarding the authoritarian nature of the Siagon government, Premier Ky's lack of a popular mandate, and the failure of his government to provide for the needs of its people. On a more pragmatic level, General Wallace M. Green, Jr., U.S. Marine Corps Commandant, returned from a 13-day tour of Southeast Asia and declared: "You can kill every Viet Cong and North Vietnamese and still lose the war unless" the Vietnamese villages are rehabilitated and reorganized. U.S. civilian authorities were beginning to recognize that the conflict was characterized by a mixture of conventional and guerrilla tactics. Moreover, they saw that it was not a simple civil war, but one complicated by major international involvement.

As these facts became clearer, direct U.S. military involvement in Vietnam intensified and U.S. civilian authorities became more deeply involved in Vietnamese civil affairs. In a move designed both to strengthen the joint U.S.-Vietnamese effort in the villages and to counter liberal American critics of the Saigon government, President Johnson convened a U.S.-Vietnamese summit meeting in Honolulu in early February 1965. Its purpose was to agree on plans for and publicize what Administration spokesmen dubbed, "The Other War."

The program of action set forth in the Honolulu conference communiqué was comprehensive, well-intentioned and, to those unfamiliar with Vietnamese culture and politics, impressive. Frustrated by the demands of the war in his desire to concentrate the energies of his Great Society programs at home and stung by the taunts of critics who pictured him as bloody-minded, LBJ sought to apply his populist zeal to the problems of Southeast Asia. He believed that the United States could do for Vietnam what he had seen the New Deal do for the poverty stricken rural Texas of his boyhood.

The new program of political and economic undertakings laid down in the Declaration of Honolulu incorporated and codified a number of American ideas and programs, some of which had been tried or talked about in one form or another for several years. With various refinements and name changes, the Honolulu blueprint was to set the pattern for U.S. involvement in Vietnam's internal affairs until the early 1970s. For that reason the results of the conference merit description.

The principal elements of the Honolulu program were a statement of U.S.-Vietnamese commitment to common objectives and a series of parallel undertakings by each party in support of the common goals. The shared commitments included: "defense against aggression . . . free self-government . . . social revolution . . . [an] attack on hunger, ignorance, and disease, and the unending quest for peace."

In support of these goals, the Vietnamese pledged themselves to several objectives that they previously had been reluctant to undertake. These were: the eradication of social injustice, maintenance of a viable economy, and "building true democracy." The last of these was understood to include the formulation of a "democratic constitution" and its submission to public discussion, modification and ratification, as well as the drafting of an electoral law. The Saigon authorities also promised to implement an amnesty program for suspected communists and political opponents. In return, the Washington delegation promised to provide financial and advisory support for the land reform, economic stabilization, increased food production, and education projects.

In the public presentation of the Honolulu meeting the military aspects of the war were downplayed. The final communiqué mentioned the war once, briefly, in the ninth of ten numbered paragraphs. On his return, President Johnson spoke of a war to be won on two fronts: "One front is the military. The other is the struggle against social injustice, against hunger and disease and ignorance, against political apathy and indifference."

From this formulation—taken at face value—it would appear that "The Other War" represented virtually an end in itself; that, in essence, the United States and the Saigon government were intent upon a transformation of the South

Vietnamese society and economy equal in scope to the objectives of the Communist enemy. Indeed, the Vietnamese portion of the Declaration closed with the promise that "we shall strive as we fight to bring about a true social revolution."

In retrospect, there is considerable reason to doubt whether the Vietnamese leaders who went to Honolulu on short notice at U.S. insistence were at all interested in "social revolution." On the American side, the Honolulu program was considered by the executive branch to be a necessary adjunct of the prosecution of the war and of the maintenance of public support for the war. Ironically, the criticism of American liberals about the lack of political and social reform was to contribute to a deeper American intervention in Vietnamese civilian affairs. The Vietnamese leaders, on the other hand, recognized the need to go along with the Americans, and were willing to promise them whatever was required in order to ensure continued American support.

The foregoing is not to suggest that President Johnson's espousal of democratic economic and social reforms was merely a cynical public relations move, or that it was undertaken solely because it was expected to reinforce the military effort. As noted earlier, the aims and objectives outlined at Honolulu were ones in which the President, his colleagues, and most Americans genuinely believed. Our innocence and ignorance of Indochina, however, led us to assume that concepts which had formed the core of our own political belief could be transferred to an alien society and culture. After all, we were a world power and what had been good for us should surely by good for others: we had no doubt that our concepts could be easily taught to and embraced by others. To LBJ, the Mekong and the Perdnales were not that far apart. Once these programs with their familiar sounding objectives were set in motion, we naturally assumed they were "good." But although we constantly measured their "progress," we failed to examine whether what we were attempting was possible.

We were further encouraged in our advocacy of these programs by the belated recognition that unattended economic and political grievances, coupled with a weak Saigon administrative apparatus, invited exploitation by the Vietnamese Communists. Indeed, it was felt by many that if the United States had taken a tougher line with Diem and insisted on reforms, the political deterioration which occurred between 1961 and 1965 might have been averted.

From Honolulu to the Paris agreements of 1973 the United States promoted and underwrote a vast number of political, social, and economic programs for the Vietnamese. First the Ky and later the Thieu governments went along with these programs. But they never gave strong leadership to these programs, and we failed to understand that they never would. As times passed, particularly following Tet 1968, the emphasis within the civilian program shifted decisively from economic and political reform to strengthening Saigon's control in the countryside. This redirection of effort was even more evident once "Vietnamization" was set in motion in 1969. One by one, the American-inspired innovations in local self-government disappeared as Thieu's repressive internal policies came to be accepted as a necessary means of providing, in the jargon of the time, "a screen of security behind which development could occur."

But there was never any doubt as to which objective would prevail: security was always more important than development. This was as true during the Thieu regime as it had been with Diem. Thus, well before the end of the Thieu government, reform and development became little more than slogans attached to politically expedient or security-oriented programs. And therein lies a central paradox of our Vietnam experience: our expectation that the Saigon power structure would undertake or allow the implementation of policies which would have resulted in its own demise.

After 1967 the implementation of civilian programs was entrusted by the United States to the Vietnamese Army (ARVN) in conjunction with the Civil Operations and Rural Development Support Directorate, or "CORDS." The choice of the ARVN as the instrument of social and political revolution probably was as unavoidable as it was unfortunate. There was no other nationwide bureaucracy through which the United States could work. Whenever we or reform-minded Vietnamese sought to create an alternate apparatus which would have been more sensitive to the needs and aspirations of the people, those efforts were effectively thwarted by the ARVN's grip on the civil administration and resources. Inevitably the ARVN's role as the primary channel for U.S. resources and influence enhanced the standing of its own members and strengthened their hold on effective power. As a result, the American programs promoted not change but rather a solidification, expansion, and enrichment of the existing power structure.

Those of us who knew Vietnam mainly from Washington never understood the real role of the Vietnamese military. There was insufficient reporting from the American mission in Saigon on ARVN politics, which was the only meaningful politics in the country, or on corruption. Reporting on the Vietnamese military was the responsibliity of the U.S. military; and while the military was largely insensitive to politics, it was, like the Embassy, supersensitive to charges of corruption. As a result, neither corruption nor Vietnamese military politics was adequately reported. Early on, many American officials in Vietnam seem to have decided that moral abstractions such as the honesty of a Vietnamese official should be considered on a relative basis and against "Asian standards." Many apparently considered honesty to be less important than whether a given Vietnamese official could "get the job done."

It is evident in retrospect that the South Vietnamese leadership did not believe in the principle of working for the political support of those governed. We should have under-stood that this was alien to the Vietnamese political and cultural tradition. Even if it had been a part of their belief and practices, our actions would have undermined it for, as a prominent Vietnamese told an American visitor a few days before Saigon fell, Thieu and his military colleagues never understood the need to obtain the political support of the people. "By providing him with everything he needed," the Vietnamese said, "you Americans made it unnecessary for him to listen to the people."

In both military and civilian endeavors, despite our good intentions and programs which we thought would encourage the Vietnamese to accept responsibility, our intervention stifled the emergence of new leadership and self-reliance. In order to prevent the Communists from taking power we finally, following massive efforts and equally massive frustration, opted for stability and cooperativeness rather than change and innovation. Given our objectives, we believed we had no other choice.

Yet, there were always Vietnamese—fewer as time went by—within the governing structure, who seemed to have a real sensitivity to the need for political, social, and economic reform. It is often said, though, that most of these individuals eventually wound up on the other side of the struggle—alienated by the corruption and excesses of the ARVN or the insensitivity of the Americans, or both. Those Vietnamese who were not driven across the ideological barrier either accommodated themselves to the American or Vietnamese establishment, or they wound up in exile or in Thieu's prisons.

The one area of U.S. effort that perhaps was not dominated by the Vietnamese military was the management of the economy. But even there the results were little better. The immediate effect of the massive U.S. and Vietnamese military expenditures beginning in 1964-65 was a surge of inflation which we sought to dampen by the massive importation of consumer goods. Given the quick profits which could be made from handling these commodities, there was little inducement to domestic savings or for the development of import-substitute industries. Consequently, little or no economic growth occurred. During the period of maximum American involvement, billions of dollars were spent in the Vietnamese economy. Most of this money flowed through a grossly expanded service sector and, too often, thence quickly out of the country. Those who already had money made more, while the poor bore an increasingly disproportionate burden of the war through inflation.

Given the repeated charge that the Americans ran Vietnam, it is ironic to note how seldom our leverage was used and how even less frequently it was effective. Although it may have appeared on the surface that the United States exerted great influence in Vietnamese internal affairs, most often it was the form rather than the substance which was affected. Moreover, whatever leverage we might have exercised was nullified by our own politics. The ultimate basis for our leverage would have been the threat to get out and leave the Vietnamese to their own fate unless they undertook desired efforts and reforms. But once Presidents Johnson and Nixon had staked their political futures on the "successful" or "honorable" conclusion of the war, they forfeited any possibility of using this leverage. And there was another related problem: to the extent the Vietnamese engaged in undertakings at our insistence, we considered ourselves beholden to them. This, in turn, further limited our freedom of action.

The truth of these propositions was illustrated by the problem which Henry Kissinger encountered when he sought to obtain President Thieu's assent to the Paris Accords. Thieu's agreement was essential because a deal with Hanoi over his objections could not have been portrayed by President Nixon as the "honorable" exit by the United States he had vowed to achieve. The ultimate irony was that the price of Thieu's agreement was a series of secret U.S. commitments which nullified any possibility that the Accords would accomplish the larger purposes claimed for them. Having been promised indefinite high levels of U.S. assistance and the reintervention of U.S. airpower in the event of a massive North Vietnamese attack, Thieu was able to pursue a policy of aggressive confrontation *vis à vis* the North without any compulsion to enter into the process of political compromise provided for in the Accords. In addition, the secret assurances of continued unlimited aid weakened any incentive which the Saigon government might have had to achieve self-sufficiency. The effect was to leave them tied to the American umbilical cord. On the U.S. side the corresponding effect was to prolong Washington's political responsibility for the ultimate outcome of the struggle.

There were other problems which arose as a result of the importance which the Vietnam outcome assumed in terms of U.S. domestic politics: the capacity of the Vietnamese to conduct the war successfully and implement civilian programs had a significant bearing on the political fortunes of both President Johnson and Nixon. Both Presidents behaved as though they could not afford to allow the Vietnamese to fail. Neither President wanted it on his record that the United States had lost a war. This belief drove them to assume that greater and greater inputs of American matériel, resources, and direct participation were needed and that these could compensate for an inadequate Vietnamese effort. Throughout the war we paid lip-service to the principle first invoked by President Eisenhower in October 1954 when he sought "assurances as to the standards of performance [Saigon] would be able to maintain in the event . . . aid were supplied." But there came a time when we had invested so much that we could not admit mistakes of our judgment or of Vietnamese performance.

One of our great failures was our inability to recognize that our civilian programs in Vietnam were so largely dependent upon a continuing infusion of American money, incentive, and discipline. They never became Vietnamese programs, and thus they stood little chance of becoming self-sustaining. To what extent this was our fault or the fault of the Vietnamese is not clear. Once the American support was no longer assured, it became evident that there was little inner strength or resource on the government side. The physical infrastructure which we had built, and which required only U.S. dollars and contractors, survived the withdrawal of our troops. It constitutes a rich inheritance for Thieu's successors. Our political efforts and reforms, however, which depended upon Vietnamese political performance, never even got off the ground.

II

This partial review of our civilian involvement in Vietnam should be sufficient to suggest some lessons which we should and should not learn from Vietnam. As noted at the outset, it is wrong to conclude that our military involvement in Vietnam grew by stages out of a civilian assistance program. The commitments made by Presidents Truman, Eisenhower, Kennedy and Johnson against the Vietnamese Communists were military before they were economic. They were deliberate and unequivocal. Moreover, we did not fall accidentally into the position of backing repressive or authoritarian governments. We knew quite well what we were doing, but we rationalized it in terms of what we believed were higher values. The point is not that we set out to do evil, but rather that we acted in the mistaken and uninformed belief that our civilian programs could succeed where our military programs could not or that American management could succeed where the Vietnamese had failed. We seem to have gotten things in reverse order. We all know that knowledge is power, but in Vietnam we acted as though power gave us knowledge. Therein, possibly, lay our greatest mistake.

Although in retrospect there is much fault to be found with our civilian efforts in Vietnam, it would be wrong to conclude that if we had executed our civilian programs better, Thieu would still be in power. Had our programs and reforms been pursued to their theoretical goals, the political economy of the South would have undergone a radical transformation—perhaps almost as profound a change as that sought by the Communists, but one which would have lent itself to democratic institutions. Those who constituted the Saigon power structure understood this even if we did not.

III

Vietnam was, in many ways, a unique experience. It did not differ from our other aid programs simply in its unprecedented scale; it carried with it an unprecedented ideological, political, and military commitment. Our aid programs today fall far short of that kind of involvement. Nevertheless, we can learn from Vietnam some lessons which should be useful elsewhere.

Without fully recognizing what we had done, we staked American lives, treasure, and our own political fortunes on factors which we neither understood nor totally controlled. When we realized how deeply involved we were and when we came under attack, we began to endow our Vietnamese allies with qualities and aspirations which they never had. In so doing we compounded the tragedy.

We sincerely believed that American institutions were transferable to Vietnam. This was as true of the liberal critics who insisted in 1966 and 1967 that Saigon had to have a proper constitution as it was of the American advisers who saw a stronger Vietnamese police force as a means of protecting the Vietnamese freedom of choice. Mistakes such as these should teach us humility and make us cautious about asserting what is best for others. That is, of course, up to them.

We should have learned from Vietnam that our wealth, our technology, and the idealism of our intentions is not always—or even usually—controlling. In particular, we ought to have learned that the individuals and the institutions with which we choose to work in a foreign environment can ultimately thwart our intentions and pervert the thrust of our effort.

Our willingness to assume responsibility on behalf of those whom we wish to help can be self-defeating. In Vietnam we saw it stifle the development of both civilian and military leadership. Even worse, it undermined the self-respect and integrity of those whom we meant to assist and created an almost total, and eventually fatal, psychological dependence upon the United States.

Some degree of dependence is, of course, inherent in the donor-recipient relationship. We cannot avoid the reality that we are wealthier and more powerful that the countries we are assisting. But we must learn to practice restraint even when others seem to invite us—as they have in the past and continue to do—to take a role in their affairs. When we allow ourselves to be drawn into such relationships with another government, we sometimes seem to manifest a greater sense of responsibility for their fate than do the recipients themselves.

In this connection, we must be more aware of the limits of

our ability and of how much depends upon the determination of the recipient. Successive Presidents lost sight of these limits as they saw their political futures and their places in history threatened by the prospect of being tagged as the first to "lose a war." Our loss of perspective prevented us from recognizing that neither on the battlefield nor in the villages were the Vietnamese able to make the requisite effort. Thus, it slowly became, and then remained, our war because they never made it theirs. We must remember this when we start to blame ourselves unduly. We did not lose the war—Saigon did. We did more for them than would be expected of any ally under the circumstances; indeed, we did too much.

Throughout our experience in Vietnam we felt compelled to commit ourselves unequivocaly to one Vietnamese leader after another. We equated the survival of each with the good of his country and the success of our programs. When they suffered or fell, our interests suffered and fell with them. Unfortunately, we continue to behave in this manner elsewhere. In several countries we have permitted ourselves to become closely identified with highly authoritarian leaders, usually in order to ensure short-term security objectives, mindless, apparently, of the possible long-term consequences.

At present there is a group of countries, all of them either actual or potential aid recipients, which individually and collectively present us with a difficult series of problems. Much of what we should have learned from Vietnam could be applied in our dealings with them. The countries in question are Portugal, Greece, Turkey, Indonesia, the Philippines, Korea and Chile. Although each presents its own peculiar set of problems, they share certain attributes which make them particularly interesting in this discussion.

All of these countries, except Chile, are usually considered to be of strategic importance to the United States. Almost all are faced with either real or potential instability in their internal and foreign affairs. The amount of U.S. foreign assistance provided to each is considered by the recipient to be an index of its importance to the United States. In each instance, except perhaps Greece and Turkey, the nature of the internal rule of the country concerned would, by our standards, be considered repressive or authoritarian. Finally, in all of them, the question of what the extent of U.S. involvement is or should be is a subject of controversy both in the United States and in the countries themselves.

To a certain extent, debate in the countries in question mirrors that in the United States. The United States is likely to be blamed, as it was by many Greeks during the period 1967–74, for being the primary source of support of a repressive regime. Indeed, many Greeks believed that the United States had a hand in the 1967 coup which brought the junta to power. And regardless of their views on these points, most Greeks seemed to believe that if the United States had chosen to do so, it could easily have brought down the junta. Indeed, many of them would have liked to see the United States do just that, notwithstanding their charges that U.S. interference was responsible for the junta in the first place.

Although there is no evidence to support the charge that the United States worked to install the junta, most Greeks apparently *believed* we did. Similarly, whether or not we could have brought down the colonels, many Greeks *believed* that it was within our power to do so. Perceptions, rather than facts, were more important in this instance. The pattern has been, and continues to be, repeated elsewhere.

Debate over U.S. policy with regard to the internal affairs of other countries, particularly the developing countries, likely will continue to be a prominent feature of our relations with the Third world. In most instances critics will emphasize moral considerations while the executive branch of government can be counted on to discourage anything which might disturb our existing relationships. In this sense, our policy often appears frozen, sometimes out of indifference, but on other occasions out of apparent inertia.

A growing number of Americans are concerned about the moral ambiguity of our foreign policy. The moralism of the 1970s is not to be confused with the moralistic anticommunism of the Dulles years. It is rather a genuine concern that we too often place security and economic interests first before we consider the human dimensions of our policies.

Many members of Congress also believe that our policy-makers should give more consideration to human rights issues—that we can have a foreign policy which is both pragmatic *and* moral. Those who hold such hopes are hard pressed to find means of affecting policy.

Ironically, although the liberal critics generally line up on the side of nonintervention, their frustration with human rights issues has led them increasingly to advocate the use of U.S. foreign assistance as a means of exerting political influence on aid-recipient countries. Examples of this are plentiful and have involved legislation directed specifically at countries such as Greece, Turkey, Korea and Chile, among others. Attempting to carry this approach even further, the Foreign Assistance Act of 1973 required the President to submit an annual report to the Congress setting forth the steps he had taken to deny economic and military assistance to any country that imprisons its citizens for political purposes. In 1974 Congress expressed its view that the President should substantially reduce or terminate security assistance to any government which engages in a consistent pattern of gross violations of human rights.

Unfortunately, there is little evidence that either this legislation or the few aid embargoes initiated by the executive branch for other reasons have produced any results. The executive branch has uniformly opposed such legislative initiatives and when laws have been passed, the executive has implemented them in a manner that effectively thwarted the will of the Congress. With the exception, as of this writing, of the embargo on arms shipments to Turkey, which did not relate to Turkish internal affairs, the Congress has never been willing to cut off aid to a non-Communist country on human rights grounds. Nevertheless, congressional demands that American military and economic aid be conditioned on respect for human rights can be expected to increase. The Administration has yet to understand that the indifference to human rights issues is emerging as a critical factor in public and Congressional skepticism of the President's foreign policy initiatives.

Although I would not necessarily advocate the increased

use of assistance-related threats as a means of exerting leverage on the internal policies of other nations, I believe that we are excessively timid in expressing our official disapproval of their internal policies in other ways. Secretary Kissinger's "quiet diplomacy" is too often misinterpreted as tacit approval of a repressive or authoritarian *status quo*. This is the case even in instances where it is reasonable to assume that the recipient government has its own compelling reasons to maintain ties with the United States. Although both the Nixon and Ford Administrations prided themselves on their "toughness" with our adversaries, both Presidents submitted to extortion-like tactics from our allies. In some of these instances, notably Turkey and Korea, the allies in question probably have as much or more to lose from a breakdown of relations as we do.

The Ford Administration, like its predecessor, seems unable to recognize that repressive actions on the part of regimes with which we are allied can be detrimental to our interests. In the case of Korea, for example, both American and Korean shared security interests may be seriously undermined by President Park Chung Hee's current internal policies. Despite the formal U.S. treaty commitment to Korea, future public and Congressional support for maintaining our troops there at substantial aid levels will depend upon how the American public perceives the political situation in Korea. If what they see appears to constitute a system which continues to abridge human and political liberties, their unwillingness to pay the high price of America's defense of the Korean peninsula will be substantially reduced. Thus, it would seem that the Administration has a practical responsibility as well as a moral reason for seeking to exert a moderating influence on the excesses of the Park regime. If our relationship is truly based on mutual security needs, we should not find this an insurmountable task.

There is perhaps no more complicated involvement for the United States than this one with Korea. It is not easy to find a way to apply leverage in the usual sense. Nevertheless, we are surely wrong to deal with our interests in Korea on the basis of short-term expediency. This is the error we made earlier in dealing with the Greek colonels. For years we witnessed an erosion of esteem among Greek people for the United States as a result of our unwillingness to assert ourselves against the junta. The same was true with regard to the Thieu government in Vietnam.

Over the years our freedom of action in Korea has become limited. We have permitted U.S. policy to become hostage to the continuing confrontation between the two Koreas. At present, strategic concerns seem to have overshadowed our sensitivity to human rights and to the implications of Park's domestic policies. As in the case of Thieu, we have tended to regard Park as an essential or, at least, an irreplaceable fixture. We appear to believe that if we were to exert moral pressure in the form of strongly disapproving public and private statements, Park might react by taking measures which would be tantamount to abandoning Korea's alliance with the United States.

In general, the use of aid as leverage for political action is a practice which should be employed only rarely and then with great discretion. If military aid is being provided to another government on the basis of genuine U.S. security concerns, then presumably we will not be able to terminate it without some risk to our own interests. If we are providing economic aid on the basis of need, then exacting political concessions seems inappropriate. Attaching even well-intentioned conditions may tend to make all our aid suspect. If we are genuinely interested in assisting the peoples of other nations, we should do everything we can to de-politicize our aid.

There is, however, one type of condition which I believe is not only acceptable but essential: we have a right and responsibility to insure that American aid reaches the intended recipients and is used in an effective manner which will accomplish the purposes specified by the Congress. And we must add to this condition a realistic understanding that social, economic, and political circumstances may have more to do with the improper utilization of American aid dollars than corruption and bureaucratic ineptitude. I am convinced that if the proper study were made, we would find the reluctance or failure of aid-recipient governments to make tough political-economic decisions, such as those relating to equitable tax structures, land reform, family planning or price and wage controls, is the greatest single impediment to the successful utilization of aid. For example, programs designed to help the small farmer increase his income are futile if the land tenure system is such that there is no incentive for the operator to participate.

In the past we have been reluctant, perhaps understandably, to lay down firm conditions designed to ensure the proper utilization of aid. It is almost as though we are afraid that if we insist, our aid will be refused. We should understand that fundamental reforms such as these are of great potential political impact within the recipient countries. Certainly they involve decisions which only the recipients should make. We should also understand that not all nations will be willing to pay the price required to receive our aid. In such cases we will simply have to decide whether to accept a much lower rate of benefit from our aid or whether we should apply it where it will be better used.

In general, however, if we will act to free ourselves from the bad habits of the recent past and refurbish our neglected diplomatic skills, we should be able to regain some of our lost influence without the application of crude leverage. One of our most serious errors seems to be our propensity to get too close to governments which we are aiding—not just in the sense of becoming too involved in their affairs but also in adopting the outlook of the recipient and losing our independent perspective. We do this both in terms of our excessively intimate personal relations with foreign leaders and in the identification of our policies and programs with those of the host government. In the name of promoting our own image, for example, we often allow assistance programs to be managed so as to contribute to a foreign leader's internal political objectives.

As a matter of form, we need to stand off a bit so that if the moment comes when we believe criticism is called for, we can deliver it without undue embarrassment. We need to maintain our separate identity so that we can neither be used by the local government nor damaged in the eyes of its

citizens by their leaders' excesses. If we can do this, we may
be able to regain our moral credibility and thus our ability to
exert a form of moral suasion which would be both effective
and tolerable to the pride of others.

Our influence abroad will be further enhanced if, in the
long term, we can direct our foreign assistance away from
security-oriented projects such as arms grants and sales and
into projects which will aid those most in need. In the long
term, it is more important that the people in other countries
have a good opinion of us than it is for us to enjoy intimate
relations with their rulers. Accordingly, we should shift our
foreign assistance increasingly into acitvities which can be
seen by the people of the Third World as related to their
needs and aspirations. If we can do this, we may find a new
source of security in the form of a restored image and greater
cooperation in international forums. In the coming decade
such new relationships could be as important as bases and
alliances were in another era.

In this connection the congressionally mandated "New
Directions," designed to ensure that American bilateral aid
produces maximum benefit to the poorest of the poor,
represent a start in the right direction. The new emphasis on
enabling and encouraging small landowners to increase
production and the goal of providing simple job skills to
urban unemployed represent a marked departure from the
priorities of previous years. In the past we concentrated on
major infrastructure projects such as hydroelectric dams and
airports. Still more needs to be done to wean the Agency for
International Development away from showcase projects and
toward undertakings which appear more mundane but which
will directly affect peoples' lives. The new functional categories of the foreign assistance legislation of 1973—Food and
Nutrition, Population Planning and Health, and Education
and Human Resources Development—describe the new areas
of emphasis and the shift away from resource transfers toward
human development. Illustrative projects of the new variety
are small-scale irrigation works, producer cooperatives, local
credit institutions, and local units combining preventative
medicine and family planning services.

In the same way that our assistance programs should be related more directly to other needs of the Third World's people, our government-to-government dealings must reflect greater sensitivity to these nations' rights and their respective historical experiences. This will require some forebearance on our part. We will have to learn that a great and confident nation does not intimidate weaker ones in order to demonstrate its toughness or out of fear of change. And a government such as ours, which professes to value rights and freedoms, should be able to appreciate the intensity of liberated leaders just emerged from decades of repression.

In order for us to behave in this manner, we must take the time and trouble to understand other people—something we never did in Indochina. We must be willing to limit ourselves to acting within the general parameters of what is acceptable and not behave as though the rules were not meant for us. Similarly, we do not have the option of rejecting interdependence in favor of independence simply because the rest of the world strikes us as complicated or as too demanding. The question for the future is not *whether* we will be involved, but *how*. We have no other choice, given our economic and security interests. Nor, I must add, have we a choice in terms of morality. It does matter what kind of world we live in and what standards we uphold. We must not compound the tragedy of our involvement in Vietnam by abdicating our responsibility in the great humanitarian issues of the day. The exercise of this responsibility will continue to involve us in the affairs of others. In so doing, we need neither be forever apologetic nor paralyzed by the Vietnam experience. Instead, what we must do is to translate the experience and the tragedy of the last decade into wisdom and vision that can guide us in the next.

Foreign Aid and America's Involvement in the Developing World

LUCIAN W. PYE

For the moment, the activist instinct among Americans for helping the poor is deadened. But there is mystery as to what caused the spirit of "benign neglect" to spread from domestic policies to the conduct of foreign aid. Is the story of our national disillusionment contained entirely in the frustrations of Vietnam? Or, were there other international trends completely unrelated to Vietnam which would have brought in due time an end to our enthusiastic visions of participating in the national building of the new states of Africa and Asia? Certainly the congeries of sentiments and rationales which sustained and gave respectability to foreign aid during the 1960s have been shattered; and few seem to have the spirit to try to pick up the pieces or to reason through again the problem of finding political support for transferring resources and knowledge to less developed lands.

It is tempting to attribute the withering of popularity for foreign aid entirely to our Vietnam experience. Many of the arts and techniques developed in the practice of foreign aid were massively mobilized and deployed in the Vietnam struggle, and thus quite understandably our sense of failure in our Southeast Asia endeavor has contaminated our belief in our own competence in helping others. Furthermore, the passion of our debates over Vietnam policy further addled American thinking about foreign aid: some high officials sought to justify our involvement in the Vietnam war on the grounds of our previous aid commitments, while others have argued that it was the initial decision to provide aid which dragged us into the quagmire of Vietnam.

Since it is so easy to blame so much on Vietnam, it is essential for our future policies toward the developing countries to examine first how firm was the American commitment to foreign aid prior to the Vietnam experience, and, second, to look at trends unrelated to Vietnam which may have contributed to the withering of American enthusiasm. I begin with some general observations about American thinking on foreign aid, then examine briefly our Vietnam experience with respect to civilian involvement, and finally try to outline realistic approaches for the future.

II

Even at the height of American enthusiasm for foreign aid in the 1960s, questions were constantly raised as to the precise rationale of our endeavors. As long as funding was available and programs grew, the champions of aid were prepared to accept any and all rationales which seemed to win over further supporters. We never clearly resolved whether we were giving aid primarily because it was in our immediate national interest or whether we were practicing indiscriminate worldwide generosity. Motives for supporting aid ranged from anxiety over the spread of communism to exhilaration over our presumed ability to manage economies and social processes so as to speed progress toward material advancement. Out of the confusion of reasons we were never able to untangle a clear sense of purpose either for foreign aid in general or even in particular cases. Did we expect gratitude for what we were doing? Did we believe that development would bring stability, or were we prepared to engineer social revolutions of our own design? Was foreign aid supposed to be just one more tool in our total arsenal of foreign policy instrumentalities? Or was there

something special about foreign aid which made it less immediately purposeful and more a matter of America's participation in a great historical process of modernization?

Behind these confusions and the conflicting justifications
for foreign aid, there was a fundamental ambivalence which
made it possible to vacillate between idealizing aid and denouncing its practice. Americans have a missionary spirit that
makes them believe deeply that those who are more fortunate
should manifest a sharing spirit, even make sacrifices to help
others. To hold back knowledge and understanding is to be
mean and spiteful, unneighborly and antiegalitarian. At the
next moment, however, Americans can just as firmly believe in
the doctrine of cultural relativism according to which everyone should be free to follow his own ways and no one should try
to change others or impose his practices and values on his
neighbors. The imperative of helpfulness and the principle of
not meddling ring equally valid, and the same audience can be
swayed by appeals to either instinct.

In the 1950s and early 1960s the cultural relativist strand in
American thinking was depressed to some degree, largely because the leaders of the new states of Africa and Asia seemed
to be asking for help in modernizing and changing their societies. Under those conditions, the cultural relativist response
would have seemed morally indecent because there was no
tactful way to tell them that we did not necessarily think badly
of them because it was in their nature to be poor and technologically ineffectual while it was our destiny to be rich and
powerful. The basic sense of decency of the American people
brought their missionary feelings to the fore. Now, however,
after tens of billions of dollars and hundreds of thousands of
man-years of labor and so little change in the developing
world, it is understandable that the American mood has
changed toward a revival of cultural relativism. American
emotions have adhered to unassailable logic: If we lack ready
answers, then we can hardly be missionaries, and therefore by
what right do we presume to be helping others? To recapture
our self-esteem we have had to revitalize the rationale of
cultural relativism: Each society should adhere to its own ways,

the test of American character should be in disciplining its activist instincts.

Such confusion and ambivalence quite naturally led to shifting popularity among different categories of foreign assistance. In the 1950s we made much over the distinction between economic and military aid, and Congress at different times favored the one or the other just as different countries seemed to prefer recieving one or the other. At the level of action rather than that of debate, there was often little to distinguish between what passed for either form of aid, particularly when military aid became "defense support assistance." Roads were built, harbors dredged, and industries fostered equally under either label, and the choice of which was used depended in many particular instances merely upon administrative or budgetary convenience.

Over the years, this American practice of elaborating more refined categories of aid than actual practice justified, and then debating the relative merits of the different forms, helped to create the illusion that American aid was becoming more purposeful.

Our ingenuity in intellectualizing about such distinctions did at times create the impression that we were making progress in developing better approaches to foreign assistance. Unfortunately, the practice also allowed us at times to talk more while doing less and thus delude ourselves as to the level of our actual contributions to the poor countries. Most recently we have seen a continuation of this practice in the debates about the relative merits of "multilateral" as compared with "bilateral" channels of foreign aid. The apparent consensus that the former had much merit was recently shockingly shattered by the decision of Congress to end our contribution to the International Development Association of the World Bank.

Behind all the debate about rationale, purposes, and categories of aid, the actual practice of foreign assistance ultimately comes down to the rather elementary matter of transferring resources and skills from one polity to another. Attempts at making fine distinctions obscured the basic fact that operationally, no matter how the aid was described, it involved an infusion of resources whose effects were determined more by the skills of those immediately involved than by the labels under which the aid was donated.

It is therefore significant that behind all the public furor over kinds and levels of aid, those dedicated Americans actually working in the developing countries increasingly learned the very complex skills of helping to transfer technology and of working for the economic and social development of foreign societies. By the time of Vietnam we had accumulated the most skilled and diversified pool of talent in all aspects of development of any country in the world. More than twenty years of experience in foreign assistance had produced substantial improvement in the techniques basic to development aid. At present it is fashionable to discount professionalism, particularly in the area of providing assistance for less fortunate people. But the fact remains that international assistance is an extremely complicated business in which amateurs can easily be outwitted by the unscrupulous who invariably swarm to the scene of soft money.

There is, therefore, a strange historical irony in the fact that America was able to produce a high level of professionalism in an area in which we seemed not to know what we wanted to do or why we were doing it. As those who were most directly involved improved their techniques and became more professional, there developed an increasing gap in communication between them and those who were engaged in debates about foreign aid. Thus, reality and rhetoric became increasingly divorced, and the sum effect was a steady weakening of popular understanding of foreign aid.

All these considerations would be enough to suggest that foreign aid was not on a strong footing at the time of the Vietnam war. Hence, it is not surprising that the war's frustrations produced a general sense of questioning of foreign aid. Even without Vietnam we were inevitably approaching a period when the very appropriateness of foreign aid was about to be questioned. Changes in international politics which were unrelated to Vietnam sped up the process of erosion of support and the growth of doubts. As a result of the Sino-Soviet split, and above all the border fights between Russia and China in 1969, the sense of urgency for foreign aid completely evaporated. At one time the United States did think that it was helping India in a race against China which would test the relative merits of democracy and communism. With China no longer a threat, it was possible to ask in much more realistic terms what had been accomplished in India as a result of nearly $10 billion of American assistance.

Politically, foreign aid was bound to decline at about the time of the Vietnam war because that was when the U.S. government could announce the first successful "graduates" of foreign assistance, and the awkward fact was that none of them seemed to conform to the model of democracy and progress which had explicitly or implicitly been the objective. Iran, Taiwan, South Korea, and Brazil were not quite what the enthusiasts of foreign aid seemed to have had in mind. Finally, even without Vietnam, American disenchantment with foreign aid would certainly have come as a result of the current energy crisis and the spectacular rise in affluence of those underdeveloped countries endowed with oil. The separation between the industrial rich and the nonindustrial poor is now blurred by the new rich of the oil-producing states. The energy crisis is causing a massive transferral of resources from the developed to the less developed countries. But it seems that the "wrong" states are benefiting. Some Americans now believe that others, particularly the newly rich oil states, have an obligation to help the poorer states.

In light of these considerations, it should be clear that America's disillusionment with foreign aid stems from far more profound causes than just our reactions to Vietnam, deep as these have been. Future policies toward the developing world must, therefore, be based upon more than just the lessons of Vietnam.

III

Given the jerry-built character of America's approach to foreign assistance, the trauma of our involvement in Vietnam "overkilled" by many times most of the lingering support for foreign aid. Since Vietnam, critics no longer have felt compelled to make coherent cases against foreign aid, assuming it to be self-evident that assisting the development of poor countries is a bad business which America should stay out of. Consensus seems to lie with the foes of aid rather than with its advocates. Former champions of aid are in a state of disarray, confused as to how an enterprise which once captured the most honorable dimensions of America's foreign relations and was supposedly guided by considerations which rose above the sordid calculation of the cold war could have become so cruelly dragged into our most vicious struggle with communism.

A careful examination of our developmental performance in Vietnam would reveal, in exaggerated form, the basic American paradox about foreign assistance: utter confusion of rationale and purpose but remarkable technical competence in separate specialized fields. Our undoing in Vietnam was that we sought to do too much with too many resources in too short a time. In body-building there may be merit in pressing muscle against muscle, but in nation-building an isometric approach leads to counterproductive paralysis. The tempo of American activities was geared more to the rhythm of American politics than to the slower current of Asian life.

Yet, if we examine separately various programs, ranging from land reform and local government development to medical training and the strengthening of the legal profession, much was accomplished. Those Americans who made great personal sacrifices deserve the praise of their compatriots. At the same time, needless to say, there were also many ill-conceived and poorly executed projects which in general seemed geared more to pleasing Washington than to solving local problems.

If we were to reduce the total range of America's experience in Vietnam to a single generalization which might serve as a guide to future policy, it would be an awkward and embarrassing observation given the current antiinvolvement mood of the country. Successful projects required close American-Vietnamese cooperation while the failures were characterized by either inadequate American involvement or inadequate Vietnamese participation. The projects which worked the best were generally those in which American specialists could work with the Vietnamese who had a personal or social interest in the success of the endeavor. This frequently meant that the lower the level at which Americans were working, the more likely it was that motivated Vietnamese could be tapped and mobilized. Where resources were merely provided to the Vietnamese and no sustained cooperation followed, the results were often disappointing if not disastrous.

This conclusion may at first seem trite, but its has far-ranging implications for future developmental policies. The key point is that in Vietnam, as in most new states, there is no uniformity of opinion, and effective development requires strengthening the hands of those people who are prepared to work for progress as against those who would obstruct development. As long as American involvement is limited to the governmental level of interactions, it is unlikely that American assistance will in fact reach those who are the most anxious for change. Too often in uninformed discussions about the practice of developmental aid, it is assumed that success requires that leverage be applied to those who hold the highest levels of authority in the developing country. In practice, such an approach leads to frustration and a waste of resources. Our record in Vietnam shows that we had the maximum leverage for developmental purposes when we were able to strengthen those people who had a personal commitment toward change and that we generally found it extremely difficult merely to apply pressure at the top.

If future American policies toward the developing world are to be influenced by readings of the "lessons" of our Vietnam experiences, then it would be important to document in far greater detail this conclusion about our civilian involvement. This, however, is not necessary for two reasons. First, the fact that we have a demonstrated competence for executing certain types of development programs is not in itself a valid argument for deep American involvement in the internal development of other societies. Second, and more important, it seems unnecessary to risk another debate over the meaning of Vietnam, because at this juncture we are confronting an entirely new world economic situation which raises quite different sets of problems and which is certain to cause new crises in the relations between industrial countries and developing ones. The combination of an energy crisis and worldwide food shortages does require that we think in terms of new challenges and not be governed by our experiences in a quite different international context.

To state the matter as bluntly as possible, it may be that just as Vietnam was more symbolic than real in ending the cold war phase of America's approach to development assistance, so the Vietnam experience is likely to have little relevance for the new era of foreign aid policies. The one conclusion that does carry over is that whatever beneficial influence the United States can exert will depend on our capacity to support not only heads of government, but those who can help solve social problems in their communities.

IV

The reason why it is legitimate not to allow the trauma of our total Vietnam experience to deaden our sensitivities to the passions of the developing world is that we are now suddenly thrust into an entirely new international economic situation which bears few resemblances to the familiar postwar world in which the United States was the supreme responsible actor. Unfortunately, much of the discussion of the energy crisis since the Arab-Israel war of 1973 has stimulated alarmist reactions rather than sober appraisals of the extraordinary changes in the international system. Yet these conditions are certain to do more to alter the style of America's involvement in the development of poor lands than all of our years of travail in Vietnam.

We now confront a world which is no longer neatly divided between the rich industrial countries and the poor agricultural ones. Rather, policy must be designed for a far more complex situation in which some of the rich are highly vulnerable and some of the supposedly poor have more capital than they can possibly use domestically. It is no longer appropriate to think of a Third World composed of countries whose dominant characteristics include the struggle for economic viability and the traumas of colonial experience and dependency on the industrial world. It is now necessary to distinguish at least three groupings of those countries which we formerly considered to be members of the developing world. First, there are those countries, many but not all in the Arab world and totaling nearly a quarter-billion people, which were formerly thought of as poor but are now astonishingly rich because of their oil and other natural resources. Second, there are those countries (like Taiwan and Brazil) with a slightly larger total population which after some two decades of struggle have now finally achieved a degree of economic success, so that their future problems will be less those of growth and more those of distribution and equality. Third, there is what we might call the Fourth World, those countries which remain truly poor, lack oil and other extractive resources, and have not achieved economic development. Located primarily in South Asia and Black Africa, these nations remain appropriate recipients of international assistance.

It would be foolish to pretend to be able to foresee in 1974 the full consequences of the international economic crisis which the energy squeeze is certain to produce. It is clear, however, that the poorest countries will have the most severe difficulties. James P. Grant and the Overseas Development Council had calculated that if the less developed countries of the world are to maintain in 1974 their 1973 volumes of imports, it would be necessary for them to spend $5 billion more for fertilizers, wheat and rice, and more than $15 billion additional for oil.[1] Clearly, they will not be able to do this—and the result can only be severe human suffering. In India, after nearly a decade of steady growth in the use of fertilizers, it is certain that in 1974 there will have to be a cutback of nearly 20 per cent in imports. When this is combined with the reduction in local production of fertilizer, the result will probably be a drop of over 20 per cent in the size of harvests. The increased cost of grain, oil, and fertilizers are such that for India to maintain in 1974 its previous spartan standards, it would have to spend over $1 billion more on imports, which is clearly an impossibility. The world has become somewhat hardened to forecasts of famine on the subcontinent and Africa, but it will not be able to ignore the shocking fact that decades of slow progress toward economic development are likely to be wiped out in the next year or two.

In addition to the threat of widespread human suffering, there is the danger of a breakdown in the international economic system, which may or may not seriously effect the American economy. It is not inconceivable that after a short-run crisis, and if a world depression is avoided, America's economy could emerge in a strong position because we are less dependent on oil imports, because we will be highly competitive in providing the capital and consumer goods which the oil-rich countries will want for their own development, and, above all, because we will remain an attractive investment market for the surplus capital of the oil-rich countries, particularly since the oil crisis will have made Japan and Western Europe less attractive for investment. We do not need to foresee clearly the emerging economic patterns to be able to predict a great increase in political tensions throughout the world, with the United States confronting many cross-pressures.

What this seems to mean is that in the post-Vietnam world environment, the United States will not be able to turn its back on the less developed world and plan only to provide them with marginal charitable or humanitarian assistance. It will be necessary to try to reduce tensions with the oil-producing countries, and this will in some measure require that we demonstrate a readiness to help them obtain the skills and guidance necessary for broader-based domestic economies. Needless to say, there will be no need for capital assistance but rather a willingness to make professionalism in the planning of development available to them.

With respect to the second category of developing countries which have finally achieved a degree of economic success, it will still be important for America to show concern for their problems and a readiness to provide specialized assistance where necessary. Many of these countries still have sectors of their economies which lag and continue to require technical assistance. Possibly the most important single area where American competence will be of importance is in helping them to make the transition from concentrating on economic growth to designing policies which will facilitate more equit-able income distributions. In 1973, Congress showed remark-able foresight and understanding by requiring our foreign assistance programs to concern themselves with the problems of distribution and the poorer segments of the population of developing countries. Again, as with the first category of de-veloping countries, the situation does not call for the large aid establishments which characterized American foreign assistance in the 1960s, but it does call for close relations between American specialists and those most concerned with changes in the developing countries.

The most serious problem lies, of course, with the third category of the truly poor countries. It is appropriate that the large American aid mission in India has been closed down, because India is no longer faced with the same range of prob-lems as characterized its development during the preceding two decades. On the other hand, it will be necessary for the United States to be prepared to take a positive attitude toward devising new modes of helping India if it needs assis-tance in its forthcoming crisis. In Africa, it may be necessary to take far more active measures to help the agricultural devel-opment and the food production of many of the African states.

A review of all the requirements in all the categories of developing countries suggests that American policy will have to be prepared to deal with a much wider range of problems than in the past. The very diversification in the situation of the developing countries calls for more diversified program ap-proaches. In some cases, macro-economic problems are still critical and soft loans will be needed, particularly in the face of spiraling food and energy costs. In other cases, the problem is not one of capital shortages but rather the need for institu-tion-building and specialized knowledge. In both cases, a more activist American approach is needed.

Even if we are only to make our appropriate contributions to multilateral institutions of assistance, there needs to be greater public awareness of the importance of the developing world for America. Economically, these countries remain our principal source of numerous critical raw materials. Politically, they constitute the majority of mankind, and the American spirit is based on majoritarian sentiment: the very ideal of America is that our national enterprise is relevant to the highest aspirations of the bulk of the human race. The one unambiguous lesson of Vietnam is that the American spirit cannot endure and flourish if we feel isolated from and scorned by the majority of the world. It will long be debated as to how well American arms performed in Vietnam, whether we exceeded the limits of our power, whether we lost a sense of reality and proportion, and whether our judgments were wise or evil. But what is not a matter of debate is the depression which came to the American spirit when we sensed that we were no longer speaking for the hopes of the majority of mankind. Therefore, how we conduct our responsibilities with respect to the Third World will remain crucial to the maintenance of our national sense of self-esteem.

It is to be hoped that American law-makers will rise above the trauma of Vietnam and vote the necessary funds to make our appropriate contributions to such institutions as the World Bank and its related agencies. As for direct bilateral American aid, Congress had taken the initiative in calling for innovations which would be responsive to concerns about equity and not just growth. America can also greatly help to reduce tensions between the developed and the developing countries by helping to facilitate the flow of skills and knowledge through public support for semiprivate institutions and foundations devoted to development work.

There are ways in which it will be possible to avoid the overblown character of American aid programs of the 1960s. But there will be no way in which we can avoid being involved and concerned with the progress of the poorest countries of the world. We must participate with them in trying to restructure their economies so that they will not be permanent charity cases. The Vietnam experience should teach us humility about presuming to have answers for the complex problems of others; it should make us more understanding of the limits of rapid progress and the need to harmonize with the pace of other societies. It should not, however, make us impervious to the problems of others. The posture of refusing to become involved in situations for which we manifestly have the resources and skills to be helpful can only be construed by the developing world as signs of American arrogance and contempt for the less fortunate. These are attitudes we cannot afford to encourage among the countries which contain the bulk of the world's population—and which are already larger as trading partners than Western Europe.

As we look beyond Vietnam for guidance for what our aid policies should be, it is appropriate to take as the model the diplomatic style of Secretary Henry Kissinger in striving to bring peace to the Middle East: we should earnestly endeavor to listen to problems of others, establish a spirit of mutual trust, give untiringly to our energies, but as we deeply involve ourselves in their problems, we should maintain a practice of objectivity which should not be easily swayed by immediate international political pressures. The rationale of our aid can, therefore, be unambiguously identified with the simple proposition that America is, and must remain, relevant to the pursuit of happiness in a new world which must in time touch the lives of all mankind.

Notes

1. See the Overseas Development Council's annual, *The United States and the Developing Countries: Agenda for Action 1974* (New York: Praeger, 1974), Chapter II.

PART IV

Conclusion:
New Lessons, New Mistakes?

To conclude the volume, David Abshire and Morton Halperin were asked to examine some of the "lessons" that seem to be emerging from the Indochina experience and to illuminate the dangers inherent in their adoption. Different conclusions are being drawn from the war, and the two find different dangers for the future.

Abshire disputes those who suggest that Vietnam should teach the United States to pay less attention to its "credibility" abroad. Rather, he argues, American overinvolvement in Indochina in the 1960s came through losing the sense of proportion that allowed President Eisenhower to avoid the depths of the Vietnam quagmire. Protection of the American government's credibility—with adversaries, allies, the American public and, in cases of intervention, indigenous people—should remain central in Washington's foreign policy calculations. A failure to do so, he argues, could lead to a number of mistakes: unwise retrenchment of American forces and bases abroad (especially in Europe), cuts in military assistance, and congressional overreaction against security agreements negotiated by the executive branch.

Abshire concludes his essay with some suggesttions on improving relations between Congress and the executive and on changes in the President's foreign policy apparatus. These changes would, he argues, foster the sense of proportion that should accompany continuing concern with American credibility.

While Abshire thus cautions against learning too much from our *failures* in Vietnam, Halperin is more concerned that too much will be made of the *success* claimed by the Nixon Administration in achieving the agreements of January 1973. The principles behind the Nixon-Kissinger Vietnam diplomacy of 1969-73, he suggests, were these:

- The United States must be able to project a credible intent to use force when its interests are threatened.
- Escalation must be sudden and massive.
- The very existence of the North Vietnamese government, society, and economy must be threatened.
- Indochina must be linked to other issues in dealing with the Soviet Union and with China.
- At home, support must come from the right and from patriotic "middle" America.

Similar concepts, he argues, were applied in a number of crises around the world. But he believes that they did not, in fact, prove valuable either in Indochina or elsewhere. Indeed, he suggests that they are more dangerous than useful. A policy which ties diplomacy so closely to the potential use of force "is not a structure of peace but a structure of threat," with the ever present danger of disaster.

David Abshire is Chairman of The Center for Strategic and International Studies at Georgetown University. He also serves as a member of the Congressional Commission on the Organization of the Government for the Conduct of Foreign Policy and is Chairman of the Board of International Broadcasting. From 1970 through 1972 he served as Assistant Secretary of State for Congressional Relations.

Morton H. Halperin served as a Deputy Assistant Secretary of Defense (1966-69) and as a member of the National Security Council (1969). His most recent book is *Bureaucratic Politics and Foreign Policy*. He is now directing a study of the Twentieth Century Fund on Information, National Security, and Constitutional Procedures.

Lessons of Vietnam:
Proportionality and Credibility

DAVID M. ABSHIRE

In 1964 the United States Senate, with only two dissenting votes, passed the Tonkin Gulf Resolution which stated unabashedly: "The United States regards as vital to its national interests and to world peace the maintenance of international peace and security in Southeast Asia." Regardless of the controversial circumstances behind its passage, the part of the resolution describing Southeast Asia as in America's vital interest reflected the prevailing sentiment of the times. Few political leaders had fully recognized and thought through the implications of "vital" interests. Subsequently, over a half-million Americans were committed to an indecisive land war in Asia, against the dictum of General MacArthur. Four or five years later, the Congress had concluded that the government did not have a workable strategy for success in Vietnam, and that the vital interests of the United States was to end the war or, failing that, to end America's direct participation in it.

What are the lessons of the Vietnam experience?

The foremost lesson is that wise decisions on foreign intervention require a constant accommodation of means to ends and of strategy to objectives. In short, a sense of proportion. The decision-making processes on Southeast Asia in 1954 which resulted in the abstention of U.S. power in Indochina involved a far greater sense of perspective than those of the 1960s.

In response to a letter from General Gruenther at NATO, Eisenhower elaborated his views on Indochinese policy: ". . . this Administration has been arguing that no Western power can go to Asia militarily, except as one of a concert of powers, which concert must include local Asiatic peoples. . . . the French could not win the Indochina war and particularly could not get real American support in that region unless they would unequivocally pledge independence to the Associated States upon the achievement of military victory." If these two requisites were not satisfied, even "if we could by some sudden stroke assure the saving of Dien Bien Phu garrison, I think that under the conditions proposed by the French the free world would lose more than it would gain. . . ." [1]

Eisenhower displayed a strong sense of proportion regarding intervention in Southeast Asia. He was concerned about the fate of Indochina; Communist aggression on the part of Moscow and Peking had to be met. He used what was to become the famous "falling domino" analogy. If Indochina fell, Thailand, Burma, and Malaysia would be threatened and Indonesia, as well as all South Asia, would be put at risk. He thought, however, that this could come only with general aggression in which Peking would be on a path similar to Hitler's. Such aggression was of a very different order from Viet Minh operations. Thus, the basis of his calculus during the Indochina crisis was his sense of discretion about the exact character of the Communist involvement and the appropriate means of meeting it.

Eisenhower enumerated precise criteria for U.S. intervention:

1. A legal right must exist under international law, which at that time meant a request by the French who were the established local authority;
2. America's allies must pledge united action;

3. Congress and the American people must respond favorably;

4. France must vow to grant independence so that there would be no implication of American involvement in a colonial war and so that the Indochinese would have an incentive to fight.

The first lesson of Vietnam comes from comparing the nonintervention decision of 1954 with the decisions to intervene of the 1960s. Unlike Kennedy and Johnson, Eisenhower declined to launch piecemeal military measures such as a tactical air strike on Dien Bien Phu. He held to his political requisites for intervention that required international, American domestic, congressional, and local support and consensus.

The second lesson of Vietnam involves a misapplication of the principle of maintaining the credibility of one's commitments. In January 1961, Khrushchev made what became a celebrated speech about wars of national liberation; President Kennedy perceived that Vietnam was becoming a test of America's commitments to its allies and of its ability to show that "wars of liberation" would not pay. The *credibility* of the United States' will to act was at stake.

In subsequent years, foreign policy-makers failed to discern the different kinds of credibility and their interrelationships:

• *first*, credibility to an adversary, which means a belief in the American will to act in the face of aggression;

• *second*, credibility with allies, which means their belief in America's willingness and capability to use its power in their interest;

• *third*, credibility on the domestic front, which entails the American public's belief in the worthiness of government policies and its explanations of the aims, methods, and costs of achieving them;

• *fourth*, in cases of intervention, credibility with the indigenous people, which involves their acceptance of the means and goals of American intervention.

Both Munich and the cold war have confirmed the importance of credibility to an adversary. During the cold war the "nuclear deterrent" was effective because such credibility existed. After the Bay of Pigs, when Kennedy met Khrushchev at Vienna, Kennedy returned with the feeling that he had given his adversary the impression of weakness. He felt he could regain lost credibility during the Berlin crisis by showing his determination by ordering a partial mobilization.

This quality has been placed at the heart of U.S. national security because experience teaches that even a temporary loss of credibility in the eyes of an opponent can result in tremendous diplomatic or budgetary costs. President Kennedy recognized this during the Cuban missile crisis when, in his October 22 message to Khrushchev, he stated frankly: "... The one thing that has most concerned me has been the possibility that your government would not correctly understand the will and determination of the United States in any given situation . . . ."

Vietnam was so drastic a misapplication of the concept of protecting America's credibility with its adversary and its active allies that the government's war effort lost credibility on all fronts: with the American people, with its allies, and with international opinion. Credibility evolved into an end in itself and thus became a "trap." Washington first tried to use Vietnam to make the general case for America backing its commitments. Failing that, it shifted to proving the credibility of American military power. But even larger increments of men, money, and matériel distorted the original purpose of the Vietnam involvement in the overall scheme of American policy.

The Kennedy-Johnson strategy created an American involvement entirely out of proportion to its original limited interests. The area was never vital, despite what the Tonkin Gulf Resolution stated. By striving so hard for credibility in a single place, the United States weakened and discredited its military capability to act elsewhere, and also undermined its economic capacity to sustain a forward defense posture.

In the Suez crisis of 1956, the British and French "fell" into a similar credibility "trap." No doctrine can be applied successfully without a sense of proportion, a measurement of means against ends, and a discernment of the difference between merely important and truly vital interests. To summarize the second lesson, the four interrelated areas of credibility—adversary, allied, domestic, and indigenous—must be pursued with a sense of proportion. One must not be sought in a way that distorts the others.

In its strategy, Hanoi, much more than America, showed a capacity for correctly analyzing and interrelating America's credibility factors. Recalling its 1954 victory in the frustrated and war-weary French National Assembly (which voted in a prime minister committed to settlement), Hanoi never lost sight of the problem for the U.S. government of maintaining a credible stance with its own people in a protracted war. North Vietnam skillfully combined political and military means in pursuit of clearly defined political objectives to exploit the problems of a democracy in conducting a distant war. While American military commanders believed they had been militarily successful in the Tet offensive, Hanoi believed it had been politically victorious in Washington when President Johnson's advisers lost heart and the Commander-in-Chief decided not to run for office again. Both were correct, but America's military benefit was more fleeting and its political loss was more crucial.

The third lesson of Vietnam further pertains to the importance of a democratic government's maintaining credibility with its people and legislature, for, in any protracted war, popular and congressional support is essential. In 1954, genuine advice was sought from Senators Russell, George, Saltonstall, and Johnson. President Eisenhower valued their judgments both for the experience they represented and for the weight they carried with other members of Congress. At the height of the Dien Bien Phu crisis, Eisenhower asked Secretary Dulles to invite eight congressional leaders to the State Department for frank consultations that included revelation of Operation Vulture, the contingency plan for air strikes to save the French garrison. This approach helped to preserve a "sense of proportion" throughout the government and reinforced Eisenhower's opposition to the plan.

There were no such effective consultations in the 1960s. In contrast, the institutionalized and highly publicized committee hearings of the latter part of the decade, especially those of the Foreign Relations Committee, became more of a public debate with each side trying to win points with the national audience rather than informing and advising the other. This situation continued more or less during the first four years of the Nixon Administration, mitigated only by the personal friendship and unusual effectiveness of Secretary Rogers with committee members. Even in executive session, however, a true dialogue was difficult to achieve because of institutional antagonism. On the one hand, many committee members felt that the real decisions were being cloaked under the mantle of White House secrecy and executive privilege, and on the other hand, the committee was pushing for terms of settlement of the war that were unacceptable to the President.

The fourth lesson of Vietnam concerns the credibility of a foreign government with the people in the area of intervention. It relates to the limits of political involvement that can be followed safely if there is to be legitimacy with the indigenous population. There seems to be general agreement in the Congress, from Senator Mansfield on the liberal side to the most conservative members, that escalation was the result of the mistake of being party to the overthrow of Diem. As of 1962, we were supporting South Vietnam primarily as a part of our containment strategy, and only secondarily in order to promote self-determination. Our basic consideration was our own national security, as it involved containment and credibility. If we could not countenance the Diem regime, we could have diluted our commitment and not have made it the all-out battlefield to stop Communist aggression. In order to offset any domino effect, a dilution of the Vietnam commitment could have been accomplished with a build-up in Thailand. Again, it is well to recall that in 1954 Eisenhower clearly set down his political criteria for intervention and did not allow the worsening military situation to force him to abandon them. Instead, he initiated the formation of SEATO, in part to offset the loss of North Vietnam.

A fifth lesson of Vietnam is that there was a gross "over-Americanization" of strategy and tactics. Herman Kahn began to write his scenarios on nuclear war in the late 1950s. "Escalation" became a very popular concept, and the theory of "flexible response" came into vogue among defense planners. Vietnam became a testing ground for these two untried strategies. Gradual escalation, which might have some validity in nuclear warfare, was misapplied to the ground war in Asia. With the manpower reserves and the domestic discipline of the North Vietnamese, perhaps no one should have seriously doubted their capability to meet an increased escalation of men and will. But escalation was underaken, first, to stiffen the resolve of the South Vietnamese; second, to signal the serious intent of the United States to the North Vietnamese who then might be willing to negotiate or de-escalate; and, third, to wear them down, clear out their guerrilla infrastructure and their military capability. Eventually this strategy became self-perpetuating. Escalations were invoked to protect the in-place commitments of men, money, and policy pledges. Moreover, the strategy was consistently based upon an under-evaluation of Hanoi's resolve. Washington misjudged the American attitude toward protracted, indecisive fighting. The lessons of Korea should have been given greater weight in this regard. Nevertheless, as the ineptitude of the Army of the Republic of Vietnam (ARVN) became apparent, Americans began to take over in order to "show" the South Vietnamese how the war should be fought. Thus, escalation developed into substitution until the process was halted by Johnson late in his administration.

The United States has followed its genius for mass production in its approach to fighting wars. Emphasis on massive firepower and on "kill ratios" were applications of America's "management" approach. This tendency produced the worst of all worlds in Vietnam: a strategy of attrition, piecemeal commitment, increasing Americanization, severe geographical limitations and disadvantages, and a domesitcally limited commitment against a totally committed opponent.

On the tactical level, there was both an overuse of air power and an overestimation of its effectiveness. A crude air war developed that hurt U.S. credibility among its allies and the rest of the world. Furthermore, the success of air operations in specific campaigns was badly overestimated. To take the ex-

ample of the incursion into Laos in 1971, Washington anticipated, as had the French prior to Dien Bien Phu, that if the
enemy reinforced and concentrated for major attacks, he
would be destroyed by air power. The overall problem, like so
much of Vietnam, was that once the war of attrition had been
initiated, it was difficult to give up any part of it without
drastic results, both in increased enemy infiltration and in loss
of negotiating leverage.

   In contrast to U.S. Vietnam ground actions of the early
1960s, involving the heavy Military Assistance Groups and
later search-and-destroy tactics, were American actions in
northern Laos. Here, the U.S. role was one of support in which
"advisers" made a specialty of using unsophisticated equipment. This war bred mistrust as a result of secrecy, the CIA
role, and the general attitude toward Vietnam, but the tactics
and supporting roles actually were far more in line with President Kennedy's and General Maxwell Taylor's initial concepts
of a new counterinsurgency strategy. While the Vietnam war
involved a massive commitment of Americans, the Laotian
war involved 200 American "advisers" at a peak cost of less
than $100 million a year. More importantly, it never involved
American prestige and allowed for a situation from which the
United States could easily disengage. The reasons for the more
appropriate approach in Laos are somewhat happenstance:
the Geneva Accords disallowed military assistance missions
and Congress blocked conventional U.S. military activities
there. The tactics and logistics of Laos merit future study as a
contrast to the "over-Americanized" effort in Vietnam.

   A final lesson of Vietnam that concerns the economy and
the credibility of the administration to the country can be
briefly summed up. Vietnam was a major factor behind the
decline of the dollar and its effect upon both the domestic and
international economy, as well as the politico-military posture
of the nation. The original role of the United States in Vietnam was to provide a low-level military assistance program.
With the Vietcong and North Vietnamese major offensive of
1965, that role changed; by December 1965, there were
184,000 U.S. troops in the area and by December 1966,
450,000. The data upon which the economic messages and the

defense appropriations of January 1965 were based did not fully reflect these new costs, nor were the assumptions for the future build-up accurate. Thus, fiscal policy was never brought into line with military policy; neither Congress nor the Treasury Department was given an accurate military forecast.

The lesson is that economic viability is as important as military viability. Overall national security, as well as domestic credibility, can be jeopardized when the cost of military policies are hidden from fiscal planners and the general public.

Mislearned Lessons

How might certain lessons of Vietnam be misapplied?

Future Role of Credibility. The tragic misapplication of the idea of credibility in Vietnam could lead to abandonment of its proper use.

Properly used, credibility played a key role in the international power politics of Nixon and Kissinger diplomacy. The delicacy of its use is demonstrated in the three interrelated aspects of the Nixon grand strategy: the new diplomacy with Moscow and Peking, which aimed at building a stable balance of power whose keeper would be the United States; the retrenchment, especially of American ground forces, from overseas and particularly from East Asia; and the contention that an American pull-back was not a retreat from U.S. commitments.

The pull-back posed a danger in that it might have seemed to undermine the credibility of our commitments in our negotiations with Moscow and Peking. The pull-back might have appeared as a retreat under pressure or as a consequence of overcommitment and failure in Vietnam. It might have given America's adversaries the impression of weakness and vacillation and might have engendered an isolationist America, thereby depriving the President of freedom of international action.

Nixon and Kissinger were fully aware of this pitfall. In moving toward Moscow and Peking, they achieved greater credibility with them through the new political leverage derived from operating and balancing between those adversaries. At the same time, President Nixon's visits to Peking and

Moscow enormously enhanced his domestic credibility. Had the "opening" to China not occurred in the year it did, the Senate would probably have passed a fund cut-off provision on the Vietnam war in 1971.

The balance-of-power diplomacy with Moscow and Peking involved a negotiating process that in itself attempted to set new ground rules for behavior by the use of penalties, rewards, and linkages. The credibility of this diplomacy depended on convincing Moscow and Peking that Washington would react when the balance was violated and try to reward them when the balance was maintained.

Perhaps the most dramatic example of the dynamics of this diplomacy occurred during the Indo-Pakistani war, prior to the Moscow summit. It appeared that the Soviet Union might support and encourage India in an all-out attack against West Pakistan proper. Such an attack would have disturbed the balance of power with China, possibly have brought China into the war, and could even have triggered a Russian attack on China which some Russian hawks advocated. To signal its disapproval to India and Russia, and to increase the credibility of its deterrent, the Nixon Administration called the Moscow summit meeting into question and moved the U.S.S. *Enterprise* to the Bay of Bengal.

Another case was the Jordanian crisis of 1970, during which the Administration backed up its diplomatic warnings to the Soviet Union and Syria by readying the 81st Airborne Division, reinforcing the Sixth Fleet, and concurring in the Israeli move of 400 tanks to the Golan Heights.

While the new grand strategy generated an effective balance among the superpowers, it also helped to facilitate U.S. disengagement from Vietnam. The blockading of Haiphong harbor is an excellent example. Hanoi launched a major new offensive during Easter 1972. Apparently its purpose was to create another politically damaging Tet reaction in the United States, as well as among American allies. Probably, it was designed also to pull Moscow and Peking into more active support of the fight against the United States.

However, President Nixon's Peking and Moscow initiatives had broadened the interests of Russia and China, and had removed Vietnam from their "vital interests." Thus, both China and Russia accepted the blockade and the great power balance held. Most significantly, President Nixon carried out his trip to Moscow.

These cases of the Nixon-Kissinger diplomacy were, on the whole, successful, at times brilliantly so, although controversy exist about whether some of the moves were necessary, unduly disturbing to allies, or incurred unjustified risks. For example, the Indians deeply resented the move of the U.S.S. *Enterprise* into the Bay of Bengal. The move into the Cambodian sanctuaries was primarily for military reasons, but also showed our adversaries that the United States, if threatened, would take drastic action even during its withdrawal in order to maintain credibility with its adversary. The cost in credibility with the American people, however, was the massive closing of colleges and the formation of a powerful antiwar coalition in Congress.

Overall, the Nixon Administration successfully increased the credibility of its leverage with Moscow and Peking by its global strategy of broad diplomatic initiatives. Changed circumstances, such as the Sino-Soviet conflict, which was not available for Kennedy to exploit and which Johnson could not exploit, made possible the new diplomacy.

In sum, if the concept of credibility was misapplied during the Vietnam build-up, it was successfully applied during the Nixon-Kissinger moves toward a new balance of power at the time of the Vietnam withdrawal. Credibility is a prime and perennial requirement of policy, but if policy-makers do not apply it with a "sense of proportion," with an awareness that it is not only an end but also a means, its misuses will have dire consequences.

NATO. The Congress could easily misapply the experience of Vietnamization to NATO, which has had a high degree of credibility with its adversary, its allies, and the American and European peoples. This country Americanized the military effort in Vietnam, created Vietnamese dependence upon America, and did not reverse the process until it commenced troop withdrawals and forced the Vietnamese to fight on their own. Why cannot the same be done for NATO by an American withdrawal and a Europeanization of NATO?

First, the NATO situation differs from that of Vietnam in that the former is a situation of genuine collective security; moreover, diverse historical, cultural, and political bonds form a basis for collective security that is unique to the North Atlantic region.

Second, Europe remains strategically dependent because of U.S. retention of the nuclear deterrent. With NATO, unlike Vietnam, the nuclear giants face one another. Thus, there can be no decoupling of nuclear and conventional commitments, as occurred in Indochina.

Third, the United States has initiated a new period of détente with Russia in a way that has led West Europeans to see their political, economic, and security relations with the Soviet Union as depending upon the Washington-Moscow relationship. This development has jeopardized American credibility with its allies at a time when Europe is still divided into two camps. Although good arguments may have been made that American troops in Europe should have been reduced in the mid- and late 1960s, a substantial unilateral reduction now outside the framework of Mutual Balanced Force Reductions (MBFR), when Soviet-American détente tends to restrain defense expenditures somewhat, might produce a crisis in U.S. credibility with NATO.

Foreign Assistance. The Vietnam experience can also be misapplied when one considers foreign assistance. Vietnam did much to destroy the credibility of any kind of aid, military or economic. It will be used to argue that foreign aid and military assistance are addictive, leading the United States into involvement in the domestic politics of foreign societies and then to their military defense.

When one recalls how such commitments developed in the 1960s and early 1970s, it is well to remember that Presidents Truman and Eisenhower gave sizable military assistance to Vietnam without becoming militarily involved. Still earlier, the Marshall Plan was conceived and executed without involvement in any kind of European military conflict. The last four Presidents have viewed military and support assistance, foreign military sales, and, in a different way, development aid, as conducive to self-defense and political stability.

When Cambodian military assistance was first under Congressional debate in late 1970, the issue was whether such assistance would intrinsically commit the United States to a government with which it had no defense treaty. Aid had never been a popular or very credible program in Congress or in the country. "Trimmed" bills always have managed to pass as a result of Presidential leverage or of a coalition of liberals and conservatives who wanted development and military assistance, respectively. On October 27, 1971, that coalition defeated the aid bill on the Senate floor. The new coalition against aid was quite diverse. Its members were concerned with matters not related solely to Vietnam: the state of the economy, the weakening of the anti-Communist and "stability" rationales for foreign aid, the demands of domestic commitments, antipathy for the part of the program that goes to the United Nations, and disillusionment with recipient countries—for example, India, which seemed increasingly anti-American. They felt that military assistance may distort economies or play into the hands of more dictatorial regimes. Although the aid program was resurrected, it has been on a downward spiral ever since. This disillusionment has come at a time when a requisite of the Nixon Doctrine is for the United States' allies to assume responsibility for local defense, bolstered by American military aid and sales.

Overseas Bases and Commitments. There is also the possibility of misapplication or overapplication of the lessons of Vietnam to this country's bases and overseas agreements. In 1969 and 1970, the Senate Foreign Relations Subcommittee on Security Agreements Abroad, chaired by Senator Symington, held extensive hearings on this. The hearings followed the passage of the National Commitments Resolution, which defined a national commitment as ". . . the use of the Armed Forces of the United States on foreign territory, or a promise to assist a foreign country, government, or people by the use of the Armed Forces or financial resources of the United States, either immediately or upon the happening of certain events. . . ." The resolution made clear the sense of the Senate that such a commitment could not exist without some form of congressional authorization.

Concerns had grown that the mere stationing of American troops abroad creates the danger of military involvement. In the Vietnam escalation, as noted earlier, the United States first established air bases in Vietnam, supposedly to conduct an air war in place of sending troops. But when those bases were attacked, the United States sent ground troops to protect them. General Earle Wheeler's statement in 1968 to the Spanish government, with which America has no formal treaty, was often quoted during the Symington hearings: "By the presence of United States forces in Spain, the United States gives Spain a far more visible and credible security guarantee than any written document."

President Nixon's discarding of the Tonkin Gulf Resolution as legal justification for operations in Vietnam and his reliance on his authority as Commander-in-Chief further heightened this debate on bases and overseas agreements. Such justification, his critics asserted, could be read as his right to become involved in an undeclared Presidential war any place in the world where there were American bases and troops. With this in mind, Congress moved toward legislation to restrict the President's role as Commander-in-Chief.

There is thus the danger of overreaction in Congress, especially after a long and unpopular war. Congress can tie the President's hands, destroying his flexiblity in negotiating and implementing the treaties and the agreements that it approved, in stationing troops abroad, and in redeploying troops in times of crisis for either deterrent or operational reasons. This danger exists despite the fact that when peace comes, the legislature must take an initiative to right the pendulum of power that has swung toward the executive branch during the war.

The Administration originally interpreted the War Powers Bill of 1973, passed during the Near East crisis, as a measure that would destroy its credibility to act. But the Administration's credibility, if jeopardized, was due to the uncertainties of Watergate, to America's relatively declining military capabilities in the Mediterranean area, and to lack of allied cooperation. On the other hand, the 1973 congressional restrictions against renewed bombing in Vietnam and Cambodia without formal authorization by Congress did destroy part of America's deterrent credibility in the eyes of Hanoi. Even though the Administration's resumption of bombing in Vietnam would have been imprudent, congressional restriction nonetheless reduced the uncertainty which Hanoi had to consider. Inadequate consultation with Congress during years of Vietnamese military operations and the lack of a policy with strong domestic credibility resulted in congressional action that weakened America's credibility with its adversary.

What Role for Congress? The domestic credibility of the government played a key role in its conduct of the war; congressional attitudes in turn were tied to domestic credibility. Never before had America experienced a war in which the role of Congress was so crucial: first, as a forum of national debate about the war effort; and second, through moves to cut off funding which, in effect, set terms, or at least constraints, on Dr. Kissinger's negotiating flexibility. Congress, while often claiming that its role had been denigrated, actually achieved an influence it had not known before. Its role was fully recognized in every foreign office in the world.

The real question is, where will this new role for Congress lead? Will it increase or decrease U.S. credibility in international affairs?

The new congressional role would certainly impair American credibility were the United States to try to return to those procedures and attitudes found in the Articles of Confederation and conduct either diplomacy or war by committee or by statute. Future Presidents will destroy America's credibility abroad if they do not build credibility at home by consulting Congress on international policy and by involving its leaders in an audit of policy. Another lesson of Vietnam is that Congress and its attitudes are, in fact, a part of America's deterrent.

Upon becoming Secretary of State, against the backdrop of the Vietnam divisiveness and the Watergate crisis, Henry Kissinger took unusual measures to reinvigorate a mode of consultation with Congress not known since the Eisenhower Administration. Ironically, his diplomacy with Russia was immediately circumscribed by the Jackson-Vanik amendment and the action of the Ways and Means Committee, which had never felt fully consulted on most-favored-nation treatment for the Soviet Union. The carrot of credits that had been used to reinforce U.S. credibility with Russia during the Vietnam withdrawal was denied. There may have been linkage in Kissinger's diplomacy, but not in the politics of Congress.

Part of Congress' foreign policy problem—its inability to link its consideration of political, economic, and strategic matters—is the structure of the committee system and the lack of a congressional group to oversee and integrate all elements of national security in a way analogous to the National Security Council. Considerations of economic policies should be intertwined with military ones. For example, Congressman Bolling, Chairman of a Select Committee on the reorganization of the House, has proposed that foreign trade should be under the jurisdiction of the Foreign Affairs Committee.

Some form of a National Security Committee or a Joint Group of Senate and House leaders is required, such as has been proposed by Senator Hubert Humphrey and Congressman Clement Zablocki. The committee would consult regularly with the President, develop mutual confidence and trust, and bring together all elements of policy. Such a group, by its very sensitivity, would not break confidence any more than would the CIA oversight committee, provided there are consultations and briefings on a regular basis. These meetings, however, probably should not be conducted as formally as committee proceedings.

Participation of the Chairman of the Senate Foreign Relations and the House Foreign Affairs Committees, and of both Armed Services Committees, in such a group is essential. They should not regard their participation as a downgrading of their committees; rather, it would furnish a much better understanding of policy for more institutionalized examination by these committees. Participation of the Finance and Ways and Means Committee leadership would furnish grounds for better integration of economic with national security policies and avoid the economic debacles that occurred in the mid-1960s. As for improved intelligence, the time has come for Congress to form a Joint Committee on this subject, and the new National Security Committee could well serve that additional purpose. Rather than possibly jeopardize the workings of the CIA, such a group could actually strengthen Congress' understanding and support of the agency.

Through these kinds of reform, a better sense of policy-making proportion could be developed in and between both branches of government. Thus, improved executive-congressional collaboration would benefit all aspects of the credibility equation.

Equally important is the need for reform in the executive decision-making process so that it will operate with a sense of proportion and with more discrimination between vital and important interests, and between the aspects of credibility. The experiences of the 1960s demonstrate the extreme difficulty of gaining an audit or a policy reevaluation from line policy-makers.

A separate group outside the institutionalized policy process should provide the audit. Such a provision is common practice in government and in the Inspector General's Office and in the corporate community. At the State Department, Secretary of State George Marshall established the Policy Planning Staff in the crisis year of 1947 with George Kennan at its head. The staff had a highly important role under Kennan and his successor, Paul Nitze. Its attention was devoted to major policy problems of interest to Secretaries Marshall and Acheson. Under Dulles, the group (renamed the Policy Planning Council) lost some importance; under subsequent Secretaries it was relegated to the function of coordinating study papers, often on secondary issues. Commensurate with this decline was the rise of the Office of International Security Affairs in Secretary McNamara's Department of Defense. The ISA, despite its unique role during the McNamara years, had an integral position in the Department of Defense. Under the Nixon Administration, the Kissinger National Security Council system was devised in a way that afforded a much better examination of policy options and appeared to give part of the Council staff a distinct planning function. The staff, however, was so overwhelmed by its task of executing important policies that such a role never fully materialized.

None of these approaches satisfactorily meets the need for the kind of audit that should be available to the President. Therefore, it would seem appropriate to have a very senior reviewing body at the White House level that would have the President's personal and political interests in mind. Such a group might be modeled after the President's Foreign Intelligence Advisory Board, which is charged with giving the President direct and confidential advice on the overall functioning of the government's foreign intelligence program. President Kennedy formalized that group after the Bay of Pigs fiasco, but unfortunately subsequent Presidents have not made good use of it.

A comparable group of senior adivsers should be designated to conduct a general audit of major policies and to give the President independent advice. The history of the Vietnam commitment, in which over a half-million men were ordered into a land war in Asia following policies that were disproportionate to the original objective of the involvement, is an overriding and cogent argument for such a group, despite its inevitable unpopularity with line officers or even Presidents who do not want to be second-guessed. To advocate a continual audit by a group of "wise" men is not to suggest government by committee. The opening to China and the negotiations conducted by Secretary Kissinger after the 1973 Arab-Israeli war could never have been conducted by committee. Certainly, however, the execution of America's grand strategy and diplomacy can be effectively improved by such advisers.

America must have a strong executive if it is to continue to play its role in creating a stable balance of power, in maintaining its security and its alliance system, and in standing for values that will produce more pluralistic societies around the world. Such an executive must possess and be seen to possess a sense of proportion—a sense of what is not only possible, but also sensible in accordance with America's goals and interests. The credibility of consequent policy and strategy, interwoven as it is with a "sense of proportion," will be patent to, if not unchallenged by, all with whom the government must deal: its people, its allies, its adversaries, and other nations. One very important way to insure a sense of proportion (and thus enhance the credibility) of the Presidency in the future, is to include in its organization a thorough procedure for auditing foreign policy. Also very important is the reshaping of Congress' organization and procedures for examining national security affairs.

Yet for all the new procedural reforms, America cannot meet the challenge of the 1970s without a new meeting of the minds on the grand design of its foreign policy. This has been made more difficult because to the Vietnam experience has been added the tragedy of Watergate, which has further eroded the credibility of the Presidency.

The Vietnam experience shows that the failure to examine assumptions and the obfuscation of the real facts eventually lead to a deep split in policy. In the future, an examination of assumptions must involve a true dialogue on foreign policy out of which can emerge a new and sound consensus. The best example of the efforts of governmental leadership to develop a consensus for a changed course of policy was that of Secretary of State Marshall, Robert Lovett, and Dean Acheson on behalf of a new American policy toward Europe in 1947. With Senator Vandenberg's collaboration, a bipartisan effort was developed in Congress and toward the public. These successes offer a model for the future as to how the relationships between the executive and the legislature can be strengthened to produce credibility both at home and abroad.

Notes

1. Dwight D. Eisenhower, *Mandate for Change, 1953-1956* (Garden City, N.Y.: Doubleday, 1963), p. 352.

The Lessons Nixon Learned

MORTON H. HALPERIN

While much of the foreign policy establishment was still debating what the lessons of Vietnam are and what should be done, the Nixon Administration drew its lessons, applied them in Indochina and elsewhere, and found them to be valid. But President Nixon's Vietnam lessons are profoundly misconceived and portend more tragedy for the United States and the world if pursued by his successors.

Richard Nixon came into office a critic of the Johnson Administration's Vietnam policy. His objections to the policy were not the familiar ones relating to a lack of American interests in Indochina and the inability of the United States to influence the outcome. Rather, he was appalled at the means. Throughout the Johnson years, Nixon had argued that we should do more, not less, in Vietnam. Johnson's failure convinced him that major mistakes had been made. In particular:

- Escalating gradually gave the enemy time to adjust militarily and psychologically.
- Assuring Hanoi's leadership that the United States

411

was not threatening the existence of their government took away their interest in negotiations.

   • Seeking to separate Vietnam from other issues eliminated the incentive of the Soviet Union to negotiate.

   • Refusing to deal with the People's Republic of China meant that Peking had no reason to undercut Hanoi.

From these mistakes clear lessons were derived:

   • The United States must be able to project a credible intent to use force when its interests are threatened.

   • Escalation must be sudden and massive.

   • The very existence of the North Vietnamese government, society, and economy must be threatened.

   • Indochina must be linked to other issues in dealing with the Soviet Union and with China.

   • Domestically, support must come from the right and from patriotic "middle" America.

These lessons were applied from the very beginning of the Nixon Administration and, in the eyes of the President and his principal associate, Henry Kissinger, they worked. Successive "decisive" escalations of the conflict; threats to North Vietnam; tough diplomacy with the Soviets and Chinese, based on a willingness to use force; new support at home; these combined to produce "peace with honor" in Indochina and a formula that could be applied elsewhere.

   Before considering the fallacies of this perspective, for Indochina as well as for other issues, it is important to spell out in some detail the lessons drawn from Indochina by Nixon and Kissinger and how they have been applied. These lessons relate to the role of force and relations with the Soviet Union and China.

The Role of Force

   The Johnson Administration quite obviously relied on military force in an effort to pursue American objectives in Indochina. However, to Richard Nixon, who observed the policy as a private citizen in the mid-1960s and assessed it later as President, the Johnson approach to the use of force had two basic flaws: The first derived from the theory of gradual escalation, and the second from the nature of the political threats which accompanied the escalation.

After much debate, President Johnson had approved a limited bombing of North Vietnam. The theory was that limited attacks on North Vietnamese military targets would convince the Hanoi leadership that the United States was prepared gradually to escalate the military conflict. Hanoi, to avoid this escalation, would either negotiate or fade away in the South. A sudden, massive, bombing campaign was rejected as being ineffective and too dangerous in that it ran a high risk of bringing in the Russians or Chinese. Nor would it be as effective as a slow squeeze that would present the prospect of later more extensive damage, and therefore be more convincing in influencing the Hanoi leadership to change its policy.

Accompanying Johnson's policy of gradual military escalation was a communications policy which emphasized the limited American purposes in the area. The Soviet and Chinese governments, and through them Hanoi, were reassured that the United States did not seek the destruction of the North Vietnamese regime or society. Rather, the stated American objective was simply withdrawal of North Vietnamese forces from the South. As the Administration frequently put it, Hanoi had only to leave its neighbor alone and the United States would withdraw. Hanoi could well have concluded that even if it continued to pursue the war in the South, American objectives would not expand to the point of threatening the existence of the regime in the North.

From Nixon's perspective, both of these elements of the Johnson policy on the use of force were mistakes. The step-by-step escalation of the war was a formula not for effective influence on the conflict but simply for a useless application of military force. Hanoi, Nixon pointed out at the time and in later statements as President, was given the time to adjust, both tactically and psychologically, to the stepped-up American military pressure. Logistically, Hanoi could respond to the bombing in various ways. As bridges or roads were bombed, resources could be used to repair them; as oil resources were attacked, alternate storage facilities could be developed. The gradual escalation, by putting strain on only one part of the North Vietnamese logistic system at a time, enabled the North to concentrate its resources in response. It also permitted time to allow the Russians and Chinese to send in the necessary supplies and equipment to redress the military situation. The gradual step-up of the bombing also allowed the North Vietnamese leaders to prepare themselves and their population psychologically for each new stage in the bombing.

Similarly, the assurances that American war aims would not expand to the point where they included a fundamental threat to North Vietnam removed any serious incentive for either Russia or China to press Hanoi for a settlement of the conflict. If both countries felt obliged to intervene only if Hanoi were threatened, and if the United States gave assurances that Hanoi would not be threatened, then neither country saw the Indochina conflict as a potential source of conflict with the United States. Neither, therefore, had any overriding reason to press the North Vietnamese to accept a settlement. At the same time, any group in Hanoi which might have favored a settlement was limited in its influence by the fact that there appeared to be no threat to the regime's existence, no matter how prolonged its actions in South Vietnam.

All this was seen by Richard Nixon prior to his election. In most of his public statements he contented himself with stating simply that he would be able to end the war. There is little doubt that his plan involved a rejection of the Johnson policy of gradual escalation and limited threats. In what he believed was an off-the-record discussion with Southern delegations at the time of the Republican Convention in 1968, candidate Nixon spelled out his plan. He told the delegates:

> How do you bring a war to a conclusion? I'll tell you how Korea was ended. We got in there and had this messy war on our hands. Eisenhower let the word go out—let the word go out diplomatically—to the Chinese and the North Koreans that we would not tolerate this continued ground war of attrition. And within a matter of months they negotiated. . . .

Nixon came into office hoping to emulate Eisenhower and end the Vietnam war quickly by conveying threats to Hanoi of a changed American approach to escalation. Nixon believed that Eisenhower had warned the Chinese that, if the Korean War continued, the United States would carry it into China using nuclear weapons. In Nixon's case, the parallelism did not involve, as far as one knows, a threat to use nuclear weapons. Rather, he threatened massive destruction of North Vietnamese society in a decisive escalatory move. The effort was to convince Hanoi that unless the war was settled quickly, it would result in an American attempt to destroy North Vietnam.

This policy had to be administered with considerable skill. Hanoi, Peking, and Moscow had to be convinced that the President had the determination to escalate the conflict as well as the domestic political freedom to do so. The President had to be seen as a decisive man who would pay the domestic costs, whatever they were, of an escalatory policy.

The difficulty came in part from the perception in the United States, as well as in the Communist countries, that the American people would not tolerate escalation, that Richard Nixon had been elected to end the war, and that he simply did not have the domestic flexibility which would enable him to embark on an escalatory campaign.

The Administration's problem was compounded by the fact that its ability to carry out this program depended not only on convincing Hanoi, Peking, and Moscow that the President would escalate, but also on convincing the American population that escalation of the conflict was not, in fact, planned. Most of the policy was carried out in secret. There were secret diplomatic warnings and secret military actions. There were also public statements, veiled in such a way that they could be clear to Hanoi, Moscow, and Peking in the context of the private warnings and actions, but could be ignored by an American public convinced that the President was withdrawing from Indochina.

The private warnings made in the early days of the Nixon Administration have still not been publicly revealed. However, they apparently included messages sent to the Soviet Union in the course of a number of private conversations between the President's National Security Advisor, Henry A. Kissinger, and Soviet Ambassador Anatoly P. Dobrynin. Other messages may well have been conveyed through the Rumanian Prime Minister, with whom the President met on an early trip to Europe. Other channels may also have been used. The intentions expressed were consistent with the President's view that a message similar to that sent by Eisenhower (apparently through the Indians to the Chinese) should be conveyed. The message was simple: The United States desired a quick negotiated settlement of the conflict but in the absence of such a settlement, would decisively escalate the war by massive attacks on North Vietnam.

The public statements in the first year of the Administration were more cryptic. For example, in his first major Vietnam speech in May 1969, which put forth a relatively forthcoming negotiating position, the President warned that nobody had anything to gain by delay.

Military operations were designed to convince Hanoi that the threats were credible and that the President did have the determination and the flexibility to launch attacks on North Vietnam. In the first days of the Administration American ground combat forces were sent into Laos to attack points along the Ho Chi Minh Trail in an exercise known as Dewey Canyon 1 (the forerunner of the later South Vietnamese invasion in 1971, known as Dewey Canyon 2). About the same time, according to some press reports, frogmen were sent into Hanoi Harbor in an effort to signal the possibility of a blockade and mining operation. In March 1969, a program of B-52 bombing of North Vietnamese sanctuary areas in Cambodia began. The Johnson Administration, while conducting extensive bombing in Laos and North Vietnam, as well as South Vietnam, had refrained from bombing Cambodia on the grounds that the country was neutral and had not, as the Laotian government had, given sanction for bombing operations.

These intense efforts to settle the conflict within six months, as the Administration was privately promising its critics in the Congress and the public, and as it believed the Eisenhower Administration had done, were a failure. The

Administration was still insisting upon a North Vietnamese withdrawal from South Vietnam to accompany the American withdrawal; this may well have been a key stumbling block to an early settlement. But to the President and Kissinger, the frustration of their effort flowed at least in part from the failure to make their threats credible. They therefore moved to solidify public support and to demonstrate that the United States could remain in Vietnam for an extended time by announcing in the summer of 1969 a program for the gradual withdrawal of American forces from Vietnam. At the same time, Kissinger began his secret negotiations with Le Duc Tho. This provided for the first time a direct channel through which offers to negotiate a settlement as well as threats of escalation could be conveyed directly to the highest level of the North Vietnamese government. The President also made more explicit public threats of escalation in the guise of what he would do to protect American lives. Thus, for example, on April 20, 1970, he said:

> But I again remind the leaders of North Vietnam that while we are taking these risks for peace, they would be taking grave risks should they attempt to use the occasion to jeopardize the security of our remaining forces in Vietnam by increased military action in Vietnam, Cambodia or Laos.
> I repeat what I said November 3 and December 15: If I conclude that increased enemy action jeopardizes our remaining forces in Vietnam, I shall not hesitate to take strong and effective measures to deal with that situation.

Still, these efforts were not successful, and the Administration was forced to do what it hoped to avoid: to engage in escalation so massive that it would not be possible to conceal it from the American people. Thus, in May 1970 it launched the invasion of Cambodia. The purpose was to persuade Hanoi that further escalation would occur if the North Vietnamese refused to negotiate and continued their operations in the South.

In commenting on why he thought this escalation would

succeed while Johnson's escalation had failed, Nixon stated:
". . . the difference is that he did move step-by-step. This action is a decisive move, and this action also puts the enemy on
warning that if it escalates while we are trying to de-escalate,
we will move decisively and not step-by-step."

The President also indicated the need to preserve the credibility of U.S. power. The United States, he warned, would
become a pitiful helpless giant if it did not respond in the face
of perceived provocations from Hanoi—especially after the
President had said that he would not tolerate such acts and
had privately conveyed even more explicit warnings. The invasion of Laos the following year was motivated and justified
in the same way, as was the blockade of Hanoi following the
North Vietnamese offensive in 1972 and later the Christmas
bombing of Hanoi.

The aim of each escalation was to make future escalation
credible. This led, finally, to the implicit warning in the
Christmas bombing that the United States was prepared to
destroy North Vietnam, that the President had the freedom
to use force, was prepared to pay the domestic price involved
in the use of force, and would engage in decisive escalation in
support of mounting political objectives. The twin hopes were
that this action would force Hanoi to negotiate (or to fade
away), and that Moscow and Peking would pressure their
North Vietnamese ally to reach a compromise settlement.
The policy of decisive escalation was thus linked explicitly to
the Nixon Administration's view of the relationship between
great power negotiations and local conflict.

Relationship with the Great Powers

In President Nixon's view, the Johnson Administration's
handling of its relationship with the great powers in connection with the Vietnam conflict was as faulty as its use of
escalatory pressures. The Johnson policy consisted essentially
of attempting to isolate the Vietnam war from Soviet-American relations. It sought an improvement in bilateral relations,
including strategic arms limitation talks, while continuing to
pursue the war in Vietnam. Although the Johnson Administration often expressed regret about the Soviet willingness to

supply arms to the North Vietnamese, it never sought to make a change in Soviet policy towards Indochina a precondition of improved relations. By and large, Johnson and his advisors did not count on Soviet support there, and did not want the Vietnam conflict to jeopardize efforts for improved relations in other arenas.

The Johnson Administration appears never to have seen any connection between efforts to end the Vietnam war and the opening of diplomatic contacts with Peking. Indeed, it appears to have proceeded on the assumption that a major move toward Peking would only be possible after the conflict had come to an end. Johnson and his advisors were concerned that the Soviet Union or China might be lured into the Vietnam war for fear that American escalation would threaten the existence of the Hanoi regime. Thus, as noted, one element of the Johnson policy was to reassure the Communists that American objectives in Indochina were limited; that they did not threaten the security of either Russia or China since they did not threaten the Democratic Republic of Vietnam (DRV).

The Nixon Administration took a fundamentally different approach. It was, the President believed, a mistake to try to isolate Vietnam from other issues. On the contrary, the war could be settled only if Vietnam was linked to other questions and only if the Soviet Union and the People's Republic of China could be persuaded to play a role in bringing the war to a conclusion. Again Richard Nixon spelled out this basic view in his address to the Southern delegates at the Miami convention:

> Critical to the settlement of Vietnam is relations with the Soviet Union. That is why I have said over and over again it is going to be necessary for the next President to sit down and talk with the Soviet leaders—and talk quite directly, not only about Vietnam, you've got to broaden the canvas—because in Vietnam they have no reason to end that war. It's hurting us more than it's hurting them.

From this approach came the theory which was labeled

"linkage." The Soviet and later the Chinese leaders would be told that Vietnam should not be separated from the effort to improve relations in other areas. American willingness to make progress in limiting strategic arms, on settlement of the conflict in the Middle East, and on trade and economic matters of particular importance to the Soviet Union would depend on progress toward a Vietnam settlement. This view, stated publicly and privately to the Soviet leadership, attempted to give them a different perspective on the Vietnam conflict. The aim was to provide incentives for the Soviets (and later the Chinese) to involve themselves in settling the conflict.

A second step was taken to involve the Communists in Indochina negotiations—the opening of a dialogue with Peking. In general terms, the purpose was to increase Soviet concern about American intentions, to ensure that Vietnam not stand in the way of Soviet-American rapprochement as the United States seemed to be moving closer to Moscow's principal enemy.

At the same time, by opening a dialogue with Peking, the United States sought to give the Chinese leaders a stake in ending the Vietnam conflict. Until then, the Chinese had no reason to be concerned about the continuation of the war, having been assured that the war would not threaten the destruction of the DRV and having been offered no alternative of improved relations with the United States.

American contacts with Peking were designed to change both calculations. On the one hand, the Chinese leaders were almost certainly warned, once direct contact was established, that if the war continued, the United States might be forced into a policy of destruction of the North Vietnamese regime. At the same time, the prospect of improved relations between Peking and the United States, perhaps in the form of a tacit alliance against potential Soviet military moves directed at China, gave the Peking leadership a positive incentive to seek a settlement of the Vietnam conflict. The promise to withdraw American forces from Taiwan if a settlement were reached increased Peking's interest in resolving the conflict.

The same threats of an expanded war were conveyed to the Soviet Union. The purpose of these policies was simply to involve the Soviet Union and China in the Vietnam negotiations, to give them an incentive to put pressure on Hanoi. Alternatively, the hope was that they would limit military supplies to Hanoi in order to prevent an offensive which would bring on a massive American response. The diplomatic maneuvering was also designed to create a sense of concern and isolation in Hanoi, to give its leaders a greater incentive to negotiate.

As noted, the Nixon Administration came into office hoping that this two-pronged policy of threats of decisive escalation and involvement with the great powers would bring an early end to the Vietnam conflict, in the same way that Richard Nixon believed it had brought an early termination to the Korean War. That these hopes foundered did not lead the Administration to abandon the basic policy. It was pursued during the four-year period which ultimately led to the signing of the Vietnam "truce" providing for the return of American prisoners-of-war.

From the perspective of Henry Kissinger and Richard Nixon, the lessons drawn from the Johnson Administration's conduct of the Vietnam war have been tested and proved to be correct. By threatening a brutal escalation of the conflict and by carrying out various "decisive" steps—the Cambodian invasion, the Laotian invasion, the mining of Haiphong, and the bombing of Hanoi—the Nixon Administration finally succeeded in convincing the leaders in Peking, Moscow, and Hanoi that the United States was serious in its threat to destroy North Vietnam if a settlement were not negotiated. This escalation was decisive; it led Hanoi to negotiate a political settlement. The policy of involving the Communist powers was also viewed as successful. By the end of the conflict, both Peking and Moscow were apparently willing to give assurances to the United States that they would seek to prevent a renewed Communist offensive. The leaders in Washington clearly believed that both major Communist powers did, in fact, put pressure on the Hanoi regime to negotiate a settlement.

The success of the policy after the cease-fire and the withdrawal of the American forces was seen to depend on the credibility of the threat to reintervene with massive power. The Christmas bombing was in fact designed to make credible this threat. If the United States was prepared to bomb Hanoi over minor clauses in the agreement, there could be little doubt that it would resume the bombing in the event of flagrant violations of the agreement. South Vietnam's President Thieu was promised in writing by President Nixon that the United States would respond with full force in the event of a North Vietnamese offensive. Similar warnings were, no doubt, conveyed to Hanoi directly and through Moscow and Peking. The Joint Chiefs were instructed to prepare contingency plans to resume the bombing.

The breakdown of the agreement in the spring of 1975 with the communist takeover of South Vietnam was attributed explicitly by Kissinger to the removal of this threat. In August 1973, without realizing the consequences of its actions on promises and threats made by the Nixon Administration, Congress voted a prohibition on American combat operations in Indochina. The Nixon Administration, weakened by Watergate, was unable to resist congressional insistence on the cut-off of funds for combat operations and unwilling to explain the importance it attached to threats of escalation. As in 1969, Congress and the public could not be informed of escalation threats while Hanoi had to believe in their credibility. A public debate on the need to threaten the reintroduction of American forces would only have underlined congressional unwillingness to approve such a course.

With the threat of escalation gone, Hanoi was free to move all its forces south and launch a final offensive. Thus, from the viewpoint of Henry Kissinger even the events of the spring of 1975 demonstrated the validity of the Nixon-Kissinger approach. The policy worked as long as the threat of decisive force was credible; it collapsed when it was withdrawn.

Application to Other Crises

The Nixon Administration's approach to the Vietnam war was a reflection of, and in turn was reflected in, its more general relations with the Soviet Union and the People's Republic of China. The basic objective was to establish a new relationship with Soviet and Chinese leaders under which they would refrain from using military force to exploit local situations, and would instead cooperate with the United States in bringing such conflicts under control. The successful application of this policy required not only an end to the Vietnam war, but more generally a conviction on the part of the Soviet leaders, especially, that the United States would use force whenever it believed it was necessary to defend its interests, even in an arbitrary and unexpected way. This in turn depended on demonstrating to the Soviet leaders that the President believed in the use of force and would not be deterred from using it by domestic political opposition.

The lessons learned from the Johnson Administration's Vietnam policy were simultaneously applied in Indochina and elsewhere. Indeed, the successful application of the lessons of Vietnam required that they be applied in each potential crisis situation. Not only were they believed to be the most likely means to bring any particular crisis under control, but the failure to use the threat of force and to hold the Communist powers responsible would undermine the credibility of the general policy. The United States might have been seen as a pitiful, helpless giant, not only if it had failed to invade Cambodia, but also if it did not take credible steps indicating its willingness to use decisive military force in any potential conflict. Thus, throughout his Administration, every time the United States has seen itself on one side of a local military confrontation and the Soviet Union or China potentially on the other, President Nixon sought to convince the Soviet leadership that the United States would intervene militarily if the Soviets themselves threatened to challenge our interests.

The first incident of this kind occurred in the early months of the Nixon Administration when the North Koreans shot down an American reconnaissance plane operating in international waters off the coast of North Korea. The initial plans to respond forcefully were checked by the lack of readiness of American forces. Washington simply did not have the capability to intervene quickly. Moreover, procedures for devising a quick response were not well developed. Hasty efforts to put together a retaliatory capability resulted in the assembly of the largest naval armada in history which set sail from stations elsewhere in the Pacific, including the Indochina theater, for the seas off North Korea. Initial plans to carry out a strike using aircraft from these carriers were called off, but not until the Soviets had expressed grave concern to the United States about the purposes and intentions of this fleet. As a result of this experience, the White House was determined to improve the quick-reaction capability of American forces. In addition, the Washington Special Action Group was created to provide a mechanism by which the White House could plan for and coordinate the American response to military crises, and monitor the readiness of forces.

The next crisis involved the apparent attempt by the Soviet Union in the summer of 1972 to establish Cuba as a base for the refueling of its nuclear missile submarines. Here the United States moved quickly to convey threats to the Soviet leadership that it would view this as a breach of the agreements reached at the time of the 1962 missile crisis and would lead to an American reaction equally as strong. In this case, the threats seemed to work without any mobilization of American military forces.

At the same time a crisis erupted in the Middle East. A Jordanian effort to put controls on guerrilla forces operating within Jordan threatened to bring on a Syrian invasion of Jordan. American military forces were put on alert, and the United States issued warnings both publicly and privately that it would intervene or support an Israeli intervention if necessary to prevent a Syrian invasion of Jordan. Similarly, in the Indo-Pakistani war of 1971, the United States sent a nuclear task force into the Indian Ocean to make credible its threats delivered to India and the Soviet Union that it would intervene if Indian forces threatened the existence of West Pakistan.

The application of this approach in the Middle East crisis of 1973 was fundamentally the same. The United States sought to convince the Russians that the two superpowers had to work together to curtail military conflict. The Soviet Union indicated that it would, if necessary, intervene with its own forces to prevent the Egyptians from being cut off on the East

Bank of the Suez Canal, and to prevent the Israelis from moving toward Cairo. The United States reacted in a typical fashion by putting its forces on alert and threatening a massive American counterattack if the Soviets moved. But it also offered political concessions, in this case assurance that the Israelis would permit the trapped Egyptian third army on the East Bank of the Suez Canal to be resupplied. These latter moves were carried out quietly.

Lessons of the Lessons Learned

Henry Kissinger and significant parts of the permanent bureaucracy, including substantial parts of the military services, are convinced that the lessons of Vietnam learned by the Nixon Administration were correct, and that their application in Indochina and elsewhere have been effective.

But have they been? As regards Vietnam, the basic argument is that the policy would have worked if not for congressional interference. It permitted American troop withdrawal, secured the release of American prisoners-of-war, and would have permitted the Thieu government to remain in power. The breakdown of the cease-fire occurred only because the threat of escalation was withdrawn. Even if one accepted this argument, there are other shortcomings to the policy.

As noted, the hope that this strategy would bring a quick end to this crisis was not fulfilled. President Nixon recognized that he was elected to end the war and hoped to do so within six months, but it took more than four years. The domestic consensus on means and ends which would make possible any effective foreign policy in the future continued to erode. The United States inflicted enormous destruction on the populations of Laos, Cambodia, and North Vietnam, as well as South Vietnam, and itself sustained severe losses. The strategy of escalation led to massive bombings in Laotian areas not related to the Ho Chi Minh Trail, and in Cambodia where the war was brought for the first time. The Christmas bombing of Hanoi involved the release of larger quantities of explosives than had ever been dropped on any city.

The Nixon Administration's response was that it acted to limit civilian casualties and that its actions were necessary to prevent World War III. For Richard Nixon and Henry Kissinger it was axiomatic that an American withdrawal without escalation would convince Russia and China that the United States would never use force. They would then feel free to engage in adventurous policies in other areas. However, the evidence for this proposition is lacking.

The Nixon Administration failed to present a convincing case that the terms of settlement which it accepted in 1973 were significantly different from those it could have negotiated in 1969, or that the differences were important to American security. Beginning with the build-up of American forces in Vietnam in 1966, the United States position was that any withdrawal of its forces would come only after a withdrawal of the North Vietnamese forces from South Vietnam, and only after the South Vietnamese government was itself capable of dealing with the insurgency in the South. It was American insistence on mutual withdrawal which prevented negotiation of an agreed settlement from 1967 to 1973. It was only after the application of overwhelming American force destroyed much of the indigenous Vietcong capability in the South, and only after the United States ended its insistence on the withdrawal of North Vietnamese forces, that a negotiated agreement became possible. It is difficult to believe that in 1969, when the United States had 550,000 troops in Vietnam, the North Vietnamese would not have been willing to accept a settlement calling for the withdrawal of American forces in return only for the release of prisoners-of-war. Yet this is all that was obtained in 1973 after extensive escalation, destruction, and dissension. More particularly, one needs to ask whether the agreement negotiated in 1973 after the Christmas bombing was in any important way different from the agreement that had been negotiated in October 1972 and announced dramatically by Henry Kissinger in his famous "peace is at hand" press conference. The Administration has failed to release the documents which would permit any appraisal of the differences between these two agreements. Many of the issues that it identified, relating to the operation of the International Supervisory Commission, are irrelevant because of the inability of that Commission to function at all.

The primary purpose of the bombing was not to change the agreement—that was the cover story presented to the American people. Its objective was to persuade President Thieu to sign the agreement by convincing him that the United States would resume the heavy bombing if Hanoi violated the agreement. When the threat of force was removed, the Saigon regime collapsed in the face of military probes. Even if the United States continued to threaten military intervention, Hanoi might well have launched an all-out offensive if that became necessary. Alternatively, it could have proceeded with its policy of gradually eroding the Saigon regime, providing the United States with an opportunity or excuse for drastic military action.

If the Kissinger-Nixon policy ultimately failed in Indochina, it is even less clear that the policy was necessary to build a structure of peace, or had an important impact on Soviet or Chinese behavior in other areas.

Events during the Nixon Administration demonstrate that crises arise not from the deliberate decisions of the superpowers but from local developments. The Syrian-Jordanian conflict, the Indo-Pakistani conflict, the EC-121 shoot-down, and almost certainly the Middle East war of 1973 resulted not from Soviet or Chinese decisions but from the decisions of local governments based on indigenous developments. Thus, the policy of threatening escalation and linking international issues cannot serve to prevent an international crisis. Nor is the evidence clear that it has played a significant role in the settlement of these crises. In making this evaluation it is difficult to disentangle the threatening elements of the American détente policy from the carrots offered to the Soviet Union primarily in the form of increased scientific and technical exchanges and of American trade and credits.

A look at the Middle East crisis in 1973 nevertheless suggests that the pattern of Soviet behavior is not different from that in prior crises. In the early days of the war when the military situation was ambiguous and it appeared that the Egyptians and Syrians might be holding their own, the Soviet Union opposed a cease-fire, as it did in the opening days of the 1967 war. When the Arab military efforts began to collapse, the Soviets decided in both cases to support a cease-fire. When it appeared that the Israelis would not be willing to stop, the Soviets threatened intervention. The United States then acted, in 1967, to stop the advance on Damascus, and in 1973 to stop the Israeli advance on Cairo, and a cease-fire was ultimately negotiated.

The outcome in these crises depended primarily, as will the ultimate outcome in Indochina, on the strength of the indigenous forces rather than the intervention of the great powers.

Moreover, Nixon and Kissinger and the bureaucracy seem to be oblivious to the fundamental risks involved in the policy. The policy, depending as it does on secrecy, necessarily exacerbates relations with allies. It focuses attention away from the problems of our economic and political relations with our allies and with the rest of the world. According to that policy, the United States must continue to threaten the use of massive military force in order to create a structure of peace with the Soviet Union and China. This leads to the need to maintain a very large military capability, to retain it at a high degree of readiness, and to put the forces on alert in a military conflict. Thus far the use of force and the threat of force has stopped short of a confrontation with either the Soviet Union or China. The success of the policy depends on the willingness of the Soviet leaders to continue to back down in the face of American threats. Brezhnev has been willing to do so because of his personal commitment to détente and because vital Soviet interests were not as stable. And thus far Brezhnev has been able to prevail in the Kremlin. In a future crisis a dominant coalition in the Soviet Politburo might decide that it had to resist. The risk of a confrontation will therefore continue to be high, despite the rhetoric or détente and despite the efforts of leaders of both sides to prevent a conflict, if the policy of the United States continues to require massive forces put on an active alert in any military conflict accompanied by threats and ultimatums. This is not a structure of peace but a structure of threat, with the ever present danger that brinksmanship will lead to nuclear holocaust. On whether the Ford Administration recognizes these dangers and works to implement a different set of lessons could depend the ability of the world to avoid nuclear war.

Index

429